Raj Orators

Speeches of Eminent Indians During the Raj

Raj Orators

Speeches of Eminent Indians During the Raj

By

Dr. B.G. Tandon

Former Professor & Head
School of Studies in English
Vikram University, Ujjain (M.P.)

Ane Books Pvt. Ltd.

New Delhi ♦ Chennai

Raj Orators : Speeches of Eminent Indians During the Raj.

Published by

Ane Books Pvt. Ltd.
4821, Parwana Bhawan, 1st Floor, 24 Ansari Road, Darya Ganj,
New Delhi - 110 002, Tel.: +91(011) 23276843-44, Fax: +91(011) 23276863
e-mail: kapoor@anebooks.com, Website: www.anebooks.com

Branch Office:

- Avantika Niwas, 1st Floor, 19 Doraiswamy Road, T. Nagar,
  Chennai - 600 017, Tel.: +91(044) 28141554, 28141209
  e-mail: anebookschennai@gmail.com, rathinam@anebooks.com

ISBN : 978-81-8052-065-5

Printed at : R.K. Offset Process, New Delhi.

To

A foursome of kind

Women

My Mother, My Wife, and My Two Daughters

and to a Benevolent Brother

S. G. Tandon

Acknowledgements

My thankfulness to my wife Jyotsna and my daughter Loveena and Saumya is already acknowledged in the dedication, which is yet only a feeble manifestation of a boundless appreciation. To the publisher, Sunil Saxena, who is responsible for the daunting task of arranging the sketches of the Orators, and whose creative interest in the publication of this book transcends the call of duty, my debt exceeds the acknowledgement.

I am also grateful to UGC, Delhi for a Major Research Project Grant during the course of my work.

B.G. Tandon

PREFACE

English speeches of eminent Indians during the British Raj are a mine of hidden treasures containing history, political thought, biographical material, and, above all, golden literature. But ironically, they are sucking dust in the obscure recesses of libraries, old book shops, archives, museums, and in the newspaper stack rooms. It is an exigency of the moment to dig them out of this unmerited obscurity and, as Hamlet would say, "to report them aright to the World." The present work is an attempt in that direction.

B.G. Tandon

CONTENTS

PART ONE

ORATORS

I

THE ART OF ORATORY

More than a hundred years ago, in the year 1895, when Sir Surendranath Banerjea was elected President of the Indian National Congress, his first need was to prepare the presidential speech. It was, he tells us in his *A Nation in the making*, a Herculean task. He worked for two hours a day, from day to day, for six weeks with all the power of concentration he was capable of, and checked the results of his labour by turning the manuscript in his mind even while he walked, intercepting the errors and polishing the style. He delivered the memorable oration, which lasted for four hours, without referring to any notes, and compelled the attention of an assembly of five thousand people with amazing success, making even the most impatient among them unaware of the lapse of time. The atmosphere was charged with a galvanic current and the entire audience stood up in a tumult of applause. The speech had the desired effect.

Making a speech of such talismanic power is no mean task. It is true that it presupposes natural endowments on the part of the speaker, an innate ability to speak; but this alone is not enough; the seeds supplied by nature need to be fertilized by studious training and matured by unbending perseverance and practice. The example of Demosthenes (383-322 B.C.) from ancient Greece is even more edifying. He was a great orator in the same sense in which Shakespeare was a great dramatist and Gandhi a great leader, a genius who was abundantly equipped with the stuff greatness is made of. But this alone did not help him when he stood up to speak before the people for the first time. His voice was weak and breath short, but his sentences were so long that he had to stop in the midst of them for respiration. He stammered to such an extent that he could not pronounce certain letters. His pronunciation was uncouth and graceless and his gestures were crude and revolting. To make the matters worse, his study was fragmentary and style badly worked out. The result was that, to his shame and sorrow, he was hissed by the whole audience. But Demosthenes was undeterred. The way he overcame these shortcomings shows what industry and application can attain. He surmounted stammering by rehearsing his speeches with pebbles in his mouth, breathlessness by uttering them while climbing steep places, and weakness of voice and hooting of the audience by pronouncing them by the roaring seas. He improved his gestures by declaiming at a large looking-glass. He had a repulsive habit of shrugging up the shoulders which he corrected by speaking in a narrow pulpit over which hung a halbert in such a manner that if he shrugged the weapon hit him. He improved his knowledge by studying in an isolated underground room for month's together, shaving half his head and face so that he could not move out for fear of ridicule. And he perfected his style by reading old masters. It is said that he copied Thucydides' *History* eight times in order that he might become familiar with his style. His labours were amply rewarded and he became the greatest orator of Greece.

Thus, there are three requirements of a successful orator: natural propensity, artistic training and determined practice. The ultimate energy comes from nature, but it has to be harnessed by study and application. Nature gives, art regulates, practice perfects. As the Greek critic Quintilian said in *The Training of an Orator*, "Skill in speaking is made perfect by nature, art, and practice." The orator must possess all these qualities together; any estrangement in them spoils his oration.

The inevitable question now is: what are the essentials of oratory? What makes a good oration? The question was immaculately answered in Aristotle's *Rhetoric*, Cicero's *De Oratore* and Quintilian's *Institutio Oratoria*, and with minor modifications and contextual adjustments their answer holds good even today. They suggested five components of oratory: (1) Invention or finding out arguments, in modern terminology collection of material or, simply, subject-matter; (2) arrangement of the material; (3) style; (4) memory; and (5) delivery.

The first concern of an orator is the subject or what to say. In the ancient times when oratory was mainly exercised for political, legal and ceremonial purposes it was customary to classify it into three branches—deliberative or political, forensic or legal, and epideictic or ceremonial; but today the field of oratory has vastly increased and such a division, therefore, sounds too narrow and limited. One may now have to speak on any subject and anywhere. It becomes, therefore, necessary for an orator to be a man of vast knowledge and experience. Nevertheless, the ways in which he can appeal through his subject are still the same, and they are rational, emotional and ethical. He may appeal to the reason or emotion or to the moral sense of the audience. Nehru appealed to reason, Michael Madhusudan Dutt to emotion, and Gandhi to moral sense. Man is a rational being and he is well pleased to see things in the light of reason. But often enough he is swayed more by emotion than by reason. That is the reason why the emotional speech of Mark Antony moved Romans more than the rational speech of Brutus. But all of an orator's rational or emotional appeal fails if the audience does not trust his character. That is why Cicero and Quintilian considered it necessary for the speaker to be a man of high and noble moral character. Quintilian defined an orator as "a good man skilled in speaking." It was because of this that when Gandhi spoke the world listened. His word was an oracle and his wish a command. Such was the power of Christ and the persuasion of Buddha.

The second concern of an orator is the arrangement of the material into an animated whole. Every subject has constituent parts coexistent with the central substance. The skill of the orator lies in linking parts with parts and in linking the parts together with the central substance. The inter-connection of the parts produces coherence and of the parts with the whole produces unity, and coherence and unity in themselves are sources of pleasure and are extremely efficacious instruments of persuasion. Here the rhetoricians talk of the organisation of the material in terms of beginning, middle and end. But such a division seems too simplistic and self-evident. Aristotle suggested four-fold division: introduction, statement of the case, proof of the case, and conclusion. Latin rhetoricians lengthened it to six parts: introduction, statement of the case, outline of the points, proof of the case, refutation of the opposing arguments, and conclusion. Such a division may appear mechanical and dictatorial, but it at least emphasises the need of some unifying principle of organisation.

The third essential of oratory is style, a term that eludes definition, though we all seem to know what it means. The diversity of well known and standard definitions only testifies to the perplexing elusiveness of the concept: "Style is the dress of thought" (Chesterfield); it is "proper words in proper places" (Swift); "style is only the frame to hold our thoughts" (Emmons); "An author's style is a faithful copy of his mind" (Goethe); "Style is a thinking out into language" (Newman); and so on. The great ancient rhetoricians were well aware of this problem of defining style and, therefore, instead of falling into this tricky trap they discussed it at various levels. For example, in his Rhetoric Book III Aristotle considered style at the levels of words singly and in combination, rhythm, and of sentence-forms. The later rhetoricians, especially Cicero and Quintilian, added to this three-fold level the fourth dimension of figures. These levels thus went on increasing, and today stylistics and linguistics have opened many more insightful ways of exercising language and style. Of the overall qualities of style Aristotle gave foremost importance to clarity and appropriateness. Theophrastus enlarged it to four virtues, adding correctness and ornateness. And there is no end to this fixation also. The fact of the matter is that style is moulded by three factors in particular—the character of the speaker, the quality of the subject, and the level of the audience. Hence there are as many types of style as there are speakers, subjects and audiences. There can never be one style or one quality of style, there are many styles and many qualities of style. Even the time-honoured division of style into grand, middle and plain styles falls in the face of this bewildering-variety.

The fourth ingredient of oratory is memory which is indeed the receptacle of the first three. All of an orator's pains in collecting the material and arranging it logically and expressing it in the best words will collapse disastrously if in the middle of his speech his memory fails and he draws a blank. Memory is not knowledge, but what is knowledge without memory? Good orators do not memorize the entire speech, they only plant the line of argument on their mind, leaving the words to come at call while they speak. This lessens the strain on memory and also lends greater vitality and naturalness to the speech. But the help rendered by memory remains. The rhetoricians today suggest a number of mnemonic devices to sharpen memory. But to a man unaided by these, memory has four mandates: attention, interest, repetition, and confidence. An average man uses only five percent of the resources of his memory and wastes the remaining ninety-five percent by neglecting these mandates.

The fifth component of oratory is delivery, which involves training in voice and in gestures. Thomas Sheridan in his book, *Lectures on Elocution*, considers this problem under nine heads: articulation, pronunciation, accent, emphasis, tone, pause, pitch, voice control, and gesture. Many a speech, faultless in matter, arrangement and in style and well supported by memory, has fallen flat because of inept delivery. I may recall the story of a young speaker who delivered his extremely well prepared oration in such a droning voice and repulsive gestures that the gathering soon grew dull and listless, and felt relieved when he had gone. His friend and guide begged of him the loan of the same speech and after a few weeks delivered it to the same audience with such elocutionary excellence that it went unrecognized and was listened with indulgent and animated attention.

But this gathering, organizing, expressing, memorizing, and delivering the material is not an end in itself. It is done to some purpose. What is that purpose? What is, in other words, the aim or function of oratory? Why does an orator speak? The obvious answer seems, persuasion. An orator speaks in order to persuade the public to his point of view, as Aristotle said in *Rhetoric*, oratory is "the faculty of discovering all the available means of persuasion in any given situation." It is exactly this that a politician does when he contests the election. He tries to convert the voters to his ideology, to persuade him to vote for him. But this is not all. Sometimes, the end may be just pleasure. The orator may speak to please the audience. He may do so by wit or humour or witchery of words, or by some such means. Sometimes, however, his aim may be to instruct his hearers, to reform and educate them. Gandhi's orations were of this type. He moralised the masses and spiritualised politics. Still another aim of oratory may be to move the public to ecstasy, to arouse its passions to a frenzy, an objective that Hitler realised to extraordinary success. These objectives are different from each other, but for that reason they are not mutually exclusive, they do not cancel each other. In fact, they may be combined in the same speech. Take, for example, the following extract from Vivekananda's famous speech, called 'Our Motherland':

> "Up, up, the long night is passing, the day is approaching, the wave has risen, nothing will be able to resist its tidal fury. Believe, believe, the decree has gone forth, the fiat to the Lord has gone forth—India must rise, the masses and the poor are to be made happy. Rejoice! The flood of spirituality has risen. I see it is rolling over the land resistless, boundless, all-absorbing. Every man to the fore, every good will be added to its forces, every hand will smooth its way, and glory be unto the Lord!"

Here Vivekananda is persuading the audience to a belief in India's spirituality, delighting it by the music of his language, instructing it to a sense of duty to the motherland, and moving it to a high pitch of emotion. All the objectives of oratory are happily blended in these magnificent words. Thus, the aims of oratory may be persuasion, delight, instruction, and ecstasy, used singly or in combination. As George Campbell said in his *The Philosophy of Rhetoric* (1776), A speech may have any one of four ends: "to enlighten the understanding, to please the imagination, to move the passions, or to influence the will,"[1] recalling Cicero's observation in *De optima Genere Oratorurn* 1,3, that the best orator "teaches, delights, and moves the minds of his hearers; to

[1] Cited, Edwards P.J. Corbett, *Classical Rhetoric* (New York : Oxford University Press, 1965), p. 564.

teach them is his duty, to delight them is creditable to him, to move them is indispensable."

Thus, oratory is an art that needs studious preparation, but as in the other arts the artfulness must be hidden. The strains of hard work must not be visible in the speech. Though studied, it must look natural, as Aristotle said in Rhetoric, Book III, "We must disguise our art and seem to speak naturally, not artificially; the natural is persuasive, the artificial is the reverse; for men are prejudiced against it as against an insidious design." The idea has been extremely beautifully expressed by William Butler Yeats in 'Adam's Curse' where he describes an artist's painful struggle to attain an appearance of spontaneity. "A line will take us hours may be," says he, but it must "seem a moment's thought." The artist labours hard to look natural.

But who decides the ultimate merit or success of the speech—the speaker himself or another speaker or critic or the public? In all probality, the public is the best judge of public speeches. The combined wisdom of the many supersedes the wisdom of a single man however wise. Moreover, the public opinion is more crucial to oratory than to any other art because here the performance is done in full view of the audience whereas in poetry or in painting it is done in the seclusion of the study or the studio. A poet writes to the imagined audience, the orator to the live one, the currents pass directly between the two. The speaker's personality, voice, bodily gestures, facial expressions, even the movements of the eyes, directly affect the audience. And if he forgets his steps in the midst of the speech there is complete disaster. He is dangerously open to the ridicule of the public. But these things do not matter to the reading public. Besides, the evaluation of an oration is spontaneous and immediate, while tie judgement on poetry is leisurely and delayed. The critic of poetry reads at leisure and criticizes at leisure, and he can even mould the public opinion by his reviews; he decides first and the public next. In oratory the public judges first and the critic next. The public gets precedence over the critic, it is the first and the more important judge. Thus Cicero remarked in Brutus, LI, 192, "The ears of the people are the instruments on which the orator has to play;" and to what extent an audience is affected is inevitably decided by it.

But the function of the critic really begins when the orator is long dead and the world has no option but to judge him on the basis of his recorded or printed speeches. His evaluation then becomes based partly on the facts of the script and partly on the imagined personality of the speaker or on contemporary evidence. The more the distance from the speaker the greater the difficulty. In his evaluation of the English speeches of eminent Indians during the British Raj the present writer is deeply conscious of this difficulty and the consequent responsibility.

II

THE RAJ

Oratory prospers during periods of radical transformation when the one age goes out and the other comes in. During such transitional periods the temper of a nation is high and there is clear call for the services of the men whose tongues can shake the world to its foundation. For examples one may recall the Renaissance in the fifteenth century Italy when it was driving out medievalism, or the Reformation in the sixteenth century England when Henry VIII broke with Pope, or the Revolution in the eighteenth century America when Patrick Henry's fiery speeches roused the American people to their depth. Something of the same kind happened during the Raj when the forces of Renaissance, Reformation and non-violent Revolution for freedom threw up a large number of orators in India. Oratory was an exigency of the moment, an inevitable outgrowth of the combined currents of Renaissance, Reformation and Revolution that heated up the temper of the nation. Let us survey the period to see how it came about.

The first Englishman setting foot on Indian soil was Father Thomas Stevens who sailed for India from Lisbon on 4 April 1579. The first Englishmen to trade with India were eighty merchants from London who formed a company and got permission from Queen Elizabeth on 31 December 1600 for "trading into the East Indies." The first factory was started by these traders in Surat in 1612 under leave from Jahangir. By what logic of events these traders expanded into conquerors, is a story oft told by historians and need not detain us here. But what is of significance is the fact that such a thing could not have happened without some serious shortcoming in our character which lent itself to easy exploitation by the clever British. In any case, the crucial event was the Battle of Plassey between Clive and Sirajuddaula on 23 June 1757 in which the English registered an easy victory over the Nawab and sowed the seeds of the British Empire in India.

The hundred years that followed the Battle of Plassey, the years from 1757 to 1857, ushered in fourteen Governors-General and saw the British Empire grow larger and larger till the whole of India came under its servitude. The greatest single political event of this long period was the Rising of 1857 which the British historians have called the revolt of the conservative India against the reforms introduced by the rationalistic Britain, and the Indian historians have called the first war of independence. Thus, Bipan Chandra, Amales Tripathi and Barun De claimed that "it was the first great struggle of the Indian people for freedom from British imperialism."[1] On the other hand, percival Spear observed, "It is in fact an anachronism to describe the Mutiny as the first essay towards modern independence. It was rather, in its political aspect, the last effort of the old conservative India."[2]

But both are agreed about its psychological impact: it struck fear and caution in the British and anger and vengeance intensified by the memory of defeat in the Indians. Physically, its result was the passing of the movement from the Company to the Crown, which was capped by Queen Victoria's famous proclamation in 1858. The hold of the British over India became even stronger. The empire was fully consolidated, though the embers of revolt smouldered beneath the tranquil surface.

One more event from this period may be recalled, an event of far greater consequence, the adoption of the Western knowledge as the content of education and of the English language as the medium of instruction by Bentinck's Resolution of 1835 which, in its turn was based on Macaulay's Minute on Education. By this English system of education Macaulay hoped to Westernize

---

[1] *Freedom Struggle* (New Delhi: National Book Trust, 1982), p. 46.
[2] *Modern India* (London: Oxford at the Clarendon Press, 1965), p. 219.

Indians, to draw them out of medievalism, to make them see visions of a new awakened India. He feared that the British Empire might one day perish, but hoped that English would remain, that would indeed be the spiritual conquest of India. It is interesting to recall his famous speech in the House of Commons in 1833:

> "The scepter may pass away from us . . . . Victory may be inconstant to our arms. But there are triumphs which are followed by no reverse. There is an empire exempt from all natural causes of decay. Those triumphs are the pacific triumphs of reason over barbarism; that empire is the imperishable empire of our arts and our morals, our literature and our laws."[3]

In this anglicization Bentick was strongly supported by many Indians, among them by the great Raja Rammohun Roy. Much earlier, in a letter addressed to the Governor-General on 11 December 1832, he had said:

> "The Government are establishing a Sanskrit school under Hindu Pundits to impart such knowledge as is already current in India. . . . The pupils will there acquire what was known two thousand years ago. . . . Sanskrit system of education would be best calculated to keep the country in darkness." So, the Government would better "promote a more liberal and enlightened system of instruction . . . which may be accomplished by employing a few gentlemen of talents and learning educated in Europe."[4]

This led to the opening of a large number of English medium schools and colleges and in the year of rising 1857 to the establishment of three prime universities of India—Bombay, Calcutta and Madras. An English knowing public was thus created and from among them emerged eminent speakers in English who through their English speeches voiced their demand for independence,

---

[3] Cited, Michael Edwardes, *A History of India* (London: the New English Library, 1967), p. 233.

[4] *Ibid.*, p. 233.

fulfilling Macaulay's prophecy that "having become instructed in European knowledge, they may, in some future age, demand European institutions."[5] This reminds me of Caliban's cutting rejoinder to Prospero: "You taught me language; and my profit on't is, I know how to curse." (*The Tempest*, I, ii, 363-4).

The period between the Rising of 1857 and the final freedom in 1947 saw twenty Viceroys who ruled over India with stick in one hand and the healing balm in the other so that the wounds inflicted by the stick could be soothed by the balm. They alternated between coersion and conciliation, between the most stringent repressionary measures and half-hearted and reluctant reforms. This progressively heated up the temper of the nation and animated the tongue of the speakers and thus gave rise to some of the most inspiring speeches by eminent Indians.

The first few years after the Rising of 1857 were those of reorganisation on the part of the British and of uneasy peace on the part of the Indians. This was also the period of stock-taking during which the two cultures came in close contact with each other—the Western culture with its rationalism and the Indian culture entrenched in tradition. Out of the crisscross of these cultures were born three interlocked movements that changed the very face of India—Renaissance, Reformation and Nationalism. A new India was born in which every heart pulsated with fresh ideas from the West and took inspiration from its own rich past. The nation was intensely charged. It woke up from a long slumber, and such an atmosphere was bound to fire the imagination of the Indian speakers and to result into great oratory.

The seeds of Renaissance were sown by Raja Rammohun Roy (1772-1833) who is rightfully called the Father of Modern India. He had championed many social, religious and political reforms under Western influence and justified them on the basis of Upanishadik rationalism. The seedlings now started sprouting. The entire Indian society felt the impact of this transformation. *Sati* practice, child marriage, oppression of women, non-marriage

---

[5] Cited, Saumyendranath Tagore, *Raja Rammohun Roy* (New Delhi: Sahitya Akademi, 1989), p. 27.

of widows, brutalities of the caste system, ritualism, idolatry, untouchability, and many more such evil practices came under inspired attack. Nearly 500 newspapers and journals came into being during this period and a good number of schools, colleges and universities to boot, which fanned the fire of this new awakening and led to the all-round development of India.

The greatest impact of this reawakening was, however, felt in the field of religion. It was increasingly realised that various religions in India needed purification by return to their original sources and by weeding out accretions of centuries. The first of these reformist movements was *Brahmo Samaj* that was founded by Raja Rammohun Roy in 1828 and was later strengthened by Dwarkanath Tagore (1794-1846), Davendranath Tagore (1817-1905) and Keshub Chunder Sen (1838-1884). It aimed at weeding out idolatry, ritualism and belief in multiple gods in the light of the rationalistic view of Hinduism in the Upanishads. Under the spell of *Brahmo Samaj* came *Prarthana Samaj* in Maharashtra which was founded by Dr. Atmaram Pandurang (1823-1898) and supported by R. G. Bhandarkar (1837-1927) and by M. G. Ranade (1842-1901) with aims of rational worship and social reform. Even more popular and powerful than these was *Arya Samaj* started by Swami Dayananda Saraswati (1824-1883) in 1875. Its most powerful members were Lala Lajpat Rai (1865-1928) and Harbilas Sarda. Just as Raja Rammohun Roy had turned to Upanishads for justification of his reforms, Swami Dayananda turned to the four Vedas, and was even more militantly opposed to polygamy, casteism and idolatry. Another powerful Reformist Movement was *Ramkrishna Mission* started by Swami Vivekananda (1863-1902) in 1897 after his Guru Ramkrishna Paramahamsa (1834-1886). It stood for *Bhakti* or devotion as a means of God realisation and believed in the inherent sameness of all religions. Its clarion call was religious universalism. The last great religious movement of Hindus was *Theosophical Movement* started by the Russian Madame Blavatsky in the United States in 1875 and adopted to Hinduism by the Irish turned Hindu Annie Besant (1847-1933). Theosophy, meaning divine wisdom or knowledge of God, held great faith in occultism and spiritualism of the Hindu rishis.

Other religions did not lag behind in this reformist race. Dadabhai Naoroji (1825-1917) and J. B. Wacha started *Religious Reform Association* to restore Zoroastrian religion to its old glory. Sikhs started, *Chief Khalsa Diwan* at Amritsar to purify their religious and social life. Of the Muslim reformist movements may be noted *Wahabis* of Patna and *Ahmadias* of Punjab which gave a call for the simplicity and sincerity of ancient Islam. To these may be added the contribution of Sir Syed Ahmed Khan (1817-1898) who stood for the synthesis of Islam and the rational West.

This pride in India's illustrious past, coupled with rationalistic ideas about freedom and democracy from the West, and a natural discontent against a foreign power, generated nation-consciousness among the Indians, which, as the years wore on and more and more stimulants came in its wake, gathered in strength and grew into a regular movement called Nationalism. Its immediate expressions were formation of *The India Association of Calcutta* by Surendranath Banerjea (1848-1925) in 1876, *The Indian National Conference* in Calcutta in 1883, and most importantly *Indian National Congress* by A. O. Hume in 1885. In the initial stages the Congress was merely a vehicle for carrying Indian grievances to the British authorities, but in slow degrees it developed into a platform for the freedom movement.

The turning point was the *Partition of Bengal* by Curzon in 1905, ostensibly for administrative convenience but really for creating a cleavage between Hindus and Muslims. The event lashed the entire nation into a wild fury and led to a chain of reaction. The immediate result was *Swadeshi* (the use of Indian goods) and *Bahishkar* (boycott of foreign goods). In the Congress of 1906 Dadabhai Naoroji proclaimed *Swaraj* or self-rule as the political goal of India, for which he is generally regarded as the Father of Indian Nationalism. In the same year was born the *Muslim League* which ultimately led to the creation of Pakistan. In the Congress of 1907 in Surat occurred the split between the *Moderates* who stood for constitutional means of agitation and the *Extremists* who were for any means. In the midst of this ferment came the *Morley-Minto Reforms* in 1909 which provided for the association of qualified Indians with the government, which soon disenchanted both the groups. Another conciliatory measure was the *Revocation of the Partition of Bengal* in 1911. *The First World War* (1914-1918) in which India helped Britain created greater expectancy among Indians. In 1916, aided by Tilak, Annie Besant started the *Home Rule League* which drew support from both the Muslim League and the Moderates and led to a temporary union of the three. In 1918 appeared the *Montague-Chelmsford Reforms* which proposed self-government in slow degrees and again alienated the Extremists who desired violent reforms. Close at heels of conciliatory reforms came the repressionary *Rowlatt Bill* in the same year which provided for the trial of some political crimes without jury. This added fuel to fire and the entire nation was outraged.

A crucial event happened at this point of time when the country was already in high fever. It was the *Jallianwala Bagh Massacre* by General Dyre on 13 April 1919. Gandhi who had by now become a national idol launched his first *Non-Violent Non-co-operation Movement* in 1920, which required boycott of legislatures, courts, schools, colleges, and of foreign clothes. It was supported by Muslims also, for they were unhappy with the British attitude towards the Turkish Caliphate (*khilafat*). Gandhi suspended the movement when violence broke at Chauri Chaura in Uttar Pradesh. In 1923 C. R. Das and Motilal Nehru started *Swaraj Party* with blessings from Gandhi. In 1929 Lord Irwin offered the *Dominion Status* which was summarily rejected. In 1929 at the special Lahore Congress Nehru declared *Complete Independence* as the objective of India.

Event followed event in quick succession, which progressively raised the temper of the nation. In 1930 Gandhi launched the *Civil Disobedience Movement*, which demanded non-violent defiance of laws, with his *Salt March* from Ahmedabad to Dandi Coast. Between 1930 and 1932 three fruitless *Round Table Conferences* followed in London, the second of which was attended by Gandhi and which elicited Churchill's famous remark that

> "It is alarming and also nauseating to see Mr. Gandhi, a seditious Middle Temple lawyer, now posing as a fakir of the type well-known in the East, striding half-naked up the steps of the Viceregal palace, while he is still organizing and conducting

a defiant campaign of civil disobedience, to parley on equal terms with the representative of the King Emperor."[6]

In 1935 came the abortive *Government of India Act*, which was followed by the *Formation of Congress Ministries* in eight provinces in 1937 and their subsequent withdrawal in 1939. In 1940 the Muslim League reinforced its demand for *Pakistan* which had been mooted in 1933 by a student named Chaudhuri Rahmat Ali, the name given being PAKSTAN—P for Punjab, A for Afghan, K for Kashmir, S for Sind, Tan for Baluchistan. In the same year Lord Linlithgo made a second offer of *Dominion Status* which was ceremoniously turned down. In 1942 the *Quit India Movement* was launched. On 7 August, that is, a day before the resolution for Quit India was carried, Gandhi spoke inspiringly at All India Congress Committee held in Bombay:

> "Here is a *mantra*, a short one, that I give you . . . 'Do or Die'. We shall either free India or die in the attempt; we shall not live to see the perpetration of our slavery . . . . Take a pledge, with God and your own conscience as witness, that you will no longer rest till freedom is achieved He who loses his life will gain it, he who will seek to save it will lose it. Freedom is not for the coward or the faint-hearted."

All the prominent leaders were arrested forthwith. In 1944 Subhash Chandra Bose tried to liberate India through the *Indian National Army* which he had inherited from Rashbehari Bose in Japan, but failed. *Communal Riots* of the most gruesome nature occurred between 1946 and 1947. The British could not contain the freedom movement and the Indians could not contain the Hindu-Muslim riots. Thus came freedom on 15 August 1947 at the crippling cost of Pakistan.

Such were the times that produced the English speeches of the eminent Indians and we need to preserve these moments and men and their speeches.

---

[6] Cited, Geoffrey Moorhouse, *India Britannica* (London: Granada, 1984), p. 181.

III

THE PREDECESSORS OF GANDHI

Considering Gandhi as the central figure of the British Raj, we may classify the Raj orators into (1) the Predecessors of Gandhi; (2) Gandhi and His Contemporaries; and (3) the Successors of Gandhi. Historically speaking, the Predecessors of Gandhi were born between the Battle of Plassey in 1757 and the Rising of 1857; Gandhi and His Contemporaries, between 1857 and the Formation of Congress in 1885; and the Successors of Gandhi, between 1885 and our Independence in 1947. I have begun with Raja Rammohun Roy who was born 15 years after the Battle of Plessey and who died two years before English was made the medium of instruction, and ended with Shyama Prasad Mookerjee who was 45 years old in 1947.

The most glaring fact about the Predecessors of Gandhi was that nearly all of them were ardent reformers who were deeply conscious of the social, moral and religious ills that had debased India and who sincerely believed that the merciful Providence had sent the British for the needful help. India had a great past, but over the years idolatry, belief in multiple gods, priestcraft, caste system, superstition, and other ills in hundred hideous forms had degraded and demoralised her. They looked upon England for help and prayed for the continuance of the British rule in India, if not permanently, at least for a time. Political consciousness was slow to come. The demand for freedom was a later development. The early speeches amply illustrate this fact. Thus, Raja Rammohun Roy said in a public meeting in Calcutta on 15 December 1829. "The greater our intercourse with European gentlemen, the greater will be our improvement in literary, social and political affairs."[1] Dwarkanath Tagore said in 1842: "It was England who sent out Clive and Cornwallis to benefit India by their counsels and arms."[2] And in 1870 Keshub Chunder Sen said in the Calcutta Town Hall: "Fallen India cried for help, and lo! at Heaven's bidding England hastened to her rescue."[3]

No less important than this is the fact that Gandhi and Vivekananda excepted, the greatest orators in English that India has produced were from the Predecessors of Gandhi—Michael Madhusudan Dutt, Kristo Das Pal, Keshub Chunder Sen, Surendranath Banerjea, and Lal Mohan Ghose. They spoke English with such fluidity, grace and elegance as astounded the best among the cultivated English men. Take this from Michael Madhusudan Dutt: "I stand before you not as Columbus, proudly claiming the need of a discoverer of unknown worlds; I stand before you- not as a Newton, whose god-like vision penetrated the blue depths of ether and saw a new and a bright orb, cradled in infinity; I deal in no mysteries; I am no sophist, ravishing the ear with melodious yet unmeaning sounds, captivating the eye with sparkling yet meretricious ornamentalism—beautiful yet artificial flowers, glittering yet false diamonds. No ! . . . ."[4]

Notable among the Predessors of Gandhi were: Raja Rammohun Roy (1772-1833), Dwarkanath Tagore (1794-1846), Ram Gopal Ghose (1815-1868.), Michael Madhusudan Dutt (1824-1873), Rajendra Lala Mitra (1824-1891), Dada Bhai Naoroji (1825-1917), Kristo Das Pal (1838-1884), Keshub Chunder Sen (1838-1884), Mahadev Govind Ranade (1842-1901), Womesh Chunder Bonnerjee (1844-1906), Budrudin Tyabji (1884-1906), Rash

---

1 Cited, Mani Lal C. Parekh, 'Rajarshi Rammohun Roy' in *Raja Rammohun Roy*, ed. Verinder Grover (New Delhi: Deep & Deep Publications, 1992), p. 107.

2 In *Indian Speeches and Documents on British Rule*, ed. J.K. Majumdar (Calcutta: Longmans & Green, 1937), p. 51.

3 *Ibid.*, pp. 87-88.

4 'The Anglo-Saxon and the Hindu' in *Madhusudan Ratnaavali* (Calcutta: Sahitya Sansad, printed 1965), pp. 531-32.

Bihari Ghose, (1845-1921), Pheroze Shah Mehta (1845-1915), Anand Mohan Bose (1846-1906), Surendranath Banerjea (1848-1925), Romesh Chunder Dutt (1848-1909), Lal Mohan Ghose (1849-1909), and Kashinath Trimbak Telang (1850-1893). I may now consider these orators individually in their chronological order.

Raja Rammohun Roy (1772-1833)

Raja Rammohun Roy, the father of Modern India, was born in an affluent and orthodox Brahmin family in the village of Radhanagar in Burdwan district in Bengal on 22 May 1772. He learnt Bengali in the local school and Persian under a Maulvi at home. He then went to Patna to study Arabic and Persian and to Benaras to learn Sanskrit. At 16 he wrote a pamphlet condemning idolatry, ceremonialism and priestcraft so militantly that it antagonized his father and he had to quit his paternal roof. After four years of wanderings which extended to Tibet where he studied Buddhism he was restored to his father's favour and he returned home. Again his forward looking ideas repelled his father and he left for Benaras where he lived for ten or twelve years. The death of his father in 1803 brought him back home and he wrote an iconoclastic book in Persian called *Tuhfat-ul-Muwahuddin* in which he castigated polytheism, instrumentality of prophets, belief in miracles and idols, and the like accretions which had devalued Hinduism, and in their place established Upanishadic monism.

In 1805 he joined the East India Company which he served in various capacities till 1815 after which he settled in Calcutta. Here he indulged in every type of public reform—social, economic, educational, political, and, above all, religious. He opposed *suttee pratha*, polygamy, infanticide, and caste system and supported widow remarriage and the right of inheritance of women. For agriculturists he fought against rack-renting. He advocated scientific and English system of education for India. He stood for the freedom of expression, and his memorial in support of the freedom of press is regarded as the *Areopagitica* of India. Equally vehement was the war that he waged against rācial discrimination. To present true religion before the Hindus he translated Vedas into Hindi, Urdu and Bengali and some Upanishads into Bengali and

English, and established *Brahmo Samaj* which advocated the worship of one Brahma. His contribution to language and literature was immense. He knew Sanskrit, Persian, Arabic, Hebrew, Greek, Latin, Hindi, Pali, Bengali, French, English, Italian, Spanish, and Tibetan. He was the originator of Bengali prose and of Indian journalism. His Calcutta period was indeed one of rich and varied activities.

In 1830 Raja Rammohun Roy left for England to plead on behalf of the Emperor of Delhi for the increase of his allowances, to advocate the cause of the abolition of *Suttee*, and to be present in the House of Commons on the renewal of the Charter of the East India Company. He performed these three duties with great efficiency and success. Honours came to him thick and fast. But overwork strained his health, and he breathed his last at Stapleton Grove, near Bristol, on 27 September 1833.

It is interesting to note that Raja Rammohun Roy commenced his study of English language in 1794 when he was twenty-two years old. By the time the century rolled out he could speak in English just enough to be understood. In 1801 he befriended John Digby, an English officer, who drew him to a serious study of the English language and the Western classics. He took a few more years to gain command over conversational language but not enough to make public speeches. In this exercise of learning, his service in the East India Company from 1805 to 1815 was of great help. The Calcutta period from 1815 to 1830 saw him grow into a real master of the English language. In 1817 he wrote his first essay in English called 'A Defence of Hindu Theism' which was followed by a large number of books and polemical writings. His English works edited by Kalidas Nag and Debajyoti run to six volumes. By the time he reached England in April 1831 he had acquired the reputation of a great English speaker, so much so that the English philosopher Jeremy Bentham paid him a rich compliment for his style and considered it superior to that of James Mill. He spoke in transparently clear style with no effort at effect or purple patches. The ideas were arranged logically and expressed in simple, precise, but forceful language. He had a turn for balanced expressions, as in the following lines at the close of his speech at the meeting of the Unitarian Association held in his honour in London: "There is a battle going on between reason, scripture and common sense; and wealth, power and prejudice. These three have been struggling with the other three." His chief concerns were matters related to reform, but the subject on which he found full unfoldment was religion. Not many of his speeches are available today, nor do we have any report about the mode of his delivery, one can only guess that considering his total personality it must have been dignified.

Dwarkanath Tagore (1794-1846)

Dwarkanath Tagore, the grandfather of Rabindranath Tagore, was born in a prosperous and cultivated family of Bengal in 1794. He was educated at Sherbourne's School, Calcutta. He entered and left the East India Company to establish his own business which prospered immensely. His interest in journalism made him acquire a major share in a Calcutta journal called *Bengal Harkara*. He visited England in 1842 and in 1845 and died there on 1 August 1846.

The speeches of Dwarkanath were marked by extreme loyalty to the British and therefore today they sound artificial, the product of motivated labour than spontaneous effusions of genuine feelings. They were made to please the rulers, and some of them were repellingly flattering. Take the concluding part of the speech in the Town Hall of Calcutta on 15 December 1829, praising the British economy which Gandhi condemned so severely in later times: "If such beneficial effects as these I have enumerated have accrued from the bestowing of European skill in one article of production alone [indigo], what further advantages may not be anticipated from the unrestricted application of British skill, capital and industry to the very many articles which this country is capable of producing, to a great extent and of as excellent a quality as any other in the world, and which of course cannot be expected to be produced without the free recourse of Europeans."[5]

[5] *Indian Speeches and Documents on British Rules*, ed. J.K. Majumdar (Calcutta: Longmans & Green, 1937), p. 45.

The style, as we see even from this brief citation, was cold but correct, characterized by rhetorical questions and long sentences. The usual subjects of his speeches were *suttee pratha*, spread of English education and freedom of the press. His ideas on these subjects were enlightened and rationalistic.

Ram Gopal Ghose (1815-1868)

Ram Gopal Ghose, the son of a small shopkeeper, was born in Calcutta in 1814. He received his school education in Sherbourne's Institute and college education at Hindu College, Calcutta. Before he could complete his education, the straitened family circumstances compelled him to take up a job in Joseph Company, Calcutta. Later, he started his own business and earned good fortune, and became a member of the Bengal Chamber of Commerce. He started a bilingual journal called *Bengal Spectator*. He became the President of the Bengal British India Society in 1845. He was a founding member of Calcutta University. He was nominated a member of the Bengal Legislative Council in 1862. He died on 25 January 1868 at the age of fifty-three.

Ram Gopal Ghose was a man of versatile interests. His speeches covered social, economic, educational, and political reforms. His most consuming obsession was female education. He spoke also on racial discrimination, incurring the displeasure of the government. In ultimate analysis, like Dwarkanath Tagore, he too was a pro-British orator. But he was more effective and eloquent than him. He was called the Demosthenes of India. His speech on Charter Act was characterized as "a masterpiece of oratory" by *The Times*. *Indian Field* observed of his speech on the Queen's Proclamation that "if he were an Englishman, he would have been knighted."[6] The language was rhetorical and the tone flattering. Praising the Queen's proclamation as a noble utterance, he said at the end: "Let us kneel down before her with every feeling of loyalty;—let us welcome the new reign with

[6] Cited, M.K. Naik, *A History of Indian English Literature* (Delhi: Sahitya Akademi, 1995), p. 19.

the warmest sentiment of gratitude, the deepest feeling of devotion."[7]

Michael Madhusudan Dutt (1824-1873)

Michael Madhusudan Dutt was born in a small village called Sagardanri, now in Bangladesh, on 25 January 1824. He received his school education at the local school and at a Grammar school in Calcutta and college education first at Hindu College and then at Bishop's College at Sibpur near Howrah till 1847. He had already embraced Christianity in 1840; in 1847 he left for Madras where he worked as a teacher and married his own student Rebecca Mctavish from whom he had four children. For reasons not known to posterity, he left his wife and children and came back to Calcutta in 1856. Here he joined as a Head Clerk in a Police Court and then became an interpreter in English. He married again. His second wife was Henrietta from whom he had three sons. In 1862 he left for England where he qualified as bar-at-law and returned to Calcutta in 1867. His legal practice did not get him enough money to indulge his reckless Westernized life. He died in poverty on 29 June 1873. His overwhelming obsession with Westernism and equally consuming passion for extravagant living cast a doom over his life. But for the kind help from Iswar Chandra Vidyasagar, he would have been ruined long ago.

Broadly speaking, during his Madras period he wrote in English and after that in Bengali. Like Raja Rammohun Roy he was a master of many languages—English, German, French, Italian, Greek, Latin, Sanskrit, and Bengali. Most of his English speeches are not preserved, but the few that have remained testify to his extraordinary power as a speaker in English. Not one Indian till date could surpass his remarkable command of the English language, or his absorption in the Western ways of life. He had acquired the mastery in this direction as far as it could be attained by a foreigner. The motivating force came from his belief that India, once the golden pride of the world,

---

7 *Indian Speeches and Documents on British Rule*, ed. J.K. Majumdar (Calcutta : Longmans & Greens, 1937), pp. 77-78).

but now decayed through centuries of servitude and superstition, could be redeemed only by the British intervention. In his speech, 'The Anglo-Saxon and the Hindu', made in 1854, he observed: "let the sceptic doubt; let the scoffer sneer; let the thoughtless laugh; but believe me, it is the solemn mission of the Anglo-Saxon to renovate, to regenerate, to civilize-or, in a word, to Christianise the Hindu."[8] This abiding belief was both the strength and the weakness of his speeches. It filled them with passion and poetry, with fluidity and fluency which have never been equalled, far less surpassed, by any speaker in India till today. But at the same time it hurt every Indian in his seat of honour, he felt depressed than rejuvenated. A repellent thought was clothed in magnificent style—long flowing sentences, uprootingly original metaphors and similes, a string of disarming rhetorical questions, loaded with rich allusions, and bent with an overweight of beautiful and well-chosen words. His above-referred speech, 'The Anglo-Saxon and the Hindu', as it reads today, can be put alongside Goldsmith's splendid essay, 'A City Night-piece'. A brief citation will illustrate the point. He said: "You see before you, as it were, on a stage, two actors—the Anglo-Saxon and the Hindu. One of them is indeed well-graced, ravishing the eyes of the audience with his manly beauty—enchanting the ears of the audience with the dulcet tones of his voice: The other, I fear is ill-favoured, worn out by the ceaseless waves of time, hoarse and dissonant as an unturned harp, as an unstrung lute. . . . Flowering youth, decaying age; radiant beauty, hideous deformity; exulting valour, pallid fear; sparkling diamond, dim crystal;—but why should I multiply such images? The contrast is indeed very great!"[9]

Rajendra Lala Mitra (1824-1891)

Rhajendra Lala Mitra, a distinguished Indologist, was born in Calcutta in the same year as Michael Madhusudan Dutt, 1824. He was associated with the Asiatic Society in various capacities,

---

[8] *Madhusudan Ratnavali* (Calcutta: Sahitya Sansad, 1965), pp. 526-27.

[9] *Ibid.*, p. 523-524.

as philological secretary, Vice-President and President. He edited nearly 80 Sanskrit texts and wrote a large number of books. His speeches were edited by Raj Jogeshur Mitter one year after his death in 1892.

Rajendra Lala Mitra was a man of encyclopedic learning combined with startling originality. Add to this the intrepidity of his character, and we have the right view of his speeches—they were profound, original and bold. He arranged his ideas most meticulously and never deviated from the central argument of his speech into side tracks, scrupulously avoiding irrelevant matter and tiresome repetition. The word that best defines his style is 'moderation'; that is why his speeches were correct, well-regulated and cultivated, but they lacked excitement, the carrying power which was the singular feature of the speeches of Michael Madhusudan Dutt. He closed his speech at the Second National Congress with *moderation* as advice to the speakers: "Let your speakers speak moderately; let your schemes be moderate; and let your resolutions be so framed that no Government can have any occasion to complain of want of moderation."[10]

Dada Bhai Naoroji (1825-1917)

Dada Bhai Naoroji, usually regarded as the Father of Indian Nationalism, was born in a Parsi priestly family of Bombay on 4 September 1825. He graduated from Elphinstone College, Bombay in 1845 and became Professor of Mathematics and Natural Philosophy in the same college in 1854. In 1855 he joined Messrs Cama & Co., an Indian firm in England. In England he also worked as Professor of Gujarati at the University College, London. Now on he oscillated between India and England. In 1874 he became the Dewan of Baroda; in 1875, a Member of the Municipal Corporation, Bombay; in 1885, a Member of the Bombay Legislative Council; in 1886, the President of the Indian National Congress; in 1892, a Member of the House of Commons

[10] *Speeches by Raja Rajendra Lala Mitra*, ed. Raj Jogeshur Mitter (Calcutta : Messrs S.K. Lahiri & Co., 1892), pp. 200-201.

for Central Finsbury; in 1893, again the President of Indian National Congress, which honour was repeated in 1906; and these ceaseless attainments were terminated by his death on 30 June 1917. Called out of veneration as the Grand Old Man of India, today he is remembered chiefly for his "drain theory" in Economics which signified draining away our moral and material resources by the British, and for his concept of Swaraj or self-government in Politics which he promulgated in his Congress Presidential speech in 1906. His most outstanding book is *Poverty and Un-ritish Rule in India*.

The speeches of Dada Bhai Naoroji invariably veered around the problem of British Indian relationships. He believed in the British sense of justice, in the civilizing power of the English system of education, in the British contribution in establishing law and order in India, and in many other benefits that flowed from the British rule. Therefore in speech after speech he preached loyalty to England. But his loyalty was never slavish. He was also aware of the exploitation of India by the British. He maintained that they combined in them the characters of rulers and traders; as rulers they oppressed Indians and as traders they fleeced them. Their empire was built with the money of India and by the blood of Indians. The right relationship between the two countries demanded that the welfare of England should be founded upon the welfare of India. The specific subjects that he handled in his speeches recurrently were the draining of Indian earnings to England, self-government under British paramountcy and simultaneous ICS examination in England and India. Clearly, these were matter-of-fact business-like subjects; so was the style of his speeches. It was lucid, straightforward, precise, and free of all verbal overweight or ornamentation. He spoke of plain things in a plain manner. His economic speeches were loaded with statistical details. It was language of explication and illustration in which there was no place for rhetorical or sentimental outbursts. That many times made his speeches cold and colourless without any literary flavour. They epitomized business. For this extremity of coolness, his speeches could not attain great literary heights. His name cannot be bracketed with the best orators of India, even though he was surely one of the tallest men of the Raj period. It is worthwhile recalling a few lines from his Presidential address at the Lahore Congress in 1893. See how plainly he opened his speech: "I am much pleased that I have the privilege of presiding at the very first Congress held in Punjab, as I had at Calcutta in 1886. I have taken, as you may be aware, some interest in the material condition of Punjab. In my first letter to the Secretary of State for India, in 1880, on the material condition of India, I took Punjab for my illustration, and worked out in detail its total annual income . . ."[11]

Kristo Das Pal (1838-1884)

The son of a *tili* (oilman) who worked in a small shop at fifteen rupees per month, Kristo Das Pal was born in Calcutta in April 1838. He was educated at the Oriental Seminary and the Hindu Metroploitan College, Calcutta. In 1858 he became Assistant Secretary and in 1879 Secretary to the British India Association. He got Editorship of *Hindu Patriot* in 1861 to which post he continued till his death in 1884. In 1863 he was nominated to the Municipal Council, Calcutta. In 1872 he became a member of the Bengal Legislative Council. In 1883 he was nominated to the Viceroy's Legislative Council as the representative of the Bengal Zamindars. In 1884 he got the honour of elevation to CIE. He died on 24 July 1884.

Kristo Das Pal was another unwavering British loyalist. He lost no opportunity of praising his white master. In his speech in Calcutta on 31 July 1875 he burst into a panegyric on the British rule: "She [Victoria] stands forth as the representative of a power which has re-kindled the East with the light that had been borrowed from it to resume the West; which has, with the extension of its arms, extended the arts and commerce of civilized life wherever it has gone; which has resucitated the dead bones of the ancient civilization of India, breathed the breath of life into its inert masses, given a healthy impulse to their legitimate

---

[11] *Political Thinkers of Modern India: Dada Bhai Naoroji*, ed. Verinder Grover (New Delhi: Deep & Deep Publication, 1992), p. 165.

aspirations for social and political advancement, and enabled them to enjoy the fruits of their honest labour, the yield of their enterprise and the rights of humanity and the citizenship of a free state in peace and tranquillity, with perfect liberty, and with the utmost advantage."[12]

The editor that he was, his favourite subject of speech making was the freedom of the press. Again and again he said in his speeches that the press was not meant to circulate only tales of adulation, its function was to make unvarnished statement of facts, to check the ruler if he erred, and to communicate the just grievances of the public to him. And for this also he lavished unstinted praise on the British. In his speech at the Calcutta Traders Association's Dinner in February 1880 he said: "The millions of India are dumb. But the Press gives them a tongue; though poets sang and philosophers spoke, when India was under her national dynasty, and though literary activity was not unknown, when the Moslems held sway over her, the people then knew not the blessings of a free press, and therefore remained mute. The right of the free speech is a glorious heritage, which you, Englishmen, and your ancestors, have brought into this country; it is a jewel above all price."[13]

Another subject on which his tongue became animated was the English system of education. He considered it a boon to India, but at the same time he was fully conscious of the value of the mother-tongue to the greatness of a nation. In his speech in Calcutta in February 1879 he said: "I am an advocate of English education. I hold that the wider are the blessings of English education diffused, the more effectually will the best interests of the country be subserved—but . . . no nation could attain to real greatness without a literature of its own; the masses must express their thoughts and feelings through the tongue which they learn at their mother's breast."[14]

---

[12] *Indian Speeches and Documents on British Rule*, ed. J.K. Majumdar (Calcutta : Longmans & Greens, 1937), p. 100.

[13] *Ibid.*, p. 125.

[14] *Ibid.*, p. 121.

Though Kristo Das Pal was a staunch loyalist, he aimed even during those remote days at self-government. He felt that the British rulers wanted Indians to learn the art of self-governance. One more citation will not be out of place. In his speech in Calcutta in February 1883 he said this on self-government: "Measures are being matured for the extension of local self-government in this country upon a national basis, for the elevation of the native to high standard of political education. . . . For a century and a quarter has England ruled India, but hitherto she sought to rule it by the sword, and not by striking a chord of sympathy in the national heart . . . . This is the first time England is essaying to fulfil her mission in the East in the highest sense of that term" (128-9).

Kristo Das Pal was among the first few great orators in India. His eloquence compelled admiration even of the English administrators. They listened to him with rapt attention. His style was marked by elegance, effortless ease and flowing gracefulness. An outstanding feature of his oratory was the combination of long with short sentences. Sometimes the sentences run to nearly one full printed page. How he kept the track was a marvel. Another striking feature was appropriateness of words. The words matched the thought most aptly. Even more important than these qualities was the rhythmical arrangement of words, phrases and clauses in a sentence. This rendered liquidity to the speech. There is no record of how they sounded to the hearers, but I visualise it must have been music to them, for the applause he received was tremendous. His speeches make a marvelous reading, though much in them is ephemeral today. The only grating note is his extreme loyalism. But during those days of British rule when the uprising of 1857 was just quashed by force and cunning such acquiescence was natural.

Keshub Chunder Sen (1838-1884)

Keshub Chunder Sen, a torch-bearer of *Sadharan Brahmo Samaj*, was born in a distinguished family of Bengal on 19 November 1878 (coincidentally the year of Bankim Chandra Chatterjee's birth) in Calcutta. He studied Mental and Moral Philosophy at

Hindu College, Calcutta, till 1858. In 1859 he joined as Clerk in the Bank of Bengal. He left this job in 1861 and started an English fortnightly called *Indian Mirror*. Thereafter he gave himself wholeheartedly to social, educational and religious reforms, the one important occupation being the promotion of *Brahmo Samaj*. In 1870 he visited England and lectured profusely on God, religion and Indo-British Relationship. In 1878, at the behest of the British Government, he solemnised the betrothal ceremony of his minor daughter to the Prince of Coochbehar who also was minor. This antagonized his admirers who condemned it as a retrograde step. It did not match with his crusade against child-marriage. He died on 8 January 1884, a year before the birth of the Congress.

Keshub Chunder Sen was a superb orator. He was regarded as the "Thunderbolt of Bengal". The *Statesman* observed: "When Keshub speaks, the world listens."[15] He was compared with Gladstone and Cicero. Surendranath Banerjea praised his eloquence thus in his autobiography: "His address drew a large audience (Indians and Europeans of all shades of opinion). They created a deep and abiding impression on young minds. His marvelous oratory, set forth with all the accessories of a sonorous voice, a noble diction and a commanding presence, and inspired by the fervour of a deep and burning conviction, fascinated his hearers. I was often at his meetings and listened with breathless attention and ever-increasing admiration."[16]

It is said that "Keshub used to commence his lectures with a short prayer, hardly audible to all till gradually the pitch of his voice rose and filled the hall to the remotest corner. Dressed in simple *choga* and *chapkan* of black surge, extempore in delivery without notes, without gesticulation or haranguing he spoke fluently in Bengali, English or Hindi, carrying the whole audience."[17]

---

[15] Cited, Publisher's Note in *Kedhub Speaks* (Bombay: Navavidhan Chittabinodini Trust, 1971), viii.

[16] *A Nation in Making* (Bombay : OUP., 1925, reset and reprinted 1963), p. 6.

[17] Publisher's Note in *Keshub Speaks* (Bombay: Navavidhan Chittavinodini Trust, 1971), x.

What was the secret of his oratory? This is how he himself explained it in one of his lectures: "When I am excited you will hear burning words. I will then speak with power and I will certainly crush into atoms the most impregnable strongholds of error. Because it is not my force, my power, which then make me speak, but the Lord's."[18]

Keshub Chunder Sen was a social, educational and religious reformer. He believed that the English system of education was instrumental in obliterating evils like polytheism, idolatry, superstition, repression of women, caste system, and so on. But more efficacious than even English rationalistic and true liberal education was faith in God or religion. In India, he maintained, social reform was to be routed through religious reform. Thus, he combined the reason of science with the faith of religion, faith in one universal God. In his speech, "Religious and Social Reformation", in Bombay on 24 March 1868, he said: "If you wish to regenerate this country, make religion the basis of all your reform movements. Hindu society has a very peculiar structure. Here in India we do not see religion on one side, society on the other; but religion and society are interwoven with each other. If, therefore, you wish to reform the social organism of India, you must, in the first instance, give her true religion, or else your attempt will be ineffectual."[19] The very titles of his speeches recalled at random testify to his religious outlook: 'Regenerating Faith', 'Behold the Light of Heaven in India', 'Our Faith and Experiences', 'Philosophy and Madness in Religion', 'Am I an Inspired Prophet?', 'India Asks, Who Is Christ?', 'God-Vision in the XIX Century', 'The Living God', 'Christ and Christianity', 'Hindu Theism', 'Religious and Social Liberty', and the like. His patent slogan was "Fatherhood of God and Brotherhood of Man".

Besides being a reformer, Keshub Chunder Sen was a British loyalist who thought that Providence had placed the debased India under the paternal and redeeming care of England. In

---

[18] *Ibid.*, cited, x.

[19] Cited, Arun Kumar Mukherjee, *Keshub Chunder Sen* (Delhi: Publications Division, 1992), p. 66.

speech after speech he referred to our indebtedness to the British rule. Take the following extract from his speech in London on 12 April 1870: "When India lay sunk in the mire of idolatry and superstition, when Mahomedan oppression and misrule had almost extinguished the last spark of hope in the native Indian mind, when Hinduism, once a pure system of Monotheism, had degenerated into a most horrid and abominable system of idolatry and polytheism, when the priests were exceedingly powerful, and were reveller in their triumphs over down-trodden humanity, the Lord in His mercy sent out the British nation to rescue India. In obedience to God's injunction, England came and knocked at the doors of India, and said, 'Noble sister, rise! thou hast slept too long.' And India rose."[20]

Keshub appealed to all the three senses of his audience—rational, ethical and emotional. His impact was, therefore, total, not one-sided. The ideas were always organized methodically, and that promoted clarity. The style was lucid and easy to understand, and yet it was elevated, poetical and sonorous. All in all, he was a perfect orator.

Mahadev Govind Ranade (1842-1901)

Mahadev Govind Ranade was born in a middle class Brahmin family at Niphad in Nasik district on 18 January 1842. He passed M.A. in History and LL.B. from Elphinstone College in 1865 and 1866 respectively. In the same year he got the job of Marathi Translator. Soon after he became a judge in the Kolhapur State. His next appointment was as a Professor at Elphinstone College, Bombay. In 1871 he passed the Advocate's Examination and entered the Judicial Service and ultimately rose to the position of a High Court Judge. He was an active member of a religious Organisation called *Prarthana Samaj* and of a public Organisation called *Sarvajanik Sabha*. He was a founder of Deccan Educational Society which later started Fergusson College, Puna, and one of

---

[20] *Indian Speeches and Documents*, ed. J.K. Majumdar (Calcutta: Longmans, 1937), pp. 88-89.

the founders of the *Indian National Congress* and its wing the *Indian National Social Conference*. His was an immaculate life except for one blot in it. When he was thirty-three his wife died and at his father's threat of disowning him he married a girl just eleven. He lived to the age of 59 and died in harness on 16 January 1901.

Ranade spoke on a wide variety of subjects—social reform, religious reform, politics, education, economics, history, and more. He was the secretary of the *Indian Social Conference* and year after year under its aegis he spoke on social problems that confronted India. He respected India's long past but condemned the parasitical growths that had encrusted it and sucked the life out of it. He was specially hard on female problems. In religious matters also, he castigated India's immediate past, not the ancient times when our rishis preached faith in one formless God. Polytheism and priestly dominance, superstition and idolatry were later excrescences. His lectures 'Indian Theism', 'Hindu Protestantism' and 'Theist's Confession of Faith' were intensely illuminating addresses on religious reform. In Politics, Ranade was a Moderate believing in change through constitutional method. He discarded aggressive and extreme measures of change. He followed the middle course. While he praised the British contribution towards the regeneration of India, he was fully aware of its chilling pitfalls. In the field of education, he was an ardent believer in the usefulness of the Western system of education for the uplift of India from her medieval outlook. His lectures on Indian economic problems earned him the title of "the Father of Indian Economics". In the two forceful lectures on India's Foreign Trade delivered under the auspices of *Poona Vyaparottejak Mandali*, he recommended mechanised industries to combat the problem of the imbalance created by India exporting raw materials and importing finished goods. Finally, his lectures on Indian History, especially that period of Indian History which was connected with the Marathas and Shivaji, were full of vivid argumentation and deep erudition.

Ranade was a rationalist and this gave his speeches a delightful luminosity. His choice of words was appropriate. The words always measured up to the ideas they negotiated. We are told that "he usually spoke extempore, without any notes or manuscripts.

His captivating eloquence held the audience spellbound. They were so attentive that they never cheered or laughed while he was speaking."[21] The ultimate power of his speeches, however, came from his intellectualism than from his appeal to emotion. His speeches were well-structured, substantial in thought, convincing in argumentation, and precise in expression, but they lacked fire. They were treat to the elitists, but of lesser interest to a commoner. A sample may be given to illustrate this. In the Ninth Social Conference at Puna in 1895, Ranade said: "One of the ways in which reform movements are being worked out in India is the method of rebellion. We go into another camp on a religious basis and a social structure is built upon it. The other way of introducing reform is by utilising caste organisations for the purpose of reform. The third is to go to the Acharyas and try to see that they are animated with a high purpose and move about the country and purify us and themselves in the bargain. The fourth way is to appeal to men's sense of honour and make them pledge themselves to certain reforms. The fifth and the least eligible way is to seek legislative help. But in order to work out reforms on any of these lines all of us must work together."[22]

Womesh Chunder Bonnerjee (1844-1906)

Womesh Chunder Bonnerjee was born in a family of lawyers at Kiderpore in Bengal in December 1844. He was educated first at the Oriental Seminary and then at the Hindu School, but before he could clear his matriculation examination he was withdrawn from the school to be articled as a clerk under an attorney. In 1864 he joined the Middle Temple, England, for studying law. In 1868 he started practice at the Calcutta High Court which turned out to be extremely lucrative, so much so that he rejected

[21] P.J. Mascreen, Makers of Modern India (New Delhi: Kalyani Publishers, 1983), p. 71.

[22] The Miscellaneous Writings of the Late Hon'ble Mr. Justice Ran-ade with an Introduction by D.E. Wacha and Address by Sri-nivasa Sastri (New Delhi: Sahitya Akademi, 1915, rept. 1992), p. 158.

the offer of Judgeship that had been made to him three times. In 1880 he became a Fellow of the University of Calcutta. In 1885 and then in 1892 he was elected the President of the *Indian National Congress*. In 1902 he left India for England where his practice at the bar of the Privy Council turned out to be equally prosperous. He died on 21 July 1906 and was cremated at Golder's Green.

Bonnerjee differed from his predecessors in that he was not a social reformer. He was of the opinion that social reform was not necessary for political reform. In his Congress Presidential Lecture of 1892, he said: "I for one, have no patience with those who say we shall not be fit for political reform until we reform our social system. . . . Are we not fit for them [political reforms], because our widows remain unmarried and girls are given in marriage earlier than in other countries?—because our wives and daughters do not drive about with us visiting our friends?—because we do not send our daughters to oxford or Cambridge?"[23] Nor was he an ardent nationalist; rather he believed in the efficacy of the British Raj with surprising certitude. He went to the extent of attributing the success of the Congress to the British rule in India. In the above cited Congress Address of 1892, he observed: "It is not the influence of this man or of that man or of any third man that has made the Congress what it is. It is the British professors who have discoursed eloquently to us on the glorious constitution of their country; it is the British merchants who have shown to us how well to deal with the commodities of our country; it is the British engineers who have annihilated distance and enabled us to come together for our deliberation from all parts of the empire; it is the British planters who have shown us how best to raise the products of our soil; it is all these, in other words, it is all the influences which emanate from British rule in India that have made the Congress the success it is."[24] Not a social reformer, nor a great

---

[23] *The Life of W.C. Bonnerjee* by Sadhona Bonnerjee (Calcutta, 1944), pp. 82-83.

[24] *Ibid.*, p. 77-78.

nationalist, Bonnerjee is remembered today for being one of the greatest mentors of the *Indian National Congress*. He wanted Congress to bring about political reforms, and his most abiding concern in politics was what he called representative principle", by which he meant "allowing the people to select their own representatives for the purpose of taking part in the making of laws which governed the country." And it was exactly this that was denied to Indians on the ground that they were not fit to govern themselves. In a public meeting held at Wainfleet, England, in August 1888, he said:, The officials say to us, 'You are not fit for the representative Government.' That has always been the excuse of those who do not wish to extend freedom. . . . They remind me of the parent who would not allow his son to go to the water because he could not swim. How can a person learn to swim if he never enters water? How can we learn to be fit for representative Government . . . if they do not give us representative rights?"[25]

As a speaker Womesh Chunder Bonnerjee was nothing compared to Michael Madhusudan Dutt or Kristo Das Pal. He could not hynotize the audience by the witchery of his words or by the flow of his eloquence, but he could cast a spell on the intellect by the substance of his thought and the logic of his argument. Clarity, conviction and confidence were the virtues of his oratory. He spoke like a successful advocate than an overpowering genius. His place was at the second rung of the ladder.

Budrudin Tyabji (1844-1906)

Budrudin Tyabji was born in a wealthy business family of Bombay on 8 October 1844. He passed his matriculation from London University and Bar-at-Law from Middle Temple. In 1867 he started his practice at the Bombay High Court which terminated at his elevation to Judgeship in 1895. His public services were crowned earlier in 1887 when he had been elected as the President of the Indian National Congress and had also established

[25] *Ibid*., p. 51.

himself as a secular Muslim leader. He died in England on 22 August 1906. His dead body was brought back to Bombay and from there taken to Badar Bagh where he was buried with honours due to a great man.

Like most of his eminent predecessors, Tyabji was an ardent reformer and his special areas of interest and speech were Muslim social reform, politics and education. But unlike his great contemporary Womesh Chunder Bonnerjee, he was of the opinion that social and political reforms went hand in hand, one could not be executed without the other. He once remarked: "I am afraid that young India has fixed its attention too exclusively upon politics, and too little upon education and social reform. I am one of those who think that our improvement and progress lies not in our efforts simply in one direction, but in various directions, and that we ought to move side by side for the purpose of improving our social status quite as much as our political status."[26] He spoke fervently to promote Muslim education and to eradicate evils like purdah system and neglect of women among Muslims. In Politics, he was the admirer of the British benevolence and sense of justice, though he did not hesitate to check them whenever they violated Indian interest. Speaking about the loyalty of the educated Indians to the British empire in his Presidential Address at the third Indian National Congress held in Madras in 1887, he observed: "Who will better appreciate the advantages of good roads, railways, telegraphs and post offices, schools, colleges and universities, hospitals, good laws and impartial courts of justice?—the educated natives or the ignorant peasants of this country?. . . we, the educated natives, by the mere force of our education, must be the best appreciators of the blessings of a civilized enlightened Government, and, therefore, in our own interests, the best and staunchest supporters of the British Government in India."[27] His political principle was one of moderation. He wanted the Congress proceedings to be

---

[26] *The Indian Nation Builders* (earlier Natesan, Madras Publication; rpt. Delhi : Mittal Publications, 1989), ii, 131-132.

[27] *Ibid.*, pp. 141-142.

marked by moderation which he thought to be the offspring of political wisdom and political experience. In the above cited Congress Presidential Address, he advised the Congressmen thus: "Be moderate in your demands, be just in your criticism, be accurate in your facts, be logical in your conclusion, and you may be rest assured that any propositions you make to our rulers will be received with that benign consideration which is the characteristic of a strong and enlightened Government."[28]

The speeches of Budrudin Tyabji, as we can clearly see from the brief citations from them given above, were characterized by the power of reasoning, moderation, clarity of presentation, and by logical marshalling of facts and ideas. It is said that three of them which created an overmastering impact were "his speech on the Indian Civil Service question delivered in 1883 in the Framjee Cowasjee Hall, his speech on the Native Jurisdiction Bill delivered in the same year in the Town Hall at Bombay and in the same historic Hall the speech he made on Lord Ripon's memorable administration in December 1884."[29]

Rash Bihari Ghose (1845-1921)

Born in a small village, Torekona, in Burdwan district, in West Bengal, Rash Bihari Ghose passed M.A. in English in 1866 and LL.B. in 1867 from Presidency College, Calcutta. In the same year he entered the High Court of Calcutta as an advocate. In 1871 he passed Honours-in-Law Examination from Calcutta University. In 1875 he became Tagore Professor of Law in which capacity he delivered lectures on 'Law of Mortgages in British India'. The lectures were published in the form of a book which got him great name. In 1884 Calcutta University conferred the degree of the Doctor of Laws upon him. In 1891 he became a Member, Governor-General's Legislative Council; in 1906, Chairman, Reception Committee of the Congress and in 1907 and 1908, President of the Surat and Madras Congress Session respectively. His legal

---

[28] *Ibid.*, p. 147.

[29] *Ibid.*, p. 129. The name of the reviewer is not given.

practice was so lucrative that in those days he could give the donation of Rs. 30,00000/- to the University of Calcutta. He died in 1821 at the age of seventy-six.

The speeches of Rash Bihari Ghose were generally on law, administration, politics, and on eminent individuals. All his Congress speeches (Welcome Address to the Calcutta Congress in 1906, Presidential Address at the Surat Congress in 1907 and Presidential Address at the Madras Congress in !908) were masterpieces of oratory, sound in subject, immaculate in Organisation, lucid in style, and graceful in delivery. Equally remarkable were his Budget Speech, 1894-1895, Budget Speech, 1907-1908 and his speech against Seditious Meetings Act, 1907. All these speeches were marked by his philosophy of moderation in Politics and in life. He was a loyalist but not of the cringing type: a good example of his intrepidity was his Reply to Lord Curzon's Speech at the Calcutta University Convocation in 1905 in which he had denigrated the Indians by saying that Asians were less truthful than the Europeans. Ghose's reply was devastatingly hard-hitting and sarcastic. A brief passage may be recalled: "His Lordship, if I may say so without impertinence, is undoubtedly possessed of great and varied gifts, but the Gods are jealous and it would be flattery which, as we all know, his Lordship hates, to affirm that he possesses in any large measure those qualities which are so essential in the representative of His Majesty in this country. Does anybody doubt it? Let him read the Chancellor's speech on the last Convocation day of Calcutta University. The style of that speech was certainly not Asiatic. Nobody could accuse Lord Curzon of such an offence against good taste. But did it possess the Attic grace and lightness? Decidedly not. The whole speech was in, what Matthew Arnold calls the Corinthion style—a style which his Lordship strongly urged our young men to avoid."[30] This speech also illustrates his ability in handling the art of characterization. He could make a mincemeat of a person if he did not like him. But if he admired him, he could be equally

[30] *The Indian Nation Builders* (earlier Natesan, Madra Publication; rpt. Delhi : Mittal Publications, 1989), i, 311-312.

humble and respectful. Such were his memorial speeches on A. O. Hume, Sister Nivedita and on Gokhale made on 27 March 1912, 28 August 1912 and on 2 March 1915 respectively. They were sincere, intense and dignified.

One stylistic feature of Ghose's speeches was so well-marked and abiding that it needs to be singled out for special mention—it was his tendency to allude to literary classics. His speeches were distinguished by rich allusiveness. They reverberated with references to the classics from English literature. His Presidential Address at the Madras Session of the Congress in 1908 was rich in quotations from the Bible. It was a remarkably literary address.

Pherozeshah Merwanji Mehta (1845-1915)

Pherozeshah Merwanji Mehta was born in a Parsi business family in Bombay on 4 August 1845. After passing his M.A. Examination from Elphinstone College, Bombay, in 1864, he went to England to join Lincoln's Inn and was called to Bar in 1868. On his return, he combined his practice at the High Court, Bombay, with participation in municipal activities. He became a member of the Bombay Corporation in 1870 and was three times elected its Chairman, in 1884, 1885 and in 1905. His political attainments were no less. In 1886 he became a member of the Bombay Legislative Council, in 1893 of the Provincial Legislative Council and in 1894 of the Imperial Legislative Council. He was a founding member of the Indian National Congress. In 1889 and in 1904, he chaired the Reception Committee of the Congress, and in 1890 he became its President at the Calcutta Session. He was President of the political Organisation named Bombay Presidency Association and started an English Daily called *The Bombay Chronicle* in 1913. In 1915 he was nominated as Vice Chancellor of Bombay University, and before long he breathed his last on 5 November 1915, attaining the stature of the greatest Parsi leader after Dada Bhai Naoroji, who always claimed that he was an Indian first and a Parsi next.

The first and indeed the most outstanding feature of Pherozeshah Mehta's oratory was its soundness of the subject matter. He never allowed mere rhetoric to outface the subject or ideas. His favourite subjects were Education, Indian Civil Service, Municipal Reforms, Indian National Congress, and the British Rule. His two abiding convictions about education were the primacy of higher education and the necessity of English as the medium of instruction. In respect of ICS, he spoke for holding simultaneous competitions in England and in India. Regarding municipal reforms, of which he is called the father, he opined that for efficient municipal administration it was necessary to have a regular Bench of elected Justices, a Consultative Town Council elected from among them, an Executive officer appointed by Government, and a Controller of Accounts appointed by the Bench. In the Congress Politics, he was a moderate who believed in constitutional progress. He was loyal to the British rule but never hesitated to expose its pitfalls. Reinforcing his steadfast loyalty to the British Government, he said in his Welcome Speech at the Bombay Congress in 1904: "I accept British rule, as Ranade did, as a dispensation so wonderful, a little island at one end of the world establishing itself in a far continent as different as difference could be, that it would be folly not to accept it as a declaration of God's will."[31]

Besides being sound in subject matter, Mehta's speeches were superb in the Organisation of facts and ideas and extremely impressive in language. He did not indulge in flatulent verbiage or showy ornamentation. His aim was forceful and clear presentation. Sound ideas in clear and convincing language was what he aimed at. C.Y. Chintamani who collected his speeches in 1905 remarked in the Preface to his anthology: "His speeches and writings, which have always attracted considerable attention, are admired no less for their literary charm than for the soundness of his opinions—closely argued, expressed in earnest language and breathing conviction in every syllable."[32] Comparing Mehta with Gladstone, Chintamani further observed: "What has been said of the oratory

---

[31] *Ibid.*, p. 191.

[32] *Speeches and Writings of Sir Pherozeshah Mehta* (Allahabad, 1905), i.

of Gladstone [by James Bryce] is applicable to Sir Pherozeshah Mehta as well: 'There was a lively imagination, which enabled him to relieve even dull matter by pleasing figures, together with a large command of quotations and illustrations. There were powers of sarcasm, powers, however, which he rarely used, preferring the summer lightning of banter to the thunderbolts of invective. There was admirable lucidity and accuracy in exposition. There was art in the disposition and marshalling of his arguments, and finally there was a delightful variety and grace of appropriate gestures. But above and beyond everything else which enthralled the listener, there stood out four qualities. Two of them were merits of substance—inventiveness and elevation; two were merits of delivery—force in the manner, expressive modulation in the voice."[33] It is worthwhile quoting one more contemporary of Mehta on his art of oratory. This was Jeejeebhoy who anthologised some unpublished and post-1905 speeches of Perozeshah Mehta. In the Preface to the Anthology he commented: "Sir Pherozeshah Mehta was admittedly the greatest orator that this Presidency has ever produced. His speeches captivated his hearers to such an extent that whenever it was announced that Pherozeshah Mehta was to speak in public, people flocked together from far and near to admire his mastery of rhetoric. . . . He addressed cultured audiences and held them spellbound with his sonorous eloquence, his inexhaustible wit and his cutting satire. To the last his utterances were characterized by the same loftiness of style and force of reasoning, the same mastery of facts and clearness of exposition as he displayed in his prime."[34]

Special mention may be made of his Congress Speeches of 1889, 1890, 1903, and of 1904 which were received with roaring applause. In 1889 he spoke as Chairman of the Reception Committee. The venue was Bombay and the audience comprised 6,000 delegates. In this speech he bandied sarcasm and humour

---

[33] James Bryce, *Studies in Contemporary Biography*, p. 430, cited by Chintamani, *Ibid.*, ii.

[34] *Some Unpublished and Later Speeches & Writings of Pherozeshah Mehta* (Bombay: The Commercial Press, 1918), p. 5.

with deadly effect. The entire audience burst into laughter recurrently and clapped in a high strain of enthusiasm. In 1890 he spoke in the capacity of the Congress President, Calcutta session. His commanding voice, dignified delivery, the weight of facts, and overmastering logic of arguments enforced breathless admiration. An exceptional moment was his ardent defence of Parsi nationalism. He said,—"To my mind, a Parsi is a better and truer Parsi, as a Mohamedan, or a Hindu, is a better and truer Mohamedan or Hindu, the more he is attached to the land which gave him birth, the more he is bound in brotherly relations and affection to all the children of the soil, the more he recognises the fraternity of all the native communities of the country, and the immutable bond which binds them together in the pursuit of common aims and objects under a common government."[35] In 1903 he created laughter at the cost of Lal Mohan Ghose who had been elected President. The venue was Madras and Mehta commented on the printed speech of Ghose, calling him a leader who had come out of his political *Yogism*. In 1904 he was the Chairman of the Reception Committee. It was the Bombay session. Mehta's welcome address held the audience in thrall. It was a splendid speech in terms of both language and sentiment. It overflowed with robust optimism and was an antidote to those who had preached the gospel of despondency. *The Times of India* praised it for its pungent wit and for never being dull.

Ananda Mohan Bose (1846-1906)

Born in a small village, Joysiddhi, in Mymensingh District in East Bengal, Ananda Mohan Bose got his M.A. degree in Mathematics from Calcutta University. For a time he worked as a Professor of Mathematics in the Engineering College, but left it to join Christ's College, Cambridge in 1870. In 1873 he passed Mathematical Tripos and became the first Indian Wrangler. After qualifying himself for the Bar, he returned to India in 1874 and started

[35] Cited, Homi Modi, *Sir Pherozeshah Mehta: A Political Biography* (Bombay : Asia Publishing House, 1921, reprinted 1963), pp. 141-142.

legal practice at the Calcutta High Court. In 1876 he became the Secretary of the Indian Association, Calcutta. In 1877 he was appointed Fellow of Calcutta University. In 1880 he founded the City School, Calcutta. In 1886 he became a member of the Bengal Legislative Council. In 1898 he was elected the President of the Madras Session of the Indian National Congress. He died on 27 December 1906.

His biographer, Hem Chandra Sarkar, who was his associate during the last years of his life, lamented in the Preface to his life that a very few of his speeches were preserved. Most of them centred on education, politics and religion. Ananda Mohan Bose was an intensely religious man and long before Gandhi appeared on the Indian political scene he tried to spiritualise politics. His religious disposition made him give up his legal practice and devote himself wholeheartedly to public activities. He was a *Brahmo Samaji* in his religious principles and this coloured his political and educational beliefs also.

Ananda Mohan Bose's speeches differed drastically from those of his contemporaries and most predecessors in that they were deeply emotional and spiritual. They were drenched in feelings and often drifted to poetry and lyricism. They were never coldly matter of fact. But more striking than their emotionalism was their intense spirituality and moral fervour. At the Madras Congress in 1898 in response to a vote of thanks he suggested a motto for the coming year, rather the century, which was "Love and Service". He said: "Love the country, love your countrymen, the children of the common mother. Be they Hindus, Mahommedans, or Christians or whatever be their religious persuasion, matters not, they are all brothers. Love them with that brotherly love."—"If indeed, friends, you cultivate that spirit of love, then from the beautiful flowers of love, will come, in time, a naturally beautiful fruit, and the fruition of the other word which I put before you—'service.'"[36] His Presidential speech was a model of oratory and created a marvellous effect upon the audience. The introduction

[36] Anthologised by Hem Chandra Sarkar in *A Life of Anand Mohan Bose* (Calcutta: A.C. Sarkar, 1910), lv-lvii.

to the Congress Report of the year thus commented on the speech: "Whether as an oratorical effort or as a survey of the political situation of the country at the moment, it stands unsurpassed even among the high class performances of his predecessors. . . . His simple manners and engaging appearance, his musical voice and the grace of his delivery combined to create a sympathetic bias in the audience, and the impression of his masterly performance from the President's Chair will be remembered long by those that witnessed it."[37] Even his political speeches were made in a spiritual key and their ultimate power came from there. We may recall for further illustration the profoundly moving and elevating peroration of his speech at the Federation Hall, Calcutta, on 16 October 1905 at the sundering of Bengal. They were indeed his farewell words, for he died a year after in 1906: "And now, farewell my friends with these, which may, perchance, be the last words which I shall utter to you on this side of eternity . . . . Let us all pray that the grace of God may bless our course, direct our steps, and steel our hearts. Let action, and not words, be our motto and inspiring guide. And then shall my dream be realised of a beauteous land, blessed by nature, and filled by men true and manly, and heroic in every good cause—true children of the Motherland. Let us see in our heart of hearts the Heavens opening and the angels descending. In ancient books the gods are described as showering flowers and garlands on the scene of a notable battle. See we not, my friends, those flowers dropped today from self-same hands, welcoming us to the new battle, not of blood, but manly effort and stern resolve in the country's cause?"[38]

Surendranath Banerjea (1848-1925)

Surendranath Banerjea, called the 'Indian Burke', was born in a middle class Brahmin family in Calcutta on 10 November 1848. He graduated from Doveton College, Calcutta in 1868. In 1869

---

[37] Cited, *Indian Nation Builders* (earlier Natesan, Madras Publication; rpt. Delhi : Mittal Publications, 1989), i, 38-39.

[38] *Ibid.*, p. 49-50.

he cleared ICS Competitive Examination and joined as an Assistant Magistrate at Sylhet but was dismissed from his services on the framed up charge of dereliction of duty. In 1875 he joined as professor of English at Metropolitan Institution, Calcutta. In 1885 he shifted to Ripon College, his own creation, and worked there as a Professor till 1912. He combined teaching with numerous other activities—journalism, legislature, politics, congress movement, and writing in particular. He became the Editor of a newspaper named *Bengalee*, was elected to the Imperial Legislative Council, organized *Swadeshi* and *Boycott Movements*, started with other leaders *The Indian Association* in 1876, got elevated to Congress Presidentship twice, in the Poona session in 1895 and in the Ahmedabad session in 1902, nailed the British Government on the Partition of Bengal in 1905 by Lord Curzon, became a Minister in the Bengal Cabinet in 1921, and completed his classic autobiography, *A Nation in Making*, before his death on 6 August 1925 at the age of seventy-seven.

Surendranath Banerjea was a versatile speaker. Administration, education, journalism, legislation, history, politics, economics, congress, personalities—all imaginable subjects came under his fiery speeches. On all these subjects he had mature and well crystallised ideas which won him natural reverence, and these ideas had their source in overall philosophy of life and of national politics that he nourished throughout his long public career. His speeches illustrate his ideology, but it is best expressed in the concluding chapter of his political autobiography, *A Nation in Making*, bearing these captions: "The secret of long life—my views on Hindu social problems—the conservatism of the Hindu—a moral and a message to my countrymen."[39] I may summarise his message given in the last six pages, 369-374: We should aim at Dominion Status, that is, Self-Government as members of the British Commonwealth; this will give us independence as also continuous British help, whereas complete severance will entail permanent British opposition. Complete freedom will follow

---

[39] *A Nation in Making* (Bombay: OUP, 1925, rept. 1963), p. 363.

in due course when we are fit for it. This Dominion Status is to be attained by a process of orderly evolution, not by revolution, for revolution unleashes bloody forces; "We Hindus abhor revolution. . . . Evolution is our motto."[40] We must avoid even Non-Co-operation, for it isolates us from the civilizing forces of the world. Further, we must draw from the past, but should not remain wedded to it, for there is no standing still in this world: "Move on we must, with eyes reverentially fixed on the past, with a living concern for the present and with deep solicitude for the future."[41] "Thus, co-operation and not non-co-operation, association and not isolation, must be a living and a growing factor in the evolution of our people. . . . That is my message to my countrymen."[42]

Surendranath Banerjea is generally regarded as the greatest Indian orator in English. He was indeed a splendid orator, but in my opinion the appellation of "the best", as far as the style of oratory is concerned, must go to Michael Madhusudan Dutt whose speeches were pure and powerful literature. He handled English language as no Indian has ever done from the arrival of the Englishmen on the Indian soil till date. That a foreign language could so easefully and magnificently flow from the mouth of an Indian fills us with a sense of awe and wonder. And all in all, the best Indian orator was Vivekananda. But this is not to minimise the talent of Banerjea. He was an extraordinarily eloquent and forceful orator in English. An Englishman who heard him speak thus commented on his oratorical skill: "Experienced speakers in and out of parliament found in Surendranath a great deal that recalled the sonorous thunders of William Pitt, the dialectical skill of Fox, the rich freshness of illustration of Burke and the keen wit of Sheridan."[43] Dr. Sachidananda Sinha (1871-1950) who heard him speak many times and who was also a great

---

[40] *Ibid.*, pp. 372-373.

[41] *Ibid.*, p. 373.

[42] *Ibid.*, p. 373-374.

[43] Cited, T.V. Parvate, *Makers of Modern India* (Jullundur: University Publishers, 1964), p. 26.

statesman was equally lavish in his praise of Banerjea's eloquence: "For over forty years Surendranath's supremacy as the most eloquent Indian orator in English remained unchallenged." He praised his energy and ideas, moral and intellectual powers, appropriate gestures and vibrating voice, and dignified delivery that swayed vast masses, thrilling their imagination and holding it spellbound. He further observed: oratory demands and Surendranath had in ample measure "dignity, elevation, lucid exposition of complicated facts, sustained and fiery declamations, impassioned apostrophes, the power to touch the emotions—making the hearers laugh and weep as occasion may demand,—rallying battle-cries, and the thunderbolt of invective, and not merely meek-spirited, dull, prosy sermons."—"Almost all Surendranath's greatest orations were set speeches—very carefully prepared, written out word for word, committed to memory and then faultlessly produced, making the audience marvel as much at his oratorical powers as his mnemonic feat."[44] So, in Sachidananda's judgment based on his personal experience Surendranath's speeches had all the virtues of great oratory—thought, arrangement, elevated style, and the support of appropriate delivery and extraordinary memory. He was a perfect orator.

Now let us see how Surendranath Banerjea himself explained his art of oratory. About the secret of his being able to make long speeches without reference to a single note, his answer was that it came from rhythmical arrangement of sentences which aided memory. The impact on the audience flowed from his moral stance. In his own Words.—"Much depends upon the arrangement and upon the construction of the sentences. If the order be natural, logical and consistent, it is an aid to memory. If the sentences are rhythmical, they imprint themselves on the mind, the cadence helping the memory. After all, preparation is the great thing. It is indeed the one thing needed."[45] Further,

---

[44] Dr. Sachidananda Sinha, *Some Eminent Indian Contemporaries* (Patna: Janaki Prakashan, 1976), pp. 41-43.

[45] *A Nation in Making* (Bombay: OUP, 1925, reset and reprinted in 1963), pp. 129-133.

the ultimate power of the orator came from his moral and emotional character. Surendranath identified this with ardent patriotism, the moral emotion of love for the country. He said, "The qualifications of the orator are moral rather than intellectual. It is the emotions that inspire the noblest thoughts and invest them with their colour and their distinctive character. Let no one aspire to be an orator who does not love his country, love her indeed with a true and soul-absorbing love. Country first, all other things next, is the creed of the orator. Unless he has been indoctrinated in it, baptized with the holy fire of love of country, the highest intellectual gifts will not qualify him to be an orator."[46] This is not to say that intellectual equipment is of no avail; "His intellectual equipment, though important, is subsidiary. The moral takes precedence." Among the intellectual qualifications the most significant thing was the power of concentration, another was reading classics. These were the qualities that characterized the orations of Surendranath Banerjea in his own estimate—rhythmical arrangement aiding memory, patriotism, the power of concentration, saturation in classics, above all, determined preparation.

Surendranath's presidential speeches at Puna Congress in 1895 and at Ahmedabad Congress in 1902 are generally regarded as his best speeches. Each of them took about four hours to deliver which he did without referring to written notes even for once. Dr. Sachidananda Sinha who had listened to these speeches with bated breath remarked: "I marvelled not so much at his rolling and rounded periods of sublime rhetoric, as at his independence of notes to assist memory, and also his sonorous intonation which neither failed nor flagged in the long ordeal."[47] Two brief passages from these speeches may be recalled. Talking about the sympathies of the good and the true in all parts of the world for India's struggle for emancipation, he said in the Puna Congress: "They will welcome as glad tidings of great joy the birth of an

---

[46] *A Nation in Making* (Bombay: OUP, 1925, reset and reprinted in 1963), pp. 129-133.

[47] *Some Eminent Indian Contemporaries* (Patna: Janaki Prakashan, 1976), p. 44.

emancipated people on the banks of the Ganges. For have they not all read about our ancient civilization; how, in the morning of the world, before the Eternal City had been built upon the Seven Hills, before Alexander had marched his army to the banks of the Tigris, before Babylonian astronomers had learnt to gaze upon the starry world, our ancestors had developed a great civilization, and how that civilization has profoundly influenced the course of modern thought is the highest concern of man?"[48] Take this from his Ahmedabad Congress speech: "India is the cradle of true religions. It is the holy land of the East. Here knowledge first lit her torch. Here, in the morning of the world, the Vedic Rishis sang those hymns which represent the first yearnings of infant humanity towards the divine ideal. Here was developed a literature and a language which still excites the admiration of mankind—a philosophy which pondered deep over the problems of life and evolved solutions which satisfied the highest yearnings of the loftiest minds. . . "[49]

Romesh Chunder Dutt (1848-1909)

Born in Calcutta on 13 August 1848, Romesh Chunder Dutt did his matriculation from Hare School and Graduation from Presidency College, Calcutta. In 1868 he joined University College, London and in 1869 he cleared ICS competitive examination. As an ICS officer he rose to the position of the Commissioner, Orissa in 1895. In 1897 he resigned ICS and joined as a Lecturer in Indian History at the University College, London where he taught for seven years. In 1899 he became the President of the Indian National Congress held at Lucknow. In 1904 he became first the Revenue Minister and later the Prime Minister of the Baroda State. In 1907 he was appointed the Member of the Royal Commission on Decentralisation in India, and after two years of rigorous work, he died on 30 November 1909.

---

[48] *Indian Nation Builders* (earlier Natesan, Madras Publication; rpt. Delhi: Mittal Publications, 1989), i, 64.

[49] *Ibid.*, p. 79.

Romesh Chunder Dutt was a prolific writer. His chief writings were *Three Years in Europe, Famines and Land Assessment in India, The Peasantry of Bengal, Literature of Bengal*, Bengali translation of *Rig Veda, The History of Civilization in Ancient India,* condensed *Ramayana* and *Mahabharata* in English, *The Economic History of India, Lays of Ancient India, Brief History of Ancient and Modern India, Rambles in India*, not to mention his numerous novels and other works in Bengali. His English speeches generally centred on Administration, Economics, and Indian History. His Congress Presidential speech at Lucknow in 1899 dealt with administrative reforms and with agrarian and economic problems. He maintained that the Civil Service did not represent the Indian point of view; it stood for the official view with no mass base. On the economic problems he was more vocal. His opinion was that the cause of Indian poverty lay in the decay of Indian industries, overpopulation and excessive land tax. On Indian history, like many of his great predecessors, he also felt that the glory of ancient India was extinguished through the accretions of the centuries and needed to be revitalised. But he never preached the philosophy of despair. His message was always one of hope and faith, hard work and courage. See his inspiring exhortation to his countrymen in the following extract taken from his speech from the platform of *Mahajana Sabha* at Madras on 4 February 1902: "My friends and Countrymen, my first and last word to you is this: Let us have faith in ourselves! Our future depends on us; our fate is in our own hands; our destiny rests on our labours! Do not, for one moment, despond, for despondency in such a cause is a sin. Do not be intemperate and violent for hysteric shams are the signs of weakness, not of strength. Strong in our determination, calms in our conviction, let us speak temperately, clearly, and unmistakably; and let us work steadily and silently, swerving neither to the right nor to the left from the path of our duty to our country."[50]

Two qualities of Dutt's language as also thought are borne

[50] *Indian Nation Builders* (earlier Natesan, Madras Publication; rpt. Delhi: Mittal Publications, 1989), ii, 427.

out even from the brief citation given above—his simplicity and moderation. He was always simple and to the point, never high-flown or exhibitive. Likewise, he avoided the extremes and steered the middle path, "swerving neither to the right nor to the left." He was certainly no match to Surendranath Banerjea, his batch mate and life long friend, in oratory, but he was assuredly great in the second order of speakers in English. He was simple and dignified.

Lal Mohan Ghose (1849-1909)

Lal Mohan Ghose was born in an elitist family of Bengal on 17 December 1849. After passing the Entrance Examination of Calcutta University he sailed for England in 1869, joined the Middle Temple, was called to the Bar in 1873, and started his practice at Calcutta. In 1879 he went to England again to plead for the admission of Indians to ICS. This was on behalf of the Indian Association, a political organisation of great name and influence. Twice he attempted to enter the British parliament as a Liberal candidate from Deptford, but lost the election. In 1903 he was elected President of the Indian National Congress held at Madras. He died in 1909 at the age of sixty.

Lal Mohan Ghose is regarded as an equal of Surendranath Banerjea as an orator, though some of his admirers considered him his superior. His first great speech was made in London on ICS and created a remarkable effect. John Bright presided and was all admiration for him. The Indian Association on whose behalf he had made this speech in 1879 was gratified. Recalling it, Surendranath wrote in *A Nation in Making*: "His marvellous gifts of oratory were unknown to us, for he had never taken to public life as a serious occupation; and when they were displayed in a manner that extorted the admiration of his audience, among whom was the greatest of living orators, John Bright, the revelation was a bewildering and an agreeable surprise."[51] Thereafter whenever

[51] (Bombay: OUP, 1925, reset and reprinted in 1963), p. 48.

he spoke attention watched his lips and conviction closed his periods. His speech on the repeal of Vernacular Press Act in 1882 was another sensation in the field of oratory. Still another was his speech on the Ilbert Bill at Dacca on 29 March 1883. The indignation with which he satirised the Anglo-Indians who had agitated against the Bill could be cited as a telling example of a powerful invective: "We will not permit any pseudo-Englishman, any Brummagem Britisher, who is neither fish nor flesh nor good red herring, who is disowned by both England and India alike,—we will not permit such a man to slander our nation and insult our country. If such a person dares to hold the language of contumely and insult towards us, we shall make an example of him. We shall not disgrace our cause by doing anything unlawful or improper; but we shall only give him, free of charge, the immortality which an admiring correspondent of the *Englishman* has proposed to confer upon him by means of a statue, but it shall be the immortality of infamy. Our platforms will ring with denunciations; our newspapers shall keep alive the memory of the outrage; and our poets shall sing of his infamy until his name shall become a bye-word and a hissing reproach to after ages and to generations yet unborn."[52]

Such citations could be culled from any number of his speeches, but even this is enough to testify to his tremendous power of oratory. He was a forceful and eloquent speaker and he knew how to sway the masses or set them to laughter. He spoke English with the ease of a native and his pronunciation, it is said, was like that of a sophisticated and richly educated Englishman. He won the admiring attention of the best English orators of his time when he spoke to the English audiences in England. A well-known Colonial Premier observed: "Mr. Ghose speaks remarkably well. He speaks straight: he speaks to the point and knows when to stop."[53]

---

[52] *Indian Nation Builders* (earlier Natesan, Madras Publication; rpt. Delhi: Mittal Publications, 1989), ii, 109-110.

[53] *Ibid.*, p. 100.

Kashinath Trimbak Telang (1850-1893)

Kashinath Trimbak Telang was born in an affluent and orthodox Brahmin family of Maharashtra on 30 August 1850. He passed M.A. from Elphinstone College, Bombay in 1868. In 1872 he cleared LL.B. and the Advocate's Examination and commenced his legal career. He translated *Gita* into English and appended a learned introduction to it. For his services to Sanskrit he was elected President of the Royal Asiatic Society, Bombay. He became the High Court Judge in 1888 and the Vice Chancellor of Bombay University in 1892. He founded the Presidency Association in collaboration with Mehta and Wacha. He died on 19 September 1893 at the young of forty-three before his full potentialities could be realised.

Telang was essentially a man of law. Next to law came his interest in Sanskrit, Marathi and English literature. His speeches therefore had the argumentativeness of a lawyer and the allusiveness of a litterateur. His favourite subjects of speech making were education, social reform and politics. In education he was in favour of making western knowledge available to all Indians. In social reform his philosophy was to go slow, not headlong. In politics he combined loyalism with progress. His best speeches were made in the field of politics, and in politics one of his best speeches was on the Ilbert Bill in Bombay in 1883. It was marked by an extraordinary power of reasoning, tremendous self-restraint, dignity, and clear and simple expression. The testimony of Dinshaw Edulji Wacha (1844-1936) who attended the lecture is well worth recalling: "Mr. Telang's speech was one sustained stream of consummate reasoning to delight the hearts of all lovers of dialectics. . . . A calmer and more solid piece of forensic ratiocination in the midst of the fiery whirlwind of passion and prejudice raging outside the presidency was never heard before. It was also a fine example of that intense self-restraint which the serene and far-sighted statesman who is not merely the politician puts upon himself during an eventful crisis."[54] On

[54] Cited, *The Indian Nation Builders* (earlier Natesan, Madras Publication; rpt. Delhi: Mittal Publications, 1888), iii, 14-15.

the quality of the language Sir Raymond West commented: "Mr. Telang's language of a limpid purity would have done credit to an English-born orator."—"His style was formed on the classic writers and expressed his meaning with admirable force and clearness."[55] Telang's speeches lacked in emotional fire, rhetorical gestures, long declamations, swelling phrases, and compelling decorations, but they were rich in the qualities of the mind. An example may be recalled. This is from his speech on the retirement of Lord Ripon from the Viceroyalty, at the Town Hall of Bombay in December 1884: "There are two tests, I think, by which you can judge, whether anyone who has been entrusted with the government of men has or has not acquired a title to the gratitude of his subjects. We may form our judgment either from the views of those over whom he has borne sway, or from a careful analysis and examination of the measures of his administration, and after striking a balance between their merits and defects. Gentlemen, I venture to say that tried by both tests; Lord Ripon's regime will come out triumphant. Whether we look to the popularity which his Lordship has won among the people over whom he has borne sway for the last four years, or whether we consider the various measures of his administration, the conclusion is forced upon all unbiased minds that Lord Ripon's Government has been most successful."[56] We clearly see that the style lacks fire but amply possesses reason and lucidity.

Overview

We have considered eighteen eminent predecessors of Gandhi. They were all born nearly a generation before him. Historically speaking, they were born between the Battle of Plassey in 1757 and the uprising of 1857. Raja Rammohun Roy, the first in our survey, was born fifteen years after the Battle of Plassey, and Kashinath Trimbak Telang, the last in our survey, was seven years old when the uprising of 1857 broke.

---

[55] Cited, *The Indian Nation Builders* (earlier Natesan, Madras Publication; rpt. Delhi: Mittal Publications, 1888), iii, 14-15.

[56] *Ibid.*, pp. 26-27.

These great Indians had learnt two lessons from the times. The first was the futility of armed revolution. They had known it from the experience of their countrymen that the violent revolution against the British could not succeed. They were in fact coerced into non-violent resistance. For Gandhi later it became a creed based on higher and sounder moral principles. The second lesson was the realisation that the fallen India needed western rationalistic outlook for her rejuvenation. That was the worst period in Indian History when the recurrent defeats in the battle-fields had crushed their spirits, and thousands of years of priestly exploitation of the common man had perverted religion, reducing it to ritualism or mindless superstition. Belief in one formless God was replaced by the worship of multiple god's ceremoniosly. Ironically, even today we have not advanced from this debasement.

The inevitable outgrowth of these two realisations were two more mechanisms of behaviour—British loyalism and the desire for reform and not revolution. The speeches by the great Indians clearly testify to the loyalty of the Indians towards the British. The Englishmen could not have ruled over Indians if they had not been loyal to them. One and all vouchsafed their support to them, stressed the beneficence of the British rule and prayed for its continuance. Without the Indian desire for the British rule thirty-thousand Englishmen could not have ruled over thirty-crore Indians. They only wanted British help in weeding out religious, social and political ills. They considered the advent of English rule in India as a divine dispensation. It was slowly and gradually that they moved away from this position and claimed independence. The erosion of their faith in the justness of the English rule was slow in coming. The early speakers were loyalists and reformers. That formed the substance of their speeches.

Thus, the subjects of Indian speeches were non-violent change, western enlightenment, British loyalism, and social, religious and political reforms. Their mode of appeal was usually rationalistic. Michael Madhusudan Dutt was an exception: he was essentially emotional. This rationalism was at the root of the organisational aspect of their speeches also. They were logically marshalled. Part of the charm of these speeches came from their orderly arrangement. Moreover, most of the speakers were lawyers and therefore they knew how to handle arguments reasonably and logically.

Closely related to this is the fact that the Indian speakers were elitists. They spoke in the halls to learned gatherings. Their speeches did not have mass base. This was natural also, because English knowing audience itself was bound to be elitistic. The masses could be addressed only in the vernaculars. That was one reason why they could not create much impact on the masses.

The style of these orations was marked by simplicity, clarity, precision, and restraint. In some cases it was bare simplicity, while in others it was inspired simplicity. The orators were concerned more with content than with form. The style rarely outfaced the thought. The thought was rational, the arrangement logical, and the language simple. Only in case of Michael Madhusudan Dutt there was indulgence in verbal profusion, in the silks and satins of style. In Kristo Das Pal there was some overflow of rhetorics and surging declamation. On the whole, the orators kept to the Aristotelean virtues of simplicity, clarity and correctness. This avoidance of extremes and of flamboyance accounted for the lack of fire in their speeches. They were cautiously correct and temperate. This was the defect of their quality.

Surendranath Banerjea is customarily regarded as the greatest orator among the predecessors of Gandhi, but in my assessment that title must go to Michael Madhusudan Dutt. He alone among Indians spoke English like an exceptional English orator. His speech, 'The Anglo-Saxon and tie Hindu', remains unsurpassed till date, and fancy pleases me to think that it can never be surpassed. In the splendour of language and in the royal wealth of metaphors it can be bracketed with the best speeches of the world, only that the British stance in it may hurt us in our seat of honour. It is simply ambrosial.

The credit for saving many of these speeches from sinking into oblivion goes to two intrepid publishers of Madras—G.A. Natesan and S. Ganesan. They were friendly with Gandhi who referred to them again and again in his writings and letters now published in one hundred volumes by Navajivan Trust, Ahmedabad.

G.A. Natesan was a publisher and politician and also a founder and the Editor of the *Indian Review*. S. Ganesan was a publisher and patriot who published the speeches of the Indian freedom fighters when it was really dangerous to publish them. Posterity owes a debt of gratitude to them.

IV

GANDHI AND HIS CONTEMPORARIES

The contemporaries of Gandhi include those eminent Indians who were born between the rising of 1857 and the formation of the Indian National Congress in 1885. The only exception is made in case of Tilak who, though born an year before the rising of 1857, is considered in this chapter, the reason being that Lal-Bal-Pal made an inseparable trio those days and need to be bracketed together in any discussion of the period. Pal was two years younger than Bal, Lal nine years, and Gandhi thirteen years. So, I have begun with Tilak who was one year old at the time of the rising of 1857, and ended with C. Rajagopalachari who was six years old in 1885 when the Congress was founded.

The predecessors of Gandhi usually spoke on socio-religious reforms, though as time advanced their interest started shifting to politico-economic reform. This shift continued in the Gandhian era until at last the political stance occupied the central stage. One common subject of speeches was whether political change should precede social reform, or social reform should come first and political next. There was a similar shift from loyalism to nationalism. The predecessors of Gandhi had unwavering faith in the British sense of justice and fair play and they had prayed for the continuance of the British rule in India; but this faith was gradually eroded and replaced by the feeling of self-help, and nationalism was promoted. Good government was considered less important than self-government. Likewise, there was a shift from elitism to mass mobilisation. Tilak was the first great mass leader and Gandhi, of course, the greatest. The English speeches necessarily continued to be addressed to elitistic English knowing audience, but these enlightened hearers were galvanized to awaken the masses.

The outstanding speakers in English among tie contemporaries of Gandhi were: Bal Gangadhar Tilak (1856-1920), Bipin Chandra pal (1858-1932), Motilal Nehru (1861-1931), Madan Mohan Malaviya (1861-1946), Rabindranath Tagore (1861-1941), Swami Vivekananda (1863-1902), Lala Lajpat Rai (1865-1928), Gopal Krishna Gokhale (1866-1915), Srinivasa Sastri (1869-1948), Chittaranjan Das (1870-1925), Sri Aurobindo Ghose (1872-1950), Bhula Bhai Desai (1877-1946), Sarojini Naidu (1879-1949), and Rajagopalachari (1879-1972).

Bal Gangadhar Tilak (1856-1920)

Known variously as "the father of Indian unrest", "an extremist with the slogan freedom is my birthright" and "lokmanya, that is respected of the people", Bal Gangadhar Tilak was born on 23 July 1856 at Ratnagiri in Maharashtra where his father was a primary school teacher. After passing B.A. in 1876 and LL.B. in 1879 as a student of Deccan College, Pune, he started with the help of his friends New English School, Deccan Education Society and Fergusson College in Pune. He edited two weekly newspapers *Kesari* and *Mahratta* in Marathi and English respectively. He set afoot Ganesh and Shivaji festivals to forge Indian nationalism. He was elected Member of Pune Municipal Council and of Bombay Legislative Council in 1895. In 1896 he did his best to assuage Famine and Plague in Pune. He actively participated in the Congress movement and was responsible for the Surat Split between the Moderates and the Extremists in 1907. He was imprisoned thrice for sedition charges. The one unwholesome distraction in his life was his involvement in litigation for private or public interests. Of his numerous political activities the most memorable was combating the Partition of Bengal with his four-fold scheme of Swaraj, Swadeshi, Boycott, and National Education. He wrote three scholarly books, *Orion, Arctic Home in the Vedas* and *Gita Rahasya*. He died on 1 August 1920, the day Gandhi launched his non-violent non-co-operation movement.

Let me recall some subjects of Tilak's speeches at random: 'Common Language', 'The Bharata Dharma Mahamandala', 'Gita Rahasya', 'The Political Situation', 'Tenets of the New Party', 'National

Education', 'Swarajya', 'Self-Government', 'Home Rule', and the like. Even these titles reveal that Tilak's consuming interests were language, religion and politics. About language his abiding strain was the necessity of Hindi as a national language. About religion he had no doubt of any kind whatsoever: he believed in the greatness of Hinduism, and Hinduism he thought was epitomized in *Gita*. His interpretation of *Gita* was different from that of Shankaracharya. According to him, *Gita* taught action first and *gnana* (knowledge) and *bhakti* (devotion) next. In his speech entitled 'Gita Rahasya' he said: "The *Gita* advocates the performance of action in this world even after the actor has achieved the highest union with the Supreme Deity by *Gnana* (knowledge) or *Bhakti* (devotion) . . . . *Gnanayoga* there is, yes. *Bhaktiyoga* there is, yes. Who says not? But they are both subservient to the *Karmayoga* preached in the *Gita*."[1] That was the essence of Hinduism and Tilak applied it to politics. In Indian Politics Tilak was the first national leader to break off from cringing British loyalism. He opined that in the early days of the British Empire Indians welcomed the change from the Muslim rule to the English rule. They pinned great hopes on it. They hoped that their arts and industries would be fostered by their new rulers. But they were soon disenchanted, and felt the need of fighting against them, against their exploitation of them. How would they fight against them? Tilak ruled out armed revolution, for he felt that India was not yet prepared for it. He therefore recommended passive resistance, and passive resistance meant *swadeshi* (resort to home goods), *bahishkar* (boycott of foreign goods) and *rashtriya kshikshan* (national education, that is, education in religion, industry, politics, and in vernacular). This will promote nationalism, the energy thus coming from both the Indian and the Western source. And nationalism would bring *swaraj*, that is, Home-Rule within the British Empire, the defence and foreign affairs being looked after by the British and the home affairs by the Indian themselves. Once the political power was in our hands, social reform would follow. Tilak thought that political reform preceded social reform, so the first thing was political power. From passive resistance to

---

[1] *Bal Gangadhar Tilak*, ed. Verinder Grover (New Delhi: Deep & Deep Publications, 1992), pp. 213-14.

nationalism to home-rule to social reform was his political creed for India.

In the expression of his thought Tilak was simple, clear and forthright. His strength came from simplicity in style, logicality in arrangement of ideas and from his intellectualism. He eschewed emotion and ornamentation in his speeches. Another source of his strength was his absolute sincerity, his moral character. This is the testimony of Aurobindo Ghose: "Tilak's speeches are, like the featureless *Brahman*, self-luminous, straightforward, lucid, never turning aside from the point which they mean to hammer in or wrapping it up in ornamental verbiage; they read like a series of self-evident propositions."[2] —"Mr. Tilak has none of the gifts of the orator which many lesser men have possessed, but his force of thought and personality made him in his own way a powerful speaker. He was at his best in his own Marathi tongue rather than in English; for there he found always the apt and telling phrase, the striking application, the vigorous figure which went straight home to the popular mind. But there is essentially the same power in both. His words had directness and force—no force could be greater—of sincere and powerful mind always going immediately to the aim in view, the point before it, expressing it with a bare, concentrated economy of phrase and the insistence of the hammer so full on the head of the nail which drives it in with a few blows."[3] Take another testimony, that of N.G. Jog: "Not for him stylistic graces or emotional appeals. . . . In his speeches Tilak was simple and direct. There was nothing of the orator or demagogue about him, no high-sounding phrases, no impassioned appeals or flights of rhetoric. In this he was complete contrast to Gokhale with his persuasive tongue, rounded periods and purple patches. Tilak put every issue plainly and uncompromisingly, without any 'ifs' or 'buts'. He demolished the position of his opponents and established his own in the light of reason and by the force of logic. It was the content of his speech and not the manner of its delivery which mattered. Tilak

[2] 'Tilak as a Writer and Orator' in *Life and Works of Lal, Bal and Pal*, ed. Dr. P.D. Saggi (New Delhi: Overseas Publishing House, 1962), p. 123.

[3] *Ibid.*, p. 131.

believed with Lord Morley that 'political oratory is action, not words; action, character, will, purpose, and personality.'"[4] I may cite as example the following passage from his speech entitled 'Tenets of the New party' made by him at Calcutta on 2 January 1907: "What the New Party wants you to do is to realize the fact that your future rests entirely in you own hands. If you mean to be free, you can be free; if you do not mean to be free, you will fall and be forever fallen. So many of you need not like arms; but if you have not the power of active resistance, have you not the power of self-denial and self-abstinence in such a way as not to assist this foreign Government to rule over you? This is boycott and this is what is meant when we say, boycott is a political weapon."[5] From the same speech I may quote one more passage to illustrate another quality of Tilak's oration which is not mentioned either by Aurobindo or by Jog, the power of sarcasm: 'He [Dada Bhai Naoroji] has come here at the age of 82 to tell us that he is bitterly disappointed [by the British rule]. Mr. Gokhale, I know, is not disappointed. He is a friend of mine and I believe that this is his honest conviction. Mr. Gokhale is not disappointed but is ready to wait another 80 years till he is disappointed like Mr. Dada Bhai."[6]

Bipin Chandra Pal (1858-1932)

Bipin Chandra Pal, the son of a district munsiff, was born in Sylhet in Bengal on 7 November 1858. After passing his matriculation at the age of sixteen, he entered the Presidency College, Calcutta. He could not complete his college education because his father disinherited him for joining *Brahmo Samaj*. After leaving the college, he joined as a Headmaster, first at the Cuttack Academy, then at the National School in Sylhet, and finally at a school in Bangalore. He combined teaching with journalism, starting and editing numerous journals and

---

[4] *Lokmanya Balgangadhar Tilak* (Delhi : Publication Division, 1990), pp. 183-4.

[5] *An Anthology of Modern Indian Eloquence*, ed. R.K. Prabhu (Bombay: Bharatiya Vidya Bhavan, 1960), p. 58.

[6] *Ibid.*, p. 53.

newspapers from time to time, particularly *New India and Bandemataram*. From journalism to politics was an easy advance. He joined the Congress in 1886, left it at the Surat split in 1907, rejoined it in 1916 at the Lucknow session, and left it again in 1921. Thrice he visited England, in 1896, 1908 and in 1919. An important incident in his life was his refusal to give witness against Aurobindo Ghose in a sedition case against him in 1907 for which he suffered imprisonment for six months. But this made him a national hero. His last days were passed in poverty. He died on 20 May 1932, a sad and disenchanted man.

As is evident even from the titles of some of his speeches recalled at random, Bipin spoke chiefly on religious, social, economic, and political subjects: 'Brahmo Samaj', 'Social Reform', 'Case of Hindu Widowhood', 'Unemployment among the Middle Classes', 'Indian Nationalism', 'Swaraj and Swadharma', 'Present Political Situation', 'Freedom Movement in India', 'Swadeshi and Swaraj', 'Contribution of Islam to Indian Nationality', 'Responsible Government', 'Magic Preferred to Logic', and the like. In religion, Bipin was a *Brahmo Samaji* joined to *Vaishnavism*. He thus combined the rationalism of the former with the emotionalism or *bhakti* cult of the latter. Besides, he was secular, showing equal respect to all religions. In social matters he spoke against female suppression, child marriage, polygamy, temperance, untouchability, and such subjects. His speeches on temperance under the aegis of National Temperance Society of Scotland compelled universal admiration. Of his lecture at the public hall of Glasgow, Bipin himself said: "It was crowded by an audience of nearly three thousand men and women gathered from all parts of Scotland . . . . When I got up to speak, this audience gave me a rousing reception, the like of which I never had in my life before."[7] In his lectures on Economics he indicted the British for their exploitation of India, specially condemning the investment of foreign capital in India, export of raw material from India to England and the import of finished goods from there, and the cheapness of Indian labour. But his most powerful speeches were made in the field of politics. His

[7] Cited, Saral Kumar Chatterjee, *Bipin Chandra Pal* (Delhi: Publications Division, 1984), p. 69.

political thought passed through three stages. In the first stage, which ended in 1904 with the commencement of the preliminary home work of the British government on the partition of Bengal, Bipin was a loyalist speaking for the perpetuation of the British rule in India. In the second stage, which began in 1904 and ended in 1908 when he left for England, he was a militant nationalist speaking for complete independence of India with no connections with England. Complete autonomy for India without the British control was the political ideal and the method of attaining it was passive resistance, not armed confrontation for which he thought with Tilak that India was not prepared. The tools of passive resistance were swadeshi, boycott and national education, that is, education through our own language and promoting our own heritage. This went by the name of radical extremism those days. In the third stage which began in 1908 and ended with him in 1932, he was a federal internationalist, by which was meant equal partnership of India in the British Empire. India, with the other British colonies, was to be a federated part whose freedom was to be realised through the unity of the federated whole. Bipin explained it beautifully when he said in 1911: "If God were to appear before me with the gift of absolute but isolated sovereign independence for India in the right hand, and of an equal partnership with Great Britain and her colonies in the present association called the British empire in his left hand, I would unhesitatingly say, Father, give us the gift in your left hand."[8] This was no different from Tilak and Annie Besant's concept of Home Rule. Thus, Tilak shifted from loyalism to nationalism to internationalism. In another phraseology, he shifted from moderatism to extremism to moderatism again. In the end he became a moderate of moderates, rejecting Gandhi's non-co-operation movement and thereby incurring the wrath of the nation. When Gandhi promised immediate freedom, subject to the fulfilment of certain necessary conditions, his cryptic comment was, "I do not know magic, but I know logic." His two visits to England, in 1908 and in 1919, had tamed him.

In the style of his oratory Bipin was different from Tilak. Whereas

[8] Cited, *Ibid.*, p. 105.

Tilak was absolutely straight, economical and simple, without any emotional outbursts or stylistic flourishes, Bipin combined simplicity with subtlety, reason with emotion, and logic of organisation with irresistible inspiration. I may give two testimonies of his two great contemporaries who had heard him speak many times. Aurobindo said: "He spoke under an inspiration, which he himself was unable to resist."[9] Srinivasa Sastri who had attended some of his Madras lectures commented: "For several days on the sands of the beach, he spoke words hot with emotion and subtly logical which were wafted by the soft evening breeze to tens of thousands of hearers, invading their whole souls and setting them aflame with the fervour of a wild consuming desire. Oratory had never dreamed of such triumphs in India; the power of the spoken word had never been demonstrated on such a scale."[10] I may recall a passage from his speech on Shivaji in which reason is blended with inspired love for the motherland, and clarity of expression with power of words and of rhythm: "Though the Hindus do not racially lack either military skill or capacity for statecraft, these are not, we must frankly and freely admit, their special gifts. It is not by these that they stand, apart from the rest of humanity. Their specialty is not in arms nor in statecraft, but in spirituality. While other nations have gone in for wealth or beauty, or for the glories of conquests, the Hindu from time immemorial has gone in for the riches and acquisitions of the life of the spirit. When the Hindu ceases to be spiritual, he also ceases to be a Hindu. He must seek wealth, and apply himself to the development of the economic resources of his country; he must cultivate statesmanship and develop the virtues of good citizenship; he must train his body and attain health, and beauty, and strength, and military skill also; but these are not, and cannot be, the ends, but only the means to the realisation of the higher life of the spirit."[11]

---

[9] Cited, T.V. Parvate, *Makers of Modern India* (Jullundur: University Publishers, 1964), p. 78.

[10] Cited, Sankar Ghose, *Leaders of Modern India* (Delhi: Allied Publishers, 1980), p. 96.

[11] *Life and Works of Lal, Bal and Pal*, ed. Dr. P.D. Saggi (Delhi: Overseas Publishig House, 1962), p. 257.

Motilal Nehru (1861-1931)

The posthumous son of Gangadhar Nehru, the Kotwal of Delhi, Motilal Nehru was born at Agra on 6 May 1861. We learn from Jawaharlal Nehru's *Autobiography* that his early education was confined to Persian and Arabic, that he began learning English in his early teens, and that he did not appear at his B.A. examination for the fear of failing. However, he passed the High Court Vakil's examination in 1883 and started his practice first at Kanpur and then at Allahabad and attained great success. He became a member of the United Provinces Legislative Council in 1910. In 1917 he was elected President of the UP Wing of the Home Rule League of Mrs. Annie Besant. In 1919 he started a paper called *The Independent* which was discontinued in 1923 for the want of money. In 1919 he became the President of the Congress and in the following year actively participated in Gandhi's non-co-operation movement. In 1922 he started the *Swaraj* Party as the parliamentary wing of the Congress with Gandhi's concurrence. In 1923 he was elected to the Central Legislative Council. In 1928 he drafted the future Indian Constitution called the Nehru Report which was not accepted by all parties. In the same year he was again given the honour of the Congress Presidentship. In that session the Congress demanded Dominion Status for India. He was jailed numerous times. This wrecked his health and he died on 4 February 1931. He differed from Gandhi on many matters and yet adored him like a disciple, though he was eight years older than him.

Liberal in his social outlook and secular in his religious thinking, the two most obsessive passions of Motilal were law and politics, politics, of course, after 1919. He spoke on these two subjects with invincible authority if not with great fire. Though he amassed a huge fortune through legal practice, he believed in avoiding litigation in favour of settling disputes by mutual compromise or private arbitration or by diverting the case to *panchayats*. In politics he was a moderate till 1920, but after that he gave up moderatism and subscribed to even unconstitutional methods of compelling reform. He joined non-co-operation movement with its triple boycott of college, court and council.

Motilal was not really an orator of the stature of Gokhale or Bipin Chandra Pal, for his speeches were too fact based and argumentative to animate the audience. Nor did they have the charm of language. On the whole, they were colourless and lacked vitality. But sometimes when he was touched, his soul became vibrant and tongue animated. Such was his reference to *Jallianwala Bagh* Tragedy in his Public Speech at Allahabad on 20 September 1919: "An enormous crowd in which there were children and boys, consisting of at least 20 thousand souls, had assembled, may be in ignorance, may be in defiance of some order of prohibition; a number of soldiers were marched to the place; they took their stand upon an eminence and fired into the thickest of the crowd. . . . You can well imagine the feelings of the mother, the wife, the sister, or the daughter who waited all through that dreadful night for the return home of the son, the husband, the brother or the father, little knowing that he was either shot dead or left dying at the *Jallianwala Bagh* in the name of law and order. . . . No doctor, no policeman, not even a municipal sweeper visited the place that night or the next day. The wounded of the afternoon were only relieved by death during the night."[12] Or take this passage from his Presidential Address at the Amritsar Congress in 1919 embodying his dream of future India: "We must aim at an India where all are free and have the fullest opportunities of development; where women have ceased to be in bondage, and rigours of the caste system have disappeared; where there are no privileged classes or communities; where education is free and open to all; where the capitalist and the landlord do not oppress the labourer and the *ryot*; where labour is respected and well paid, and poverty, the nightmare of the present generation, is a thing of the past. Life will then be worth living in this country, it will be inspired by joy and hope, and the terrible misery we see around us will become a bad dream which has faded away from our memory, on our awakening to welcome the morning sun. But that day is yet distant. We have still a difficult path, full of obstacles and pitfalls before us. Let us march ahead with truth for our

[12] *Selected Work of Motilal Nehru*, ed. Ravinder Kumar and D.N. Panigrahi (Delhi: Vikas Publishing House, 1984), ii, 258-259.

guide and courage our watchword and before long we shall reach the promised land."[13]

Madan Mohan Malaviya (1861-1946)

Madan Mohan Malaviya was born in a scholarly Brahmin family at Allahabad on 25 December 1861. He passed B.A. as a student of Muir Central College in 1881 and LL.B. in 1891. He joined the Government High School, Allahabad as an Assistant Master in 1884. He left this job to become an Editor of *Hindustan* in 1887. He later became Editor of *Indian Union* also. In 1893 he started legal practice at Allahabad High Court. Earlier in 1886 he had made an impromptu speech at the Calcutta session of the Congress which was greatly applauded by Hume. He was elected President of the Indian National Congress four times: (1) Lahore, 1909; (2) Delhi, 1918; (3) Delhi, 1932; and (4) Calcutta, 1933. He, however, organized the Indian National Party to protect Hindu interest. In 1931 he attended the Second Round Table Conference with Gandhi. He also became a Member of the Central Legislative Council. But his crowning attainment was the establishment of the Benaras Hindu University in 1915. He died in November 1946, an immensely loved and respected national leader.

Three subjects took the strongest hold of his attention throughout his life, religion, politics and education. In religion he was an orthodox Brahmin holding full faith in ritualism. In politics he was a moderate supporting *swadeshi* but not the boycott of Councils. In education he believed in the blending of scientific, technical and industrial education with religious instruction and classical culture.

His Congress speeches and those on Bundelkhand Land Alienation Bill and the Excise Bill and on the Repressive Measures in Bengal were received in a high strain of applause, yet on the whole he was not by any chance an extraordinary speaker. You look for flashes of eloquence in his speeches in vain. Each speech was an example of sustained argument without life or verbal enchantment. But the argument

---

[13] *Ibid.*, p. 305.

was soundly substantiated and immaculately organized. That was all its beauty. I may cite for example a passage from his speech 'Repressive Measures in Bengal' at the Benaras Session of the Congress in 1905: "I do not want to keep up boycott of foreign goods. What is desirable so far as the Swadeshi Movement is concerned, is quite another matter. That has gone on and will go on. As far as boycott is concerned, I think I express the sense of all of you when I say that the Congress would rejoice to see boycott come to an end, if the cause which has given rise to it were to cease to exist. It is, therefore, entirely in the power of the Government to put an end of this boycott."[14]

Rabindranath Tagore (1861-1941)

The fourteenth child of Maharshi Debendranath Tagore, Rabindranath was born in Calcutta on 6 May 1861. Averse to formal education, he could neither complete his school or college education, in India or in England, nor qualify for the bar. In 1883 he married a girl of 10. Soon after, his sister-in-law Kadambari Devi to whom he was most deeply attached died, leaving him broken and desolate. In 1890 he visited England again, and this was followed by numerous such visits or lecture tours to England, Japan, America, China, Italy, Switzerland, Germany, Russia, Persia, Iran, and many more in subsequent years. He never had to work for his livelihood, the only distraction being the management of his paternal estate in Shelaidaha for some years. In 1901 he founded Shantiniketan near Bolpur which in 1920 was elevated to the status of a university called *Visvabharati*. In 1905 he participated in anti-partition movement. In 1911 he wrote 'Janaganamana' for the current congress session. In 1913 he was awarded Nobel Prize for literature on his English translation of *Gitanjali* which made him an international celebrity. On 6 March 1915 he met Gandhi for the first time at Shantiniketan. The same year he was conferred knighthood which he surrendered in

---

[14] *An Anthology of Indian Eloquence*, ed. R.K. Prabhu (Bombay: Bharatiya Vidya Bhavan, 1960), p. 82.

1919 because of *Jallianwalla Bagh* tragedy. Notwithstanding his profound respect for Gandhi, he did not support his non-co-operation movement. In 1940 the university of Oxford conferred D.Litt. degree upon him. He died on 7 August 1941. Gandhi said that though dead, Gurudev lives significantly; his tendencies were heavenly.

Though known chiefly as a poet, playwright, novelist, and a short story writer, Tagore was a prolific speaker. *Nationalism* (1917), *Personality* (1917), *Creative Unity* (1922), *Talks in China* (1922), *The Religion of Man* (1930), *Man* (1937), *Crisis in Civilization* (1937), are some of the collections of his English speeches. Tagore was a total personality and there was hardly any vital subject on which he did not speak. God, religion, ethics, aesthetics, politics, society, economics, education, metaphysics, nature, personalities, countries,—all animated his tongue. His ideology was throughout touched by an extraordinary poetic sensitivity and compassion for all human beings; it was never a result of bare intellectual dilettantism. He believed in personal God Who is interested in the joys and aspirations of all human beings, not in the impersonal God of Sankara-Vedant. He was opposed to orthodox Hinduism with its faith in multiple gods, ritualism, taboos, idolatry, caste system, and in such externals. He, on the other hand, believed in the religion of mankind, in universal humanism, and thought that the aim of life was the realisation of the divine in man. In the field of morality, he avoided the extremes of asceticism and of indulgence, of complete self-denial and of reckless physical enjoyment. Renunciation not of the entire world of sensuous delight but only of pride, ignorance and lust, and embracing the thousand bonds of delight with love and compassion for all mankind, were the planks of his ethical thought. In aesthetics, he was for both the external harmony or proportion and the internal harmony or grace. With these two aids he tried to blend the human and the divine elements in art, saving it from degrading into either the love of pure expression or of pure emotion. In politics, he was opposed to aggressive nationalism or cruel imperialism, and believed in internationalism. He did not accept Gandhi's non-co-operation movement. He did not agree with his mandate of the boycott of foreign cloth or of colleges or of the entire western civilization. Nor did he accept Gandhi's economic ideas completely. He was not enamoured of his passion for the spinning wheel. He agreed with his insistence on small-scale industries, but he wanted it to be combined with industrialisation. He advised co-operative farming and was all for the extension of rural development schemes. His concept of education had four vital planks—closeness to nature, closeness to life, delight in studies, and creativity. He denounced artificial education based on mechanical memorization of dead facts which he said propagated parrot-learning, or "culture, captured and caged." *Visvabharati* was his attempt at translating these dreams into living reality. One more subject that figured in his speeches recurrently was 'synthesis of the East and the West'. He maintained that the East was excessively taken up with spirit and the West with matter; the one was inordinately other-worldly and the other inordinately this-worldly. It was necessary that the twain met and corrected and balanced each other.

Tagore was essentially a poet, and most of us who are fed on the mysticism and music of the God-songs of *Gitanjali*, or the intoxicating lyricism of the love-songs of the *Gardener*, or on the melting tenderness of the child-songs of the *Crescent Moon*, will find the spacious wisdom of his written speeches a little too taxing and tedious. But they did cast a magical spell on his hearers. His foreign audiences were intensely excited and ecstatic about them and surged to the lecture halls in overwhelming number. His exotic oriental costume, flashing eyes, silver locks, long flowing beard, broad forehead, and sweet musical voice,—all of which made him look like a rishi come from some ancient *tapovana*, added to the mesmerism. His spoken prose, though not as rhythmical and mellifluous as the strains of his splendid lyrics, had a charm of its own. It was natural, simple, fresh, full of spiritual suggestiveness, studded with honeyed phrases and sustained all through with golden music. Occasionally his English listeners complained of a subterranean mysticism which made it difficult to understand, but that was when he spoke of such subjects as God, religion and Vedantic metaphysics. Otherwise he was easy to understand and delightful to the heart. Take this extract on Mahatma Gandhi's spiritual power from his address in New York on 1 December 1930: "He has neither physical nor material power, but through his great influence people who have been in subjection to all kinds of tyrannical power have stood up; and he is the strongest spiritual power in this world today. Not because of his political prudence, but for his spiritual influence the people believe in him, and they are ready to die for their faith. They are ready to suffer. It is a miracle that these people, downtrodden for centuries, are coming out, and without doing any injury to others, they suffer and through suffering, conquer. And our women, . . . have come out to follow this man, this leader. Not an association, not an organisation, not a politician, but a man! And his message goes deep into our veins. He attacks the enemies that are within us."[15]

Swami Vivekananda (1863-1902)

Narendra Nath Dutt, later called Vivekananda (the combination of 'viveka' or discrimination and 'ananda' or joy) was the son of an attorney-at-law and was born in Calcutta on 12 January 1863. After passing B.A. from Calcutta University in 1884 he tried to get a job to support his family, the father being dead, but could not succeed. The depression this caused was mitigated by his master Ramakrishna whom he had met in 1881. He left the world to become his avowed disciple. On 16 August 1886 Ramakrishna died and Vivekananda took charge of his monastery at Barangapore. From 1882 to 1893 he travelled through India as a monk seeking truth. On 31 May 1893 he left India for Chicago where he addressed a Parliament of Religions, from 11 to 27 September 1893, and became an international celebrity. He also visited England and Switzerland. In December 1896 he returned to India, receiving a hero's welcome. In 1898 he established Ramakrishna Mission with the twin aims of social service and the spread of Vedantism and opened two monasteries at Belur in Calcutta and at Mayavati in Almora. He undertook another lecture tour to America from 1899 to 1900 and died of the complications caused by diabetes on 4 July 1902.

Advaita Ashrama, Calcutta, has published the complete works of Swami Vivekananda in 8 volumes which contain all his speeches alongwith the reports in foreign newspapers on them. Even a cursory

[15] *The English Writings of Rabindranath Tagore*, ed. Sisir Kumar Das (New Delhi: Sahitya Akademi, 1996), iii, 633.

look at them reveals that ninety-five percent of them were on religion and spirituality and a bare five percent on subjects like poverty, education, morality, social reform, India and the west, and none on politics. We may summarise his thought on these subjects one by one. Vivekananda's concept of God was best expressed in his lecture on Vedanta delivered at Lahore on 12 November 1897 where he said that there are three perceptions of God: the first is that God is outside the universe; the second is that God is inside the universe; and the third is that God is neither outside the universe nor inside the universe, but God and universe and soul are all one. He is the reality in everything. This is *Advaitwad* or monism. The aim of life is to realise God, and there are four ways of God-realisation—*jnana yoga, bhakti yoga, karma yoga*, and *raja yoga*. The thinkers realise God through *jnana*, the devotees through *bhakti*, the workers through *karma*, and the mystics through *raja yoga*. Religion is faith in God. It is realisation, not reasoning. In this religion of realisation two ideals are most prominent: the first is renunciation; the second is unity of all religions. He found that his master Ramakrishna was the embodiment of both renunciation and religious universalism. Religious isolationism was, however, extremely dangerous. He said: "Though there is nothing that has brought to man more blessing than religion, yet at the same time there is nothing that has brought more horror than religion. Nothing has brought more peace and love than religion; nothing has engendered fiercer hatred than religion. Nothing has made the brotherhood of man more tangible than religion; nothing has bred more bitter enmity between man and man than religion. Nothing has built more charitable institutions, more hospitals for men, and even for animals, than religion; nothing has deluged the world with more blood than religion."[16]

Notwithstanding his deep faith in God and in religion, Vivekananda believed that there was no use talking of religion to a hungry man. First bread and then religion was his motto. The root causes of

---

[16] Cited, Dr. A.D. Pusalkar, 'Swami Vivekananda' in *Pageants of Great Lives*, edited by K.M. Munshi and R.R. Diwakar (Bombay: Bharatiya Vidya Bhavan, 1964), iii, 25.

Indian poverty were priestly and foreign exploitation, ignorance, superstition, and inaction, and the only way it could be redeemed was proper education. By proper education he meant education that combined Indian culture with western science and technology. Besides, it should build character, and the four virtues that he considered primary for the cultivation of character were strength, fearlessness, faith, and courage. Good education, he further believed, would not only eradicate poverty but also dilute social ills like untouchability, degradation of women, petrification of the caste system, and the like. But more important than social reform was social service. Vivekananda was the one thinker in India who stood not only for personal liberation or *moksha* but also for social liberation, the salvation of society through service of our fellow beings. He raised social service to the level of religion. As for politics, it was an anathema to him. Patriotism, not politics, he thought was the exigency of the moment. However, he advised his countrymen never to live in isolation. East and West must complement each other. Western science and Indian spirituality must combine and in that combination lay the salvation of humanity.

These subjects were of such vital interest to the people, and the ideas that Vivekananda raised on them of such profound substance that they drew large audiences to the lecture halls. One patent comment of the American newspapers was that the halls were filled to capacity because of the importance of the subject and the wisdom of the Hindu monk. To add to this was the logic of the argument. He spoke with such lucidity and logic that even a subject like vedanticism appeared like plain commonsense.

The press was equally lavish in its praise of his language and delivery. Even his personality, voice and dress elicited the admiring attention of the listeners. The following report on his lecture 'Plea for Tolerance' at Memphis on 17 January 1894 is representative of the usual American reviews of his speeches:

> "The eminent oriental was received with liberal applause, and heard with attentive interest throughout. He is a man of fine physical presence, with regular bronze feature and form of fine proportions. He wore a robe of pink silk, fastened at the waist

with a black slash, black trousers and about his head was gracefully draped a turban of yellow India silk. His delivery is very good, his use of English being perfect as regards choice of words and correctness of grammar and construction. The only inaccuracy of pronunciation is in the accenting of words at times upon a wrong syllable. Attentive listeners, however, probably lost few words, and their attention was well rewarded by an address full of original thought, information and broad wisdom."

(*Mempis Commercial*)[17]

No evaluation of Vivekananda as a speaker can be complete without a reference to his celebrated speeches at THE PARLIAMENT OF RELIGIONS, CHICAGO in September 1893. When he began his address with "Sisters and Brothers of America", hundreds of members of audience sprang to their feet and gave him a standing ovation. When the applause died down to an expectant silence, he thanked the audience, and in the course of his address pleaded for universal religion, ending up with the stirring words: "May he who is the Brahman of the Hindus, the Ahura Mazda of Zoroastrians, the Buddha of the Buddhists, the Jehovah of the Jews, the Father in leaven of the Christians, give strength to you. . . . The Christian is not to become a Hindu or a Buddhist, nor a Hindu or a Buddhist to become a Christian. Upon the banner of every religion will soon be written in spite of resistance: 'Help and not fight,' 'Assimilation and not Destruction,' 'Harmony and Peace and not Dissension'."[18] "His speech," said Romain Rolland, "was like a tongue of flame."[19] He was called variously as "an orator by divine right", "a perfect master of English language", "the sensation of the world's fair parliament," and so on.

Vivekananda was indeed an inspired spiritualist in thought, a logician in argument, an angel in appearance, and a dramatist on the platform. A greater orator it is difficult to find.

---

[17] *The Complete Works of Swami Vivekananda* (Calcutta: Advaita Ashrama, 1964), iii, 486.

[18] *Ibid.*, iii, 3-24.

[19] *The Life of Vivekananda* (Calcutta: Advaita Ashrama, 1988 edition), p. 37.

Lala Lajpat Rai (1865-1928)

The son of an Urdu teacher, Lala Lajpat Rai was born at a small village called Jagraon in district Ludhiana, the Punjab. In 1885 he passed the Law examination of the Punjab University and began his legal practice at Hissar which in 1892 he shifted to Lahore. In 1905 he went to England to represent the Congress. In 1907 he was deported to Mandalay jail in Burma. In 1914 he went to England as a Congress delegate and from there left for the United States where he stayed till 1920, mobilizing public opinion in favour of Indian Freedom Movement. In 1920 he presided over the special congress session in Calcutta. In 1925 he joined *Swaraj Party* only to leave it in 1926. In 1925 he joined the *Hindu Mahasabha* also and became its President. He died on 17 November 1928 as a consequence of grievous injury caused by the lathi blows he had sustained while heading a procession against the Simon Commission.

An extremist in politics, an *Aryasamajist* in religion, Lajpat Rai was an enlightened thinker. He was neither a blind revivalist nor a slavish anglicist: he took the best of the Vedas and combined it with the humanism of the West. This is best reflected in his view of education: the education must be national, yet it should be secular and scientific. Likewise, in Economics he was neither a believer in capitalism nor in communism, he preached *Swadeshism*. He adored Gandhi, yet did not hesitate to disagree with him when he withdrew Non-Cooperation Movement. For his intrepid ideas and actions he was called the 'Lion of the Punjab.' There was fire in his speeches, nevertheless, C. Y. Chintamani drove his admiration for him too far when he said that "as a public speaker I think of Lloyd George and Lajpat Rai together. They had equal capacity for rousing the indignation of the masses."[20] His orations were plain and straightforward but full of deep sincerity and power. Take this extract from his speech on *Swadeshi* Movement delivered at Surat in 1907: "It will be an evil day for the Hindus, the Mahomedans and the Parsis when they allow their national characteristics to be entirely swept away by Western

---

[20] Cited, Sankar Ghose, *Leaders of Modern India* (New Delhi: Allied Publishers, 1980), p. 109.

manners and methods. Let us never forget that we are not an upstart people having no traditions and no past to boast of. Respect for age, regard for sincerity, reverence for ties of blood and relationship, constitute the most valuable heritage bequeathed to us by our forefathers, and we shall be going backward than forward in exchanging them for the noisy and at times undesirably pushful manners of the West."[21]

Gopal Krishna Gokhale (1866-1915)

The son of a clerk who later became a sub-inspector of police, Gopal Krishna Gokhale was born on 9 May 1866 at a village named Kotluk in Ratnagiri district of what was then called Bombay Presidency. He took his B.A. degree as a student of Elphinstone College, Bombay in 1884. In 1885 he joined as an Assistant Master at New English School at Poona and in two years time became Professor of English at Fergusson College from where he retired as a Principal in 1902 to participate in political activities with greater involvement. His professorial life coincided with much journalistic and social work. In 1902 he was elected to the Imperial Legislative Council and in 1904 the title C.I.E. was conferred on him. In 1905 he founded the Servants of India Society given to selfless service. In the same year he presided over the Benaras session of the Congress. In 1912 he visited South Africa at the behest of Gandhi. He visited England seven times for political purposes. The year 1912 was marked also for his appointment to the Public Service Commission. He died on 19 February 1915 at the young age of 48.

The speeches of Gokhale were rich in political, social, economic, and educational thought. In politics he was a moderate believing in gradual constitutional progress. His opposition to Tilak in this regard marked the high watermark of Indian political life. In his social thought he was militantly opposed to Casteism which he considered the ultimate source of most social evils. He was a staunch

---

[21] *The Indian Nation Builders* (earlier Natesan, Madras Publication; rept. Delhi: Mittal Publications, 1989), i, 339-340.

secularist who indefatigably worked for Hindu-Muslim amity. In Economics he subscribed to Dada Bhai Naoroji's 'drain theory' but not with the same emphasis. He also condemned what he called 'absentee capitalism' and the British racial arrogance. He believed that rationalistic education was necessary for the upliftment of Indian society. He also moved a resolution in the Imperial Legislative Council in favour of free and compulsory primary education. Over and above everything, he was a great proponent of the spiritualisation of public life. These ideas lent substance to his speeches and made them intellectually heavy, and that is why his appeal was more to the elitists than to the masses.

In his excellent analysis of Gokhale's art of oratory in his address delivered to the Annamalai University Union on the 19 February 1940 V. S. Srinivasa Sastri remarked: "When he had to make an appearance on the public platform he took the greatest care to inform himself thoroughly of the subject matter and he was not content with his work until he had given it the best possible form. He had a fine taste for English, not only for its Grammar and for its idiom but for its inner and more subtle beauties. People wondered how he found time to prepare his speeches with such marvellous care. When he delivered them, although he scarcely referred to notes, he seldom hesitated or paused for words: they came readily all through his speech. Although there was not anything to light up the subject matter, any flash of humour, any brilliance of wit, still he was able to keep the audience keyed up to a high pitch of expectancy, for his subject was full, his manner earnest, and his style elevated." About the arrangement of Gokhale's speeches, his style and his delivery, Sastri further observed: "Every speech had a carefully constructed beginning; it went through its course stage by stage and then it rose up to a conclusion generally couched in language of high power and appeal. His conclusions therefore could be called by the dignified name of perorations. His main quality as a speaker was fluency. He spoke rather fast and although there was distinctness of utterance you could now and then see that he was anxious to push on to the end, and when the end came it came so naturally that you would not know where the peroration began." Sastri who was always present among the audience when Gokhale spoke, especially after 1906, said that his delivery was always animated and earnest and accompanied by minimum gestures:

"When he began to speak there was animation in his countenance which communicated itself to the listeners. It would almost seem that his chief power lay in his earnestness. Every word that he spoke was charged with sincerity, you could see his soul as it were trying to escape through his lips. He had not any gestures, nor had he those arts of ornamental speech." As for the emotion underlying his speeches, Sastri observed: "There was no marked sensitiveness in the words themselves but there was emotion overfull in the utterance itself; and both in the words and in the sentiments there was a pregnancy which indicated the depth of his feeling."[22] This testimony of an equally great contemporary who was also by all standards of oratory among the world's foremost speakers of the time is indeed of great significance and therefore I have cited it in more detail. I may now give a somewhat long extract to illustrate the above evaluation. It is from his Elementary Education Bill of 1911: "This bill, thrown out today, will come back again and again, till on the stepping-stones of its dead self, a measure ultimately rises which will spread the light of knowledge throughout the land. It may be that this anticipation will not come true. It may be that our efforts may not conduce even indirectly to the promotion of the great cause which we have all at heart and that they may turn out after all to be nothing better than the mere ploughing of the sands of the sea-shore. But, my Lord, whatever fate awaits our labours, one thing is clear . We shall be entitled to feel that we have done our duty, it is better even to labour and fail than not to labour at all."[23] Serious in thought, restrained in emotion, luminously logical in organisation, fluent in style, and dignified in delivery, Gokhale was an orator par excellence.

Srinivasa Sastri (1869-1946)

Srinivasa Sastri was born on 22 September 1869 at Valangaiman in Tanjore district: thus he was only ten days older than Gandhi who

---

[22] *My Master Gokhale: A Selection from the Speeches and Writings of Rt. Hon'ble V.S. Srinivasa Sastri*, ed. T.N. Jagadisan (Madras: Model Publications, 1946), pp. 224-225.

[23] *Ibid*., pp. 239-240.

was born on 2 October in the same year. After passing B.A. in 1887, he joined as a teacher in Municipal High School, Mayavaram. In 1893 he became lecturer in English, Municipal College, Salem. In 1907 he was admitted to the Servants of India Society of Gokhale. In 1913 he was nominated to the Legislative Council, Madras. In 1915 he succeeded Gokhale as the President of the Servants of India Society. In 1916 he was elected to the Imperial Legislative Council. In 1927 he became the Agent-General of the Government of India in South Africa. In 1929 he was made a Companion of Honour. In 1930 he attended the First Round Table Conference in London. In 1932 he was a member of the Second Round Table Conference on Indo-African Affairs at Capedown. In 1935 he was appointed Vice Chancellor of Annamalai University. In 1945 he opposed Jinnah's demand for the formation of Pakistan. He died on 17 April 1946, a little over one year before Indian Independence.

Srinivasa Sastri was an orator of international eminence. Especially notable were his Kamala Lectures at Calcutta University on the 'Rights and Duties of Citizenship' (1925), Mysore University Extension Lectures on Gokhale (1935), Dr. Abayambal Memorial Lectures on the status of women at Mysore University, Lectures on Pheroze Shah Mehta (1943), Lectures on the *Ramayana* (1944), though the speech that had established him as great orator was a much earlier one, the celebrated speech opposing Rowlatt Bill in the Imperial Legislative Council (1918). His favorite subjects of oratory were politics, personalities, religion, and education. In politics Sastri was a moderate believing with Gokhale that an inscrutable providence had designed that India should regain freedom only in conjunction with her British master. Among the personalities Gokhale was the one he adored. He called him his master. For Gandhi he had immeasurable regard, though he differed from him on many crucial matters. The others for whom he had immense respect were Ranade and Sir Pherozeshah Mehta. In religion he was a sceptic. As an educationist, the one thing on which he spoke with greatest fervour was the participation of students in politics which he condemned.

Sastri was a great name as an orator. His speeches in England won the admiration of the best of Englishmen. It is human that he enjoyed this universal acclaim. In a letter to his son V.S. Sankaran on 10 July 1921 he confided: "Sir Maurice Hankey is lost in admiration of my English and says he envies my faculty of getting the right word in the right place . . . . He just now said my speech on Friday in moving the resolution on the status of Indians was most eloquent. Hughes called it great. Meighen pronounced it a moving plea. Balfour declared it very brilliant. The Prime Minister came up in the afternoon to where I stood and said, 'It is a very fine speech, careful and guarded, therefore the more effective.' . . . Then the British Prime Minister said my speech gladdened the hearts of the British Cabinent Ministers, for I arraigned General smuts, who used on every occasion to preach the Sermon on the Mount with a sanctimonious air."[24]

What was the secret of Sastri's power of oratory? It lay in two qualities: first, the logic of persuasive argument; second, the purism of his language. He conquered the audience by appealing to its reason through rich argument logically organized and presented in pure, polished and restrained language. In this connection it is interesting to recall a letter that he wrote to Gandhi. It illustrates his purism in language. Gandhi had written to him for a message to the *Harijan* and this was what He got in return: "You are an extraordinarily correct writer of English. The ordinary reader will not detect any slips on your part. They are not only rare but of a subtle nature. The eye of a schoolmaster, made acute by dwelling on trivialities of grammar, can alone see them." Then he pointed out eight grammatical errors in the first number of the *Harijan* of which the space permits me to recall only one: "Page 4. 'Caste Hindus have to open their temples to Harijans, precisely on the same terms as the other Hindus.' (Say 'the same terms as "to" the other Hindus. Else it would mean that the other Hindus opened their temples on certain terms to Harijans)." After identifying the linguistic lapses in Gandhi's prose Sastri added some criticism of substance: "You are obscure and even baffling when you say that your policy of non-cooperation with Government allows of your seeking its cooperation whenever your purpose is, in your opinion, 'very sacred and altogether good.' Most sensible people follow this

---

[24] *Letters of the Right Honourable V.S. Srinivasa Sastri,* ed. P.N. Jagadisan (Bombay: Asia Publishing House, 1963), p. 77.

rule in ordinary life, not seeking cooperation when they don't care and seeking it when they care. They don't proclaim it as a policy or give it a grand name."[25] Gandhi found the letter too good to suppress. He wired permission to publish it. The reply was equally typical of Sastri: "Firstly inappropriate to *Harijan*, secondly offensive to partisans, ill-requital for your steadfast affection. However, if perchance useful, please publish." Gandhi published the letter, commenting: "Let the student note in passing Sastri's love for the language he has mastered as few men have done. He is a purist in everything. We badly need *purists* in our country."[26]

Let me now recall a passage from Sastri's speech, 'Democracy and Truth', delivered at the Convocation of Annamalai University on 7 November 1940 as a sample of his oratorical style; the central point of the speech was the malady of party system in democracy which in practice amounted to the surrender not only of the individual but also of the nation to the interests of the party: "I advise you [the graduates of the year] to be faithful to party, but always to put the nation above it. I advise you, when you become leaders, to circumscribe within well-defined limits the jurisdiction of your party, to demand of your followers due respect for this jurisdiction, but scrupulously to allow them full discretion outside that jurisdiction. I advise you not to look upon members of other parties as enemies to be avoided, denounced and injured, but as fellow-travellers choosing different routes to reach the same goal, *viz.*, the common good. I advise you, above all, to cherish your personal freedom as a birthright and guard it jealously except in a limited sphere, so that in your public activities you may be true to yourself."[27]

Mahatma Gandhi (1869-1948)

Mahatma Gandhi's life is so well known and so oft told that it seems redundant to retail it. However, it may be recalled in the barest

---

[25] *Ibid.*, pp. 249-250.

[26] *Ibid.*, pp. 248-251.

[27] *Indian Oratory: Vivekananda to Indira Gandhi*, ed. B.K. Ahluwalia (Delhi : Kalyani Publishers, 1977), p. 154.

outline for form sake. He was born on 2 October 1869 in Porbandar. When thirteen, he was married to Kasturba who was of the same age. After matriculating at the age of eighteen, he qualified as a barrister from England and started legal practice at Rajkot. In 1893 he went to South Africa to work for Dada Abdullah & Co. but got involved in non-violent struggle against racial discrimination and but for very brief visits to India remained there till 1914, December 19. In India by slow degrees he became the undisputed leader of the freedom movement which he firmly led from Non-Violent Non-Co-operation Campaign (1920) to Civil Disobedience Movement (1930) to Quit India Movement (1942) to crippled Independence (1947). How all this came about makes high drama. On 30 January 1948 he was assassinated by Nathuram Vinayak Godse on the foolish notion that he was excessively pro-muslim. It is sad to recall that Gandhi was shot dead on Friday, the same day on which Christ was crucified. Christ had preached Sermon on the amount, Gandhi lived it.

Before I set out to describe the thought underlying Gandhi's speeches and writings and actions, I consider it absolutely necessary to clarify what I regard the ultimate source of misunderstanding about him. It is pointed out by some of his critics that he preached impossible ideals and is therefore worthy of respect but of no relevance in the present day world. It is true that many of the ideals voiced by him are unattainable, such is for example the ideal of non-violence or the concept of stateless state. Gandhi was fully aware of this. His answer was that if we could not draw a straight line, for that reason the definition of the straight line did not need to be changed. What really signified was the effort to approximate the ideal. Gandhi only gave the direction where the truth lay, he knew that its full realisation was beyond the imperfect human instrumentality. We cannot realise truth or ahimsa fully, but for that account should not cease to seek it. The stateless state is an impossible goal, but in our effort to realise it we can to an extent minimise excessive state interference in individual life: Gandhi gave the direction towards minimal state control, or maximum self-control or *swaraj*. That is, the more we reduce the state control, the better, that will be a happy direction towards the goal of statelessness. Applying the same principle to *Brahmacharya*, Gandhi said: "*Brahmacharya* means perfect control over all the senses and organs. For a perfect *brahmachari* nothing is impossible. But it is an ideal state which is rarely realised. It is almost like Euclid's line which exists only in imagination, never capable of being physically drawn. It is nevertheless an important definition in geometry yielding great results. So may a perfect *brahmachari* exist only in imagination. But if we do not keep him constantly before our mind's eye, we should be like a rudderless ship. The nearer the approach to the imaginary state, the greater the perfection."[28]

The entire thought of Gandhi, be it religious or ethical or political or social or economic or educational, or any other thought, was ultimately rooted in his belief in God. This may be briefly stated. What is God? God is Truth. What is Truth? Truth is what the purified inner voice says. How can inner voice be purified? The inner voice can be purified through five vows—truth, non-violence, self-control, fearlessness, and non-possession. These five principles are the five cardinal virtues of Gandhi's ethics. What is religion? Religion is being bound to God. Organized religions are imperfect because they are the products of imperfect human beings and therefore need to be reformed from time to time. The essence of Hinduism lies in the first *mantra* of *Ishopanishad* which gives four messages: (1) God pervades the universe; (2) renounce everything, for all belongs to God; (3) enjoy what you need for sustenance, that is God's gift to you; (4) never covet anybody's possession. Temple-going is not necessary, for God pervades everywhere, but if one does there is no harm. Likewise, idol-worship is irrational, but if it aids a simple man in worship, that simple faith does not need to be disturbed. Rama is a name for truth, he is an embodiment of truth. Caste system is based on a healthy division of work not on arrogant superiority. Untouchability is a later excrescence, a blot on Hinduism. A scavenger is as worthy of his hire as a lawyer or our President. This in fine is Gandhi's philosophy of God, morality and religion from which all his other thought is coloured.

Essentially, Gandhi's political thought had three planks: (1) *satyagraha*

[28] *The Collected Works of Mahatma Gandhi* (Delhi: Publications Division, 1994), xviii, 345.

(truthful action); (2) purity of end and means; and (3) concept of stateless state. *Satyagraha* is the application of the principles of truth and non-violence to political and public affairs: passive resistance, non-cooperation, civil disobedience, and individual civil disobedience are its offshoots. Purity of end and means implies that end is always infected by means and therefore both must be equally good. The ideal of stateless state, of minimal state interference in individual life, can be realised by the development of village republics leading to the decentralisation of power.

Gandhi's social thought could be summarised in one word, SARVODAYA, that is welfare of all. In his scheme of things there was no marginalisation of the weak or the unprivileged. All created beings are equal and deserve equal justice. He did not tolerate lower status to untouchables or minorities or blacks or women or rural folk. Not only are all men equal, but all work too is equal. Here Gandhi was deeply influenced by Ruskin's *Unto This Last* which he translated entitling it *Sarvodaya*. He summarised the teachings of the book into three clear statements. "(1) The good of the individual is contained in the good of all; (2) a lawyer's work has the same value as the barber's, in as much as all have the same right of earning their livelihood from their work; (3) a life of labour, *i.e.*, the life of the tiller of the soil and the handicraftsman, is the life worth living."[29] There is dignity in manual labour, and earning bread by it is what Gandhi called bread labour. This takes us to Gandhi's economic thought and also shows how in his philosophy all thoughts were interrelated.

In Gandhi's economic thought the greatest place was occupied by *Charkha* or the spinning wheel: he maintained that the study of Indian Economics was the study of the spinning wheel. It alone could solve the problem of the deepening poverty of India. It supplemented the agriculture of the villagers and was a saving talisman for the Indian widows or the under-privileged. It was the truest method of industrialising India. It alone gave meaning to the boycott of foreign and the use of *swadeshi* or homemade goods. One more economic principle of

[29] *An Autobiography*, trans. Mahadev Desai (Ahmedabad: Navajivan Trust, 1927, rept. 1995), p. 250.

Gandhi may be recalled, the principle of trusteeship, that is, what a man earns in excess of his needs must be given in trust to the society, must be used for social welfare.

Gandhi's educational thought may be reduced to five pivotal statements: (1) Education should ensure the harmonious growth of body, mind and soul, that is, it should involve manual labour, sharpen the mind and develop character; (2) it should be rooted in Indian culture and be related to the immediate surroundings; (3) it should be self-financing by being made craft-centred; (4) the medium of instruction should be the mother-tongue, the national language must be Hindi, and English may be made optional; and (5) adult women and harijan education should not be neglected. It may be added that he was not in favour of compulsory education which he felt created a distaste for it.

There is hardly any subject on which Gandhi did not write; his written and spoken words fill one hundred volumes printed by Publications Division, the Government of India. Besides, it is not always easy to distinguish between his English and Hindi speeches, for they are translated to both the languages. But the saving grace is that the translations are usually indicated. His mass speeches were mostly in Hindi and the speeches given in England, Africa and to some exclusive audiences in India, in English. He rarely enjoyed lecturing in English to Indian audiences. His Benaras speech in English in 1916, for example, began with an apology: "It is a matter of deep humiliation and shame for us that I am compelled this evening . . . to address my countrymen in a language that is foreign to me."[30]

Gandhi was not a deliberate speaker; he did not speak for the sake of speaking. His aim was never to project himself or to create effect. That way he had completely exorcised his personality from his speeches. He spoke simply to communicate what welled inside him for the good of his country and countrymen: his motive was altruistic, not personal glory. And yet wherever he spoke, in the large grounds

[30] *The Collected Works of Mahatma Gandhi* (Delhi: Publications Division, 1964, rept. 1990), xiii, p. 211.

or in the select halls, to whomsoever he spoke, to the masses or to the elitists, people listened to him with rapt and respectful attention. Whether they agreed with him or disagreed with him, they could never turn their ear from him. His was the final word, a judgment.

What was the secret of this extraordinary power of his spoken word? Why was it that Gandhi spoke and the world listened? Trying to explain it is trying to say why space is majestic or time so fascinating. To attempt it is arrogance, but not to do it is dereliction of duty; I can afford the former, but not the latter.

I believe that the first secret of Gandhi's holy charm was his abiding religiosity. As I have already said his entire thought flowed from his intensely religious faith in the existence of God, and even today religion compels the greatest attention. Nothing in this world is as overpowering as religion not even love; the reason may be that it addresses itself to man's sense of mystery or wonder about the unknown. And whether Gandhi spoke on politics or economics, his motive was essentially and predominantly religious. In his speech at Y.M.C.A. at Madras on 4 September 1927 he admitted: "I do not know a single speech of mine or a talk of mine, within my own recollection, which has not been a religious discourse."[31]

The second source of the extraordinary power of Gandhi's speeches came from his weighty thought. He possessed the supreme gift of stripping every thought of its inessentials, reducing it to its elements and of making the audience face the truth about it in its utter nakedness, in its pure essence. He penetrated through the external trappings to the core of whatever he spoke; the audience got the essential truth and its overpowering effect could not be escaped. Gandhi never appealed to the easily inflammable emotion of his audience; this he knew had quick and immediate effect, but he was always for lasting impact. Emotion subsided as quickly as it was aroused but a weighty and truthful thought stayed, as J. McCosh observed. "In the end, thought rules the world. There are times when

[31] *Ibid.*, xxxiv, 450.

impulses and passions are more powerful, but they soon expend themselves; while mind, acting constantly, is ever ready to drive them back and work when their energy is exhausted."[32] A solid evidence of the soundness and substantiality of Gandhi's thought lies in the numerous books of quotations that have appeared bearing his name; the quotations culled from his speeches would make an encyclopaedia.

The third secret of Gandhian power sprang from his scriptural sincerity. The animation in his speeches was the result of his downright earnestness. His words were the messengers of his soul. They were never made up or artificial or cunningly sugarcoated for the occasion. He spoke as he thought; he was as he seemed. He wore his heart on his lips and could say with Hamlet, "Seems, Madam; Nay, it is; I know not 'seems'."

Closely allied to these three secrets of the extraordinary power of Gandhi's speeches (his religiosity, thought, sincerity) was the fourth one, his Christ-like character. Quintilian, the great Greek critic of ancient times, had said that an orator must be a man of strong moral character, for the speaker's reputation for a virtuous life would have a persuasive effect on the audience. In this regard Gandhi could be bracketed with Buddha or Christ or Nanak. Much of the force of his speeches came from his immaculate character.

These were the inner qualities of Gandhi's speeches. I may now mention two qualities that concerned the external features of oratory: the first of these was the relentless logic of his organisation. He arranged his ideas so logically and lucidly that the audience not only comprehended them easily but they were imprinted on its mind indelibly. It was an old adage that 'truth lies in a well'; to carry the metaphor further it could be added that logic provides us with steps through whose aid we could climb down to reach the water: Gandhi helped us reach his thought through his meticulous organisation.

---

[32] Cited, Tryon Edwards, ed. *The New Dictionary of Thoughts* (USA: Standard Book, 1992 reprint based on the revised edition done by Ralph Emerson Browns et al.), p. 668.

The second of these external virtues of his speeches was his transparently clear and simple style, he who ran could understand them. He spoke in short, lucid and artless sentences which fell upon the ears of the audience like the commands from the Bible. There was scriptural grace about his language which endeared him the more for it to his listeners. But it should be remembered that this simplicity was invariably combined with overmastering power. Gandhi was simple but powerful. It is appropriate at this point to recall the testimony of a European contemporary of Gandhi, Joseph J. Doke: "He is not a passionate orator; his manner is calm and serene and he appeals particularly to the intelligence. But his serenity places the subject he discusses in the clearest light. The inflexions of his voice are not varied, but they are intensely sincere. He never makes any gestures with his arms, in fact he rarely even moves a finger. But his luminous words, expressed in terse, concise sentences, carry conviction. He never abandons a subject before he feels that he has made it perfectly clear."[33] I may now cite a rather long extract to illustrate the quality of Gandhi's English oratory: this is from his speech at Benares Hindu University on 6 February 1916.

> "His Highness the Maharajah, who presided over our deliberations, spoke about the poverty of India. Other speakers laid great stress upon it. But what did we witness in the great pandal in which the foundation ceremony was performed by the Viceroy? Certainly a most gorgeous show, an exhibition of jewellery which made a splendid feast for the eyes of the greatest jeweller who chose to come from Paris. I compare with the richly bedecked noblemen the millions of the poor. And I feel like saying to these noblemen: 'There is no salvation for India unless you strip yourselves of this jewellery and hold it in trust for your countrymen in India.' I am sure it is not the desire of the King Emperor or Lord Hardinge that in order to show the truest loyalty to our King-Emperor, it is necessary for us to ransack our jewellery-boxes and to appear bedecked from top to toe, I would undertake

[33] Cited, Romain Rolland, *Mahatma Gandhi*, trans. C.D. Groth (1924; rpt. Delhi: Publications Division, 1990), p. 2, fn.

at the peril of my life to bring to you the message from King George himself that he expects nothing of this kind. Sir, whenever I hear of a great palace rising in any great city of India, be it in British India or be it in India which is ruled by our great chiefs, I become jealous at once and I say; 'Oh, it is the money that has come from the Agriculturists.'"[34]

Chittaranjan Das (1870-1925)

Chittaranjan Das was born in Calcutta on 5 November 1870. He Graduated from the Presidency College, Calcutta at the age of twenty. He was called to the Bar from the Middle Temple in 1892 and thereafter enrolled as a Barrister in the Calcutta High Court. He rose to fame in 1908 when he defended Aurobindo in the Alipore Bomb Conspiracy Case. In 1917 he became President of the Bengal Provincial Conference, Bhowanipur. He first opposed and then accepted the non-cooperation movement launched by Gandhi in 1920. In 1921 he gave up practice at the Bar and was elected President of the Ahmedabad Congress but could not preside over it because he was then an under-trial prisoner. In the succeeding year he presided over the Gaya Congress and also founded the *Swaraj* Party with Moti Lal Nehru. The *Swarajists* entered the Council in 1923. He presided over the A.I.T.U.C. at Lahore in 1923 and in Calcutta in 1924. He was elected the first Mayor of Calcutta Corporation in 1924 and was elected again in 1925. In 1925 he became the President of the Bengal Provincial Conference, Faridpore. He died at Darjeeling on 16 June 1925.

Chittaranjan Das had four passions—law, journalism, poetry, and politics, and in each of these he acquired considerable excellence, though his fame as a lawyer and as a politician eclipsed everything else in his life. In politics he was an extremist. He supported Gandhi's views about decentralisation and the development of village industries. Like him he repudiated violence and bloody

[34] *The Collected Works of Mahatma Gandhi* (Delhi: Publicaitons Division, 1964, rpt. 1990), xiii, 213-214.

revolution. Subhas Chandra Bose regarded him as his political mentor. His first speeches were made in England in connection with the election campaign of Dada Bhai Naoroji who had contested for a seat in the House of Commons. His Presidential address at Bengal Provincial Congress in 1917 on the Culture of Bengal, at Ahmedabad Congress in 1921 on the Meaning of Freedom, and at Bengal Provincial Congress, Faridpore, in 1925 on *Swaraj* and Dominion Status, are generally considered his best speeches by his admirers. His speeches were published by Banerjee Das & Co., Calcutta and by Natesan, Madras.

However, I may recall an earlier speech of Chittaranjan Das, the concluding part of his defence of Aurobindo in 1909; it was a unique blend of passion and argument and masterly prose: "Long after this controversy is hushed in silence, long after this turmoil ceases, long after Aurobindo is dead and gone, he will be looked upon as the poet of patriotism, as the prophet of nationalism, and the lover of humanity. Long after the mortal in him has perished, his words will be echoed and reechoed across distant seas and lands."[35]

His Presidential speech at Bengal Provincial Conference in Calcutta in 1917 romanticized Bengal's golden past and attributed India's fall to her acceptance of the materialism of the West: "I have found out the true soul of Bengal. I have learnt to appreciate the real history of Bengal. The images of Buddha of the Buddhists, of Siva of the Saivas, of Sakti of the Saktas and of the devotional love of the Vaishnavas rise up before my vision. I think of the immortal songs of Vidyapati and Chandidas and feel myself glorified by the glorious life of Shri Chaitanya. The songs of Jnanadas, Govindadas and Lochan Das vibrate in my heart's core."—"Mimic Anglicism has become an obsession with us; we find its black footprint in every walk and endeavour of our life."[36] In his book *The Heart of Aryavarta*, Lord Ronaldshay made the following comment on this speech: "Mr. Das

---

[35] Cited, Dr. Sachidananda Sinha, *Some Eminent Indian Contemporaries* (Patna : Janaki Prakashan, 1976), p. 108.

[36] Cited, Hemendranath Das Gupta, *Deshbandhu Chittaranjan Das* (Delhi: Publications Division, 1977), p. 31 and pp. 143-144.

spoke indeed with all the ardour of a missionary. He smote in pieces the golden calf which he set up as symbolical of the idea of Europe and with the fervour of a seer he promised the way to a promised land."[37]

These citations could be multiplied but even these two are enough to illustrate the greatness of Chittaranjan Das's eloquence both in respect of its inner quality and linguistic expression. He was indeed a remarkable orator.

Sri Aurobindo Ghose (1872-1950)

The son of a prosperous doctor, Sri Aurobindo Ghose was born in Calcutta on 15 August 1872. He graduated from King's College, Cambridge, in 1892, obtaining, a first class in the classical tripos. In 1893 he joined Baroda Service and rose to the position of the Vice Principal, Baroda College. He combined his Baroda Service with much radical writing and revolutionary activities. In 1906 he resigned his Baroda job to join as principal, National College, Calcutta. The same year he declared complete independence as the goal of Indians and in the year following contributed to the split of the congress at Surat. In 1908 he was arrested in the Alipore Conspiracy Case and was released in 1909 on account of his strong defence by Chittaranjan Das. Soon after his release he started editing *Karmayogin* from Calcutta. In 1910 he was secretly informed by sister Nivedita that he was going to be rearrested for writing seditious articles. In April 1910 he left Bengal and his family in the assumed name of Jytindranath Mitter for Pondicherry which was a French territory and engrossed himself in the pursuit of divine life till his death on 5 December 1950.

There were two distinct phases in 'Aurobindo's life—political (up to 1910) and spiritual (after 1910). Politically, he was an extremist, believing in boycott, swadeshi and in national education. He agreed that freedom could be won through passive resistance, but at the same time he maintained that if passive resistance failed armed revolt

[37] *Ibid.*, p. 32.

could be resorted to. He also believed that political freedom should precede other reforms. He said: "Political freedom is the life-breath of a nation; to attempt social reform, educational reform,, industrial expansion, the moral improvement of the race without aiming first and foremost at political freedom, is the very height of ignorance and futility."[38] His spiritual philosophy is extremely difficult to follow. He confessed it was so, as did Mirra Richard, later known as the Mother.[39] Subhas Chandra Bose found it even revolting; he said it was weakness to seek refuge in contemplation when we are hemmed in on all sides by dangers and difficulties. Hitting him straight, he observed. "In this holy land of ours Ashrams are not new institutions and ascetics and yogis are not novel phenomena; they have held and they will continue to hold an honoured place in society. But it is not their lead that we shall have to follow if we are to create a new India, at once free, happy and great."[40] Gandhi, on the other called Aurobindo a "sage", a "humble devotee, without any hatred in his heart, even though he had refused to grant him interview on the ground that it would interfere with his *Sadhna*.[41] Notwithstanding these differing responses to his philosophy, it may be briefly recalled. But this is no easy matter: Carlyle wrote thirty volumes to preach the gospel of silence; Aurobindo wrote twenty-nine volumes to explain his system of philosophy. To reduce it to a few words has the danger of misrepresentation. However, this

[38] Cited, Sankar Ghose, *Leaders of Modern India* (Delhi: Allied Publishers, 1980), p. 126.

[39] *Ibid.*, p. 129.

[40] *Selected Speeches of Subhas Chandra Bose*, ed. S.A. Ayer (Delhi: Publications Division, 1974 rpt. 1992), p. 44.

[41] Aurobindo wrote to the Mother in Pencil to communicate it to Gandhi that "I am unable to see him because for a long time past I have made it an absolute rule not to have any interview with anyone.—that I do not even speak with my disciples and only give silent blessings to them three times a year. All requests for an interview from others I have been obliged to refuse. The rule has been imposed on me by the necessity of my *Sadhna* and is not at all a matter of convenience or anything else. The time has not come when I can depart from it" (*The Collected Works of Mahatma Gandhi*, Delhi: Publications Division, 1973, rpt. 1994), Lvi, 499.

needs to be done. Possibly, Aurobindo said that the aim of life is God-realisation, and God can be realised through the medium of supermind which has to be reached through *yoga*. Supermind is the link between man and God. God comes down to man through the supermind and man goes up to Him through the supermind. There are many stages between this ascent and descent. The idea which sounds fanciful is best developed in *The Life Divine*. Martin Seymour Smith comments. "Sri Aurobindo Ghose presents a notoriously difficult case. He was a learned and worthy man who cannot be laughed away—although some have tried. He will have to be re-evaluated."[42]

The political speeches of Aurobindo were immensely impressive. They were given in forceful and elevated style. His English upbringing produced a certain native ease or familiarity in the language which is wanting in many other Indian speakers. He spoke English with native ease and fluency. The diction was chaste and well-chosen. Let me recall an extract from his Uttarpara speech delivered on 30 May 1909 after his acquittal in the Alipore Bomb Case: "When I went to jail the whole country was alive with the cry of *Bande Mataram*, alive with the hope of a nation, the hope of millions of men who had newly risen out of degradation. When I came out of jail I listened for that cry, but there was instead a silence. A hush had fallen on the country and men seemed bewildered."[43] My other example is from his Jhalakati Speech delivered on 19 June 1909 in the district of Barisal. "Storm has swept over us today. I saw it come, I saw the striding of the storm-blast and the rush of the rain and as I saw it an idea came to me. What is this storm that is so mighty and sweeps with such fury upon us? And I said in my heart, 'It is God who rides abroad on the wings of the hurricane—it is the might and force of the Lord that manifested itself and His almighty hands that seized and shook the roof so violently over our heads today.' A storm like this has swept also our national life. This too was the manifestation of the Almighty."[44]

---

[42] *Guide to Modern World Literature* (London: Macmillan, 1986), p. 719.

[43] *Sri Aurobindo Birth Centenary Library Popular Edition: Karmayogin* (Pondicherry: Sri Aurobindo Ashram Trust, 1972), p. 1.

[44] *Ibid.*, p. 61.

Bhula Bhai Desai (1877-1946)

Born at Surat in 1877, educated at Bombay University, Bhula Bhai Desai began his professional life as a professor but gave it up to join legal practice in 1905. Here he rose to a great height and in 1923 he was offered High Court Judgeship which he did not accept. He combined his legal practice with active participation in Congress affairs and freedom movement. He was a member of the Congress Working Committee. He displayed extraordinary forensic eloquence in his defence of I.N.A. prisoners. He died in May 1946.

Broadly speaking, the speeches of Bhula Bhai Desai can be classified into three groups—political, economic and legal. His outstanding economic and legal speeches were delivered in the Legislative Assembly and those on budget, finance, criminal law, and on law in general were received with unusual admiration. His political speeches were mostly freedom-centred: they gave a call for freedom, awakening the people to their sense of present ills and invoking India's glorious past. Some of these memorable speeches were: 'We Are not Faint-hearted' (Coimbatore, 1934), 'India's Mission in the World' (Madras, 1934), 'Vindicate the Name of Our Motherland' (Bezwada, 1934), 'Freedom Cannot be Won by Arguments' (Vizagapatam, 1934), 'Why Is India What She Is Today' (Nagpur, 1934), 'We Can never Be Divided' (Nagpur, 1934), 'Work for the Larger Freedom That Is to Come' (Nagpur, 1934), and many more. In his stimulating lecture at Nagpur in 1934 he analysed the degraded state of India to three sources or 'dominations' as he called them. "Why is India what it is today? It is because of three dominations . . . the domination of the Indian mind by its society, the domination of the Indian spirit by its present religion, and the domination of the people by the foreign races."[45] His thought was invariably bold and convincing and the expression exceedingly simple and lucid. He used mono-syllabic words and was deeply conscious about the wave length of his listeners' comprehension. He always spoke to his audience, never above it. Every word that he spoke went home to it. There was no ambiguity, no straining after effect, no desire to flash his knowledge upon them. It was as if a kind

[45] *Speeches of Bhula Bhai J. Desai* (Madras: G.A. Natesan, 1938), p. 41.

teacher was speaking to the students he loved. But this was blended with power and conviction, intrepidity and righteous indignation. I give two brief samples of his speeches. The first is from his speech 'Freedom Cannot Be Won by Arguments' delivered at Vizagapatam on 24 July 1934: "15 years ago it was impossible to consider anything else but the blessings and security provided by Pax Britannica. . . If India exists merely in order that her children may be bled to the last drop they possess, in order that there may be an efficient administration in this country, we may as well submit to an immediate destruction of ourselves. If I did not believe that we still have a future, I would have preferred that as a genuine and real consummation. For on examining the history of the world, I have asked myself the question, Rome has gone, Greece has gone, Egypt has gone, Assyria has gone, why is it that Indian civilization, perhaps the most ancient civilization, continues to survive?"[46] My second sample is from his speech 'Why Is India What She Is Today' delivered in 1934 at Nagpur. "If freedom is a virtue, it cannot be a virtue for only a limited part of the human race. Why is freedom a virtue to be fought for so far as the West is concerned so that they may be men, so that they may be masters in their own countries, and why is it a crime so far as India is concerned? For it was considered a crime during the last three years of history of this country when people who dared to fight for their liberty were punished, were thrown into prison, and the spirit of freedom was considered a crime and sought to be suppressed as a crime. If freedom is a virtue, it is a virtue for all mankind."[47] Every word of this speech was drenched in patriotism and in righteous anger against the double standards of the British. It was a trumpet call to Indians to rise and fight for their justful right for freedom.

Sarojini Naidu (1879-1949)

Sarojini Naidu was born in Hyderabad on 13 February 1879. Her father, Aghorenath Chattopadhya was an educationist and a writer of a sort. She matriculated from Madras at the age of twelve and

[46] *Ibid.*, p. 28.
[47] *Ibid.*, pp. 41-42.

thereafter joined first King's College, London, and then Girton College, Cambridge, but ended up without a degree. On her return to India, she married Dr. Govindarajulu Naidu on 2 December 1898. In the years that followed she wrote poetry and participated in politics, befriending stalwarts like Gokhale, Gandhi and Jinnah. In 1924 she presided over the East African Indian Congress at Mombasa. In 1925 she took over the charge of Congress Presidentship from Mahatma Gandhi. In March 1947 she presided over the Asian Relations Conference at Delhi. On the eve of Independence she was made the Governor of U.P., this being an apt responsibility after her numerous trips abroad as India's cultural ambassador and a good respite after being in and out of jails countless times as a political prisoner. She died on 2 March 1949, aged 70.

Sarojini Naidu was a ceaseless speaker. No one has kept count of the innumerable speeches that she gave at different colleges, universities, conferences, public gatherings, foreign countries, and at many other platforms. G. A. Natesan, Madras, have published only a very limited number of them, and since most of her speeches were given extemporaneously, they are either lost or must be lying in the stack rooms of the contemporary newspapers from where they can be retrieved only by a determined government. No single individual can do it. Moreover, her reputation as a poet so far outdistanced her fame as an orator that such an exercise has not found favour with anyone so far, though the quality of the speeches more than justifies it.

There is hardly any subject on which Sarojini Naidu did not speak, nevertheless, the largest number of her speeches were on emancipation of women, Hindu-Muslim unity and on India. Her first important speech on women was made at the Calcutta session of the Congress in 1917 in which she said: "Womanhood of Indiastands by you today when your hour strikes, when you need torchbearers in the darkness, standard bearers to uphold your honour . . . the womanhood of India will be with you as holders of your banner, sustainers of your strength."[48] The titles of some of the lectures on

[48] Cited, V.S. Naravane, *Sarojini Naidu: Her Life, Work and Poetry* (Delhi: Orient Longman, 1980, rpt. 1996), p. 95.

women she gave in America were: 'The Veiled Pageant', 'Guardians of the Flame', 'A Garden Enclosed', and 'The Sceptre of Service.' However, it must be remembered that she was not a militant or acrimonious female liberator but only a soft proponent of her rights. On the subject of Hindu-Muslim unity Mrs. Naidu waxed equally eloquent. In her lecture at Patna in 1917 she remarked: "Centuries ago when the first Islamic army came to India, they pitched their caravans on the banks of the Ganges and tempered and cooled their swords in the sacred waters. It was the baptism of the Ganges that gave the first welcome to the Islamic invaders that became the children of India as Generations went by."[49] Her speeches on India were drenched in poetry, passion and patriotism. Nehru was moved by her nationalistic speeches. He wrote in his *Autobiography*: "I remember being moved also, in those days after the Lucknow Congress, by a member of eloquent speeches delivered by Sarojini Naidu in Allahabad. It was all nationalism and patriotism."[50] Like Nehru Sarojini Naidu also thought that the ultimate oneness of India lies in her cultural unity.

Sarojini Naidu's speeches were remarkable not for their thought but for their style. V.S. Naravane who had attended one of her speeches at Allahabad when he was a young student remarked to his Professor A.N. Jha: "Sir, I must confess that I did not quite follow her argument." And Jha quickly added: "Nor could I . . . .Who needs arguments from poets?"[51] She spoke in lyrical prose marked by verbal exuberance and rich ornamentation. She was a magnificent drunkard of words and jewelled phrases. Her surging eloquence and fluent lyricism enchanted the hearers. She spoke words, and words, more words, and still more words, many times empty of ideas, but never wanting in enthralling sweetness, It is worthwhile recalling the impression of Professor Bhattacharya who heard her many times at Allahabad. "That unbroken flow of sonorous and dignified language, the symmetry, the verve, the passion and sensitiveness of her utterance,

---

[49] Cited, Padmini Sen Gupta, *Sarojini Naidu* (Delhi: Sahitya Akademi, 1974, rpt. 1989), pp. 32-33.

[50] (1936; rpt. Delhi: Oxford, 1962), p. 35.

[51] V.S. Naravane, p. 3.

her vivid imagery, her modulations, her silvery voice sometimes waxing warm and becoming piercing, sometimes mellowed, would keep the audience all the time in a state of animation."[52] Of her delivery and mannerisms Eleanor Morton, her friend, observed: "Her graceful hands moved in gestures of appeal, a lift of an eyebrow emphasing an inflection, a turn of glance giving fuller meaning to a word. These were mannerisms of a great lady, taught since infancy to plead without speech. Men realized the magic of her effortless charm."[53]

An illustrative passage may be cited. This is from her speech as the President of Asian Relations Conference in March 1947 at Delhi: "I wonder how many of you who have come journeying across steep mountain passes, floating on the vast bosom of many coloured seas, riding amid the clouds of dawn and darkness, realise that we stand today, here and now, not only in the heart of Asia, but the very core and centre of India's heart . . . We have come here to take an indestructible pledge of unity of Asia so that the world in ruin could be redeemed from sorrow, unhappiness, exploitation, misery, poverty, ignorance, disaster and death."[54] No orator before Sarojini Naidu ever luxuriated in the giddying pleasures of style without any regard for substance. She spoke airy nothings, and this was all her virtue and all her vice.

Chakravarti Rajagopalachari (1879-1972)

Called by Gandhi as his 'conscience-keeper' and by Melville de Mello as 'Chanakya of the Century', Chakravarti Rajagopalachari was born at Salem, Madras, on 8 December 1879. Passing B.A. from Central College, Bangalore, and B.L. from Law College, Madras, he joined the Bar at Salem in 1900. He gave up legal practice to strengthen the hands of Gandhi in his struggle for freedom in 1921. On 13 April 1930 he led a march from Tiruchi to Vedaranyam to disobey the British Salt Law. In 1937 be became the first Congress

---

[52] *Ibid.*, p. 147.
[53] *Ibid.*, pp. 147-48.
[54] Padmini Sen Gupta, p. 68.

Chief Minister of Madras but resigned this post in 1939. He resigned from the congress in 1942 for not joining the Quit India Movement: he had persuaded the Madras Legislature party to pass a resolution accepting the formation of Pakistan in order to reconcile the congress and the Muslim League. But he rejoined the congress in 1946 as a member of the working committee. After independence he became a member of the Nehru Cabinet, then the Governor of West Bengal, and in 1948 the Governor-General of India. On 26 January 1950 he relinquished the Governor-Generalship to become the Chief Minister of Madras. In 1954 he was awarded Bharat Ratna. In 1959 he started Swatantra Party in opposition to Nehruvian socialism. In 1962 he led Anti-Nuclear Mission to America, England and to France. He died on 25 December 1972 at the age of 93 plus.

In his long life of more than ninety years Rajagopalacharya spoke on a wide variety of subjects covering religion, social reform, politics, economics, education, disarmament, and lot more. Essentially, like Gandhi he was an intensely religious man, believing in God, oneness of all organized religions and in the moralising and spiritualising power of religion. He said again and again that all holy books—*Gita, Bible, Koran, Granth Sahib, Dhammapada*—taught universal love. The rationalists took religion for ritualism and tried to dislodge it and in the process degenerated into rank individualism. 'Back to basic religion, to Vedantism' must be our slogan. In the field of social reform his two obsessive passions were Harijan Uplift and Prohibition. He was also a great proponent of inter-caste marriage. In politics he was an ardent opponent of communism which he considered his number one enemy. He opposed the formation of states on linguistic basis, frequent constitutional reforms curtailing individual freedom, policy of non-allignment, and the tendency to centralisation. In economics, he supported *laisse faire* and free enterprise and condemned the policy of controls and permits. He was an invincible opponent of co-operative farming. In the field of education his primary concern was the language problem: he was pro-English and did not approve of its violent and hurried replacement by Hindi, though it is true that during the freedom movement he had supported Hindi. His last abiding and strong concern was nuclear disarmament. In his address to the Madras Christian College Union on 16 August 1945 he decried the use of the atom bomb in the second world war which resulted into the fall of Japan; he said that the process of making such a bomb was a secret but it would soon become world knowledge. He observed: "When men have discovered a wicked thing, it would not remain a secret for long. The data available are quite enough for people to develop it further. No doubt, the war had ended, but it has ended in a terrible way and people are not inclined to be jolly about it."[55] So much about the subjects on which he spoke and about his ideas on them.

As an organizer of his speeches Rajagopalachari was a redoubtable logician. His logic was irresitible and had the force of inevitability. Once his premises were established, the arguments that followed and the conclusions that were arrived seemed natural and incontrovertible. The middle flowed from the beginning, and the end flowed front the middle; the logical unity or order was meticulously maintained. His language was marked by four striking qualities—lucidity, economy, precision, and simplicity. There were no superfluous but flowery decorations. Like the man, his style too was straight and unambiguous. But sometimes when he was stimulated he could be unbearably incisive and pungent. His wit was sharp and came handy to him in his speeches. He was full of humility and gentleness, but at the same time he could not be taken for granted, he was strong and insurmountable. To students he was always authoritative and parental: his speeches to them were like sermons. As a sample of his art of speech making I give an excerpt from his address at Jamshedpur on 21 November 1946: "Take the recent World War. The fighting nations thought it was peace they were fighting for. They thought the world would be all beautiful as soon as they had won the war. But what has happened? We find peace more difficult than war. It is easy to fight, it is easy to win a war, but it is difficult to rebuild after the war is over. And I think I tell the truth when I say that many people who fought and won this war, especially the leading people, must be mentally regretting now why they ever fought and won it. They must be feeling that they

---

[55] *The Voice of the Uninvolved: Speeches and Statements on Atomic Warfare and Test Explosions* (New Delhi: National Book Trust India, 1960), p. 2.

might have been happier if there had been no war, or at least, if they had not won the war and had to be responsible for peace."[56]

From Bal Gangadhar Tilak to Chakravarti Rajagopalacharya is a long journey and with this our story of the English oratory of Gandhi and his contemporaries comes to an end. During this period nationalism became completely entrenched in the Indian psyche. British loyalism was eroded by *Jallianwala Bagh* Tragedy in 1919 and in the Lahore Congress Jawaharlal Nehru demanded complete independence for India. Gandhian thought of truth and nonviolence and the realisation of its value in politics gradually superseded every other philosophy. Indian oratory thereby gained in political substance. In style three modes reached their acme—the grand style climaxed in Vivekananda, simple style in Gandhi, and lyrical style in Sarojini Naidu. All in all, it was a momentous period for Indian eloquence in English.

[56] *An Anthology of Modern Indian Eloquence*, ed. R.K. Prabhu (Bombay: Bharatiya Vidya Bhavan, 1960), p. 155.

V

SUCCESSORS OF GANDHI

Successors of Gandhi comprise those great Indians who were born after 1885 and were in their middle age or at the threshold of old age in 1947. Some of them came to eminence at the time of Non-co-operation Movement in 1920 and some after it; thus they made their speeches between the short period of twenty-seven years at the most. By this time the venue of speeches had shifted from halls to *pandals* or even open grounds; not that they were not made in the halls, but that they generally took place in the open. With this the medium of oratory changed from English to Hindi or local languages. Moreover, Gandhi encouraged his followers to speak in Hindustani as a part of Hindustani Movement. Besides, the speeches of this period became politics-centred: the speakers continued to speak on all kinds of subjects, but their commanding subject was political freedom.

Some eminent men of this period who were stirring public speakers thus did not speak in English. Among them the greatest was Maulana Abul Kalam Azad (1888-1958), an Islamic scholar and nationalist Muslim. Some others spoke in English but not in English that could be called literature: of them I could recall M.N.Roy (1886-1954), a Marxist turned Liberal Humanist; Dr. Zakir Hussain (1897-1969), an educationist and Gandhian who made the famous remark that "he wished there was more education in our politics and less politics in our education;" and Jayaprakash Narayan (1902-1979) who changed his political position from Marxism to Socialism to Gandhism. In politics another tall man was V.K. Krishna Menon (1896-1974) who lived mostly in England and whose thundering speeches on India from the platform of India League in London in the thirties earned him the encomium of Nehru, but these speeches are not preserved, or that I could not lay my hands on them. His post-independence speeches made in the Security Council are currently not our concern. Three more speakers whom I heard myself and who were any day better as orators than most statesmen and thinkers of the past, were S.C.Deb, Professor of English, Allahabad University, Ishwari Prasad, Professor of History, Allahabad University and General Cariappa who wore his heart on his lips and spoke like a master. But even their speeches are lost to the world. Of the remaining speakers the most outstanding were Sarvepalli Radhakrishnan (1888-1975), Jawaharlal Nehru (1889-1964), Bhimrao Ramji Ambedkar (1891-1956), Subhas Chandra Bose (1897-1945), and Shyama Prasad Mookerjee (1905-1953).

Sarvepalli Radhakrishnan (1888-1975)

Sarvepalli Radhakrishnan was born in a conservative middle class family at Tiruttani near Madras on 5 September 1888. After passing M.A. in Philosophy from Madras Christian College, he joined as a Lecturer at Madras Presidency College in 1909, became Professor at Mysore University in 1918 and at Calcutta University in 1920, and rose to the position of the Vice-Chancellor, Mysore University, in 1931 and Benaras University in 1939, with a three year spell from 1936 to 1939 as the Spalding Professor of Eastern Religion at the University of Oxford. In 1948 he headed Universities Commission which brought out an excellent report on higher education. The same year he became the Chairman of the UNESCO and of the UGC. In 1949 he was made India's Ambassador to the Soviet Union. In 1952 he was elected the Vice-President of India and in 1962 the President. He retired in 1967 and died on 17 April 1975.

Radhakrishnan was a prolific writer and a fluent speaker. He generally spoke on philosophy, religion and on education but sometimes on politics too. But his political lectures were the products of his post-independence period. In 1927 he delivered the Upton lectures at Oxford in which he defended Hinduism against the charges of illusionism, fatalism and of ritualism and presented it as scientifically viable, making the characteristic observation that religious experience must be in conformity with the findings of science. The lectures were published as *The Hindu View of Life*. From England he went to USA to deliver Haskell Lectures at Chicago and to speak in the International Congress of Philosophy at Harvard. Here he focussed on the role of philosophy in the growth of human civilization. Commenting on these lectures, Prema Nandakumar says: "He mesmerized his audiences with a judicious mixture of irony and humour while expounding the most abstruse philosophical problems in sonorous English garnished with Sanskrit phrases."[1] Then he delivered the Hibbert Lectures at Manchester and London Universities which were published as *An Ideal View of Life*. Here he explicated Advaita Vedanta with extraordinary eloquence and clarity. In 1937 he delivered the British Academy lecture on Buddha extemporaneously without consulting any notes and enchanted the audience by his exquisite presentation of Buddha as a corrector of Vedic ritualism. He observed: "The quiet end of the Buddha contrasts vividly with the martyr's deaths of Socrates and Jesus. All the three undermined, in different degrees, the orthodoxies of their time. As a matter of fact, the Buddha was more definitely opposed to Vedic orthodoxy and ceremonialism than was Socrates to the state religion of Athens, or Jesus to Judaism and yet he lived till eighty, gathered a large number of disciples, and founded a religious order in his own life-time. Perhaps, the Indian temper of religion is responsible for the difference in the treatment of unorthodoxies."[2] In his educational lectures he stressed the need of autonomy for the universities. His Convocation Address at Andhra University in 1927 was an embodiment of mature thought on education. He advised universities to assume the leadership in the world of ideas, and ideals, in both the rational ideas and the religious values. He accepted what he called the constructive conservatism of the past but at the same time did not reject the scientific and technological advances: he was for an integral system of education.

Radhakrisnan could render the mystical and the mystifying easily intelligible. He never used three words when two were enough. There were no surplus words or ornaments that lengthened the sentences, nor uncommon expressions or egocentric phraseology that rendered

---

[1] *S. Radhakrishnan* (Delhi: Sahitya Akademi, 1992), p. 17.

[2] Cited, Prema Nandkumar, p. 26.

the simple difficult and obfuscating. Similarly, in his delivery he was sparing in the use of physical gestures; he was serene, composed and commanding. I heard him many times and was always impressed by his dignified posture and by the majesty of his language, but I must confess that I was disenchanted when I heard his broadcast on the death of Nehru, it lacked in the soulful warmth which marked every word that Nehru spoke on the death of Gandhi. I had heard both of these broadcasts and had found Nehru's infinitely more moving and kathartic.

Jawaharlal Nehru (1889-1964)

Jawaharlal Nehru was born at Allahabad on 14 November 1889. After an undistinguished career at Harrow School and Trinity College, Cambridge, where he took the natural sciences tripos, he was called to the bar in 1912 before returning to Allahabad to practice at the high court there. During Christmas of the same year he commenced his political career by attending the Bankipore Congress as a delegate. He met Gandhi at the Lucknow Congress in 1916 and under his magic spell participated in the Non-cooperation Movement in 1920. He was arrested in 1921 and thereafter gaol became his second home. In 1929 he presided over the Lahore Congress and he was elected to this office many times since then. He became the first Prime Minister of India in 1947 and continued in this office till his death on 27 May 1964. He would have lived longer if his policy of friendship with China had not been falsified by the Chinese Aggression in 1962.

Nehru's pre-independence speeches collected by J.S.Bright in *Before and After Independence: Collected Speeches, 1922-1950*, 1950, covered a staggering variety of subjects, but whatever be these subjects, they drew their sustenance from some root ideas. These root ideas being given, one could even anticipate what he was to say on a particular subject. The substance of his speeches came from those fundamental thoughts or seed ideas. What were they? In my evaluation the most overmastering of these was his RATIONALISM. This made him discard organized religion as blind belief, superstition, exploitation, and a force that divided man from man. In India it created insensate strife between brother and brother.

The second seed idea was INTERNATIONALISM. He was opposed to narrow nationalism. Nationalism had a vital place in every country, but it could not be allowed to become aggressive and come in the way of international development. Indian nationalism was only an enforced necessity, a passing phase in her fight against British Imperialism. An independent India would be linked to the whole world in peace and amity.

The third root thought was the thought of freedom, freedom of every type—political, social, economic. He hated domination of any kind. In the Lahore Congress in 1929 in which he proclaimed complete independence as the goal of India he decried the domination of kings as well as of the modern kings of industry who were no less predatory. It was his love of freedom that made him oppose imperialism and fascism.

The fourth encircling thought of Nehru was PACIFISM, the belief in the preservation of peace. He knew it well that the forces of aggression had to be repulsed by military power, but he maintained that even while we resist aggression we should keep the temper of peace. Non-violence was an impossible ideal, but non-violent temper could surely be cultivated.

The fifth pervasive thought of Nehru was DEMOCRATIC SOCIALISM: in the words of S.Gopal, "Democracy, as adapted to an under-privileged society; socialism, indistinct in outline, but not necessarily, therefore, disadvantageous, and not conceived as a backward and poverty-striken socialism but linked with production rather than distribution."[3] He disregarded the argument that democracy and socialism were contradictory.

Nehru generally spoke extemporaneously. Even on formal occasions he did not like to speak from written speeches. Nor did he organize his ideas laboriously. The result was that his speeches were natural but rambling. They pleased not by their orderliness but by their disarming friendliness and informality. He spoke in two styles: when in emotion, he spoke in lyrical prose, but when he spoke from cool reason and explicated some intellectual problem, his style became

[3] *The Mind of Jawaharlal Nehru* (Madras: Sangam Books, 1980), p. 47.

sparse, all the silks and satins of beauty and all the verbal enchantments were dropped, and his language became as translucent as clear water over pebbles. As for memory, Nehru's mind was a storehouse of knowledge and he could draw from it at will: he needed no notes to aid his memory. He spoke from the fullness of ideas and emotions. As for delivery, his voice was feminine and his gestures were limited to the waving of hand. I heard him times out of number and what impressed me most was his angelic appearance and the child-like sincerity of tone. D.P. Mukerji has this to say about his voice: "It is probably the most cultured voice in India. Tagore's was a piping one and often ended in a shrill. Gandhiji carried persuasion through directness. Mrs. Besant had a feminine roundure; Mrs. Naidu's was clear and melodious; Shastri's had grace; Surendranath's had thunder; Malaviya's was mellifluous, but Jawaharlal has the somewhat cloudy overtones of a cultured man's voice without being gorgeous. That voice speaks with the sensitive hesitancy of thought process and a slight sensuality that is not quite male and yet must be very attractive for a female. It is definitely melancholy even when it lashes out in anger."[4] Frank Moraes who has written an admirable biography of Nehru has this judgement on Nehru's art of oratory: "Nehru is no great orator by classical or even conventional standards. But when the mood and occasion move him his eloquence takes wing in limpid, often moving prose."[5] Such was his famous 'Tryst with Destiny' speech on the night of 14 August 1947 or his inaugural speech at the first Asian Relations Conference in November 1946. I cite the following passage from his Broadcast from New Delhi on 7 September 1946 on the Interim National Government: "India is on the move and the old order passes. Too long have we been passive spectators of events, the plaything of others. The initiative comes to our people now and we shall make the history of our choice. Let us all join in this mighty task and make India, the pride of our heart, great among nations, foremost in the arts of peace and progress. The door is open and destiny beckons to all. There is no question of who wins and who

---

[4] Cited, C.D. Narasimhaiiah, *Selection from Speeches by Jawaharlal Nehru* (Madras: Macmillan, 1959), p. 44.

[5] *Jawaharlal Nehru* (Bombay: Jaico, 1959, rpt. 1978), p. 486.

loses, for we have to go forward and together as comrades and either all of us win or we all go down together. But there is going to be no failure. We go forward to success, to independence and to the freedom and well-being of the four hundred millions of India. JAI HIND."[6]

Bhimrao Ramji Ambedkar (1891-1956)

Bhimrao Ramji Ambedkar was born at Mhow in Madhya Pradesh on 14 April 1891 in a low-caste Mahar family. He was the fourteenth child of a Subedar-Major who lived on a meagre pension of Rs. 50 per month when Bhimrao was born. So, from childhood he had to face poverty and caste discrimination which embittered his character. After passing B.A. from Elphinstone College in 1912, he did M.A. in Economics in 1915 and Ph. D. in 1916 from Columbia, the U.S.A., on a Baroda State Scholarship. On his return to India, he worked as a Professor at Sydenham College of Commerce, Bombay from 1918 to 1920. Thereafter he did his M.Sc. and D.Sc. from London School of Economics and qualified as a barrister from Gray's Inn and started legal practice at the Bombay High Court. Then he rose through many spirited struggles for the upliftment of untouchables to the Bombay Legislative Council (1926-34) and attended the three sessions of the Round Table Conference, London (1930-32) as a delegate of the depressed classes. He founded independent Labour Party in 1936, Scheduled Caste Federation in 1942 and People's Education in 1945. On India attaining freedom, he became a Law Minister in the Nehru Cabinet (1947-51) and resigned it to become the Opposition Leader. He was also a Member of the Constituent Assembly (1947-50) and had the distinction of drafting the Indian Constitution as the Chairman of the Drafting Committee. Disenchanted by Hinduism, he embraced Buddhism on 14 October 1956 alongwith 10 lac of his followers and died a non-Hindu on 6 December 1956.

Ambedkar was an intensely learned man: he had one lac books in his personal library. He was at the same time a much anguished

---

[6] *Jawaharlal Nehru's Speeches* (Delhi: Publications Division, 1993), i, 5.

victim of heartless Hindu Casteism. These two facts affected his public speeches, making them both knowledgeable and fiery. The subjects on which he spoke with special ire or excitement were the depressed state of untouchables, the rottenness of Hinduism, and the conservatism of Gandhi. His speeches on politics, economics and education too need special mention.

Ambedkar was of the opinion that untouchability started in A.D. 400 out of the conflict between Buddhism and Brahminism. The Brahmins wrote scriptures to swindle the ignorant masses and to exploit them to their material ends. In his speech at Kanpur in 1944 he said: "The root of the untouchability is the caste system, the root of the caste system is religion attached to *Varna* and *Ashram*; and the root of *Varnashram* is Brahmanical religion; and the root of the Brahmanical religion is authoritarianism or political power."[7] He discarded Hinduism to embrace Buddhism because he thought that Hinduism believed in God, Soul and in Caste System, while Buddhism set aside these to emphasise knowledge, love and equality. And since Gandhi was a devout Hindu who believed in caste system as an expression of the division of labour he derided his Harijan movement as a hypocritical mask, saying that Mahatmas have come and Mahatmas have gone, but the untouchables have remained untouchables. Nor did he appreciate Gandhian economics or sociology: he thought that Gandhism reduced man to the position of two bullocks yoked to his plough, and enclosed woman in the cottage to make her cook and procreate and ply on the spinning wheel, depriving both man and woman of all culture that can develop only by using the brain and mental faculties. So he concluded that a worse person than Gandhi could not have been chosen to guide India's destiny. Ambedkar did not, or could not, combine sweetness with light; he spoke bitterly.

In Economics, Ambedkar condemned capitalism and supported progressive socialism and considered parliamentary democracy as a means to realise socialism. He further believed that to reduce social inequality it was necessary to tax agriculture. In politics, he firmly

[7] Cited, W.N. Kuber, *B.R. Ambedkar* (Delhi: Publications Div., 1990), p. 104.

believed in democracy and hated the cult of hero-worship; he favoured progress and agitation through constitutional means and considered civil disobedience and non-co-operation as grammar of anarchy. In the field of education Ambedkar championed female education. In his speech in Depressed Class Women's Conference at Nagpur in 1942 he said that he weighed the progress of a community by the education of the women.

Ambedkar's speeches were thus rich in substance; they were logical in organisation and simple in language; but the language was too bare and matter of fact to be called literary. Its one abiding feature was its hitting tone; it was too forthright and blunt. No palliatives: No sweeteners! It was straight and persuasive. Here is an example from his speech, 'The Annihilation of Caste', delivered at Lahore on 15 May 1936: "It is a pity that even today the caste system has its defenders. It is defended on the ground that the caste system is but another name for division of labour and if division of labour is a necessary feature of every civilized society then it is argued that there is nothing wrong in the caste system. The first thing to be argued against this view is that the caste system is not merely a division of labour. It is also a division of labourers."[8]

Subhas Chandra Bose (1897-1945)

The ninth of the fourteen children of Janakinath, a lawyer, Subhas Chandra Bose was born at Cuttack on 27 January 1897. After graduating from the Scottish Church College, he cleared the ICS examination in 1920 but left it before completing the probationary period and joined as a Principal, National College, Calcutta. He plunged into India's struggle for freedom under the guidance of C.R. Das and was arrested in December 1921 and that ended his work as Principal. Thereafter he was arrested eleven times. He belonged to the left wing of the Congress. In 1927 he was elected as President of the Bengal Provincial Congress Committee. In 1933 he went to Vienna for the treatment of tuberculosis and there married Emilie

[8] *100 Best Pre-Independence Speeches: 1870-1947*, ed. H.D. Sharma (Delhi : Harper Collins, 1998), p. 270.

Schenkl from whom he had a daughter whom he named Anita. In 1938 he was elected President of the Congress and he repeated this feat in 1939, defeating Gandhi's candidate Dr. Pattabhi Sitaramayya, but had to resign on account of differences with Gandhi. Early in 1941 he escaped to Germany where he met Hitler and thereafter to Japan where he assumed command of the Indian National Army organized by Captain Mohan Singh and Rash Behari Bose and manned by prisoners of war. He thought that an armed revolt could succeed, but he had to retreat when Japan fell and it was said that he died in an air crash at Taihoku in Formosa on 18 August 1945, though the legend still lingers that the story of the aircrash was made up.

Even a cursory glance at the speeches of Subhas makes it evident that the two subjects that took possession of his mind like an obsession were freedom and India. The first speech in the *Selected Speeches of Subhas Chandra Bose* edited by S.A. Ayer for Publications Division, Government of India, is called 'Vision of a Free India'. And the first thing that strikes our mind as we go through these speeches is his anti-Gandhian thought. In his concept of freedom and of the means of attaining it, as also in his view of the reconstruction of India, he thought differently from Gandhi. Whereas Gandhi was for non-violent means, Subhas was for armed revolution. Gandhi stood for openness and truth in his dealings with the British, Subhas adumbrated shrewdness and diplomacy: one criticism that he persistently lodged against Gandhi was that he put all his cards on the table and lacked the art of diplomacy which was so essential in political thought. Besides, Gandhi believed in self-help in the fight for freedom, while Subhas looked for outside help also. In his broadcast from Berlin called 'Outside Help for Freedom Fight' on 17 June 1942 he said: "The Indian people must fight for and win their liberty but in this fight some help from abroad will be necessary."[9] But it must be remembered that his reverence for Gandhi never became the less for these differences. He called him 'India's greatest man', 'the father of the nation', and the like. In his Haripura Congress Address on 19 February 1938 he said: "We need Gandhi to keep our struggle free from bitterness and

---

9 *Selected Speeches of Subhas Chandra Bose*, ed. S.A. Ayer (Delhi: Publications Division, 1992), p. 136.

hatred. We need him for the cause of humanity."[10] In his broadcast from Bangkok on Gandhiji's birthday on 2 October 1943 he said: "The service which Mahatma Gandhi has rendered to India and to the cause of India's freedom is so unique and unparalleled that his name will be written in letters of gold in our national history for all time."[11] To top it all, in his broadcast from Azad Hind Radio on 6 July 1944 he prayed to him, "Father of our nation! In this holy war of India's liberation, we ask for your blessings and good wishes."[12]

Likewise, in his economic thought Subhas was anti-Gandhian. He felt that Gandhi was backward-looking and medieval: he was taking India to the days of bullock-cart or the spinning wheel. India had to resort to modern and scientific means of growth and go for large scale industrialisation and agricultural reform. In everything our approach must be rational, not mystical or medieval. India does not need saints. We have had enough of them. She needs practical, dynamic, down to earth thinkers and doers. In his political thought too Subhas was Gandhi's opposite number. While Gandhi was for stateless state, that is, for the minimum state interference in the individual affairs, Subhas was for a strong Central Government with dictatorial powers for some years to come in order that India may be put on her feet. The country needed a strong party with a strong leader with strict military discipline. It was a sort of a queer blend of communism and fascism which he called *Samyavad* or synthesis or equality.

Subhas was not an intellectual of the level of Nehru or Ambedkar or Radhakrishnan. Nor was he a fluent and graceful stylist like Surendranath Banerjea or Srinivasa Sastri or Sarojini Naidu. One looked for bright and beautiful flowers in vain in his speeches. Nor was his voice mellifluous or smooth-flowing. He loaded each sentence-end with a big heavy stress which made it blunt and unmusical. Yet his speeches were effective and they swayed the audience. What was the secret of their moving power? I believe it came from his character, from his ardent patriotism, his utter sincerity, his dynamic activism, and his love and respect for the audience. He was impetuous but full

---

[10] *Ibid.*, p. 87.
[11] *Ibid.*, p. 209.
[12] *Ibid.*, p. 235.

of deep humility. It was the man Subhas who lent power to his speeches. I recall the judgment of Dr. Girija K. Mookerjee on this: "Subhas was not a great orator. He could never come near to such great orators as Surendranath Banerjea, C.R. Das or Srinivasa Sastri. He spoke too slowly; his images were often faulty and his choice of words was far from being dynamic. Still he was effective and he could move people. This success lay only in the directness of his speech and the homeliness with which he touched unsophisticated hearts."[13] Anyone who hears his speeches collected and edited by Netaji Research Bureau, Calcutta and recorded by the Gramophone Co. of India Ltd., will endorse this judgment. I now give two examples from his better-known speeches. The first example is from his celebrated speech, 'To Delhi, To Delhi' at a military review of the Indian National Army on 5 July 1943, "When France declared war on Germany in 1939 and the campaign began, there was but one cry which rose from the lips of German soldiers—"To Paris, To Paris". When the brave soldiers of Nippon set out on their march in December 1941 there was but one cry which rose from their lips—"To Singapore, To Singapore!" Comrades! Soldiers! Let your battle-cry be—"To Delhi, To Delhi!"[14] My second example is from his speech 'India Shall Be Free' delivered when INA had failed, on 16 August 1945, two days before his reported death: "In this unprecedented crisis in our history, I hope only one word to say. Do not be depressed at our temporary failure. Be of good cheer and keep up your spirits. Above all, never for a moment falter in your faith in India's destiny. There is no power on earth that can keep India enslaved. *India shall be free, and before long*. Jai Hind"[15] These were the last words of his last speech! Exactly two years after, India became free.

Shyama Prasad Mookerjee (1901-1953)

The son of Ashutosh Mookerjee, the great judge and educationist, Shyama Prasad Mookerjee was born at Calcutta on 6 July 1901. He

---

[13] *Subhas Chandra Bose* (Delhi: Publications Div., 1992), p. 94.
[14] *Selected Speeches*, p. 193.
[15] *Ibid.*, p. 266.

studied at Presidency College, Calcutta and was called to the Bar at London in 1927. In 1929 he was elected to the Bengal Legislative Council. In 1934 he became the Vice-Chancellor of Calcutta University. In 1941 he was inducted to the Fazul Haq Cabinet as Finance Minister. He was militantly opposed to partition and spoke against it in the Cabinet Mission in 1946. After independence he became a Minister of Industries in the Nehru Cabinet, but resigned on account of differences with Nehru. He was the founder of *Jana Sangh* and became its President. He was elected to the Parliament in 1952. In 1953 he was put under house arrest at Srinagar on the Kashmir issue and there he died in, what some people suspected then, dubious circumstances. He was one of the outstanding parliamentarians of his times.

The one subject that animated the tongue of Shyama Prasad Mookerjee was India's glorious past. We never revelled in destruction; we believed in assimilation and improvement. Those who came here to conquer and slay remained to wonder and pray. To strangers too we ungrudgingly gave of our best. If we lost our political independence it was mainly because at the critical hour we were divided and disorganised. The internal strife led to our fall. Such were his views.

Another subject on which Shyama Prasad spoke movingly was freedom. No man should be stifled by the cramping restrictions of bondage, poverty, overwork and of environment. Freedom is not merely absence of restraints, it is also the presence of opportunity. It is not a single conception; it has four elements—national, political, personal, and economic. Unless such a freedom was regained, India would not attain the true splendour of her past civilization.

Apart from these, Shyama Prasad Mookerjee's educational speeches were immensely popular and forceful. His approach here was balanced. He stood for equal emphasis on primary, secondary and on higher education. Similarly, scientific and literary education should be equally valued. Female education needed special impetus. A reconciliation between English and indigenous languages was necessary for national growth. And most importantly, education must strengthen character and obliterate the nullities of cliquism, communalism and cabalism; it must produce soldiers in the war of liberation so that we might march proudly for the promised land of the *swaraj*.

Shyama prasad Mookerjee was a great orator. The three qualities that marked his style were fluidity, grace and clarity. His diction was chaste and apt, Organisation logical and lucid, and prose rhythm elegant and flowing. Here is an example from his speech 'Hindu Nationalism' delivered at Amritsar on 26 December 1943: "Indian culture has remained unconquered from generation to generation. The invaders came and went. Kings, emperors and generals appeared and disappeared but the soul of India remains unconquered. It is her remarkable spirit of assimilation which turned generations of invaders into ultimate contributors to the growth of the mighty Indian civilization. Hindus and Muslims sometimes fought with each other and at other times lived together in amity and brotherhood, while contributing to India's welfare. I believe now that . . . peace will reign again in India."[16]

Of the successors of Gandhi Radhakrisnan was most erudite, Nehru sensitive, Ambedkar blunt, Bose earnest, and Mookerjee persuasive. The speeches of each one of them carried the impress of his exceptional personality and gained in power by it. None of them really matched the earlier stalwarts like Michael Madhusudan Dutt, Surendranath Banerjea or Vivekananda. It was more their personality than their speeches that swayed the audience. Moreover, their comparative proximity to us weighs in our more favourable evaluation of them as orators.

---

[16] *100 Best Pre-Independence Speeches: 1870-1947*, ed. H.D. Sharma (Delhi : Harper Collins, 1998), pp. 143-144.

VI

AN OVERVIEW

In the preceding chapters I reflected upon the art of oratory, its five components (thought, arrangement, style, memory and delivery) and three appeals (rational, emotional and moral); on the Raj and how the reform and the revolution that marked it combined to animate the tongue of the orators; on the predecessors, contemporaries and the successors of Gandhi who moved from loyalism to nationalism, reform to revolution and from elitism to mass mobilisation, and how they thought and arranged their thought, and how they spoke in varying styles. It now remains for me to take an overview of these orators and evaluate their comparative merit; I have counted the trees and have now to look at the forest.

Thought

I am only repeating a platitude when I say that the best thought of the period climaxed in the speeches of Mahatma Gandhi. He was the soul of India and his thought was rooted in all that was the best in her past: ancient India sowed the seed and modern India reaped Gandhi. But to say that he was antiquated is to miss the eternal in him. He was as old as India and as fresh as each new dawn, and in that dichotomy lay his abiding charm.

Arrangement

In the arrangement of thought no Indian orator could excel Mahadev Govind Ranade. He was luminously clear in his ideas and he arranged them logically, step for step. In fact, this aspect of oratory was better attended by the predecessors of Gandhi. And the man who least attended it was Nehru. He mostly spoke extemporaneously and therefore his speeches were prolix and rambling.

Style

Broadly speaking, the greatest stylist among the India orators in English was Michael Madhusudan Dutt who spoke English with the ease of a native and whose speech 'The Anglo Saxon and the Hindu' could be bracketed with the best speeches in the English language. In the choice of words, in the freshness of phraseology, in grace and elegance, and in rhythmical flow and liquidity, it remains the best Indian speech till date. Its pro-British stance hurts us in our seat of honour, but its style is a perennial source of delight.

Memory

We have no record of the memory of every orator, but from whatever material that is available to us we may say that the best in this respect was Surendranath Banerjea. We are told by him in his autobiography *The Nation in Making* that he delivered his four hour long Congress Presidential Speech at Poona in 1895 from memory without consulting notes even for once. He prepared his speeches most meticulously and committed them to memory if the occasion demanded it.

Delivery

No record of how different orators delivered their speeches is available to us today, but from the notices that appeared in the foreign press of Vivekananda's delivery of his Chicago Speech in 1893 we can speculate that none could surpass him in this regard. His majestic appearance, oriental dress, dignified gestures, and mellifluous voice cast a magic spell on the audience. There was a charisma about him that is not given to ordinary mortals.

Appeal

Of the three appeals of orators (rational, emotional and moral) the best in rational appeal was Mahadev Govind Ranade, in emotional appeal Sarojini Naidu, and in moral appeal Mahatma Gandhi. Here it should be remembered that the stamp of the personality on the speeches did weigh upon their appeal to the audience: many times, it was more the personality of the speaker than his words that carried the audience. This was true of the speeches of Subhas Chandra Bose. He was freedom incarnate, and this aspect of his personality endeared him to the audience and was at the root of his immense appeal. This is true of the speeches of Mahatma Gandhi also: the nation held him in such reverence that every word that fell from his lips descended upon the audience like an oracle. No Indian could ever surpass him in mass appeal which was infinite.

Inborn Propensity

Who was an inborn orator? Who spoke from nature? The answer is obvious; it was Vivekananda. He spoke effortlessly, from his inner self, and it was good for the world that this innate gift in him was amply strengthened by knowledge and recurrent speaking. Surendranath Banerjea was a great orator, but he was not an orator by nature; his speeches smacked of midnight oil, they were laboriously prepared and delivered with an eye on the audience, as if he loved his own voice and was always conscious of his performance, and this is evident from his self-conscious observations on his speeches in his autobiography. Vivekananda never spoke for self-glory but from an inner urge to redeem humanity: he was a born orator.

The Greatest Orator

Who was the greatest orator during the Raj period? There are many contenders for this honour—Michael Madhusudan Dutt, Kristo Das Pal, Keshub Chunder Sen, Surendranath Banerjea, Lal Mohan Ghose, Swami Vivekananda, and Srinivasa Sastri. I keep Gandhi out of the race, for he can be bracketed only with Buddha and Christ. His word carried the same weight and in future times he will have his place by them, the dissenting voices will in time wither away. The more I read him, the more my conviction grows. Every word that he wrote or spoke carried with it the impress of sainthood. He went as close to truth as a mortal can go. He lived scripture and spoke scripture, he was scripture incarnate. Oratory is too small a word for him, and so I keep him out of comparison. He excepted, the greatest orator in the British India was Vivekananda. Different orators excelled him in different departments of oratory: in thought Aurobindo was no less profound; in the organisation of thought Ranade carried the day; in the splendour of language none could touch Michael Madhusudan Dutt; and in memory Surendranath Banerjea was unsurpassable. But in oratory taken as a whole Vivekananda stood the tallest, and this was amply proved by the overwhelming impact he created upon the audience. Every speech that he delivered in England or in the U.S.A. won the heart of the audience and was noticed by the European and the American newspapers in a high strain of admiration. An added advantage was that he spoke on a subject that has ever had the greatest potential of winning the audience, that is, religion. Religion is man's first answer about the unknown and the unknowable and therefore it is the most lasting and the most obdurate; like the sap of a tree it reaches the most distant branches. No wonder Vivekananda reached all audiences, near and distant, and created a lasting impact on them. His intense religiosity, marvellous explication of Vedantic philosophy, and noble sentiments dressed in noble words and delivered with quiet poise and dignity, spread an enchantment over the hearers and made him the most coveted speaker of the time. And his child-like acceptance of the applause, without a shade of conceit or egotism, endeared him the more to the audience. It is well to end this resume with an inspiring extract from his address called 'Why We Disagree' delivered at the Parliament of Religions at Chicago on 15 September 1893 in which he gave a call for Universal Religion:

> "If there is ever to be a universal religion, it must be one which will have no location in place or time; which will be infinite like the God it will preach, and whose sun will shine upon the followers of Krishna and Christ, on saints and sinners alike; which will not be Brahminic or Buddhistic, Christian or Mohamedan, but the sum total of all these, and still have infinite space for development; which in its catholicity will embrace in its infinite arms, and find a place for, every human being, from the lowest grovelling savage not far removed from the brute, to the highest man towering by the virtues of his head and heart almost above humanity, making society stand in awe of him and doubt his human nature. It will

be a religion which will have no place for persecution or intolerance in its polity, which will recognise divinity in every man and woman, and whose scope, whose whole force, will be created in aiding humanity to realise its own true, divine nature."[1]

[1] The Complete Works of Swami Vivekananda (Calcutta: Advaita Ashrama, 1992), i, 19.

PART TWO

ORATIONS

RAJA RAMMOHUN ROY
(1772-1833)

RAJA RAMMOHUN ROY

Principles of Unitarian Christianity

Speech at the Meeting of the Unitarian Association Held in London in His honour

I am too unwell and too much exhausted to take any active part in this meeting; but I am much indebted to Dr. Kirkland and Dr. Bowring for the honour they have conferred on me by calling me their fellow-labourer, and to you for admitting me to this Society as a brother, and one of your fellowlabourers. I am not sensible that I have done anything to deserve being called a promoter of this cause; but with respect to your faith I may observe, that I too believe in the one God, and that I believe in almost all the doctrines that you do: but I do this for my own salvation and for my own peace. For the objects of your Society I must confess that I have done very little to entitle me to your gratitude or such admiration of my conduct. What have I done?—I do not know what I have done!—If I have ever rendered you any services they must be very trifling—very trifling I am sure. I laboured under many disadvantages. In the first instance, the Hindus and the Brahmins, to whom I am related, are all hostile to the cause; and even many Christians there are more hostile to our common cause than the Hindus and the Brahmins. I have honour for the appellation of Christians; but they always tried to throw difficulties and obstacles in the way of the principles of Unitarian Christianity. I have found some of these here; but more there. They abhor the notion of simple precepts. They always lay a stress on mystery and mystical points, which serve to delude their followers; and the consequence is, that we meet with such opposition in India that our progress is very slight; and I feel ashamed on my side that I have not made any progress that might have placed me on a footing with my fellow-labourers in this part of the globe. However, if this is the true system of Christianity, it will prevail, notwithstanding all the opposition that may be made to it. Scripture seconds your system of religion, common sense is also on your side; while power and prejudice are on the side of your opponents. There is a battle going on between reason, scripture and common sense; and wealth, power and prejudice. These three have been struggling with the other three; but I am convinced that your success, sooner or later, is certain. I feel over-exhausted, and therefore conclude with an expression of my heartfelt thanks for the honour that from time to time you have conferred on me, and which I shalt never forget to the last moment of my existence.

DWARKANATH TAGORE
(1794-1846)

DWARKANATH TAGORE

A Grateful Appreciation

Speech at a Meeting Held in Edinburgh in 1842 by the Lord Provost, the Magistrates and Council of the City to Confer upon Him the Freedom of the City

My Lord Provost and Gentlemen,—I appreciate more highly than I can express, the distinction which has this day been so unexpectedly conferred upon me by the Lord Provost, the Magistrates, and Council of this ancient and learned city. Though not permitted, till yesterday, to behold any part of the beautiful and romantic country of which this city is the proud and justly celebrated metropolis, I was not a stranger to your eventful history, nor to the labours of your men of science and literature, and least of all to the enterprise, the talents, and the patriotism of the many sons of Scotland, who have distinguished themselves in that part of Her Majesty's dominions, with which by birth, by fortune, and by strong affection, I am connected. Let me take this opportunity of gratefully acknowledging, that the first wish which rose in my bosom to tread the shores of the British Isles, was inspired by a friend, who was a native of this country. I am happy that I cherished, and have lived to fulfil that wish (cheers). The reception I have uniformly experienced from the first moment of my arrival in Great Britain until the present, and the facilities now afforded, and still increasing, for visiting this country, will, I confidently trust, operate as an inducement to many others of my countrymen to follow my example, and have the effect of uniting still more closely, in the bonds of mutual interest, acquaintanceship, and good feeling, the natives of the most distant parts of Her Majesty's possessions (applause). My Lord Provost and Gentlemen, permit me to assure you, that it will be to me a source of no ordinary gratification on my return to India, to know that, though far away from you, I am enrolled among you as a fellow-citizen. Allow me to say, too, that I shall eagerly embrace every opportunity of discharging the duties of a fellow-citizen to the sons of your soil, whom it may be my happiness to meet in my native land. It shall be my endeavour to make such feel as much at home in Calcutta as I have been made to feel in Edinburgh. If, in years that are past, I have felt it to be alike my duty and my privilege to advance the common interests of this country, and of that to which I more peculiarly belong, whose destinies have been committed to your control, I shall henceforward find an additional motive in the remembrance of this day's transactions, since I am now not merely your fellow-subject, but your fellow-citizen (loud cheers). My Lord Provost and Gentlemen, I return you my most grateful thanks for the flattering compliment you have bestowed upon me, the value of which will be much augmented if you will permit me to regard it as a token of the interest with which you view the country of my birth, and a pledge that you will co-operate in all, wise and peaceable measures for its improvement and happiness (cheers). In conclusion, I would express my earnest wish for the prosperity of Edinburgh, and of this kingdom at large, and my fervent hope that under the mild, enlightened, and benignant sway of that gracious Sovereign whom you are about to welcome to your city, the various parts of this vast empire, and all its dependencies, may be firmly consolidated, and all classes of Her Majesty's subjects have cause to rejoice that so extensive a dominion has been entrusted to the Government under which it is our happiness to live (cheers).

We regret to inform our readers about the non-availability of any photograph / sketch of Shri **Ram Gopal Ghose.** In case the reader finds any such photograph from his archives and is willing to pass on the same to the publisher, we shall acknowledge the same in our next edition when published.

RAM GOPAL GHOSE

On Queen Victoria's Proclamation

Speech at a Public Meeting Held in Calcutta on 3 November 1858 on the Occasion of the Queen Taking upon Herself the Government of India

Gentlemen, since I came into the room, I have been requested to second the Resolution which you have just heard read. I consider it a privilege and an honor to have been requested to do so. I feel that I am somewhat in a false position, inasmuch as I see around me many of higher rank, and of greater influence among my countrymen who would have more worthily and ably represented the Native community on the important occasion than I can pretend to do. But at the same time, my intercourse in life has been so much with Englishmen, and I know so much of the vast resources, the great power, and the great goodness of the English people, that I do not think myself altogether incompetent to offer an opinion on those points. (Cheers) If I had power and influence, I would proclaim through the length and breadth of this land—from the Himalayas to Cape Comorin,—from Bermapootra to the Bay of Cambay, that never were the Natives more grievously mistaken than they have been in adopting the notion foisted upon them by designing and ambitious men that their religion was at stake;—for that notion I believe to be at the root of the late rebellion. (Cheers.) They do not understand the English character; (hear, hear);—they do not understand the generosity, the benevolence of the governing Power,—the even-handed Justice with which that Power is willing and anxious always to do that which is right between man and man, without any reference whatever to the fact whether the men belonged to the governing or to the governed class. (Cheers.) If all this were known, where would be rebellion in this land? Certainly, there would have been no such outbreak as that which recently shook the foundations of this Empire. The only remedy is Education. (Hear, hear, hear.) Nothing has distressed me more among the late acts of Government, than the positive prohibition against incurring any expense on the score of Education. (Hear, hear, hear.) Lord William Bentinck, a name which must ever be remembered with reverence, in his reply to the Address which was presented to him on the occasion of his departure from India, said, after enumerating all the evils, all the oppressions, all the grievances under which India labours, that the first remedy was Education,—that the second remedy was Education,—and that the third remedy was Education. (Cheers.)

But to come round to the point, I have read the Proclamation of Her Majesty with great pleasure,—with awakened feeling,—with tears when I came to the last paragraph. (Cheers.) A nobler production, it has not been my lot ever to have met with in my life. The justest, the broadest principles are enumerated therein. Humanity, Mercy, Justice breathe through every line, and we ought all to welcome it with the highest hope and the liveliest gratitude. Depend upon it when our Sovereign Queen tells us—"In your prosperity is our strength; in your contentment, our security; and in your gratitude, our best reward." The future of India is full of encouragement and hope to her children. What could have been nobler or more beautiful, what could have dignified even the tongue of a Queen than language such as that! Let us kneel down before her with every feeling of loyalty;—let us welcome the new reign with the warmest sentiment of gratitude—the deepest feeling of devotion. (Cheers.)

Gentlemen, I came perfectly unprepared to address you, and will detain you no longer, but conclude by saying that I feel no small pleasure in having had the opportunity and the honour of seconding this Resolution. (Cheers.)

MICHAEL MADHUSUDAN DUTT
(1824-1873)

MICHAEL MADHUSUDAN DUTT

The Anglo-Saxon and the Hindu

Speech in Madras in 1854

The fair queen of Carthage, captivated by the manly beauty of the heroic son of Aphrodites, asked her sister Anna—"Who is this stranger that has come to our dwelling?" In her widowed heart—hitherto a vacant temple—she found the image of this man mysteriously enshrined; and it was thus that her adoring yet wondering soul hymned forth its deep, its impassioned, its fervent devotion—"Who is the stranger that has come to our dwelling?"

Now—though I cannot conscientiously say that the Anglo-Saxon stranger has created in the bosom of this magnificent land of the sun, this queenly Hindustan—that profound, that fervent, that all-absorbing feeling of love, which immolated the hapless Dido on the blazing pyre, and sent her to the hades, an unblest, a melancholy ghost—yet well may she ask—well may this queenly Hindustan—ask in the language of the love-sick Phoenician—"Who is this stranger that has come to our dwelling? Well, methinks, may she ask—who is this fair-haired stranger that has come to our shores? Who is this stranger that has in the course of a solitary century reared among us a fabric of power the most wondrous and glorious? Who is the stranger that is lord of our sunny fields, of our shady groves, of our woody hills, of our wells of crystals water, of our mossy fountains, of our bowers of roses? Who is this stranger, for whom the most radiant diamonds are sought from the sunless depths of our mines; for whom the gold and silver, hidden in our treasure-caves, are brought forth to blush in the light of the sun? Who is this stranger that has bound us, as it were, with chains of adamant, and whose bright sword gleams before our eyes like a fiery meteor—terrifying us into submission and humbling us to the dust? "Who is this stranger that has come to our dwelling?"—Well, methinks may she ask and wonder !

For look around you. From where the silvery waves kiss the brow of the virgin Bride—to where the stupendous Himalayas rise in airy grandeur, with summits untrod, but by the shadow of the Deity—from the deep—blue Bay, to which the greenest and palmiest of countries give its name—to the mighty Indus, look around you. Empires and kingdoms, such as would have gratified the boundless ambition of that earth-born Titan—Napoleon the grand; rich valleys, fertile plains, wide table-lands, copious rivers, extensive woods, exhaustless mines, piny hills, and all that Nature can and does bestow, when in her most beautiful mood: populous cities, busy towns, marts, for which the white-winged ships of proud America war with and conquer the stormy waters of the illimitable Atlantic—for which the Arab, the Persian the Tartar, journey through the shrubless, the arid, the dismal deserts of Northern, of Western, and of Eastern Asia—for which the son of the flowery kingdom forsakes his fatherland to which the haughty Europe—the Parvenu—does not despise to send her jewels of silver, and her jewels of gold, her robes of silk and her garments of linen, the choicest, the most sparkling, the most purple juice of her vines, the most brilliant fabrics of her thousand manufacturers, where the tawny copt is no stranger, and the swarthy Abyssinian brings the riches of his far land !—Look around you and ask, to whom do these belong—whose are they? The Anglo-Saxon's—the pale-faced stranger's,—the stranger, who came to these shores as a nameless wanderer ! What destiny is this ? "Who is this stranger that has come to our dwelling?" Is not his career the realization of a dream, such as Ambition herself would shrink from indulging even when in her wildest mood? Does not the history of his career sound like a tale of Romance, woven by a visionary, a rhapsodist, a rapt bard, who wanders in the vast realm of imagination and culls from it materials, wherewith to build some glorious, some wondrous fabric of song? Fly back through the dim, the shadowy, the chaotic regions of the past; survey the earth, vast, dreary, lonesome, baptized by the terrible waters of the Deluge; behold the second father of mankind, pale and yet with the light of confident hope beaming from his eyes, presiding over his meek and pious family, his diminutive kingdom. Invoke the great Angel Michael,—let him guide you to the summit of the airy hill whence Adam saw, and sighed and wept and smiled to see the future drama of life; and look before you. See the Mighty Hunter, hewing down men, like the beasts of the forest, for a diadem; see the Amazonian Semiramis, blending the softest enchantments of woman's beauty with the sternest virtues of man; see the Hybrid Cyrus, issuing forth like a strong man—refreshed with wine, to slay and to conquer; see the wild Macedonian rushing forth like a mountain-torrent, carrying everything before him as the tempestuous wind carries the dark cloud onward, see laurelled Caesar, gasping out his proud soul at the feet of statued Pompey, forgetting his mighty dream of empire, and reposing on the calm bosom of his mother earth, all besmeared with blood; see the grandest of warriors, the loftiest of mortals, the most glorious, the most awful the most mystical the most inconceivably sublime Brim of heroworshippers—the son of the Corsican Attorney—surrounded by his eagles with their terrific beaks drying the blood torrents which flowed at Austerlitz, at Jena, at Wigram, at Friedland, at Borodino and then pining away in the solitude of St. Helena—his island prison in the midst of the vast Atlantic—look at all these. They were great, they were mighty; but here is one greater, mightier still. In him, you do not find the majesty, the might, the genius of a whole nation centered, developed, incarnated (if I may use such a word,) assuming a sublime individuality, blazing forth for a season, like a wild comet, like a sudden, a luminous but a transient burst of light, like a terrific out-belching of some volcano dazzling and confounding the sight of the beholder and then fading away into the gloom of night. No !—In him, you see the majesty, the might, the genius of a race, bequeathed from father to son—unimpaired, unenfeebled, through every stage of transmission, through every stage of existence! These men were like rivers, which suck their mother-clouds on their rocky cradles; acquire strength and then journey on; sometimes with impetuosity, felling down wide forests; subduing obstinate hills; sometimes, gently, warbling liquid melody, loving flowery mead's, watering golden cornfields; and at last they melt away and vanish in the embrace of Ocean, their father. They have a beginning, a middle, and an end. But look at the Anglo-Saxon; look at the Nile, which has covered the sunny plains of Hindustan with its waters. Its source is known to us—we know where it rises, we know where the dews of heaven foster its growth. But after it leaves its parent rock, what becomes of it? For fifteen thousand miles it is nowhere seen! The blue waters of the Rhone are lost in the liquid wilderness of the glassy constance ! And then, with what magnificence, what grandeur does he burst forth—removing ancient landmarks, sweeping away Thrones, Dominations, Princedoms, Powers; irresistible, unresisted! What destiny is this? The heroic son of Aphrodites (to revert once more to the story of Dido) won a woman's heart—a rich treasure, to be sure a beautiful mine, with its gemlike affections, its stores of sweet and sunny hopes, and gentle aspirations, and rosy dreams; but look at the stranger that has come to our dwelling ! The nameless vagrant of the other day, the pale-faced stranger from the west, on whom the haughty Moslem scarcely deigned to cast his eyes, by whom even the timid Hindu passed heedlessly, is now the heir of Victorious Baber, of sagacious Akbar, of lofty Jehangir, the lord of millions,—nay, more; he is greater—far greater than victorious Baber, than sagacious Akbar, than lofty Jehangir ! The fabric of his power vaster; bayonet-wall which glitters round the citadel of his power, firmer. Well, methinks, may this queenly Hindustan ask in the language of the love-sick Phoenician—"Who is this stranger that has come to out dwelling?" Well, methinks, may she ask and wonder !

I need not waste your time with a lengthened narrative of the advent of the Anglo-Saxon to this broad land of the sun—the destined scene of his glory. I need not remind you how, while the haughty, the imperious, the virgin Elizabeth sat on the English throne, winning the admiration of Europe as a sovereign, subduing rebellion, crushing treason, frowning disaffection into moody submission, battling with a ruthless hand against Heresy and Schism, defying the invincible Armada, humbling the lofty pride of Spain, and at the same time wondrous to relate!—deluding herself into the flattering belief that the glances of her eyes kindled a quenchless flame in the bosom of the accomplished, the graceful, the elegant, the manly Devereux; that her grey tresses, woven in the language of a Persian poet—into chains, had bound that proud Earl to the car of her triumphant beauty; that the melody of her virginal ravished the hearts of his courtiers, falling upon their ears like the sweet south breathing upon a bank of violets, stealing and giving odour; that the bloom of her cheeks—they were faded flowers—outvied that of the rose.—I need not remind you how the breezes of the West, wafted across the pathless Atlantic, the Anglo-Saxon; how the acorn was sown, out of which has sprung forth the gigantic oak, which now overshadows this land; how the mysterious hand of Providence hurled the little stone, destined to crush to atoms the golden image of Moslem power, to become a great mountain, to fill the whole land; how the Anglo-Saxon first ascended the Indian horizon, a faint, a dim streak of light, how the little cloud-herald of a mighty storm, of a terrific elemental commotion—rose from out the sea; how the son of Kish came to seek his father's asses, his unconscious royalty veiled in the coarse garb of a shephered:— I need not remind you how he toiled and sweated in his factory—now overwhelmed by the oppressive tyranny of the captious lordlings around him, now basking in the dubious rays of their shortlived favour, harassed and despised—but working on with an unsinking soul, a buoyancy of spirit, which nothing could repress; a secret daringness of purpose which nothing could daunt: I need not dwell on the career of Clive, that basest, that grandest of Indian Statemen, how he went forth making the path straight, levelling and beating down inequalities, that the chariot-wheels of victory and of conquest might roll on unimpeded: I need not call to your minds the brilliant triumphs, the wondrous achievements which annihilated the turbulent and restless Mahratta, paled the blooded glare of the tremendous Crescent, humbling the soaring pride of the Rajpoot, drove the wild and wily Goorka to the solitude of his mountain-girt home, razed to the ground the structure which the Lion of the North—prophetically named—when an helpless infant in his nurse's arms—"the Victorious in war,"—had laboured to build: I need not name Plassey—the dawn of an era of splendour, an age of glory: I need not name Assaye, where the future Victor of the Titanic Corsican—himself the Victor of combined Europe, won fadeless laurels: I need not name Seringapatam, where the blood of his bigoted, his infatuated, his ill starred son flowed freely, but flowed in vain, to save the house of the illiterate, the drunken, but the great Hyder from the desecrating feet of the alien and the infidel. I need not name Feroz Sur, Aliwal, Moodkee, Sobraon, Mooltan, Guzerat, where blood libations were copiously poured forth to the ruthless god of war. As the sons and the daughters of the Anglo-Saxon, these names, however uncouth, are, I presume, familiar in your mouths as household words. Do they not sound like bursts of triumphant music, swelling on the air, thrilling the heart, breathing heroic ardour, to adventurous deeds? Do they not sound like trumpet calls which summon the brave to the battlefield? I need not, I repeat, waste your time with a lengthened narrative of the advent of the Anglo-Saxon to this broad, this magnificent land of the sun; nor need I dwell on his brilliant career, his wondrous achievements, his proud triumphs. Behold him here, sceptered and crowned—with his feet on the jewelled neck of fallen Hindustan! Verily the destiny of this stranger that has come to our dwelling—is a mysterious destiny !

Let us now turn for a moment from this magnificent picture—the master-piece of Nature ! Let us now turn for a moment from the contemplation of the splendour and the richness of its colourings, the delicacy, the beauty, and the symmetry of its proportions—to another—far inferior, to be sure, but not altogether destitute of interest. When Hamlet saw the picture of his royal father and of his despicable guilty, and hated uncle in the chamber of his erring and queenly mother, he indignantly pointed them out to her and exclaimed in a tone of withering contempt—"Look on this picture and that !" Now—we shall not imitate the prince of Denmark—we shall not point that finger of scorn towards the Hindu. No. Fallen, obscured as he is—shorn of his beams, he does not deserve it. Men do not gaze on the ruins of Babylon with contempt; nor ridicule the massy, the blackened, the huge, the shapeless things, which were once towers and temples and palaces in the imperial city of Caesars, the mistress of the world of her days ! The faithless Volney sat by the ruins of Empires and wept—for the thought of the instability of human grandeur, the vanity of human glory ! We have seen the Anglo-Saxon, crowned and sceptered and seated on his throne, let us now look at the millions, who kneel before him.

I need not here enter into a disquisition on the origin of this singular, the primitive race, (I say, "race" for the sake of convenience, for it must be known to you that India is inhabited by a variety of races, differing as much from each other as does the Anglo-Saxon from the Celt; the Celt from the Teuton, the Teuton from the Hun and the Hun from the Etruscan, and so on.)—I need not here enter into a disquisition on the origin of this singular, this primitive race. That origin is curtained round by the most obscure clouds of mythism. I need not labour up the blue stream of the Nile, to unravel the mystery connected with its hidden source; I need not breathe the difficult air of the iced mountain-tops; I need not ascend airy precipices, nor wonder in lonesome, vast and dreary valleys to reach for its coy source which in the language of poetry, may be said to have concealed its Naiad and maiden beauty in some sacred and solemn grove, which the human eye may not penetrate.

The Hindu !—Alas ! Centuries of servitude and oppression; the predominance of a superstition, dismal and blasting; a fatal adherence to institutions whose cruel tendency ever it is to curb and to restrain the onward march of man as a social, as an intellectual pilgrim, tracing round him a wizard ring solemnly believed to be impassable and violently repressing every inborn longing to be free; these alas ! have rendered that name a name of reproach and astonishment, a proverb and a byword among the nations! But—do not despise him.

Cedric—the sturdy Saxon, whose patriotism was a bigotry and a frenzy looked with a softened heart on the guilty, the degraded, the fallen, Ulrica, in the crime-desecrated halls of Torquilstone.

As the hot Simoom pales the blooming cheeks of the queenly rose; as the cold breath of winter robs each tree of its verdant robe; as the insatiable locust mars the golden pride of the most fertile field; as the rust corrodes the brightest, the most polished steel; as the terrible fire of leprosy consumes the beauty of man transforming it to hideous deformity; as the wail of sorrow hushes the sweet voice of music, as concealed love feeds on the damask cheek of the maiden like a worm in the bud; as the guilt clouds the warm sunshine of the heart, so servitude and bondage eat into the soul, crushing its hopes, fettering its aspirations, quenching its lustre into a dim twilight, robbing it of its giant strength. What wonder then that the Hindu should be what he is? The furious waves of fanaticism, of oppression, have swept over his hapless soul for a thousand years ! Iron shod conquerors have trampled upon his hapless soul for a thousand years! From the day that the blood-thirsty wolf of Ghiznee bounded across the stupendous rocky barriers of the west, desolating her homes, flinging to the dust her idol-gods from their glorious temples, leading her sons and daughters captive, ill-fated Hindustan has been the prey of the invader, the sport of the ambitious and the rapacious Zenobia—chained, not to the chariot of a single conqueror, but to those of a hundred, to grace their triumphs! Alas! for the fallen queen: Alas! for the widowed bride ! Alas for the ravished maiden ! The pilgrim Harold wept over desolate Rome for he was an orphan of the heart and turned to her; and the eloquence of his grief, the sweet and soft voice of his sorrow, swelling like a stream of rich yet mournful music, still saddens the soul; and yet he was an alien, a wanderer from a colder, a cloudier clime ! What would he have done, had he stood where I stand; had he been what I am? Believe it not that we have no love of country—that out heart strings do not cling round the land of our fathers ! I say, believe it not. But let that pass.

The Hindu, as he stands before you, is a fallen being;—Once—a green, a beautiful, a tall, a majestical, a flowering tree—but now—blasted by lightning! This is no idle boast, no vaunting fiction. When Moses journeyed feebly through the vast, the dreary, the desolate, the arid deserts of Arabia, with a murmuring, a rebellious host behind him, the land of the Hindus was a populous, a mighty land! Nay, when Abraham surrendered the fair Sarah to the amorous and puissant pharaoh of his day—mightier and far more puissant kings ruled over the broader, the sunnier, the more fertile plains of Hindustan! Long before the blind beggar Homer told the tale of "Troy divine" enchanting the fairland of Greece—bards as sublime, breathing music as sonorous, as dulcet, had built the lofty rhyme in Hindustan! Behold the Vedas; and adore the Shekina of Intellect which fills them with a golden and a rosy light —Long before the beautiful but frail Helen kindled the flame which consumed to the dust the proud city of Priam, the faithless Seeta had deserted the arms of her exile-husband, and brought desolations and disaster and woe to the spicy and pearly shores of Lunka ! But why need I dwell on such themes? Volumes could be written on the glories of Old India—volumes could be written on achievements in love and war of her heroic sons and lotus-eyed daughters. She is indeed an exhaustless mine for the Poet, the Romanticist, the Historian, the Philosopher. But let me pass on—let me turn away my eyes from the dazzling and tempting field—let me close my ears against the syren-music which ravish my soul and softly call me to wander away from the path I am pursuing !

The Hindu, as he stands before you, is a fallen being—once—a green, a beautiful, a tall, a majestical flowering tree; now—blasted by lightning ! Who can recall him to life?

You now see before you, as it were, on a stage, two actors—the Anglo-Saxon and the Hindu. One of them is indeed well-graced, ravishing the eyes of the audience with his manly beauty—enchanting the ears of the audience with the dulcet tones of his voice! The other, I fear, is ill favoured, wornout by the ceaseless waves of time, hoarse and dissonant as an untuned harp, as an unstrung lute. Joyous Bolingbroke, the proud rose of the house of Lancaster, blooming with the gorgeous honours of new Royalty and the pensive and crownless and sceptreless son of the sable-armoured victor of Cressy and Poictiers; Sylla in his chariot, rolling on the wheels of fortune; Marius seated in voiceless sorrow in the midst of the lonely and sad ruins of carthage, himself a lonelier, a sadder ruin! Caesar weaving for his bald brow, a crown of blood-stained laurels reaped from the deadly plain of Pharsalia; Pompey wandering in the silent, but lovely vale of Tempe, mingling his tears with the murmuring waters of the meandering Peneus! Octavius feasting in the tent of the luxurious Antony, the golden goblet blushing and sparkling with the delicious blood of the vine of sunny Italy in his hand, the chaplet of dewy roses on his head; Brutus sternly watches the purple current of life, ebbing out from the ghastly wound inflicted by his own suicidal hands! Eva, with the transplanted rose of the West, blooming on her cheek, the blue heaven of her eyes beaming with cloudless sun light; and poor Topsy—the degraded daughter of a degraded race, standing before her like a ghastly phantom, an unearthly vision ! Flowering Youth, decaying age; radiant beauty, hideous deformity; exulting valour, pallid fear; sparkling diamond, dim crystal;—but why should I multiply such images? The contrast is indeed very great! 'Tis a foolish bird, says the proverb, which fouls its own nest. But there are occasions, when—to borrow the significant image of the Latin poet—a man cannot help plucking the leaves of his own vine trees! In a physical and moral point of view, the contrast is startling; it is painful; though by no means unaccountable. But it is not my object at present, to permit myself to be detained by such a subject. Let me sail on and woo the breezes of heaven to hurry me to the appointed port still afar off. He is no navigator, destined to affect a speedy passage, who suffers every glassy creek of the sea he careers over, to seduce him to shorten sail and drop anchor. He is no charioteer, destined to reach the appointed goal in time, the glowing wheels of whose chariot raise the dust of every by-path diverging from his course.

You see before you, as it were on a stage two actors, the Anglo-Saxon and the Hindu and believe me, it is a sublime, a solemn, a grand, a wondrous Drama they are destined to act.

A nation, like a man, has its infancy, its youth, its manhood, its age;—its faint dawn, its dewy morn, its effulgent noon, its solemn, and dim and dusky eve. Behold the shepherd Romulus, building him a little city to dwell in with his lawless companions; see how proudly, how scornfully the Sabine maiden spurns him as he timidly solicits her love; and then harken to the shriek of terror, the voice of agony, the wail of sorrow, the cry of rage, the shout of triumph, the clash of swords, the twanging of bows, the whizzing of winged shafts which lend an unearthly, a terrific pomp to the nuptial rites of the youthful fathers of Rome ! Look on. See the young eagle on his hill throne; surveying with wistful eyes the sunny fields, the viny hills, the silver streams of fair Italy, how soon his growing wings overshadow them; how soon his kindling eyes look beyond the blue waves of the Mediterranean, the stupendous and avalanche—peopled summits of the everlasting Alps, beyond the glassy expanse of the Adriatic—the future bride of the purple-clad Doge; beyond the sleepless Tyrrhenian. See the Anglo-Saxon of the Past, of an older world, growing apace. Why should I dwell on the glories of his manhood? Behold that golden barque sailing down the beautiful-flowing Cydnus, with sails of purple silk; with oars of bright silver; hearken to the melody of flutes and of cymbals; what perfumes fill the air ! Know ye that queen of beauty—that earth-born Venus, seated on her throne spangled with stars of gold, and gems, and pearls, and diamonds, surrounded by her nymph-like train? It is the voluptuous, the glorious daughter of Ptolemies—the divine and yet frail Cleopatra, voyaging to kneel at the feet of Antony—the descendant of the man whom in days gone by, a petty Sabine maiden has listened with contempt ! Then look at the sun set hour of the great Roman. Lowering clouds, deepening the gloom of a lightless sky; the Goth; the Vandal; nameless hordes from nameless regions; the awful "Scourge of God". Alaric the terrible ! Look at the expiring lamp; now blazing up with unwonted splendour,—the hectic flush painting with roseate hues, the sallow cheek of consumption—now sinking to dimness, and then fading away into the darkness of night ! A cowled and tonsured Priest seated on the throne of the Caesars! The barbarians of Austria crossing with unpaled brow the Rubicon, on whose bank the mighty heart of the mightiest Caesar, quailed!

A nation, like a man, has its infancy, its youth, its manhood, its age—its faint dawn; its dewy morn; its effulgent noon; its solemn, and dim and dusky eve. Sometimes it dies away, and its place knoweth it no wore; sometimes it lingers on—the pallid hues of death on its brow; the dim, unearthly light of the charnel house gleaming forth from its eyes ! Look at the Greek of the present day. Look at the sons of the men who fought and bled at Thermopylae, who empurpled the rippling waters of Salamis with Persian gore. How changed ! How changed from Hector, who was wont to return from the battle field, laden with the spoils of Achilles, or hurl Phrygian fires at the ships of the Achaians ! This, of course, is a mystery but is not this world full of mysteries? "The wind bloweth where it listeth; and thou hearest the sound thereof, but canst not tell whence it cometh or whither it goeth."—Why it has pleased the Great maker so to ordain, we cannot tell. We see it, and that is enough. Let us bow and humbly adore !

We may sigh over the instability of human grandeur; the vanity of human wishes; the evanescence of earthly glory; we may weep over nations fallen from their high estate; but it were impiety to question the justice of Providence, it were impiety to murmur. How wondrous are the ways of God ! In the mournful language of the Persian Poet the spider weaves its funeral pall in the palace of the Caesars; the owl hoots from the high watch-tower of Afrasiab ! Well has the royal son of David said—"all is vanity !"

Now—it does not require much thought, much observation, much historical and ethnological lore, to come to the conclusion that the nation among whom your lot has been cast, is in its old age; that nameless centuries of obscurity, of glory, of shame that untold years of helpless infancy, of kindling and blossoming youth, of brilliant and fructiferous manhood, have landed it on that state of existence which is the sunset period of a nation's life. The Hindu is an aged, a decayed race. Look at the old oak, the monarch for hundred years, of the green wood !—Where are the broad and verdant leaves which the dew-drop and the raindrop loved to empearl? Where are the giant arms, which warred for centuries with the howling storm? The leaves are faded and fallen; the arms, withered! Listen to the night-wind which sighs around the desolate trunk. It is a death-wail—the coronach of viewless spirits ! Alas ! for the great of old ! O Lucifer ! Son of the morning, how art thou fallen ! Rome, Rome, thou art no more, what thou hast been—on thy seven hills of yore, thou sat'st a queen !—as the plaintive chorus of the Roman pastoral song has it. In the sweet language of sweet but hapless Ophelia—"O ! What a noble mind is here o'erthrown ! the courtier's, soldier's scholar's eye, tongue, sword, the glass of fashion, and the mould of form, the observed of all observers;" I repeat, this is no idle boast, no vaunting fiction. Who has not heard the greatness of the fathers of those on whom, I fear, many of you are now tempted to cast a look of disdain and contempt? Is not the glory of great fathers of the Hindu race enstarred in the Temple of Fame? the burden of the trumpetblast of Fame? Have they not bequeathed to mankind deathless gifts ?

But to return—the Hindu, I say, is an aged race—tottering on the verge of a mortal grave. It must die, for the ponderous and marble jaws of that grave are hideously yawning to swallow it, and it is descending into the grave. The irresistible and fatal current destined to dash the once beautiful and proud vessel against the rock of destruction has set in—the train destined to blow up to atom the vast and antique fabric, once so superb, and so magnificent, is already fired. Who will recall the dead from the grave to a brighter existence? Whose hands will gather up the fragments, therewith to build a more beautiful, a prouder vessel to walk again the waters of the shorereless sea of life in glory and in joy? Whose hand will seek the scattered materials, therewith to re-erect a fabric more superb and more magnificent, whose airy towers and lofty battlements, whose massy and yet graceful pillars shall woo the eye of the beholder, and fill his soul with wonderment, not unmixed with awe?

I pore over the annals of mankind, crimsoned with blood, peopled with the most appalling pictures of guilt, and of shames and of sin; burdened with tales, which in the language of the Persian Poet—are full of the tears of the eye—I feel like one, who stands on the borders of a vast, a boundless wilderness—I see before me hideous and ghastly pyramids of human skulls, grinning as in mockery;—stupendous heaps of human bones—bleaching in the sun; I see blackened and shapeless masses, which mark the path of the devouring element; I see rivers of blood, I turn me to the East, to the West, to the North, to the South; the same horrible spectacle greets mine eye and chills my heart ! Such is history. Nations wade through blood to the dazzling throne of glory; and are again swept away by impetuous torrents of blood from the fatal Seat ! Such is the burden of the song of the Muse of History. There is no verdant oasis in that boundless wilderness; no burst of joyous melody in that song. History telleth us not of national rejuvenescence. The Sadducee dreams not, knows not of the resurrection of the dead. With him, there is no life beyond the grave—his is the dark tale of death, of annihilation. Like the unhappy hermit of Beattie—he looks on nature with morbid, with unschooled feelings. He sees the tree; to day-leaf-crowned and flower-crowned, and fruit-crowned, beautiful and verdant; tomorrow-leafless, and flowerless and fruitless, drooping, as the dismal and chilling blasts of winter howl around it. And again, when sweet, and rosy and gentle spring comes, how it revives ! What fresh glories deck it ! The maiden who had bewailed in silent solitude, the absence of her lover, blushes again in his eager, his impassioned embrance. He sees the silvery orb of the moon, to-day—shining in the fulness of her splendour—and the lesser lights of heaven are lost in her blaze; to-morrow—pale and waning like widowed beauty. And again how soon does she re-ascend her deep-blue throne—majestic on high, throwing her silver mantle over the rejoicing earth ! He looks on man, and in the bitterness of his heart exclaims—"When shall spring revisit the mouldering urn; when shall day dawn on the night of the grave !" But away with the creed of the moral Sadducee; away with the creed of the historical Sadducee ! History telleth us not of national rejuvenescene; we never read in history of a nation waning to re-appear on the horizon of the world, first a faint streak of light; then a well-defined crescent, and gradually assuming a bright gibbosity, till the fullness of its renovated splendour, redazzles the eyes of mankind. But what of that? With the Great Architect of the Universe nothing is impossible.

It is the mission, and mark my words, ye manly sons and ye fair daughters of the Anglo-Saxon, it is the glorious mission of the Anglo-Saxon to regenerate, to renovate the Hindu race ! The trumpet-call of the Anglo-Saxon, is destined to rouse from his grave the Hindu, to a brighter, a fairer existence; the mystic wand of the Anglo-Saxon, is destined to break the dreamless slumber which now curtains him round. The progress of Society is a grand revelation of the will and the design of the Great Maker of us all; and the history of the rise, and the onward march, and the fall of each nation, is a distinct chapter of that sublime and mysterious Apocalypse—that vast and sacred volume the characters on whose pages are traced by the finger of the deity himself ! I say, it is the mission of the Anglo-Saxon race to renovate, to regenerate the Hindu. Methinks, I already see the hue of life blushing—though but faintly—on the pale and cadaverous cheeks of the widow's son; the sunny morn of life dawning in the lightless eyes of the widow's son—why came the prophet to Sarepta? Was it chance that guided his steps thitherward? No !—Now—if this be a vain thought, a wild, an improbable theory—a fond imagination, then—what shall we say then? The moral world is a dismal chaos—the realm of law-despising anarchy; inharmonious and dark as the dreary region in which the proud and dauntless monarch of Hell found himself, when its hideous and mis-shapen portress opened the eternal and wide gates of his terrific and fiery dungeon ! But what soul dare harbour such treason; what tongue dare utter such blasphemy?

Like the prophet of old, methinks, I stand in the midst of a valley, full of dry bones—the silent realm of Death, the lonely, but vast sepulchre of a nation. And I stand—not to look on and sigh over the glories of the Past, now obscured and dimmed; to listen to the voiceless yet sad and solemn eloquence of nature telling me of the utter vanity of the hopes, of the aspirations, of the ambition of humanity. No !—Other sights invite my eyes; other sounds fill my ear. I behold a shaking, and the dry bones coming together—bone to his bone; and I hear a clear voice echoed far and near—come from the four winds, O breath ! and breathe upon these slain, that they may live ! Whose voice is that? It is the Anglo-Saxon's ! Harken to the fair-haired son of far Albion, prophesying in the valley of the broad Ganges, on the banks of the mighty Indus ! What a wondrous mission is thine, thou stranger ! That hast come to our dwelling !

Ages ago, when the bloom on the cheeks of this fair earth was fresher; the light of her eyes, more lustrous; a shepherd youth built him a city—a little city—a rude and scanty collection of lowly huts—on the green and reedy banks of the yellow-waved Tiber. Did the boundless East, with her thousand monarchs, surrounded by barbaric pomp; did Africa, along whose northern shores the blue and limpid bosom of the Mediterrannean reflected the images of flourishing kingdoms; did Europe, peopled by a hundred hardy races, wild and free as the breezes which fanned the brows of her lofty mountains; fierce as the wolf which howled in her dim and vast and solemn forests—did sunny Asia, did arid Africa, did cold Europe, believe that on the day—when the shepherd youth saw the ominous flight of vultures, and crimsoned his hands with a brother's blood; that on that day, was born a queen—their future and imperious mistress ? Yet—how soon did they quail to hear her voice—mighty as the sound of many waters; how many did they pale at the sight of her terrific eagles—with their beaks empurpled, encarnadined by the blood of nations; how soon did they prostrate themselves before her throne—presenting unto her gifts—gold, frankincense, and myrrh? What was the mission of this queen; what was the mission of Rome—eternal Rome, as the fond and blind vanity of her sons had baptized her? Read the history of the Church; the history of the sorrowings, the sufferings, the tribulations, the trials, and the triumphs of the spouse ! Look at the glorious stream, which two thousand years ago, issued from the consecrated and hallowed recesses of Calvary! The idol worshipping Roman, who knelt before the soulless image of Jupiter; and in fancied visions, saw a beardless and beauty-limbed youth with his silver bow and fiery steeds, in the stupendous and radiant orb of the sun; or rapturously echoed the unmeaning, the idiot-cry—Great is the Diana of the Ephesians; the idol worshipping Roman unconsciously paved the way for the onward march of the Truth. From the fabled pillar of Hercules, to the far banks of Euphrates; from the rock-girt and inhospitable shores of Britannia to the vast and solitary mountain-range, which veiled the lovelier, the sunnier, the more fertile regions of central and southern Africa from the eyes of men in those days, it was one grand empire—myriad kingdoms, and princedoms, and powers and principalities melted—as it were, in some Titanic crucible—to form one stupendous, one magnificent whole !—The rugged inequalities, the almost impassable barriers, presented by difference of race, of language, of government, were all beaten down and levelled; and the majestic car of the Truth, issuing forth from hilly Palestine rolled on; the Ark was borne forward, humbling to the dust the vile Dragon of the Pagan; the seed was sown on ploughed ground—ploughed by hands, which knew not what they did. Such was the mission of imperial Rome. See ye not on whom the mantle has fallen issuing forth from hilly Palestine? Where is the tremendous crescent, which turned fiery red at the sight of the hated Cross? Where is the brave but idolatrous and priest-ridden Mahratta? Where is the stern, monotheistic, yet superstitious Seikh? The sound of the Church-going bell—as Cowper calls it—mingles with the solemn melody of the Muezzin, and the barbaric and dissonant music of idol-temples ! Let the sceptic doubt; let the scoffer sneer; let the thoughtless laugh; but believe me, it is the Solemn Mission of the Anglo-Saxon to renovate, to regenerate, to civilize—or, in one word, to christianize the Hindu! The Anglo-Saxon is the soldier of the cross—the Crusader, who has come to the sunny East to carry on a bloodless, though a far more glorious war, than did the lion-hearted Richard, than did the puissant Edward-first of that name.

After quelling the obstinate antagonism, after crushing of the stout resistance of European Paynimrie, the victorious gonfalon of the Cross is now unfurled before the mighty and vast citadel of Braminism, and it is the hand of the Anglo-Saxon which must plant it on the embattled towers of that citadel. Behold that banner ! Trace ye not on it in letters of gold, the words—Conquer in this—as did purple-clad and imperial Constantine?

It were a mere waste of time, to adduce argument in support of a self-evident truth. I must not, therefore, detain you by efforts to prove what needs no proof. He is no wise man, who soils his clothes by carrying coals to New Castle; or wears out his shoes by journeying to far Athens, with cages full of moon-eyed, and solemn owls !

I stand before you—not as a Columbus, proudly claiming the mead of a discover of unknown worlds; I stand before you not as a Newton, whose god like vision penetrated the blue depths of ether and saw a new and a bright orb, cradled in infinity; I deal in no mysteries; I am no sophist, ravishing the ear with melodious yet unmeaning sounds; captivating the eye with sparkling yet meretricious ornamentalism—beautiful, yet artificial flowers, glittering yet false diamonds. No !—The fact I enunciate, is a simple one; even he who runneth may read it. But its simplicity ought not to destroy its grave importance. You all know it—you all see it. Why has Providence given this queenly, this majestic land for a prey and a spoil to the Anglo-Saxon? Why? I say—it is the Mission of the Anglo-Saxon to renovate, to regenerate, to Christianize the Hindu—to churn this vast ocean, that it may restore the things of beauty now buried in its liquid wilderness; and nobly is he seconded—will he be seconded, by the Science and the Literature of his sea-girt fatherland—the Literature of his country—baptized in the pure fountain of Eternal Love ! And here let me pause for a moment.

When a man suddenly stands before her, to the golden shrine of whose beauty, his impassioned soul kneels in the sinless idolatry of love; the lustre of whose eyes is dearer far to him than the light of sun, or moon, or star; the sound of whose voice is sweeter far to him than strains from angel harps; a lock of whose raven hair—in the enthusiastic words of the Prince of the Persian Lyre—is far more priceless to him than Samarcand and Bokhara—he is as one dumb. What tongue can utter the thoughts of delirious joy, which oppress his bosom? I acknowledge to you, and I need not blush to do so—that I love the language of the Anglo-Saxon. Yes—I love the language,—the glorious language of the Anglo-Saxon ! My imagination visions forth before me the language of the Anglo-Saxon in all its radiant beauty, and I feel silenced and abashed.

I have heard the pastoral pipe of the Mantuan Swain; I have heard that Mantuan Strike, with a bolder hand, the lyre of heroic poesy, and sing of arms and the man whom the hatred of white-armed Juno imperiled both by land and by sea! I have listened to the melodies of gay Flaccus, that lover of the sparkling bowl, and the joyous banquet: I have heard of bloody Pharsalia, and learned to love Epicurus, the honour of the Greek race: I have sighed over the sad strains of him, who in his cheerless exile, sang of the hapless and the absent lover: The harp of the blind old man of Scio's rocky isle, singing of the wrath of Achilles, the direful spring of woes unnumbered to Greece, has often hushed my soul to awe: I have seen gorgeous Tragedy, in sceptered pall come sweeping by presenting Thebes' or Pelop's line: I am no stranger to the eloquence of fiery Demosthenes, of calm and philosophic Cicero: I am no stranger to marvel-relating Livy; to sententious Thucydides; to the delightful outpourings of the father of historic novelists—the man of Halicarnassus: I have heard the melodious voice of him who from the green tree of Poesy sang of Rama like a Kokila: I have wept over the fatal war of the implacable Courava and the heroic Pandava: I have grieved over the sufferings of her who wore and lost the fatal ring: I have wandered with Hafiz on the banks of Rocknabad and the rose-bowers of Mosellay: I have moralized with Saddi, and seen Roustum shedding tears of agony over his brave but halpless son: I have laughed with Moliere: the melody from the dismal prison-cell of Torquato Tasso, has soothed my ears: I have visited the lightless regions of Hades with Dante: I know Lama's sad lover who gave himself to fame with melodious tears: but give me the literature, the language of the Anglo Saxon! Banish Peto, banish Bardolph, banish Poins: but for sweet Jack Falstaff, kind Jack Falstaff, banish him not thy Harry's company; banish plump Jack and banish all the world ! I say, give me the language—the beautiful language of the Anglo-Saxon !

I have heard would-be Quinctilians talk disparagingly of this magnificent language as irregular, as anomalous. I disdain such petty cavilers ! It laughs at the limit which the tyrant Grammar, would set to it—it nobly spurns the thought of being circumscribed. It flows on like a glorious, a broad river, and in its royal mood, it does not despise the tribute waters which a thousand streams bring to it. Why should it? There is no one to say to it—thus far shalt thou go, and no farther ! Give me, I say, the beautiful language of the Anglo-Saxon.

It is the glorious mission, I repeat, of the Anglo-Saxon to renovate, to regenerate, or—in one word, to Christianize the Hindu. How he is fulfilling that mission, must, with your permission, form the subject of a future discourse.

RAJA RAJENDRA LALA MITRA
(1824-1891)

RAJA RAJENDRA LALA MITRA

Adulteration of Ghee

Speech at a Half-yearly Meeting of the British Association Held in the Hall of the Association on 6 September 1886

Gentlemen,—Before I put the resolution to the vote, I think it necessary to explain to you the reason why this report has been delayed. It embraces the period from January to June and the proper time for the submission of it was July, but it so happened that in July, your house was under repairs, and consequently it was not possible to convene a meeting. The repairs took up the whole of August, and therefore your Committee was compelled to defer the meeting to this day. On that ground, however, your Committee did not feel it desirable to extend this report to the end of August. Usually our reports embrace six months, and consequently this report is just three months after time, and it does not give you any information with regard to what has been done during the last three months. The last three months, however, have not been altogether uneventful, and I shall attempt to give you an outline of what engaged their attention during that period. The first question to which your Committee directed their attention during the last three months was the exodus of Government from Calcutta. The question was first suggested to us by the Chamber of Commerce, and a meeting of the representatives of the Chamber of Commerce, of the Trades' Association, of this Association and of the Indian Association, was held in the rooms of the Chamber of Commerce for devising means for a proper representation to Government of the grievances we complain of on account of this exodus. The Chamber of Commerce in this instance evinced the warmest sympathy for the people, and the unity of sentiment which prevailed was highly gratifying in every way. The meeting, convened by the united Committee in the Town Hall, was of a highly satisfactory kind. The unity was perfect, and the effect of the meeting, I have reason to believe, will be good. You have already seen from one of the late telegrams from England, that the Under-Secretary of State has said that there was no intention to transfer the seat of the metropolis from Calcutta to Simla. Upon this telegram, I should not be justified in expressing a definite opinion. It may mean anything or nothing. The subject will, no doubt, be discussed in a quiet way, when everything is ready for discussion. But the telegram shows that the meeting must have had an effect for good. The Government of England are not yet prepared to assert positively and finally what they want to do. The matter will take much time before a decision is finally arrived at. I can easily conceive how strong must be the opposition in official quarters to the giving up of this prolonged nine months' picnic on the hills for the benefit of nobody but the picnicians, at the cost of the public. It is satisfactory to know that the public have done their duty, and have entered their most earnest protest against the conduct of Government in forsaking Calcutta, the metropolis, for their Simla retreat. If you could conceive Lord Salisbury seated in his chalet Cecil and the whole of Downing Street carried with him to the shores of the Mediterranean, and ruling England therefrom, you would have some idea how Government is conducted in this country; with this difference, that in regard to England, it would be the Riviera; here you have the crest of the Jakko Hill, leaving the people hundreds of miles away from the ruler. In the case of Bengal, you have the Lieutenant-Governor on the top of Birch Hill at Darjeeling, surrounded by Lepchas and Bhooteas, ruling the whole race of Hindus and Mahomedans 300 miles away from him. You can also imagine in the same way Mr. Grant-Duff in the Neilgheries, or at Ootacamund, and the people of Madras left to take care of themselves. Could any Government in England have dared to insult the community at large by taking their perch on the top of Ben Nevis, and ruling England, Wales and Ireland? Such a thing would be preposterous; but that is exactly what is done in this country, and in protesting against what has been done, and which is pretty well becoming an institution, have you done what is the duty of your, as people of the country, feeling strongly the advantage of good government and the disadvantage of bad government.

The next subject which engaged the attention of your Committee, was a domestic one—in reference to the annoyance felt by the people on account of the adulteration of *ghee*, one of the main necessaries of Hindu dietary. In its simplest form, *ghee* is nothing but butter, and yet there is a difference. In ordinary language, when we talk of butter, we mean something very emollient and agreeable, and we often say one has been buttered when we mean he has been flattered, but it comes to something greasy and obnoxious if we change butter into *ghee*. I am sure if I could butter well, I could win the good graces of a great many; but I would jeopardise my skin if I tried to ply rancid *ghee* instead. To Indians, *ghee* may be welcome as an article of food, but *ghee* by itself is one thing, and quite another, when a quantity of tallow or some other fat, or some other fatty oil, is put into it, and this is what the tradesmen of Calcutta have been doing for some months, not only to the injury of the health of the people, but also to the injury of the religious feelings of the community. It is gratifying to me to notice that His Honour the Lieutenant-Governor has taken the subject into his earnest consideration, and has gone so far as to leave his delightful residence at Darjeeling, and come down to Calcutta for the express purpose of passing a Law on the subject. I am sure that the whole of the Hindu community of Calcutta are deeply thankful for this prompt action of the Lieutenant-Governor (hear, hear). Your Association took the matter up with, as usual, very great promptness, and, after deliberation, they submitted a representation to Government praying that as the matter was of great urgency, it should at once be taken notice of and an ordinance issued to put a stop to it. The Government thought a different course desirable. They published a draft of an Act in the local newspapers for any suggestions that might be offered at any time. The objection to the present course of legislation, is that we cannot accept this hasty legislation, and enter, as we have hitherto done, our most emphatic protest against legislation in a hurry. It is usual to take the greatest care to give permanency to the laws of a nation, and every caution against the liability of laws being frequently and readily changed. The form and procedure prescribed for making laws require much deliberation and much time, and they are the best safeguards against hasty legislation, and nothing should be done to undo that. Is it then desirable, is it prudent, that the people at large should set aside all checks and go and ask the Government to pass a law in 24 hours' time for their own benefit? Doubtless they may be benefited in this instance; but they should not forget that if they give up the principle for their own benefit, and accept a principle fraught with mischief, it can be brought into play against them quite as effectually as to their benefit. I am, therefore, strongly opposed to the system of legislation in a hurry. I would have infinitely preferred an ordinance which could have been set aside at any time on objection. The Bill as it is drafted is a very unsatisfactory one (hear, hear). In the first place, it is limited to Calcutta only, where people are dissatisfied with larded *ghee*; but are not the people living on the east side and west side of Calcutta equally dissatisfied? And if they are, they should have the same benefit from the law; but as the law stands, they most be content with, larded *ghee*. We, the inhabitants of Calcutta, have no special right to get a law to which the others have no claim. The Government should treat the Hindoos and the Mahomedans alike, and give the benefit of the law on the other side of the river as well as on this side. But the Government is not going to do this, and have not told us why. Some say the law is not going to be made general, because it is not convenient to obtain chemical analysis of *ghee* in the mufussil. I should not think this is a valid reason, and therefore strongly advise your Committee to submit a representation to Government that the law may be more general. In one section of the Draft Bill,—I forget which, it is the 3rd or 4th—the wording is very defective. It says "articles unfit for human food." What is unfit? In ordinary parlance that is unfit which is prejudicial to health. A sirloin of beef or a shoulder of mutton is "unfit" when it is too stringy or tough. We don't say it is unfit, because some Hindus won't touch it. The word simply applies to what is wholesome as opposed to what is unwholesome We complain of what is prejudicial to our religion. Lard is not prejudicial to health, suet is not prejudicial to health. Doctors, in ninety-nine cases in every hundred, recommend the use of mutton, and seldom denounce it as unfit, but it is prejudicial to religion, and the wording should have been very different. The duty of your Committee is to call the attention of the Government to that clause. It is quite true that a Bill hastily put up and passed will require an amendment in a short time, and our-Council is like a tinker's shop where our legal utensils are repaired every month; but that is not what we want. We want abiding laws and matured laws.

The next subject, and that is one on which no action has of late been taken by you, there having been no opportunity for it, is that of the increase of the income-tax. You have all heard that the prospect is not cheering about the balancing of our income and expenditure in the next Budget. There is sure to be a heavy deficit, and to meet that deficit, the rumour is that the rate of the income-tax is to be considerably increased. Very unwelcome news to you; but you must be prepared to face it, and the sooner you take care to meet this, the better.

For your friends, the zemindars, there is yet another matter. It is said that the Government contemplates taking revenue in gold—to be calculated in gold. What disastrous effects this change will have, my friends, the zemindars, know well. For my part, if such a change is desirable, I hope that Government will likewise make it applicable to the Government securities, reckon the promissory notes in gold, and pay us interest and capital in gold. This has not yet been developed; it is yet in its infancy; but we must be prepared for the contingency. When I will have the opportunity of addressing you again some time in the beginning of next year, I am afraid that I shall have to talk on this subject in greater detail. Before putting the resolution to the vote, I should have said something about the exchange, but the appointment of the Royal Commission for enquiry into the currency, has already had the effect of slightly improving the rate of exchange, I therefore put it off to another occasion. (Loud applause).

DADABHAI NAOROJI
(1825-1917)

DADABHAI NAOROJI

India Must Be Bled

Speech at the United Methodist Free Church, Walthamstow on I July 1900 in Aid of the Indian Famine Relief Fund

Mr. Chairman, I feel exceedingly pleased at having to address so large a meeting of English ladies and gentlemen. I assure you it is a great consolation to me that English people are willing to hear what Indians have to say. I will make bold to speak fully and heartily, in order that you may know the truth. I will take as a text the following true words: "India must be bled." These words were delivered by a Secretary of State for India, Lord Salisbury himself. i don't mention them as any complaint against Lord Salisbury. On the contrary, I give him credit for saying the truth. I want to impress upon you what these important words mean. Let us clearly understand what is meant by bleeding a nation. It is perfectly true that when government is carried on people must pay taxes. But there is a great difference between taxing a people and bleeding a people. You in England pay something like fifty shillings, or more now, of taxes per head per annum. We in India pay only three to four shillings per head per annum. From this you may conclude that we must be the most lightly taxed people in the world. That is not the case, however; our burden is nearly twice as heavy as yours. The taxes you pay in this country go from the hands of the taxpayers into the hands of the Government, from which they flow back into the country again in various shapes, fertilising trade and returning to the people themselves. There is no diminution of your wealth; your taxes simply change hands. Whatever you give out you must get back. Any deficit means so much loss of strength. Supposing you pay a hundred million pounds every year, and the Government uses that money in such a way that part only returns to you, the other part going out of the country. In that case you are being bled, part of your life is going away. Suppose, out of the hundred million pounds only eighty million pounds return to you in the shape of salaries, commerce, or manufactures. You will have lost twenty million pounds. Next year you will be so much the weaker; and so on each year. This is the difference between taxing people and bleeding people. Suppose a body of Frenchmen were your rulers, and that out of the hundred million pounds of taxes they book ten to twenty million pounds each year; you would then be said to be bleeding. The nation would then be losing a portion of its life. How is India bled? I suppose your own case with Frenchmen as your rulers. We Indians are governed by you. You manage our expenditure and our taxes in such a way that while we pay a hundred million pounds of taxation, this hundred million never returns to us intact. Only about eighty million returns to us. There is a continual bleeding of about twenty millions annually from the revenues. Ever since you obtained territorial jurisdiction and power in India, in the middle of last century, Englishmen and other Europeans that went to India have treated that country in the most oppressive way. I will quote a few words of the Court of Directors at the time to show this. "The vast fortunes acquired in the inland trade have been obtained by the most oppressive conduct that ever was known in any country or age." The most oppressive means were adopted in order to bring away from the country enormous quantities of wealth. How was the Indian Empire obtained by you? It has been generally said that you have won it by the sword, and that you will keep it by the sword. The people who say this do not know what they are talking about. They also forget that you may lose "it by force". You have not won the Indian Empire by the sword. During these hundred and fifty years you have carried on wars by which this great Empire has been built up, it has cost hundreds of millions of money. Have you paid a single farthing of it? You have made the Indians pay every farthing. You have formed this great British Empire at our expense, and you will hear what reward we have received from you. The European army in India at any time was comparatively insignificant. In the time of the Indian Mutiny you had only forty thousand troops there. It was the two hundred thousand Indian troops that shed their blood and fought your battles and that gave you this magnificent Empire. It is at India's cost and blood that this Empire has been formed and maintained up to the present day. It is in consequence of the tremendous cost of these wars and, because of the millions on millions you draw from us year by year that India is so completely exhausted and bled. It is no wonder that the time has come when India is bleeding to death. You have brought India to this condition by the constant drain upon the wealth of that country. I ask any one of you whether it is possible for any nation on the face of the earth to live under these conditions. Take your own nation. If you were subjected to such a process of exhaustion for years, you would come down yourselves to the condition in which India now finds herself. How then is this drain made? You impose upon us an immense European military and civil service, you draw from us a heavy taxation. But in the disbursement and the disposal of that taxation we have not the slightest voice. I ask anyone here to stand up and say that he would be satisfied, if, having to pay a heavy taxation, he had no voice in the government of the country. We have not the slightest voice. The Indian Government are the masters of all our resources, and they may do what they like with them. We have simply to submit and be bled. I hope I have made it quite clear to you, that the words of Lord Salisbury which I have quoted are most significant; that the words are true and most appropriate when applied to India. It is the principle on which the system of British Government has been carried on during these 150 years. What has been the consequence? I shall again quote from Lord Salisbury. He says: "That as India must be bled the lancet should be directed to the parts where the blood is congested or at least sufficient, not to those parts already feeble from the want of it." Lord Salisbury declared that the agricultural population, the largest portion of the population of India, was feeble from the want of blood. This was said twenty-five years ago; and that blood has been more and more drawn upon during the past quarter of a century. The result is that they have bled to death; and why? A large proportion of our resources and wealth is clean carried away never to return to us. This is the process of bleeding. Lord Salisbury himself says: "So much of the revenue is exported without a direct equivalent." I ask any one of you whether there is any great mystery in these dire famines and plagues? No other country, exhausted as India has been exhausted by an evil system of government, would have stood it, half the time. It is extraordinary that the loyalty of the Indians who are bled by you is still so great. The reason of it is that among the Hindus it is one of their most cherished and religious duties that they should give obedience and loyalty to the powers that govern them. And they have been loyal to that sentiment, and you have derived the benefit of it. It is a true and genuine loyalty. But do not expect that that loyalty can not fail, that it will continue in the same condition in which it is at the present time. It is for the British to rouse themselves and to open their minds, and to think whether they are doing their duty in India. The theory maintained by statesmen is that India is governed for the benefit of India. They say that they do not derive any benefit from the taxation. But this is erroneous. The reality is that India, up to the present day, has been governed so as to bring about the impoverishment of the people. I ask you whether this is to continue. Is it necessary, that for your benefit, we must be destroyed? Is it a natural consequence, is it a necessary consequence? Not at all. If it were British rule and not un-British rule which governed us England would be benefited ten times more than it is. You could benefit yourselves a great deal more than you are doing if your Executive Government did not persist in their evil system, by which you derive some benefit, but by which we are destroyed. I say let the British public thoroughly understand this question, that by destroying us you will ultimately destroy yourselves. Mr. Bright knew this, and this is an extract from one of his speeches. He said, "By all means seek your own benefit and your own good in connection with India; but you can not derive any good except by doing good to India. If you do good to India you will do good to yourselves." He said there were two ways of doing good to yourselves, either by plunder or by trade. And he said he would prefer trade. Now, I will explain how it would benefit you. At the present time you are exporting to the whole world something like three hundred millions worth of your produce a year. Here is a country under your control with a population of three hundred millions of human souls, not savages of Africa. Here is India, with a perfectly free trade entirely under your control, and what do you send out to her? Only eighteen pence per year per head. If you could send goods to the extent of £ 1 per head per annum India would be a market for your whole commerce. If such were the case you would draw immense wealth from India, besides benefiting the people. I say that if the British public do not rouse themselves, the blood of every man that dies there will lie on their head. You may prosper for a time, but a time must come when you must suffer the retribution that comes from this evil system of government. What I quoted to you from Lord Salisbury explains the real condition of India. It is not the first time that English statesmen have declared this as absolutely as Lord Salisbury has done. During the whole century Englishmen and statesmen of conscience and thought have time after time declared the same thing, that India is being exhausted and drained, and that India must ultimately die. Our misery is owing to this exhaustion. You are drawing year by year thirty millions of our wealth from us in various ways. The Government of India's resources simply mean that the Government is despotic and that it can put any tax it chooses on the people. Is it too much to ask that when we are reduced by famine and plague you should pay for these dire calamities ! You are bound in justice and in common duty to humanity to pay the cost of these dire calamities with which we are afflicted. I will conclude with Lord Salisbury's other true words: "Injustice will bring down the mightiest to ruin."

KRISTO DAS PAL
(1834-1889)

KRISTODAS PAL

The Achievement of the Indian Press

The speech at the Calcutta Trade's Dinner on I February 1875

Master of the Trades Association and Gentlemen—I thank you most heartily and sincerely for again inviting me to this your very interesting annual re-union, and again allowing me the privilege of acknowledging the compliment to the Native Press. Last year, as several speakers, who have preceded me, have reminded you, we met under the shadow of a dire calamity threatening millions of my fellow-countrymen with starvation and death, but thanks to the All-Merciful Providence, the sore trial with which it had pleased Him to visit us, has ended; the gloom which hung over us has given place to sunshine; the anxiety and sorrow, which it brought us have been succeeded by the hope that cheers, and the joy that gladdens. (Cheers.) Plenty now smiles over the land and the poor men, women, and children, who, pinched by that dread enemy, hunger, had last year by thousands and tens of thousands crowded at the relief centres for the daily pittance to keep their body and soul together, have with the return of Nature's favour, gone back to their homes and avocations. Gentlemen, we hear much of the want of sympathy between the European and the Native, but whatever may be the feelings of individuals, no one can deny that the British Government and the British nation have shown a most lively and generous sympathy for their Indian subjects in this hour of adversity, and I can assure you that my countrymen feel deeply grateful for it. (Hear, hear.) Rich as you are in the traditions of your prowess and power, nothing can exceed the glory of the trophy, which the Indian Government has achieved in fighting so skilfully and successfully the battle of humanity. While history records the triumphs of British arms at Assaye and Laswaree, on the plains of Chillianwalla and Loodiana, in the re-capture of Delhi and the relief of Lucknow, in the memorable war of the Sepoy Mutiny, no page in the annals of British progress in the East will shine with greater lustre than that in which she will chronicle the brilliant achievements accomplished in the campaign against the Bengal Famine of 1874—with the calm courage, untiring energy, and noble self-sacrifice with which all from the highest to the lowest worked in this good cause. (Cheers). Here was a demonstration of sympathy not confined by geographical boundaries or partitions of race and religion, not flowing from the lip, but gushing from the heart, not shown to the rich who could always exact their dues, but the poor and forlorn, to dumb millions, who could not speak, whose voice could not reach their august rulers, but who, in the heart of their hearts, blessed the fatherly hand that gave them rice while they were hungry, and water while they were thirsty. (Cheers.) Such sympathy constitutes the golden chain, which will securely bind India to England, despite the storm of political tumult and the war of foreign aggression. (Hear, hear.) Gentlemen, the place which you have assigned for several years past to the Native Press in your toasts implies that you have confidence in that press, and I thank you for it not only on my own behalf, but also on behalf of the whole body of my brethren of the Native Press. Until the advent of the British, as the proposer of the toast has rightly observed, the press as an institution, as a vehicle of the thoughts, sentiments and feelings of the nation was unknown in this country; the tongue was always tied under the Oriental Government; the people, when oppressed beyond endurance, did not resort to the pen, but the sword for the vindication of their rights. But under the happy auspices of the British Government that state of things has changed. (Hear, hear.) There is now no restraint upon the tongue or pen of the Indian to express his inmost thoughts, to represent his grievances, to seek for redress, so long as he does not forget his duty as a loyal subject of the Queen. (Cheers.) And I am proud to say that whatever may be the shortcomings of the Native Press, it has rarely been found wanting in that prime qualification for the liberty which it enjoys, I mean loyalty to the Crown. Gentlemen, I need not urge upon you difficulties which beset the conductors of the Native Press. They are inseparable from the government of this country by a foreign nation. However intelligent, sagacious, and sympathetic, the English in India labour under a peculiar disadvantage. Though descended from the same stock which, in the dawn of human history, sent forth its teeming millions westward to people Europe and southward to people India, they are for all practical purposes alien by birth, language, customs, and religion: they are necessarily perplexed in mastering the complicated problems of Indian administration, and are consequently under the necessity of employing interpreters to interpret the rulers to the ruled and vice versa. Marvellous as has been the success of British rule in the East, I believe I do not exaggerate when I say, and I am glad to find my statement corroborated by our distinguished Foreign Secretary, that success could hardly have been achieved if the English rulers of India had not from the beginning availed themselves of Indian experience, Indian counsel, and Indian co-operation. The Indian holds the key, wherewith to open the gate of the East, and if our Western rulers had not used that key, not all the bayonets and guns of England, not all her countless treasures, would have sufficed to build up her magnificent Eastern Empire, justly prized as the brightest jewel in her diadem. The conductors of the Native press are the unpaid interpreters of the Government and the nation: they may be misinformed, misled and mistaken, but they act in good faith, and endeavour to interpret the Governors to the governed and the governed to the Governors, loyally and faithfully. In discharging their duties it not often falls to their lot to expose abuses and oppressions to lay bare the failings of individual officers, and to criticize unreservedly both measures and men, and in doing so, they not unfrequently incur the displeasure, I regret to add sometimes, the personal hostility of those upon whose corns they tread, and possibly the hue and cry now and then raised against the Native Press proceed from these sources. But I believe really thoughtful and enlightened Englishmen, who care more for the character and permanency of British rule as an engine of good for the millions under its sway, than for their own temporary and limited interests, like such outspokenness, though the language may resemble the feeble utterances of those who have but learnt to lisp. If the Native Press were to circulate only tales of adulation, what would the Government or the people gain? For my part I believe that the real usefulness of the Native Press consists in an unvarnished statement of facts, illustrative of the working of the laws of the action of the vast administrative machinery, and the under-current of the social and political feelings of the people directed by such laws and actions—facts which the Government and the European public have no other means of ascertaining, and if it sometimes errs in making such statements, there are many forces at work for its correction. But, Gentlemen, bear in mind that the Native Press of India is a plant peculiarly entitled to your fostering care; it has grown from a seed which has been brought from the west: the manure which has contributed to its growth is derived from that fertilizing knowledge which Englishmen have diffused in this country—it is a knowledge drawn not from your books only, but also from your precepts, from your examples, from your personal influences, and if the tree now presents a goodly appearance, the glory is the greater to you to whom it owes its existence, to the liberality of your principles, to the kindliness of your feelings, and to the high-minded statesmanship, which characterize your rule of this country. (Cheers.) Gentlemen, this is not the place to exchange with Jupiter Junior the thunderbolts which he has thought fit to hurl against the Native Press, but permit me to say that he is about as well-informed of the circulation as of the politics of the *Patriot*. (Laughter and Loud Cheers).

KESHUB CHUNDER SEN
(1838-1884)

KESHUB CHUNDER SEN

The Religious and Social Conditions of India

Speech at the Philosophical Institution, Queen Street Hall, Edinburgh on 19 August 1870

Mr. Chairman, I thankfully appreciate the kind words with which you have introduced me to this meeting. They embolden me, however unworthy I may feel I am of the position which I occupy tonight. It is interesting to observe the present religious and social condition of India. The eye, and no less the heart, loves to expatiate on the solemn sublimity of the spectacle of an ancient nation advancing under the enlightening and civilizing influences of the present day. In that remote country and in that vast peninsula we see the union of the East and the West—the union of the past and the present. It is this which invests the subject with peculiar interest, and, I may add, renders it profitable and instructive to us all. In that great country, we find the results of an ancient civilization lying side by side with the achievements of modem thought and refinement. The mists of superstition and idolatry are vanishing before the light of modern science. We see schools and colleges multiplying throughout the length and breadth of the land. Idolatry and caste are being imperceptibly undermined by the effects of English education. The people are hankering after, and in many cases successfully achieving, a better and more improved social and domestic economy. Thus, intellectually, morally, and religiously, the country is making great strides,—to say nothing of material improvement; for we see already, spread over the length and breadth of the country, a vast network of railways and telegraphs, and neglected wastes are being converted into smiling fields, and intercommunication with distant races is being established. But is not all this, one may ask, "the baseless fabric of a vision?" Is it not the false glitter, the temporary gloss of mere outward and borrowed refinement? Is the work of reformation that is going on in India really abiding and permanent, or is it only the innovation of the moment? A few individuals may have received education; but may they not one day go back to the ancient system of things, forget the effects of education, and obliterate the influence of modern civilization? I would not for a moment rejoice in the work of Indian reformation were it but the importation of foreign customs and manners—if it were merely the outward and temporary gloss of borrowed civilization. It is certainly interesting to see a number of flower-pots, but the question is—are the beautiful flowers that we see, permanent—have the plants struck their roots deep into the country's soil? Is civilization an indigenous growth of the country, or has it been forced upon the people of India? Anything that is forced upon a nation, however good and grand it may be, does not and cannot last long. (Applause). True reformation, in order to be lasting, must come from within. (Applause). The English people are trying to carry into India the machinery of the present day with the view of more effectually and rapidly developing the physical resources of the country; and thus able and efficient teachers are going forward with the view of cultivating the intellectual and moral resources of the country. The results already achieved are indeed wonderful; but still the question stares us in the face, whether after all we have succeeded in planting in the country a radical and abiding civilization. Many are apt to congratulate themselves on anything that is new and good; but we, natives of the country, must look into the depth of the matter. We cannot congratulate ourselves upon those excellent things which float always on the surface of society. We must go down in order to see whether there are pearls below. It is true that to-day India sits in a state of abject humiliation at the feet of modern nations and is content to receive lessons which she ought to receive, which she cannot reject for her own interest. But yesterday, what was she? Though in her infancy in relation to modern civilization, she was in ancient times the parent of a more grand and sublime civilization. When your ancestors were enveloped in the darkness of ignorance and barbarism, my ancestors boasted of a really grand civilization. (Applause). The ancient Hindus had a better literature, better scientific ideas, and better and purer social and domestic customs and manners. They had better education and enlightenment amongst themselves, at least amongst the higher and middle classes. They had no idolatry—no idol-worship—no caste distinctions to fetter them—no priestcraft to keep them down in a state of spiritual destitution and slavery. (Applause). My countrymen in ancient times were famous for their philosophy and even theology. But to-day, India's face is changed. She is not now what she was centuries ago. Superstitious and idolatrous notions crept in. It was found that the people could not be made to climb up to true conceptions of a personal and spiritual God, and hence idol-worship was invented and fabricated by crafty priests. Distinctions of caste were established. The liberty which was accorded to women was withdrawn under the rule of the Mahomedans, so oppressive and tyrannical they were. And so, in the course of time, under an ignorant and bigoted priesthood, and under Mahomedan misrule and oppression, even the last vestiges of the ancient civilization of India seemed well nigh obliterated. So to-day India is looking forward to you, and to all civilized nations in the world for help, in order that she may regain her former greatness. In regard to India, therefore, you must not look only into her condition to-day but travel back in imagination thousands of years, and see what she was in the ancient times of primitive Hindu simplicity and purity. (Hear, and applause). Even in the earliest books of the Hindus, the *Vedas*, which must be regarded as the earliest record of Aryan faith—even in them you find glimpses of high moral and religious truths which are unmistakable—not duly formed and organized religious thought, but the crude instincts and aspirations of the human mind, in a state of religious infancy, seeking after the Deity. "Who knows," says, the *Rig Veda*, "whence this manifold creation sprang? The gods themselves came later into being. Who knows from whence this great creation sprang? He from whom all this great creation came, whether His will created or was created, the Most High Seer that is in highest heaven, He knows it—or perchance He knows it not." It has been said that the *Vedas* teach nature-worship and polytheism; but it is clearly proved in many passages that the One True God was worshipped under the different names—under the names of the various deities presiding over the different departments of physical Nature, but still the same God. This will be evident to you from such passages as these:—"They called Him *Indra, Mitra, Varuna*, and *Agni*;" "That which is One the wise call by diverse names." Later on we find these crude instincts and intuitions taking form, and assuming definite shape; and, coming to the later books, called the *Vedanta*, which contain simply the philosophy of the ancient Vedic

Scriptures, we find the Hindu mind has already attained much clearer notions of the One Creator of the universe. In the early theological state of Hinduism we see only vague ideas scattered about here and there; but in the later books of the *Upanishads* we find clearer notions and a more developed system of theology. I do not think there is anything in any other book which can be compared to this—"Let us endeavour to know the Ruler of the universe, who is the God of gods, the Deity of deities, the Lord of lords—above all, who manifests Himself, and is worthy of all reverence." Passages like these are clear and unmistakable proofs that the Hindus, at one time in the history of their religious development, did worship the One True God of the universe, and not only theoretically but practically protested against and denounced all manner of idol worship. If, therefore, you wish to accuse my countrymen of being idolatrous and superstitious, you should lay the charge at the doors of modern Hindus. So far as my ancestors are concerned, I may say the charge does not belong to them. (Applause). And as in religion, so in morality. The ancient Hindus possessed a high standard of ethical rules, and always tried to carry out those principles into practice. Everybody knows that the Hindus are celebrated for their meekness, for their simplicity of character, their devotion to God, their resignation to His divine will, their deep faith in immortality, and constant endeavour to lay up provision for the future life. Every one knows that whatever shortcomings the Hindu may have, he is ever endeavouring to serve God in a gentle, pious and devout spirit, and to perform the duties of social and domestic life according to His will. "Every householder must be devoted to his God. Whatever work he does, he must do unto the glory of God." (Applause). If you admit that there was a pure religion and pure morality among the Hindus, you must also admit that the system of caste distinctions was not known to my ancestors. It is said,—"This is my friend,—that is not,—so counteth the man of narrow heart; but to men of large hearts all mankind are kinsmen." (Applause). I hope I have conclusively shown there are truths, sublime and practical, in the Scriptures of the Hindus, which we cannot but revere. These constitute the precious legacy which our ancestors have bequeathed to us for enjoyment and use, and he is a traitor to his country and to his noble ancestry who, being an Indian, would cast away such precepts—such noble and deep principles of morality and religion. (Applause). Thus in India, in the early books and institutions of the Hindus, there is a substratum for future reforms as strong and firm as a rock. We find unmistakably the principles of pure Theistic religion and morality; and the duty of all those who are trying to enlighten, educate, and civilize that great country ought to be to establish modem civilization upon a firm and enduring national basis. (Applause). The country will reject any other basis. Foreign customs a few of my countrymen may admire; a few, addicted to apishness, may adopt them; but after a time, all that will be gone—it will be altogether effaced. But if you succeed in establishing the work of reformation on the platform of national instincts and national ideas, and if you succeed in establishing all that is good and grand in England and Europe in the heart of India, then, I say, the work done will last for centuries. (Applause). India will attain true greatness and civilization, if only the basis on which we build this vast fabric is national and firm. And such a basis we have in the great ideas of the past.

But these great ideas were swept away for a time, as I have said, by Mahomedan misrule, and by that system of idolatry and superstition which cropped up in later times. Yet every now and then, through the impenetrable darkness of superstition, the Hindu mind struggled in order to vindicate, and revive its national Theism; every now and then amid cimmerian gloom you see the rays of national Monotheism shining forth. About four hundred years ago, when the mind of Luther was revolutionizing Europe, Nanak, who has been justly called "the Luther of the Punjab," boldly declared a crusade against idolatry. He succeeded in establishing that noble Indian sect, known as the Sikhs, in the Punjab, and gave them a better and purer social and domestic economy, and he succeeded in some measure in bringing together the hitherto antagonistic sects of Hindus and Mahomedans. Almost at the same time in Bengal, Chaitanya declared a crusade against caste. He preached the equality of men. He told the proud Brahmin to go down to the level of the lowest Sudra, and he exhorted them to sing together with one heart and with one voice the name of their common God of Love. Even at the present moment in Bengal you see the effects of his teaching and of his own personal influence. Thus you see that every now and then pure Theism has been trying to vindicate itself and clear itself from the incrustations of later superstitions. But it was not until the English established their power in India that these desultory revival movements were organized into one mighty and compact institution. When Raja Rammohun Roy, with whose name many of you are, I dare say, familiar, received the influence of English education, it pleased God to foster and excite in his mind a desire to form a pure monotheistic national Church. He dived into the Vedas and earlier Scriptures of the Hindus, and at the same time he read that wonderful book, the Bible; and while he published extracts from those Scriptures, he at the same time published a book, containing extracts from the Bible, called *The Precepts of Jesus; Being a Guide to Peace and Happiness*. He tried to take advantage of the influence of both these great movements—the Hindu and the Christian. He tried to unite the East and the West, for in his own mind the results of English education and Vedic training had harmonized, and he could not be unfaithful or untrue to either. He upheld the authority of the earlier books of the Hindus, and exhorted his countrymen throughout the length and breadth of Bengal to renounce later idolatry, and offer their adoration and prayers to the one living God described in the ancient books. He founded the Church called the Brahmo Samaj, in Calcutta, where all religious sects and denominations, and all castes, races, and tribes, might unite at least once every week to worship devoutly and prayerfully the One Supreme Ruler of the universe. (Applause). He succeeded in gathering together a few enlightened men of the age, and after a time he came over to England where unfortunately he died. It was subsequently found that a mere congregation of worshippers could not long continue in a land given up to idolatry and superstition; that a dozen earnest-minded young men would not be able to stand their ground against multitudinous adversaries; that the glimmering light of this small monotheistic Church in one comer of India would not succeed in scattering away the mists of superstition and idolatry which spread darkness over the land. So, after a time, the movement seemed to decline; but fortunately, under God's providence, nothing that is good or great meets with untimely death, and the movement fell into the hands of a good successor. He gave form and organization to the movement; he converted worshippers into believers; he converted a place of worship into a society; and he converted a system of weekly preaching into a religion of life. (Applause). Year after year the movement spread in its organized form; branches and small prayer-meetings were established in different parts of the country;

men of character and intelligence were called upon to do the work of preaching; and so, from city to city, from province to province, from district to district, the movement rolled on, assuming grand proportions, and extending its influence far and wide. In the natural course of things, the movement shorty entered upon a third stage of progressive development. True, the new reformers worshipped one God, and cherished a definite system of theology, and a definite code of moral rules; but they were not practically bold enough to throw away the fetters of caste, and remove those pernicious social customs from which the country was suffering. I am sure you are aware of the painful fact that in that great country there are at the present moment such injurious customs as premature marriage, polygamy, and the custom which prohibits the remarriage of widows. These customs must be abolished. Lamentable and gross ignorance prevails amongst the masses; we must educate them. We must give education not only to the men, but also to the women in India. (Applause). We must improve and reform the marriage customs—we must make the people understand, the sacred duties and responsibilities of marriage. In fact, we must not rest satisfied with offering weekly prayers at churches and prayer-meetings, but we must bring true religion into our homes, and improve and purify our daily life. We must ask fathers and mothers, brothers and sisters, daughters and sons, to sing with united voice the name of their beloved and common Father, and discountenance, theoretically and practically, the distinctions of caste and all impure social customs. Led by these considerations, the advanced section of the Brahmos united and came forward about six years ago to carry their principles into practice. What are the results of their endeavours? God be thanked, we have already succeeded in forming a good number of Theistic families, where not only men, but even the ladies set their faces completely against idolatry and superstition, and regularly and systematically in their own homes offer their heartfelt prayers and thanksgivings to the One True God. They have given up caste. The number of such Theistic families is steadily increasing in the country. We have also succeeded in promoting marriages between members of different castes. High-caste Brahmins have already married low-caste Sudras—a thing which people could not even have dreamt of ten years ago. Men and women are now made to understand their duties before they are allowed to marry. I could quote to you passages from the Hindu books inculcating the principle that no girl ought to be given in marriage unless and until she knows fully the duties of married life. Thus, ladies and gentlemen, at present the Brahmo Samaj is not merely a body of worshippers, but also the national centre of social and moral improvement.

The number of adherents as yet is small, I must say. Perhaps it does not yet exceed six thousand. But we thank God that we have succeeded during the last few years in achieving even such results as these. We feel confident that the work will advance under Gods providence, and we feel encouraged by the facts which we see around us to-day in all parts of Bengal. We have also branches of our Church in the Punjab, Bombay, Madras, and many of the important cities in the North-Western Provinces. In fact, wherever you plant an English school to-day, tomorrow rises, side by side, a Brahmo Samaj; wherever you send good books, there you see their influence manifested within a short time in a Brahmo crusade against idolatry and caste. If you send good missionaries to India, what do they do? Have they done nothing to deserve the gratitude of that country? The members of the Brahmo Samaj extend their right hand of fellowship to all those who can co-operate with them in promoting the spiritual, moral, and intellectual welfare of the people. (Applause). They are ready,—and I may confidently say in this assembly they have always been ready—to offer the tribute of their gratitude to those Christian missionaries who have shed their blood for rescuing the people of India from the thraldom of idolatry and superstition. (Applause). Grateful to Christian missionaries, loyal to Her Majesty Queen Victoria (applause) for all the religious and political blessings that have been derived from British rule, the members of the Brahmo Samaj are carrying on under Divine guidance the great work of national, religious, social and moral reformation. (Applause). I come to this country to thank the British public for all those blessings which you have conferred on my country. I come here to effect, so far as is possible, with my humble means and powers, a moral and social union and intercourse between India and England—between the East and the West. (Applause). I come to guard and warn you against that fatal mistake into which, I am sorry to say, many Englishmen in India have fallen, of forcing upon the myriads of the Indian population, customs, manners and institutions, which belong altogether to different races. (Applause). I do not wish you to go to my country to teach the people to eat and drink or dress just as you do in this country; and I do not exhort you to go and teach them outward refinement of manners. Every nation must stick to its own nationality for ever and ever. (Applause). If you, Scotchmen, are proud of your dear Scotland, I, too, am equally fond and proud of my beloved India. (Loud applause). Give us all that is good and great in your religion, in your social life and we shall be thankful. But have you done so? Have you not given us evils of which you yourselves should be ashamed? (Applause). What as the effect of that fatal and iniquitous liquor traffic in India? (Applause). Does it not tend to demoralize the people? I have seen with my own eyes the awful effects of intemperance and drunkenness amongst my people. While I joyfully behold the progress of English education throughout my country, I feel grieved when I see how some of my own countrymen, boasting of their English education, take advantage of the liberty which education affords them, and go forward madly, recklessly in a career of moral infatuation and iniquity to what, alas ! is the end—untimely and ignominious death. Brethren, as one man rise and protest against this liquor traffic. (Applause). You should not force upon our people the dreadful custom of drinking. (Applause). Even here I see that temperance societies are being established in order to stem the tide of this gigantic evil; and if it is such a frightful curse in England, why should you extend it to my fair and dear country, India? (Applause). All that is grand and good we are prepared to accept, for we feet the need of your help. God has placed us under your protection, and as beggars we ask for your help. I wish I could go throughout the length and breadth of England and Scotland, in order to rouse and animate the hearts of all Englishmen and English women, and Scotchmen and Scotch women, and excite their pity and commisseration for the millions of helpless souls in India. (Applause). Give me assurance of your sympathy, kindness, and brotherly love. My countrymen will rejoice to hear that in the far West there are so many friends and brethren desirous and anxious to help them on. But give us something more. Give us personal influence—the influence of character. Tell all those Englishmen who are at present in India to feel their responsibility to God. If they do anything wrong, they not only defile themselves, but they send forth a cursed contagion of evil example which cannot but prove detrimental to the moral interests of those millions of people who surround them. Exhort them to cultivate friendly intercourse with the natives of the soil. It is God's desire that England and India should no longer remain apart from each other. (Applause). The English must depend on India; and the people of India must depend on England. If God, then, in the inscrutable designs of His providence, has knit together politically these great representatives of Asia and Europe—of the East and the West—namely, India and England—is there no moral significance in the fact? Will you go there only to make money, and then come home; and will you not feel a moral interest in that country, in the welfare of its people?—(Applause)—will you not endeavour to bring about a harmonious feeling between the two races, conducive to mutual good? I am sorry such good relations do not at present exist. I know my countrymen are to blame. Their social customs are in a great measure obstacles in the way of friendly intercourse with foreigners; but, at the same time, I cannot altogether exculpate the British settlers in India, for they are sufficiently enlightened to feel that unless they come forward and practically show their sympathy, the natives of the soil cannot come forward even to ask for their help. (Applause). Therefore, Christian men and women in India ought always to cultivate intercourse with educated natives of the country anxious to receive the influence of their life and character. They should do so both privately and publicly. Let public and private meetings be every now and then held simply with a view to make Indians and Europeans friends to each other. But you in England also possess great influence, and that influence you should exert in the cause of universal education all over India. Up to the present moment the blessings of education are restricted to the upper ten thousand; but the mass of the people are really ignorant—most painfully ignorant. Let them have the benefits of true intellectual culture. You should also call upon Parliament to abolish forthwith the opium trade and liquor traffic. (Applause). You should ask Government to do all in their power to improve the marriage customs of the country. The iniquitous and cruel custom of *suttee* or widow burning has already been abolished. Government has by a legislative enactment already encouraged and promoted the remarriage of Hindu widows. Now, it is for Government, at the instance of the members of the Brahmo Samaj to legalize marriages solemnized according to the reformed ritual prescribed by the church, without any of the rites of idolatry and superstition, and thus put down polygamy, bigamy, premature marriage and caste. (Applause). Humbly I beseech you to give these improvements to India, and God will bless you. Ladies and Gentlemen, I have not come to your country to offend any political party or religious denomination. Ever since my arrival in this country—thousands will bear testimony—I have taken my stand on a catholic and comprehensive platform, and have extended my hand of friendship and brotherhood to all men, whatever their religious and political opinions might be—(applause)—and I am glad to say that I have received in return sympathy and kindness from all. The high and the low, the rich and the poor, the Low Church and the Broad Church, the Quakers and the Methodists, the friends of temperance and the friends of peace, have all extended to me the right hand of fellowship. (Applause). This is a fact which speaks volumes in favour of the generosity of the British nation. I admire the liberality of feeling and sentiment with which I have been greeted and encouraged by men of all classes in this great country; and I hope and trust they will cultivate friendly intercourse not merely with me, but with those whom I humbly represent to-night. Let India have your sympathy and patronage and kind cooperation, and millions of her sons and daughters will bless you and honour you. May the God of mercy bless England and India; May the East and the West unite in true spiritual and social fellowship. (Loud applause).

MAHADEV GOVIND RANADE
(1842-1901)

MAHADEV GOVIND RANADE

India a Thousand Years Ago

Speech at the Indian Social Conference, Lucknow in 1900

This time last year, I had occasion, at the inauguration of the conference held at Madras, to speak on the subject of "Southern India a Hundred Years Ago". Today I find myself far away in the North, surrounded on all sides by the traditions of a civilization older than the oldest known to history, the land of the Aryan race settled in India, tracing its descent from the self-born *Swayambhu* Manu, where the solar dynasty flourished for thousands of years, the land of the Ekshwakus, of Dilip and Raghu, of Dasharatha and the incarnate hero Rama, with his illustrious brothers and the still more honoured wife Sita; the land where Vasishtha and Viswamitra lived and flourished; the home of all that is beautiful and true, and lovely and god-like in Aryan history. This favoured land of yours gave birth also in later time to Sakyamuni Buddha, who has been well described as the perfection of humanity in its highest and noblest development, and whose "wheel of law" still regulates the thoughts and feelings of half the human race. The South and the North, thus contrasted together, suggest recollections that are so over-powering, that I am tempted on this occasion when we meet to inaugurate the work of the conference at Lucknow to dwell for a few moments on this subject, and I bespeak your thoughtful attention to the lessons it suggests. Far in the South, which is now the stronghold of Brahminical ideas uninfluenced by outside contact, the Aryan civilization, no doubt made its way, but it continued to be an exotic civilization confined to a small minority of Aryan settlers so few in numbers, that they were overwhelmed by the influences of the earlier Dravidian Dominion. It never made its home in those remote regions, and the common people continued their adhesion to their old worship and to their old faiths under new names. What the effects of this subordination were, was depicted in my address at Madras in the words of a foreign missionary, who lived and worked a hundred years ago, and who had exceptional opportunities of studying these effects. I propose this time to draw your attention to the turn which the Aryan civilization has taken under the influences represented by the conquest of this part of the country by the Mahomedans, nearly a thousand years back. The one factor which separates Northern India from its Southern neighbours, is the predominant influence of this conquest by the Mahomedans which has left its mark permanently upon the country, by the actual conversion to the Mahomedan faith of one fifth of the population, and by the imperceptible but permanent moulding of the rest of the people in the way of thought, the belief, the like of which is hard to find on the Malabar or Coromandel Coasts. I propose to draw my materials from the Mahomedan philosophers and travellers who visited India both before and after the Mahomedan conquest and changed the face of the country. Owing to the absence of the historic instinct among our people, we have necessarily to depend upon the testimony of foreign historians. That testimony is, however, unexceptional because it was for the most part given before the Mahomedan domination had effected the separation which distinguishes the old India of the past from the modem India in which we are now living. This domination also separates the line which marks off Southern India, of which I spoke last year from the North, in one of the most representative centres of which we are met here to-day. At the outset we must have a correct understanding of what Northern India was before Mahomed of Gazni made his numerous expeditions for the plunder of its far-famed cities and temples, at the commencement of the tenth century. Fortunately for us, we have a witness to this period of our history in the writings of Alberuni, whose work on India was written shortly after the time that Mahomed crossed the Indus as a conqueror of infidels. That work has been translated by Dr. Sachau, a professor in the Berlin University, and in its English form is now accessible to us all. Alberuni was a native of Khorasan, his birth place being near Khiva. Mahomed of Gazni, conquered Khorasan and alberuni had thus to shift to Gazni, which was then the seat of a flourishing empire, the rulers of which were great patrons of Mahomedan learning. Alberuni was in special favour with Masaud, the son of Mahomed, and he was thus enabled to travel throughout India, where he spent many years, having mastered the

Sanskrit language. He was a philosopher by profession and temper and had a special liking for Indian Philosophy, which he studied with the same care and attention that he bestowed on Plato and Aristotle. His work on India consists of eighty chapters relating to Religion, Philosophy, Caste, Idolatry, Civil Polity, Literature, Science, Mathematics, Medicine, Geography, Astronomy, Cosmogony, Alchemy and Astrology.

He took great pains to give a full description of all that was known to the Hindus under these several heads, and being naturally not a bigotted Mahomedan his book shows that he wrote his whole work with a single desire to promote the cause of true learning. While Alberuni shows a great regard for the Hindu Philosophy, Astronomy and Medicine, he was not slow in finding out the weak points of the Indian character. In his chapters on Caste and Idolatry, in the condemnation he pronounces on the want of practical aptitudes in our people and in their devotion to superstitious observances. Alberuni did not spare his censures. He contrasted the democratic equality of the Mahomedan people with the innumerable divisions of the Indian races. He notices the helpless position of the women of India and the filthy customs and the habits of the people in those days. He gives praise to the few educated Brahmins whom he separates from the superstitious multitudes, whose fallen condition he deplores. Even among the Brahmins, he notices the verbosity of their writings and the wordsplitting which passed for wisdom. He notices the greediness and tyranny of the Hindu princes who would not agree to join their efforts together for any common purpose, and the timidity and the submissiveness of the people who, in his expressive language, were "scattered like atoms of dust in all directions", before the invading Moslems. The prevailing feeling among the Mahomedans of the time was that the Hindus were infidels and entitled to no mercy or consideration, and the only choice to be allowed to them was that of death or conversion. Alberuni did not share in these views, but these were the views of his master Mahomed of Gazni and of the hordes who were led by him on these expeditions. Another traveller Idenbatuta, a native of Tangiers, in North Africa, visited this country about a hundred years after Kutbuddin established the Afghan kingdom at Delhi. Like him he was taken into favour by the then Delhi Emperor, Mahomed Tuglak, under whom he acted for some time as judge of Delhi. Ibenbatuta travelled more extensively than Alberuni. He travelled from the extreme West of

Africa to the extreme West of China, and went round the Coast from Malabar to Coromandel. He was, however, not a philosopher, neither a scholar. His journal of travels is interesting, but he did not observe the manners and customs of the people with the same mastery of details that Alberuni's work shows on every page. The only points which struck Ibenbatuta in the course of his travels through India were the rite of *Sati* of which he was a witness and the practice of drowning men in the Ganges both of which struck him as inhuman to the degree he could not account for. He also notices the self-mortification of the *jogees* and their juggleries, in describing which he mentions the fact that in the presence of the Emperor he saw a *jogee* raise his body up in the air, and keep it there for some time. Another traveller Abdur Razzak visited India about 1450 A. D. His travels lay chiefly in the Southern Peninsula, Calicut, Vizianagar and Mangalore. The narratives of two other travellers—one a Russian and the other a Venetian, who visited India in the fifteenths century, are published by the Hakluyt Society, which afford most interesting reading. The general impression left on the minds of these travellers was a respect for the Brahmins for their philosophy and attainments in astrology, but for the common people, the vast multitudes of men and women, their sense was one of disgust and disappointment. Abdur Razzak expressed this feeling in his own words in a reply to the invitation of the king of Vizianagar.

He said to the king: "If I have once escaped from the desert of the love and reached my country, I shall not set out on another voyage even in the company of a king." In Southern India, these travellers found that both men and women, besides being black, were almost nude, and divided into innumerable castes and sects which worshipped their own idols. This abuse of idolatry and caste struck every traveller as the peculiar characteristic of the country, and gave them offence. The practice of self-immolation or *Sati* and of human sacrifices to idols by being crushed over by the temple car are also mentioned. Finally, we have the testimony of the Emperor Babar who in his memoirs thus describes this country:—"Hindustan is a country which has few things to recommend. The people are not handsome. They have no idea of the charms of friendly society or of freely mixing together in familiar intercourse. They have no genius, no comprehension of mind, no politeness of manners, no kindness or fellow-feeling, no ingenuity or mechanical invention in planning and executing their handicraft work, no skill or knowledge in design or architecture. They have no good horses, no good flesh, no good grapes or musk melons, no good fruits, no cold water or ice, no good food or bread in their bazaars, no baths, no colleges, no candles, not even a candle stick. They have no aqueducts or canals, no gardens and no palaces; in their buildings they study neither elegance nor climate nor appearance nor regularity. Their peasants and lower classes will go about naked tying on only a *langote*. The women too, have only a *lang*." The only good points which Babar could find in favour of Hindus then were that it is a large country, and has abundance of gold and silver, and there is also an abundance of workmen of every profession and trade for any work and employment.

Such was the picture presented to the Mahomedans when they entered India through the passes in successive hordes for three or four centuries. A great portion of the disgust and disappointment felt by these Mahomedan invaders may be set down to ignorance and the pride of race. At the same time, it is always of advantage to know exactly, how India appeared in its strong and weak points to intelligent foreigners; such as those we have mentioned above. The question for consideration to us at the present moment is, whether in consequence of the predominance of the Mahomedans for five centuries which intervened from the invasion of Mahomed to the ascendancy of Akbar, the people of India were benefited by the contact thus forcibly brought together between the two races. There are those among us who think that this predominance has led to the decay and corruption of the Indian character and that the whole story of the Mahomedan ascendancy should, for all practical purposes, be regarded as a period of humiliation and sorrow. Such a view, however, appears to be unsupported by any correct appreciation of the forces which work for the elevation or depression of nations. It cannot be easily assumed that in God's Providence such vast multitudes as those who inhabit India were placed for centuries together under influences and restraints of alien domination, unless such influences and restraints were calculated to do lasting service in the building up of the strength and character of the people in directions in which the Indian races were most deficient. Of one thing we are certain, that after lasting over 500 years the Mahomedan empire gave way and made room for the establishment of the old native races in Punjab and throughout Central

Hindustan and Southern India on foundations of a much more solid character than those which yielded so easily before the assaults of early Mahomedan conquerors. The domination, therefore, had not the effect of so depressing the people that they were unable to raise their heads again in greater solidarity. If the Indian races had not benefited by the contact and example of men with stronger muscles and greater powers, they would have never been able to re-assert themselves in the way in which History bears testimony they did.

Quite independently of this evidence of the broad change that took place in the early part of the eighteenth century when the Mogul empire went to pieces, and its place was taken up not by foreign settlers but by revived native powers we have more convincing grounds to show that in a hundred ways the India of the eighteenth century, so far as the native races were concerned, was a stronger and better constituted India than met the eyes of the foreign travellers from Asia and Europe who visited it between the period of the first five centuries from 1000 to 1500. In Akbar's time this process of regenerating India first assumed a decided character which could not be well mistaken. No student of Akbar's reign will fail to notice that for the first time the conception was then realized of a United India in which Hindus and Mahomedans, such of them as had become permanently established in the country, were to take part in the building of an edifice rooted in the hearts of both by common interest and common ambitions in place of the scorn and contempt with which the Mahomedan invaders had regarded the religion of the Hindus, their forms of worship, their manners and customs, and the Hindus looked down upon them as barbarous *Mlechas,* whose touch was pollution, a better appreciation of the good points in the character of both came to be recognized as the basis of the union. Akbar was the first to see and realize the true nobility of soul and the devotion and fidelity of the Hindu character, and satisfied himself that no union was possible as long as the old bigotry and fanaticism was allowed to guide the councils of the empire. He soon gathered about him the best men of his time, men like Faizi, Abdul Fazul and their father Mubarek, the historians, Abdul Rahim, Naizamuddin Ahmad, Badauni and others. These were set to work upon the translation of the Hindu epics and Shastras and books of Science and Philosophy. The pride of the Rajput races was conciliated by taking in marriage the princesses of

Jaipur and Jodhpur, and by conferring equal or superior commands on those princes. These latter had been hitherto treated as enemies. They were now welcome as the props of the empire, and Maharaja Bhagavandas, his great nephews Mansingh, for some time Governor of Bengal and Kabul, Raja Todar Mal and the Brahmin companion of the Emperor, Raja Birbal, these were welcomed to court and trusted in the full consciousness that their interests were the same as those of the Mussalman noblemen. The Emperor himself guided by such counsel of his Hindu and Mahomedan nobles became the real founder of the union between the two races and his policy for a hundred years guided and swayed the councils of the empire. A fusion of the two races was sought to be made firmer still by the establishment of a religion of the Din-i-ilahi in which the best points both of the Mahomedan, Hindu and other faiths were sought to be incorporated. Invidious taxation and privileges were done away with, and toleration for all faiths became the universal law of the empire. To conciliate his subjects, Akbar abjured the use of flesh except on four special occasions in the year, and he joined in the religious rites observed by his Hindu queens. In regard to the particular customs of the people relating to points where natural humanity was shocked in a way to make union impossible, Akbar strove by wise encouragement, and stern control where necessary, to help the growth of better ideas. Sati was virtually abolished by being placed under restraint which nobody could find fault with. Re-marriage was encouraged, and marriage before puberty was prohibited. In these and a hundred other ways the fusion of the races and of their many faiths was sought to be accomplished with a success which was justified by the results for a hundred years. This process of removing all causes of friction and establishing accord went on without interruption during the reigns of Akbar, Jehangir and Shahjahan. Shahjahans eldest son, Dara Sheko, was himself an author of no mean repute. He translated the Upanishads, and wrote a work in which he sought to reconcile the Brahmin religion with the Mahomedan faith. He died in 1659. This period of a hundred years may be regarded as the halcyon period of Indian history when the Hindu and Mahomedan races acted in full accord. If in place of Aurangzed, Dara Sheko had succeeded to power as the eldest son of Shahjahan, the influences set on foot by the genius of Akbar would have gathered strength and possibly averted the collapse of the Mogul power for another century. This was, however, not to be so, and with Aurangzeb's ascent to the throne, a change of system commenced which gathered force during the long time that this emperor reigned. Even Aurangzeb, had, however, to follow the traditions of his three predecessors. He could not dispense with Jai Singh or Jaswant Singh who were his principal military commanders. In the reign of his son, the whole provinces under him were governed by Rajput Kayastha and other governors. The revival of fanatic bigotry was kept in check by the presence of these great Rajput chiefs, one of whom, on the re-imposition of the Zezia, addressed to the Emperor a protest couched in unmistakable terms that the God of Islam was also the God of the Hindus, and the subject of both races merited equal treatment. Aurangzeb unfortunately did not listen to this advice, and the result was, that the empire built by Akbar went to pieces even when Aurangzeb was alive. No one was more aware of his failure than Aurangzeb himself who, in his last moments, admitted that his whole life was a mistake. The Marathas in the South, the Sikhs in the North, and the Rajput States helped in the dismemberment of the empire in the reigns of his immediate successors, with the result that nearly the whole of India was restored to its native Hindu sovereigns except Bengal, Oudh and the Deccan Hyderabad. It will be seen from this that far from suffering from decay and corruption, the native races gathered strength by reason of the Mahomedan rule when it was directed by the wise counsel of those Mahomedan and Hindu statesmen who sought the weal of the country by a policy of toleration and equality. Since the time of Asoka, the element of strength born of union was wanting in the old Hindu dynasties which succumbed so easily to the Mahomedan invaders.

Besides this source of strength, there can be no doubt that in a hundred other ways the Mahomedan domination helped to refine the tastes and manners of the Hindus. The art of government was better understood by the Mahomedans than by the old Hindu sovereigns. The art was also singularly defective till the Mahomedans came. They brought in the use of gunpowder and artillery; in the words of Babar, they "taught ingenuity and mechanical invention in a number of handicraft arts"; the very nomenclature of which being made up of non-Hindu words, shows their foreign origin. They introduced candles, paper, glass and household furniture and saddlery. They improved the knowledge of the people in music—instrumental and vocal, medicine and astronomy, and their example was followed by the Hindus in the perversions of both these sciences, astrology and alchemy, geography and history were first made possible departments of knowledge and literature by their example. They made roads, aqueducts, canals, caravansaries and the post office, and introduced the best specimens of architecture, and improved our gardening and made us acquainted with a taste of new fruits and flowers. The revenue system, as introduced by Todar Mal in Akbar's time, is the basis of the revenue system up to the present day. They carried on the entire commerce by sea with distant regions, and made India feel that it was a portion of the inhabited world with relations with all and not cut off from all social intercourse. In all these respects, the civilization of the united Hindu and Muslim powers, represented by the Moguls at Delhi, was a distinct advance beyond what was possible before the tenth century of the Christian era.

More lasting benefits have, however, accrued by this contact in the higher tone it has given to the religion and thoughts of the people. In this respect both the Mahomedans and Hindus benefited by contact with one another. As regards the Mahomedans, their own historians admitted that the sufi heresy gathered strength from contact with the Hindu teachers, and made many Mahomedans believe in transmigration and in the final union of the soul with Supreme spirit. The Moharam festival and Saint worship are the best evidence of the way in which the Mahomedans were influenced by Hindu ideas. We are more directly concerned with the way in which this contact has affected the Hindus. The prevailing tone of Pantheism had established a toleration for polytheism among our most revered ancient teachers who rested content with separating the few from the many, and established no bridge between them. This separation of the old religion has prevented its higher precept from becoming the common position of whole races. Under the purely Hindu system, the intellect may admit, but the heart declines to allow a common platform to all people in the sight of God. The Vaishnava movement, however, has succeeded in establishing the bridge noted above, and there can be no doubt that the hands of the followers of Ramananda, especially the Kabir Panthis, Malikdasis, Dadu Panthis, the followers of Mirabai, of Lord Gauranga, on the Bengal side, and Baba Nanak in the punjab in the fifteenth and sixteenth centuries, the followers of Tukaram, Ekanath and Namdev, in the Deccan, Baba Lalis, Pranathis, Sadhs, the Satnamis, the Shivanarayans and the followers of Mahant Ramacharan of the last two centuries this elevation and the purification of the Hindu mind was accomplished to an extent which very few at the present moment realize in all its significance. The Brahmo and the Arya Samaj movements of this century are the continuations of this ethical and spiritual growth. Caste, idolatry, polytheism and gross conceptions of purity and pollution were the precise points in which the Mahomedans and the Hindus were most opposed to one another, and all the sects named above had this general characteristic that they were opposed to these defects in the character of our people. Nanak's watchword was that he was neither Hindu nor Mahomedan, but that he was a worshipper of the Nairankar or the formless. His first companion was a Mahomedan and his teacher is said to have been also a Mahomedan. Lord Gauranga had also Mahomedan disciples. Mahomedan saints like Shaikh Mahomed, Shaikh Farid and Mahomed Kazi were respected both by Hindus and Mahomedans. The abuses of Polytheism were checked by the devotion to one object of worship which in the case of many of these Vaishnava sects was supreme God, the Paramathma and the abuses of caste were controlled by conceding to all Hindus and Mahomedans alike the right to worship and love of one god who was the god of all. In the case of the Sikhs the Puritanic spirit even developed under persecution, into a coarse imitation of the Mahomedan fanaticism directed against the Mahomedans themselves, but in the case of the other sectaries, both old and new, tolerant and the suffering spirit of Vaishnavism has prevailed, breathing peace and goodwill towards all.

Such are the chief features of the influences resulting from the contact of Mahomedans and Hindus in Northern India. They brought about a fusion of thoughts and ideas which benefited both communities making the Mahomedans less bigoted and the Hindus more puritanic and more singleminded in their devotion. There was nothing like this to be found in Southern India as described by Dubois where the Hindu sectarian spirit intensified caste, pride and idolatrous observances. The fusion would have been more complete but for the revival of fanaticism for which Aurangzeb must be held chiefly responsible. Owing to the circumstances, the work of fusion was left incomplete; and in the course of years, both the communities have developed weaknesses of a character which still need the disciplining process to be continued for a longer time under other masters. Both Hindus and Mahomedans lack many of those virtues represented by the love of order and regulated authority. Both are wanting in the love of municipal freedom, in the exercise of virtues necessary for civic life and in aptitude for mechanical skill in the love of science and research, in the love and daring and adventurous discovery, the resolution to master difficulties and in chivalrous respect for womankind. Neither the old Hindu, nor the old Mahomedan civilization was in a condition to train these virtues in a way to bring up the races of India on a level with those of Western Europe, and so the work of education had to be renewed, and it has now been going on for the past century and more under the Pax Britannica with results which all of us have witnessed in ourselves.

If the lessons of the past have any value, one thing is quite clear, *viz.*, that in this vast country no progress is possible unless both Hindus and Mahomedans join hands together and are determined to follow the lead of the men who flourished in Akbar's time and were his chief advisors and councillors and sedulously avoid the mistakes which were committed by his great-grandson Aurangzeb. Joint action from a sense of common interest and a common desire to bring about the fusion of the thoughts and feelings of men so as to tolerate small differences and bring about concord, these were the chief aims kept in view by Akbar and formed the principle of the new divine faith formulated in the Din-i-ilahi. Every effort on the part of either Hindus or Mahomedans to regard their interests as separated and distinct and every attempt made by the two communities to create separate schools and interests among themselves, and not to heal up the wounds inflicted by mutual hatred of caste and creed, must be deprecated on all hands. It is to be feared that this lesson has not been sufficiently kept in mind by the leaders of both communities in their struggle for existence and in the acquisition of power and predominance during recent years. There is at times a great danger of the work of Akbar being undone by losing sight of this great lesson which the history of his reign and that of his two successors is so well calculated to teach. The conference which brings us together is especially intended for the propagation of this "Din" or "Dharma", and it is in connection with that message chiefly that I have ventured to speak to you to-day on this important subject. The ills that we are suffering from are most of them self-inflicted evils, the cure of which is to a large extent in our own hands. Looking at the series of measures which Akbar adopted in his time to cure these evils, one feels how correct was his vision when he and his advisers put their hands on those very defects in our national character which need to be remedied first before we venture on higher enterprises. Pursuit of high ideas, mutual sympathy and co-operation, perfect tolerance, a correct understanding of the diseases from which the body politic is suffering and an earnest desire to apply suitable remedies, this is the work cut out for the present generation. The awakening has commenced as is witnessed by the fact that we are met in this place from such distance for joint consultation and action. All that is needed is that we must put our hands to the plough and face the strife and the struggle. The success already achieved warrants to expectation that, if we persevere on right lines, the goal we have in view may be attained. That goal is not any particular advantage to be gained in power and wealth. It is represented by the efforts to attain it, the expansion and evolution of the heart and the mind which all make us stronger and braver, purer and truer men. This is at least the lesson I draw from our more recent history of the past thousand years, and if those centuries have rolled away to no purpose over our heads, our cause is no doubt hopeless beyond cure. That is, however, not the faith in me; and I feel sure it is not the faith that moves you in the great struggle against our own weak selves than which nothing is more fatal to our individual and collective growth. Both Hindus and Mahomedans have their work cutout in this struggle. In the backwardness of female education, in the disposition to overleap the bounds of their own religion, in matters of temperance, in their internal dissensions between castes and creeds, in the indulgence of impure speech, thought and action on occasions when they are disposed to enjoy themselves in the abuses of many customs in regard to unequal and polygamous marriages, in their desire to be extravagant in their expenditure on such occasions, in the neglect of regulated charity, in the decay of public spirit, in insisting on the proper management of endowments—in these and other matters, both communities are equal sinners and there is, thus, much ground for improvement on common lines. Of course, the Hindus, being by far the majority of the population, have other difficulties of their own to combat with and they are trying, in their gatherings of separate castes and communities, to remedy them each in their own way. But without co-operation and conjoined action of all communities, success is not possible, and it is on that account that the general conference is held in different places each year to rouse local interest, and help people, in their separate efforts by a knowledge of what their friends similarly situated are doing in other parts. This is the reason of our meeting here and I trust that this message I have attempted to deliver to you on this occasion will satisfy you that we cannot conceive a nobler work than the one for which we have met here to-day.

WOMESH CHUNDER BONNERJEE
(1844-1906)

WOMESH CHUNDER BONNERJEE

Indian Grievances

Speech before a Public Meeting held at the Town Hall in Northampton on 21 August 1888 to Consider 'India's Wrongs and English Remedies'

Mr. Bonnerjee who was cordially welcomed said: Mr. Mayor, Ladies and Gentlemen,—You have come to-night to hear Indian grievances discussed before you, and I shall not therefore, follow my friend, Mr. Naoroji in stating to you the great benefits which most undoubtedly you have conferred upon my country. My task is to lay before you the grievances of that country in order that you may consider them and see for yourselves whether there are no means by which to redress them. Now the first grievance that we labour under is that there is no responsible Government for India at all. ("Hear, hear" from Mr. Bradlaugh). The Government of India is in the hands of one of Her Majesty's principal Secretaries of State called the Secretary of State for India, who is assisted by a Council, but would you believe it, that this gentleman, the Secretary of State and his Council, are sometimes ignorant of things which private members of Parliament are in possession of fully? (Cries of "Shame" and laughter). The other day I had the great privilege of listening to your respected representative in the House of Commons—(loud cheers)—and in the course of his speech he was able to tell the under Secretary of State that he knew a good deal more of what was going on in connection with the Irrawaddy Flotilla Company than the Secretary and his advisers did in this country (Cheers). When any question is asked in the House of Commons of the Under-Secretary the answer invariably is—"The Secretary of State has no official knowledge of the matter"—(laughter)—and unless the honourable member putting the question is persistent, and after a short time again puts the question, it seems to me that the Secretary of State never has any official knowledge of anything under the sun in India. (Laughter and cheers). Then the Secretary of State entirely dependent upon the advice he receives from India and he does not seem to have in his possession any machinery by which it is possible for him to check what the officials in India send to him as a true account of what is taking place. ("Shame"). I need not go further than just across St. George's Channel to remind you that the official information sent over is very different from the information given from other sources you are getting daily. (Cheers). I don't for one moment mean to say that the condition of India is like the condition of Ireland. Thank goodness, we are ever so much better off than the people in Ireland (hear, hear), but I bring forward the case of Ireland for the purpose of showing you that official information is not in every instance true information. (Cheers). In India the supreme rule is in the hands of the Viceroy and his Council. They act from the information which they receive from the district officials. However clever, however able, however well-meaning, however inclined to do justice the Viceroy may be, he is more or less in the hands of those who have to administer the country in the districts, in the places where the people congregate, where the people lead their daily lives, and it is the officials who are entrusted with the charge of these districts who have the weal or woe of the country in their hands, and when you appeal against any action of theirs to the Viceroy you do not get any reply for months and months, and as a matter of fact the only reply vouchsafed is that the Viceroy sees no reason to interfere. (Cries of "Shame"). To a certain extent this state of things must be so, but it need not be so in the hard and fast way in which it is being carried out and if we had some voice in the Government of our country there is no doubt we should be able to put questions of administrative details to the officers responsible in the Council for the Government, and we should be able to stir the members of the Government up to do, what I have no doubt they conscientiously wish to do—namely, good to the people of India (Cheers). Now, I will give you two instances to show how the present system of Government has instead of advancing the country done very much to retard it for a certain time. The Legislative Councils, as my friend Mr. Naoroji has told you, pass laws—the local Councils for the Provinces represented by them, the Supreme Council for the whole of India. Now, these Councils, particularly in the Viceroy's Council, seem to be a sort of hothouse for English gentlemen going out there to carry out their own views. They try their theories in this country, and absolutely fail, but somehow they manage to get seats in the Indian Council in Calcutta, and the things that had been scouted in this country are carried out there, notwithstanding the position and clamour and protest of the people ("Shame"). From 1861 to 1872 we had in India a Criminal Procedure Code which had been drafted by no less an authority than the illustrious Thomas Babington Macaulay. It had been looked over very carefully by no less an authority than Sir Barnes Peacock, whose name you may have heard as being Chief Justice in Bengal for many years, and as now being one of the members of her Majesty's Privy Council. Several other persons well acquainted with the law had perfected this code. Under this code we were allowed trial by jury in such districts the Local Government considered we were fit to have trial by jury (Cheers). I may mention there is no single district where trial by jury may not be safely introduced at the present time (cheers), but that is, by the way. The verdicts of juries were final. The prisoner had the right of carrying his case, if convicted, to higher courts if there were any points of law to be urged on his behalf. That remained the law, and worked very well indeed to a very considerable extent. In the year 1870, to our very great misfortune, Sir James Fitzjames Stephen was appointed law member of the Viceroy's Council. He went out to India and the first thing he took in hand was called "The Amendment of the Criminal Procedure Court." That amendment consisted in this—that he took away the finality from the verdict of the jury; he gave the power which no judge in India had ever possessed before, of enhancing sentences on appeal; and he made the Criminal Procedure Code almost Draconian in its severity. (loud cries of "shame"). You have, no doubt, heard that the people of India are as law-abiding as any people on the earth—(cheers)—and yet in a country like that the Criminal Procedure Code has been made the severest of any in the civilised world. ("shame" and sensation.) I will tell you what happened under this law. This is an instance, you may call it an extreme instance, but it took place, and there are others which take place everyday, to the great oppression of the people of the country, who protest, but nobody listens to their protest. ("shame"). A man was tried in one of the districts in Bengal for murder. The trial took place, not before a jury, but before what are called assessors —two assessors and a judge, the judge concurring with the two assessors, found the man not guilty of murder, but found him guilty of manslaughter, and sentenced him to hard labour for five years. He appealed against his conviction—he had right of appeal, the trial having been held with the aid of assessors and not with the aid of a jury. The case came before the High Court of Calcutta. He was a poor man and could not be properly represented. The judges upset the conviction as regards manslaughter, found this man guilty of murder, sentenced him to be hanged, and notwithstanding petitions for mercy from nearly the whole country that man was hanged (great sensation, and loud cries of shame). He had in the meantime undergone nearly two months of imprisonment, so that he was kept in rigorous imprisonment for two month at the end of that was hanged ("shame"). Now this created such a shock in the minds of the people that it is impossible to describe the sensation in the country at the time; everybody wept aloud almost, but there was nobody to take any notice of that. Our district officers thought that the prestige of the High Court would be lost if the Government interfered and allowed that man to live. The High Court had the power, and could have sentenced him to transportation for life; but no—the man was sentenced to be hanged, and hanged he was accordingly ("shame", "shame"). There are many instances where a man has been fined; after Sir James Fitzjames Stephen's law he has appealed, and the result has been that the judges, instead of affirming the fine, have sent him to hard labour for many months ("shame"). How I saw the scenes created in this country when it was reported, and truly reported, that some Country Court judges in Ireland had enhanced the sentences on appeal. There was a tremendous outburst (cheers), and the result was that even Mr. Balfour was obliged to send instructions to his Country Court judges not to enhance sentences on appeal (cheers). But a thing like this goes on in India almost every day. The people cry aloud against, but there is nobody to pay heed to their cry ("shame"). The way in which legislation is conducted in India is such that if I gave you instances you would cry "shame." This very Sir James Fitzjames Stephen passed what is called the Evidence Act for India. It is the substance of Pitt Taylor's book boiled down considerably. Well, one clause he has introduced is that at a criminal trial the previous conviction of any prisoner may be given in evidence at any stage. That is to say in the year of grace 1888 a man is charged with picking another persons pocket, you may give evidence against him that in 1830 he was guilty of bigamy (laughter). And what do you think is the reason given for this. Sir James Fitzjames Stephen says in his report to the Legislative Council: "it is said that evidence of this description may prejudice the prisoner. My answer is that if the prisoner is guilty"—mark the logic—"if the prisoner is guilty I do not see why he should not be prejudiced, the object of giving evidence against a man being to show whether he is guilty or not." And laws of this description have been passed, people have protested, but there is no heed paid to these protests. Representative institutions and other things which go to make up a civilised country, only exist for the happiness and well-being of the people. If without giving us representative institutions you can discover something by which the people will be able to lead a happy and contented life, have all their aspirations humanly speaking satisfied, I am perfectly certain that my countrymen would rejoice at the idea; but at present no one has been able to discover anything better than such institutions as are possessed more or less by other countries in the civilized world. But it is not even representative institutions in the form that exist in this country that we want. We say whether you admit it or whether you do not admit it, you are dependent for the good Government of our country upon the advice you must necessarily seek from the people themselves (cheers). Officials in India do not admit it, but they do it. If they have a difficult question to deal with, they call together this man and that man and they call together a third man, being natives of the country, with whom they discuss the matter. These persons, as has been pointed out to you, are not responsible to anybody and they may give such answer as may chime in with the views known to be held by the district officer; and instead of getting good advice from responsible persons, the district officer generally gets advice that leads him to take action not in accord with the will of the country. The subject of India, like the country itself, is a very vast one, and I am afraid, if I were to detain you from now till the morning, I should not be able to exhaust it (cheers and a voice "go on"). You will have, I am glad to say, the opportunity of hearing my friend Mr. Bradlaugh (loud cheers), and he will make that clear to you which, I probably, have not been able to do. For good or for evil India has become bound up with you (cheers). You cannot, having carried her so far, turn her adrift, and of her own will India will never ask to be allowed to go adrift (loud cheering). It is necessary for the peace of both countries—

this great country as well as her great dependency—that some method should be devised by which the people will be more contented, the people will get more to eat (cheers), the people will be able to discharge the duties of citizenship (cheers). You are a superior nation, you are governing the country, and it behoved you, one and all, to take pride in measures which will be a blessing not only to India, but to this country (renewed cheering).

BUDRUDIN TYABJI
(1844-1906)

BUDRUDIN TYABJI

Native Press

Speech in Bombay on 8 July 1896 in a Meeting Convened to Denounce Recent Murders Which Had Been Condoned by Some Newspapers

Gentlemen:—The object of my convening this meeting is to express our abhorrence of the recent murders at Poona, and to denounce the seditious, disloyal, defamatory and mischievous writings in the Urdu newspapers. Every loyal citizen must mourn the dastardly murders and must sympathise with the families of the murdered people and with Government whom they serve so well. Our duty is plain enough. We range ourselves firmly and decidedly on the side of Government and order. We denounce the miscreants and their horrible deeds. We pray they may be speedily brought to justice and receive the punishment they so richly deserve. It Is fortunate that no suspicion rests on the Mussulmans. This is due to their well known loyalty, to the good sense and moderation of their leaders, and to the absence of any disloyal or seditious writings on their part at Poona. Fortunately there are not so far as I know, any Islami papers at Poona against which charges of disaffection or sedition can be brought. Can we say the same thing regarding all Urdu newspapers published in Bombay? I acknowledge with pride and satisfaction that, if we take India as a whole, the Mussulman newspapers are singularly free from seditious writings. I can say the same thing of many of the Mussulman newspapers published in Bombay. Unfortunately, however, there are black sheep among us in Bombay. There are some papers the editors of which seem to have no conception of their real duties. Their sole object is to malign and defame everybody provided only he is respectable and enjoys the esteem of his fellow-subjects or does his duty either as an offender of Government or as an honest public spirited and high-minded citizen. Government collectively, and the highest and most prominent officers of Government individually, are the subjects of outrageous attacks for which there can be suggested no possible justification. I do not believe they know the meaning of "disaffection," for which the offender is liable to be transported for life under section 124-A of the Indian Penal Code. They confound liberty with licence, and criticism with abuse. These papers are published by ignorant men with absolutely no knowledge of public affairs or the motives of Government and the springs which move Government. They have no sense of their responsibility and do not appear to understand the meaning or force or effect or tendency of the words they so glibly employ. They seem to think that the more they misrepresent the actions of Government or the motives of public officers, the stronger and fouler the language they use, the better their papers sell. This is all they care for. The writers, I know, take deliberate and malicious advantage of the fact that they are too contemptible to be taken notice of either by Government or by private individuals. The contemptuous tolerance has however, had a most pernicious effect upon these papers. They have become bolder and more hardened and more violent and outrageous. It is true that their scandalous writings do not circulate among the respectable classes. But, unfortunately, they circulate among the lower, more ignorant, more excitable, more inflammatory portion of our community. They are read in Bazaars and the Coffee houses, and the more violent their language, the more eagerly they are purchased. Is not this a great evil? Is it not the duty of Government and of all loyal and honest citizens to put it down? Has it not reached a point when tolerance is likely to be mistaken for weakness? What, then, is the remedy? Am I an advocate of repressive legislation? Am I suggesting the curtailment of liberty of speech by any new enactment? Certainly not. The whole object of my convening this meeting is to prove that there is no need for any such measures, that the remedy lies ready in the hands of Government and of the community, and that it has only to be used and applied to put an end to this evil. So far as Government is concerned I believe the present law is amply sufficient. It gives perfect freedom of speech, but punishes disaffection, that is to say, punishes malicious attempts to produce in the minds of people feelings of enmity, or hatred, or discontent against Government. What I should advise is this. Let bygones be bygones, but let Government, let us all watch the newspapers carefully in the future. If these seditious and defamatory writings are continued let the writers be prosecuted. We shall then see whether the present law is sufficient or not. I myself believe that there would not be the slightest difficulty in obtaining a conviction of the miscreants I have in view. But, gentlemen, in a case like this, it is not to Government that we ought to look. We have the remedy in our own hands. If none of us read them, or tolerated them directly or indirectly, these wretched papers would cease to exist to-morrow. It is to you, then, and to those whom you can influence, it is to the good common sense and to the loyalty to the community at large, it is to their sense of fairness, justice and honesty and leniency far more than to any repressive legislation that I look for the extinction of this growing evil.

RASH BIHARI GHOSE
(1845-1921)

RASH BIHARI GHOSE

The Sins of Lord Curzon

Speech at Calcutta Town Hall on 10 March 1905 Deprecating Curzon's Convocation Address at Calcutta University in which He Had Denigrated Indians

Gentlemen,

In rising to address you I must begin with a word or two about myself, but I promise to be very brief as an immoderate use of the first personal pronoun appears to me to be much more offensive than an immoderate use of adjectives. The first thing that I have to say about myself is that I cannot claim to be a hero of a hundred platforms or even of one, nor am I a habitual revealer of authority. I can also solemnly affirm that I have never taken any part in the debates of the Indian National Congress. And if I am here this afternoon, it is not because I take any delight in railing at Government but because I honestly believe that Lord Curzon is lacking in that breadth of vision, tactfulness and flexibility of temper which we naturally expect in one occupying the unique position of an Indian Viceroy.

His Lordship, if I may say so without impertinence, is undoubtedly possessed of great and varied gifts, but the gods are jealous and it would be flattery which, as we all know, his Lordship hates, to affirm that he possesses in any large measure those qualities, which are so essential in the representative of His Majesty in this country. Does anybody doubt it? Let him read the chancellor's speech on the last Convocation day of the Calcutta University. The style of that speech was certainly not Asiatic. Nobody could accuse Lord Curzon of such an offence against good taste. But did it possess the Attic grace and lightness? Decidedly not. The whole speech was in, what Matthew

Arnold calls, the Corinthion style—a style—which His Lordship strongly urged our young men to avoid.

There was not the least trace of light or sweetness in that speech which was redolent, not of the "olive grove of the Academy" but of the House of Commons, or perhaps it would be truer to say of the hustings. It was full of sarcasms, full of sneers in which sympathy with the people of this country who may be said to be wards of England was conspicuous only by its absence.

One of the greatest political figures in England said on a memorable occasion that he did not know how to frame an indictment against a whole nation but Lord Curzon, dressed in the Chancellor's robe and a brief little authority, was able to frame an indictment not only against the people of India, but also against all the various nations of Asia—Asia which gave to the world Gautama Buddha. Jesus Christ and Mahomed who may not have taught men how to rule but who certainly taught them how to live and how to die.

The truth is the theories of race, as Sir Henry Maine tells us, have little merit except the facility which they give to some persons, half educated, writers of doggerels, for instance, to build on them inferences tremendously out of proportion to the mental labour which they cost the builder. And in this context, I would venture to ask His Lordship, who is a scholar, if praise is not often given to successful deception in the ancient classical literature of the West on which the youths of Europe arc nurtured even at the present day?

In one of his numerous speeches—there are very few brilliant flashes of silence—Lord Curzon said—"You will never rule the East except through the heart." Is the Convocation speech of His Lordship likely to win our affection? And yet it is easy enough to touch our hearts, as easy, say, as it is, to pass a Validating Act through the Viceroy's Council.

One word more before I part with this painful topic. The Indian, says Lord Curzon, is most certainly a citizen of the British Empire, and His Lordship is indignant at the idea that he is a mere hewer of wood and drawer of water, but nobody, I think, would take such a statement literally any more than His Lordship's reference to High Court Judges, Ministers of Native States and High Executive and Judicial officers in the service of Government. His Lordship, however, has no reason to be surprised if in moments of spleen such expressions occasionally drop from some of my young and impulsive countrymen,—for I find that in his Guildhall speech, Lord Curzon said. "It is with Indian coolie labour that you exploit the plantations equally of Dametora and Natal, with Indian-trained officers that you irrigate Egypt and dam the Nile, with Indian forest officers that you tap the resources of Central Africa and Siam; with Indian Surveyors that you explore all the hidden places of the earth." In this picture drawn by the hand of no mean artist, the Indian stands in the foreground, it is true, but only you will notice, as a tiller of the earth, making it flow with milk and honey for strangers.

I will now pass on to some of the legislative and administrative measures of His Lordship. The history of the present Calcutta Municipal Act is familiar, to you all, and I need not relate it-, but every one of you may not know that, though Sir Alexander Mackenzie sought to make the Chairman independent of the Corporation in the discharge of his executive duties, we owe the curtailment of the elected element in the new Corporation to Lord Curzon who proposed the reduction as a most effective though "hitherto unsuggested check" upon the abuses and anomalies which, it was said, had grown up under the old system. Sir Alexander Mackenzie would have at least left us the shadow of self-government, but to Lord Curzon belongs the credit of reducing it to the shadow of a mere shade. The chastisement administered by His Lordship was thus severer than that proposed by his Lieutenant. The present Municipal Act is now generally admitted to have been a blunder which, in such cases, means a good deal.

And this leads me to remark that the proposed partition of Bengal is also an "unsuggested check", should I be very wrong in saying, on the struggling sentiments and stifled aspirations of the people of Bengal. The alarm which the proposal created is, I can solemly assert, perfectly genuine and has spread even to those who are ordinarily in the habit of regarding Government measures as the dispensations of a mysterious power. The grounds on which our opposition to the threatened partition is based were so fully discussed by Sir Henry Cotton in this very hall, a short time ago that it would be a work of supererogation to re-state them on the present occasion. The Viceroy, however, seems to have made up his mind and is determined to divide Bengal. And in connection with the question I may mention that text-books for primary schools are henceforth to be compiled in local dialects, because our administrators are particularly solicitous for the welfare of the silent and inarticulate masses who, if they learned to speak at all, should, they think, learn to speak only in their own native dialects. Whether persons who are not administrators are likely to regard the proposal in the same light is a question which I will not pause to discuss. I may, however, point out that if our officials were possessed of the gift of seeing themselves as others see them, they would command much greater respect.

The abolition of the competitive test would also seem to be another unsuggested reform. It is true the Public Service Commission, presided over by Sir Charles Aitchison, reported that in parts of the country where the general educational conditions are more advanced than elsewhere, especially the Presidencies of Madras and Bombay and the lower provinces of Bengal, a system of open competition would give satisfaction to some important classes of the community and would meet objections that are justly felt in a system of nomination. But Lord Curzon is wiser than the members of the Public Service Commission, wiser than Mill, wiser than Macaulay, wiser than the distinguished statesmen who accomplished a similar reform in the Civil Service in England. It may be true that the competitive system has some drawbacks, but experience has shown that it everywhere increases the efficiency of the public service and stimulates the acquisition of knowledge. Above all, as a thoughtful writer who is also a statesman has observed, it strengthens the social feeling for the maxim that the career should be open to the talents. Lord Curzon, however, is anxious to free the Intellectual activities of the Indian people, keen and restless as they are, from the paralysing clutch of examinations, for which every idle lad in this country ought, I think, to be grateful to him.

And this brings me to the Universities Act, one of the gifts of Lord Curzon to this country which my countrymen refuse to accept, because they regard it with distrust. By this Act the whole system of higher education has been practically placed under official control. This is not all. Lord Curzon's measure will place University education beyond the reach of many boys belonging to the middle class. And here, perhaps, I may be permitted to remark that to talk of the highest mental culture as the sole aim of University training betrays a singular misconception of the conditions of Indian life. Our students go to the Universities in such large numbers because they cannot otherwise enter any of the learned professions or even qualify themselves for service under Government. I would also point out that education, though it may not reach a very high standard, is still a desirable thing, on the principle that half a loaf is better than no bread. The fallacy that lurks in Pope's well known couplet has been so clearly exposed by Macaulay, Whately, John Stuart Mill and last though not least by Mr. Morley, and I will not occupy your time with discussing it. One word more. The standard of education will never be improved either by Universities Acts or Validating Acts. It can only be done by attracting to this country, as teachers of our youth, men distinguished by their scholarship or by their scientific attainments, like those who occupy the chairs in European Universities.

The Official Secrets Act is another measure which we owe to Lord Curzon's Government. It was passed in the face of the unanimous opposition of both communities. The *Englishman*, the leading newspaper, thus spoke of the Bill when it was before the Council: Very grave rumours, which we mention for what they are worth, credit the Government of India with bringing forward amendments to the Official Secrets Bill, which leave its principal defects untouched. What those defects are have been clearly and unmistakably pointed out and they are so serious that the Viceroy, speaking from his place in the Legislative Council December, professed to stand aghast at the picture of official Machiavellianism which they reveal. His Excellency also professed to have been moved by these criticisms and he gave a solemn pledge that so far as in him lay, the provisions which were so universally execrated would be modified or withdrawn. "I believe," said Lord Curzon, "that when the Select Committee meet they will find that their labours are neither so severe nor so contentious as has been supposed, and that a satisfactory measure can be placed upon the Statute Book which need not strike terror into the heart of a single innocent person." This meant nothing if it did not mean that the Government of India has been impressed by the arguments employed against the Bill and that it had decided to meet them in the spirit of real concession. The speech was so interpreted by the Press which, although it was absolutely unanimous in opposing the measure, decided to intermit its criticism and to wait for the promised amendments. It was so interpreted by the leading commercial bodies which have only refrained from addressing Government on the ground that, after the Viceroy's speech, this obnoxious measure was likely to be wholly recast. If it be true, however, that the divulgence of civil secrets is still to be penalized, we have not the slightest hesitation in saying that one at least of its worst features is being retained. The public is in no mood to be treated in such a manner and it becomes our duty to warn the Government that if this provision or any of the other cardinal vices of the Bill remain, it must make up its mind to the renewal of agitation which will not slacken until the measure has been withdrawn or repealed. But Lord Curzon remained unmoved and the Bill was passed into law, for His Lordship seems only to care for the opinion of the inarticulate masses—"whose hearts," I may mention in passing, according to Lord Curzon, had been touched with the idea of a common sentiment and a common claim by the Delhi Durbar and in whom His Lordship has noticed "a steady and growing advance in loyalty" during his administration.

"Public opinion in India," said His Lordship from his place as Chancellor of the Calcutta University, "cannot for a long time be the opinion of the public that is of the masses because they are uneducated and have no opinion in political matters at all." This probably is the reason why so little attention is paid to the views of the elected members in the Legislative Councils who sit there merely to play the part of the chorus in a Greek tragedy. But surely we cannot be asked to wait till the masses who do not know what it is to have a full meal from year's end to year's end cease to feel the pangs of hunger and become sufficiently educated to discuss the ways of a foreign bureaucracy. In that case we shall have to wait for that dim and distant future when, according to Lord Curzon's forecast, some approach to all Indian nation will have been evolved. His Lordship also said that public opinion if it is to have any weight must be coordinated with necessities and interests and desires of the community who are perhaps hardly capable of formulating an opinion of their own. So long as this co-ordination is not achieved no weight, it would seem, should be attached to public opinion in this country and I imagine that it was on this account that the Government of Lord Curzon paid no attention to the opinion of the educated minority of the Official

Secrets Act, the Universities Act or the recent Validating Act which compromised the dignity alike of the Legislative Council and of His Majesty's Judges.

And this reminds me that in the course of the Convocation speech Lord Curzon said, "of course, in India it is very difficult to create or to give utterance to a public opinion that is really representative because there are so many different classes whose interests do not always coincide-, for instance the English and the Indians, and the Hindus and the Mahomedans, the officials and non-officials, the agriculturists and the industrialists." If Lord Curzon is right, there can be no such thing as true public opinion even in England, for there are many questions on which controversies between different classes of the community must arise from time to time. To take one example out of many, the interests of the capitalists are frequently in conflict with those of the working man. Is it therefore to be said that public opinion in England is merely sectional. So in this country questions may arise on which the Englishman may be divided against the Indian, the Hindu against the Mahomedan, the agriculturist against the industrialist, but surely where there is no such conflict the Government cannot ignore the opinion of the educated classes as an altogether negligible quantity.

The truth is, Lord Curzon believes whatever he desires and is never troubled with any misgivings. His Lordship also seems to think that he has got, to use a homely phrase, a clean slate, and that whatever is, is wrong. Now energy and a zeal for reform are no doubt excellent things in their way, but an excess of either is not regarded as a virtue in a statesman.

Gentlemen, we all admire Lord Curzon's undoubted abilities, his intense devotion to duty and his monumental industry. Simla is certainly no longer a Cupua. We do not also distrust his love for India which he has told us is next to his own country, the nearest to his heart, nor are we offended with him because he is rather fond of playing the part of the candid friend. But we doubt, with all deference, his possession of those higher qualities of statesmanship which are essential in a ruler of men and in none perhaps more essential than in an Indian Viceroy. The Convocation speech betrays the limitation of His Lordship in a manner not to be mistaken.

To sum up, almost all His Lordship's measures have tended towards strengthening the Simla bureaucracy. I thank the Englishman for teaching me the word, our system of Administration. This has been specially shown by his attack on Municipal Self-Government in the case of the Calcutta Corporation; his Education Act, which destroys the independence of the Universities and converts them into a department of Government, and his measures against the freedom of the Press. The result has certainly not been "a steady and growing advance in the loyalty of the Indian people', of which Lord Curzon spoke with some unction to an English audience last year. Optimism, however, is blind. But the moving finger writes, and having writ moves on.

In one of his speeches Lord Curzon spoke of regard for our feelings, respect for our prejudices and deference even to our scruples. But the dominant note of his administration has been a disregard of public opinion and an impatience of criticism which betrays itself conspicuously in almost every word of his Convocation speech. It may be said of him, what Metternick said of an English statesman of the last century, that he is an audacious and passionate marksman ready to make arrows out of any wood.

In the very first speech that Lord Curzon delivered in India he said that he would act in a manner not unworthy of that august and benign sovereign whom he is privileged to represent. He also said that he would spare no efforts to fortify, to diffuse and encourage that feeling of loyalty to the English throne which holds together the diverse races and creeds of his country. Does His Lordship believe that his last Convocation speech fulfils these promises? His Lordship also said that sympathy shall be one of the key-notes of his administration. Is any sympathy discernible in his Convocation speech, any feeling for the sentiments of the people in his proposed partition of Bengal, any sympathy with the poor and struggling student who only seeks to earn a living by passing through the University? As for the educated classes all that Lord Curzon has to say is that "there are some people who clamour for boons which it is impossible to give." And here I may be permitted to remind His Lordship that though we are loyal to England, a country to which we owe so much, and though sufferance is the badge of all our tribe, we have like other men senses, affections and passions.

I trust I have not done any injustice to Lord Curzon, indeed, I think I might without any difficulty have made out a case; but the half is sometimes better than the whole. I have not said aught in malice and have carefully avoided rhetoric. Gentlemen, it Is always disagreeable to have to speak of ourselves, but I am bound to say that I am not one of those who purchase their opinions for an anna or less a day, nor am I in the habit of calumniating my opponents who consist exclusively of my learned friends at the Bar. I have also never taken part in the manufacture of public opinion, but if, in spite of my best endeavour to guard myself from those vices against which Lord Curzon raised his warning voice the other day, I have done any injustice to His Lordship, I can only console myself with the reflection that there are some infirmities from which the average man cannot altogether free himself "The contemporaries of superior men," observes Goethe, "may easily go wrong about them. Peculiarity decomposes them, the swift current of life disturbs the point of view and prevents them from understanding and appreciating such men."

PHEROZE SHAH MEHTA
(1845-1915)

PHEROZESHAH MEHTA

The Beneficent Results of the Visit of their Majesties King George and Queen Mary to India

Speech in Bombay on 3 February 1912 in a Public Meeting Convened on the Occasion of Their Majesties' Visit to India

Ladies and Gentlemen,

I am indeed as proud as I am grateful to you for the great honour you have done me in asking me to preside over a Public Meeting of the inhabitants of Bombay on so great and memorable an occasion as that which has brought us together here to-day. Perhaps the choice has fallen on me, because, with the single exception of our revered friend Mr. Dadabhai Naoroji, who, but for reasons of health, would have made an ideal Chairman on this occasion, my public life extends over that period of nearly half a century during which the drama of Indian history has unfolded itself in a marvellous manner. I may therefore be supposed to be able to realize more vividly and fully than others that wonderful transformation which, inaugurated by the sober and practical, and yet in the main, the righteous genius of British statesmanship, was fostered and promoted by the affection and sympathy of the great and good Queen Victoria, who even in the dark days of the Mutiny, inspired with her own lofty and noble spirit the policy embodied in our first Magna Charta—the Proclamation of 1858. That policy was consistently maintained and steadfastly emphasized by her great son and successor Edward VII. It has now received its culminating crown of glory at the personal hands of our illustrious Sovereign in a way that has electrified the whole country from one end to the other. His Imperial Majesty has, within the few short days of the Royal visit, revealed himself to us as one who combines in himself the sagacious head of a great and far-seeing statesman with a gentle and loving heart full of the tenderest regard and sympathy for his people. The great Poet Laureate of the Victorian era sang in prophetic strain of his "Beloved, revered" Sovereign, how

> "Statesmen at her Council met
> Who knew the seasons when to take
> Occasion by the hand, and make
> The bounds of freedom wider yet
> By shaping some august decree
> Which kept her throne unshaken still
> Broad-based upon her people's will."

Ladies and Gentlemen, the Poet-Laureate of the reign of her grandson may go still further, and say, that not only statesmen, as stalwart as of yore, met at his Council, but that he presided in person over them, the greatest statesman of them all, shaping august decrees, and coming with his Imperial Consort to announce them in his own person, proclaiming at the same time boons of far-reaching beneficence. Those boons have been rich and varied. But we must remember that the boons announced at the Coronation Durbar are not all the boons that he has conferred upon us.

Among others, there are two of priceless value, for which we are grateful. The first is the boon of the bright example which he has set as to how to regulate mutual treatment and intercourse between all his subjects—rulers and ruled—founded on mutual self-respect and human sympathy. The permeating influence of that example cannot fail to penetrate among all ranks of society and help in the solution of a problem which has caused the gravest anxiety among all friends of the British connexion, and has baffled the efforts of the best and wisest amongst us all to find a remedy. The second boon is, that, in drawing the hearts of all his subjects towards himself, their Common Sovereign, he has drawn closer the ties of peace, harmony and union among themselves, however differing in race, religion, or colour. I am confident that his parting appeal for union in his farewell speech in Bombay will not have been made in vain, and will powerfully help the efforts of men like Sir William Wedderburn, our friend Mr. Gokhale, and His Highness The Aga Khan who is proving himself not only a leader among Moslems, but a truly patriotic leader of all India. Ladies and Gentlemen, when I remember these wonderful results of the

Royal Visit, I think I may venture to claim, in some small measure, the gift of prophecy for, speaking in this very Hall at the Public Meeting convened to make arrangements for the reception of their Imperial Majesties, I ventured to say, you will pardon me for quoting from my own speech:—

> I cannot help wishing that I was a poet, a historian, and a statesman, all combined in one. For without this combination, without 'the vision and faculty divine' of the poet, the illuminating lore of the historian, and the penetrating comprehension of the statesman, it is almost impossible to give full and adequate expression to the dignity and grandeur of the occasion which we desire to celebrate, to its serious and sacred solemnity, to its pregnant and far-reaching symbolic significance for everything connected with the welfare, happiness and progress, indeed for all events moulding the lofty destinies of this magnificent land of ours. The occasion will not be a mere pageant, perhaps more gorgeous and dazzling than any that has gone before; it will not be a mere Royal visit of kindly interest and sympathy and mutual knowledge such as those we have been favoured with in the past.
>
> It will be a historic event of deeper significance and import than a pageant or a Royal Visit—this unprecedented advent of our Gracious Sovereign to announce in his own person his accession to the throne of the British Empire. It will be nothing less than an emphatic announcement that we are an equal and integral part of the British Empire, it will be a fervent and solemn and deliberate assurance that his watchful eye will be always upon us, on our weal and our woe, that his unceasing interest and sympathy will cover and envelop the development of our destinies, and will be a stimulus and example to all concerned in the administration of this country. It will be tidings of great joy for the present,—of glowing hope for the future. It will, indeed, be the perfect and practical fulfilment of the noble words—as wise as generous—uttered by that great and good Queen when she assumed the direct Sovereignty of the Indian Empire, in the Great Proclamation of 1858:—"We hold ourselves bound to the natives of our Indian Territories by the same obligations of duty which bind us to all our other subjects; and these obligations, by the blessing of Almighty God, we shall faithfully and conscientiously fulfil."

I think I can now claim to have been something of a prophet—but prophet or no prophet, I thank Providence that, working under good report and evil report for nearly half a century in company with greater men, many of whom, alas, have passed away, I have lived long enough to be blessed with a sight of the promised land. And it is to His Imperial Majesty that you and I and all of us will owe this sight. Among the many brilliant functions at the Coronation Durbar at Delhi, there was none more attractive and interesting than the presentation of colours to several British and Indian regiments with all the rites of religious incantation. But that function, splendid as it was, pales into insignificance before the presentation in Calcutta to the whole people of India of a banner, consecrated with all the multiform prayers of all his subjects of all races, creeds and religions, and embroidered with his own hands in letters of purple and gold with the soul-stirring motto and watchword of "Hope." In exhorting us to aim at higher and higher educational ideals, His Majesty presented yet another colour to the educated classes "a banner with the strange device 'Excelsior'." And Ladies and Gentlemen, we shall march under these banners in all loyalty and sincerity of heart, confident that we are marching to the promised land, to the goal of the united welfare, progress, and happiness of our Country, and, who knows perhaps towards a still higher goal, though the day may be far distant and the road long and arduous—the goal, predicted by the poet, of "The Parliament of man, the federation of the world."

Full of these great events and hopes, it is no wonder that our hearts are unutterably stirred within us, and we desire to tell the great English people of our loyalty and our gratitude to Their Imperial Majesties, whom we shall no longer continue to regard as foreign rulers, but as rulers of our own, reigning over an Empire of which we are an equal and integral portion. (Loud applause.)

ANANDA MOHAN BOSE
(1846-1906)

ANANDA MOHAN BOSE

The Indian Educational Service

Speech at the XII Congress in Calcutta in 1896 in proposing a Resolution on the Reorganization of the Higher Education Service which was as follows:

"That this Congress hereby records its protest against the scheme for reorganising the Educational Service which has just received the sanction of the Secretary of State, as being calculated to exclude natives of India, including those who have been educated in England, from the superior grade of the Education Service to which they have hitherto been admitted, for, in the words of the Resolution, "in future, natives of India, who are desirous of entering the Educational Department will usually be appointed in India and to the Provincial Service." The Congress prays that the scheme may be so recast as to afford facilities for the admission of Indian graduates to the superior grade of the Educational Service."

Mr. President, Brother-Delegates, Ladies and Gentlemen: If the preceding resolution as mentioned by its mover was a very old one, the present at any rate is brand new. I regret, therefore, all the more, that booked as a speaker last night in my absence and without my knowledge, I find myself, by a change made since I entered this hall, in the position of being the mover of this resolution. But, Sir, your mandate must be obeyed, and I must accept the situation with all the philosophy I can command. Brother-Delegates, before addressing myself to the one feature of the many featured and complicated scheme which is specially referred to in our resolution —the feature namely of extending and perpetuating the area of exclusion in regard to our countrymen in the Educational Service—

permit me to make one observation in reference to another feature of the Resolution of the Government of India on this subject. By that Resolution, amongst many changes, an important improvement is effected in the position and pay of many European members of the Educational Service; and I beg to say a word in reference to it in order to prevent any possible misapprehension of our attitude. I rejoice, Sir, that this has been done, because I look upon that improvement as an important recognition of the practical value to the country of the great Educational Service, of the work of those who are engaged in the task of furthering and fostering the cause of education. And I rejoice also, Sir, because on this platform we know no distinction of race, colour, or creed. We welcome an act of justice, though it is done to our European fellow-subjects; we welcome it as an act of justice, and this enables us to emphasise our position in the face of the world that what we contend and strive for in the Congress is not the granting of privileges to any particular sect, race, or creed, but the recognition of merit wherever it may be found, of service rendered in the cause of the country by whomsoever it may be rendered.

Coming now, gentlemen, to the resolution before us, the text on which I have to speak is set out in the words of the sentence which is quoted in it. They are: "in future natives of India who are desirous of entering the Education Department will usually be appointed in India, and to the Provincial Service." Mark the words "Provincial Service" and all that they necessarily involve, and mark also the words "in future"; and the question, Brother delegates, that I put to you is this, Is the cause of progress not only not to advance, but to be put back? Is the future to be worse than the past? Is the hand to be set back on the dial, is retrogression to mark the onward march of time, because that is what the resolution of the Government of India contemplates, what it proposes to carry out. It will be necessary, the subject being new, to place before you and explain in the fewest words I can, the particular portion of the reorganisation scheme which bears on the present resolution. What the scheme proposes is now for the first time to introduce two distinct divisions or branches in the superior Educational services of the country, the higher branch to be called the Indian Educational Service and to be filled by persons appointed in England; and the lower branch, namely the Provincial Educational Service, to be filled, by reason, I presume, of the inferiority of its position, by recruitment in India. Let us for a moment examine what are the results that follow from these two different methods of recruitment. Let me say once again, I do not grudge the better terms of what I have called the higher branch. What we regret and what adds to the keenness and bitterness of that regret is that while there has been this recognition of the claims of education in regard to the European member of the Service, as regards the people of India justice has not been done. Justice has been denied to us. In what I have called the higher branch they begin on a pay of Rs. 500; as regards the lower branch, the branch for natives of India, there is no knowing on what pay they will begin. Let me give you one or two facts only, premising that the figures and dates which will be mentioned by me relate specially to Bengal. Previous to the year 1880, the higher branch was open to natives of India and open on exactly the same pay as to a European member; and as a matter of fact it actually comprised several such Indian gentlemen. There was neither a bar to admission nor difference in the scale of pay. But in that year began the downward march, and it was declared that natives of India taken into the higher service should begin on Rs. 333 or two-thirds of Rs. 500, the pay of a European member. I will not pause to consider the invidious and the retrograde character of this distinction then introduced for the first time, or on the heart burning at the sense of degradation it was likely to cause. But, gentlemen, bad as this was, things did not stop here. The scale of 333 went on until in 1889 the initial pay was further reduced to Rs. 250; and we do not know, Sir, how far that progress may now go on, and what further reduction may yet be carried out. Not only is there no guarantee in this respect, no word of hope in the Government Resolution now before us, but so far as it is concerned, commencing pay may be so low as Rs. 150. So far then with reference to the initial salary. As regards the other, maximum limit of pay, we have more light thrown by the terms of the resolution. A native of India, however high his education may have been in the Universities of Europe, however exalted the position he may have taken in the highest competitions in England, can at the end of his life in the Provincial Service expect to rise only to Rs. 700, possibly after 25 or 30 years of service—service reckoned not only by length of years, but it may be by important researches, by unique discoveries by valuable and noteworthy work in advancing the cause of education. Whereas in the higher branch which is open only to Europeans, at the end of 10 years alone, the salary shall be Rs. I 000. This then is the difference in the position as regards these two. What I have said applies also to the graduates of our own Universities, many of them men of brilliant abilities and rare talent, who would have entered the Educational Services of the country and proved its ornaments and its most useful members but for the poor prospects held out to them and the invidious distinction between the positions of the Indian and the European members of that service.

Let me now point out how we have been actually going backwards in another most important respect by the provision of this resolution, the result of more than five years' incubation and of numerous despatches passing between India and England. Up to now there was nothing to exclude an Indian member of the Service from becoming the Principal of the highest college in this country. But under the terms of the resolution in question, you will find given in an appendix to the despatch, the list of appointments open respectively to the Indian Educational Service and to the lower Provincial Service. In the former, I am speaking only for Bengal—there are five principalships of the Colleges, under the latter not one. At the present time any Indian Professor in the Presidency College, and I know some most distinguished ones there, can become in course of time and by virtue of seniority the Principal of that College. There is absolutely nothing to prevent it. But under the new scheme we are excluded, we are debarred, from looking forward to that state of things, even if it should be that in working out the scheme some of the minor professorships of the College may, by a stretch of generosity, fall to the lot of the Provincial Service. Is this right? Are we going onwards or backwards? Is that, gentlemen, to be the fruit of that awakening of the great social, moral, and intellectual forces that are now dominating the face of this continent? Is that indeed to be the result of the onward march, of the vaunted progress and enlightenment, of the country? Is a new preserve to be created for the European members of the higher service? Is the area of exclusion for the people of the soil to be further extended? From equality in the earlier years to inequality in 1880, and now in the closing years of the century to still further and grosser inequality, is that to be the order of things, the destined course of progress under the enlightened administration of England for this great and ancient land? At any rate, by our voice and effort we shall do, I trust, all we can to prevent that state of things, and to bring home to the minds and consciences of our rulers and of the justice-loving people of England the injustice that has been done. And, Sir, let me tell the authors of this scheme that, as regards the inauguration of this backward policy in the great educational service of the country, they have selected a very inopportune moment indeed. Why, Sir, I should have thought that if the gracious words of Her Gracious Majesty's Proclamation, which is the charter of our rights, are to be belittled, if those solemn words still ringing in our ears which granted equal rights and equal privileges to all classes of her subjects irrespective of race, colours or creed are to be violated and to be departed from, then the task should be attempted not in the sixtieth year of Her Majesty's reign which we in India are celebrating, and the coming of which has filled with joy and rejoicing the minds of all Her subjects in the vast Indian Empire. Let them not select this present year of Her Majesty's beneficent and benignant rule for initiating this retrograde policy. There is, Sir, another reason also which emboldens me to say that they have been specially unhappy in the selection of their time. Why, Sir, we know the *London Times* has only the other day borne testimony to the fact that the year 1896 is an epoch-making year, as regards the intellectual advance of India. We know that the grand researches of an Indian professor in the field of invisible light, in the sublime and giddy heights of etherial vibration, have led to discoveries which have filled the mind of Lord Kelvin, the highest authority which England has produced, literally with 'wonder and admiration'. We have heard of the great and wonderful feat that another countrymen of ours has achieved in the last great competition for the Indian Civil Service. We know of the discoveries which also in the present year of grace have rewarded the genius and the patient toils of another countryman of ours in the realm of chemical research. The present year then, when India has shown that she has not forgotten the traditions of her glorious past, when the great Indian mind has awakened to the consciousness of the great destiny before it, and not only awakened to that consciousness, but has taken the first practical step towards obtaining its recognition from the generous scholars of the West, surely is not the time or the season for ushering into existence a policy of this retrograde character. We shall not, so far as in us lies, permit, without protest at any rate, the inauguration of such a policy. It is, gentlemen, rather late in the day for this policy, for this creation of a new crime of colours, for this infringement of the gracious words of Her Majesty's Proclamation.

Gentlemen, there is one other remark I have to make and that is this. If I have dwelt on the nature of this policy, on what I may venture to describe with all respect, as its audaciously retrograde character, if I have dwelt upon that, it is only right that I should draw your attention to a small word that occurs in the sentence I have placed before you. That sentence, as you know, is "that in future natives of India who are desirous of entering the Education Department will usually be appointed in India and to the Provincial Service." Perhaps the framers of the resolution thought that there was a great deal of virtue in that saving word "usually." But I will venture to prophesy, I will undertake to say, what the result of that "usually" will be. Not that the mantle of prophecy has fallen upon me or that the gift of the seer has been vouchsafed to me. But, gentlemen, the past is a guide to the future and lightens up the dark places of much that is yet to be. Let us consult that guide. As I have said, my facts specially refer to Bengal, and this is what we find in that province at the present time. I will not attempt to carry the meeting back with me to distant days. But confining our views to the time which has elapsed since the birth of the Congress, what I find is this that within the last twelve years there have been six appointments of gentlemen educated in England, and educated most successfully so far as all the tests there are concerned. These six gentlemen who have been appointed to the higher educational department in these years, have all of them been appointed in India. Not that they did not try to get appointed in England. No, gentlemen, after taking their degrees in the great English and Scotch Universities, after having won all their high distinctions—distinctions not only less high than those of their English brethren in the service, in some cases perhaps even higher, they tried their very best, they made what I may almost describe as frantic efforts at the

India Office to get an appointment from England, but all their efforts were in vain. After waiting and waiting, and after heart-rending suspense, they were told that they must ship themselves off as soon as they could to India for the Government to appoint them there. Therefore, although there is that word "usually," you may take it that that will happen in the future which has in these years happened in the past, and happened too, so far as we are, aware, in the absence of this retrograde clause now authoritatively laid down in the Resolution. For all practical purposes, you may take it, gentlemen, that 'usually' in the sentence would mean 'invariably.' I cannot venture to detain the meeting any further. I have already passed the limit of my allotted time. I will, therefore, conclude with only one more remark. There is no cause which can be dearer to the members of the Congress than the cause of education. You, gentlemen, are the fruits of that education, of that great awakening of the national mind to which I have referred. And can it possibly be that you will for a moment neglect to do all that you can, all that lies in your power, with the help of our friends in England and in India, with the help of all those, wherever they may be, who look forward to human progress as a thing to be wished for, as a thing to be fought for, to see that your children are not ostracised from those higher branches of the service with their higher opportunities of educational work and educational progress, to which, up to now, they have been appointed? There are no considerations such as those which are some times supposed, be it rightly or be it wrongly, to apply to appointments in the Indian Civil Service, which can have any application to those in the Education Service of the country. What possible shade of a shadow of Justification can there be then for this enlarged and expanded edition of the policy of exclusion? Gentlemen, I believe in the intellect of India. I believe the fire that burned so bright centuries ago has not wholy died out. I believe, there are sparks, aye more than sparks, that still exist and only require the gentle breeze of sympathetic help, of Judicious Organisation and kindly care, to burst forth once again into that glorious fire which in the past illumined not only this great continent, but shed its l ustre over other lands, into that intellectual life which achieved wonders in the field of literature and arts, in the field of mathematics and philosophy, which produced works which are even now the admiration and the wonder of the world. Fight with redoubled vigour in that cause, and then we may depend upon it that, in the Providence of God, righteousness and justice shall triumph, and this attempt to fix on the brows of the people of this ancient land a new stigma and a new disability shall fail as it deserves to fail.

SURENDRANATH BANERJEA
(1848-1925)

SURENDRANATH BANERJEA

The Situation in India

Speech at the Caxton Hall in Westminster on 13 July 1909

Mr. Chairman, Ladies and Gentlemen,—I desire at the outset to associate myself, and I can also speak on behalf of my countrymen, with the observations which you, Mr. Chairman, have been pleased to make regarding the blessed and time honoured memory of the late Marquis of Ripon. (Hear, hear) In the illustrious muster-roll of Indian Viceroys he will take his place amongst the most illustrious. His memory will for ever remain enshrined in the grateful recollections of our people. The rulers of India who cling together in our grateful affections are Bentinck, Canning, and Ripon (Cheers). I do not think it necessary to repeat the observations which I have made at other public meetings to express the horror and detestation which we have felt at the terrible tragedy which resulted in the deaths of Sir Curzon Wyllie and Dr. Lalkaka, for Indian public opinion in this country and in the home-land is clear and emphatic with regard to it. (Hear, hear).

For various reasons, some of them not of the most pleasant character, the Indian problem at the present time looms largely into the public view. Our complaint—I mean the complaint of the people of India—is that so little interest is felt in this country regarding the affairs of that great dependency. (Hear, hear). The apathy of the British public is one of our greatest grievances because the fact remains, whoever might be our governors and administrators, the British democracy, the electors of Great Britain and Ireland, are the real rulers of India. (Hear, hear). To them have been entrusted the destinies of 300,000,000 of my fellow-countrymen, not savages or barbarians but representatives of a great and ancient culture which carries the mind back to the dawn of human history. (Hear, hear). How is this awful responsibility discharged? I am reminded in this connexion of an Eastern legend, historical in its character and based upon truth. Mahmmud of Ghazni flourished in the eleventh century of the Christian era. His dominions extended far and wide. There lived in a part of his empire an elderly woman who had suffered a grievous wrong, for one night she found her house burned down, her goods plundered, and her children massacred. Overwhelmed with the awful calamity, she set out to the capital of the empire and sought her ruler's presence. She presented herself at the palace gates, was ushered into Mahmmud's presence, and laid her complaint before him. Mahmmud heard her case and its tale of sorrow and wrong, and then he remarked: "Woman, you live in remote part of my Empire. How can you expect me to extend to you the protection of my power?" And the woman, with that promptitude of resource which characterises her sex—(laughter)—replied: "Sire, why then do you conquer countries to whose affairs you cannot pay sufficient attention, and for which you cannot hold yourself answerable at the Day of Judgment?" (Applause).

Ladies and Gentlemen, I have no desire to enforce this lesson in its application to the British democracy, but I say this, and I think with your full concurrence that the responsibility of these islands as regards their great dependency is not discharged by merely appointing your governors and your administrators and leaving them to the discretion of their own sweet wills. (Hear, Hear). I have no desire to make the smallest reflection upon the men on the spot. (Hear, hear and laughter.) I am sure they do their best according to their lights and opportunities; but, after all they are human beings, dominated with ideas and sentiments and it may be with the passion of their prejudices. In the old days of the East India Company a Parliamentary Committee used to be appointed every twenty years to enquire into Indian affairs. The labours of this Committee were favourable alike to England and to India, and I do not understand why this practice should not be revived and the Government thereby exercise a beneficent sway over the people, caring for them and in turn being loved by them. There is nothing to lose but everything to gain by such an enquiry. (Hear, hear). But Governments are slow to move. They will not prepare the materials or provide the grant for impelling progress without the irresistible pressure of public opinion being brought to bear upon them (Hear, hear). Yet this is what will have to be done. (Hear, hear). I have heard it said that if such an enquiry were to take place the machinery of the Government would be dislocated. Well, all I can say is I have a far greater faith in the stability of that machinery than apparently have those who work it and are responsible for its efficiency. (Hear, hear and laughter). And this is justified by the lesson of experience. Only eighteen months ago the Decentralisation Committee was appointed to visit India and travel up and down the country, examining numerous witnesses and instituting the most searching investigation.

Ladies and gentlemen, will you believe it, the Government of India actually survived the catastrophe. (Laughter). No dislocation nor any disturbance of the existing machinery of the Government took place. There was not the slightest deviation from the normal conditions of the administration of the Government, nor was there any deviation in the uses of Indian life and society. My own belief is that if this Committee were continued and their recommendations followed, the Government of to-day would not have been confronted with excitement and unrest and all the deplorable things which have followed in their train. (Hear, hear). The Government would have been more in touch with the people. And that brings me to the subject of Indian unrest. What is the cause of that unrest, where are the circumstances contributing to it, and what is the solution of the problem? (Hear, hear). Ladies and gentlemen, I ask you to bear in mind that we in India are a law-abiding and peaceful people. (Hear, hear). Our instinct, traditions, and deepest religious feelings and affections are intimately bound up in the maintenance of law and order. Our ancestors developed a system of ethics and a code of laws upon that proclamation from on high, "Peace and good will among men," which to-day excite the admiration of mankind and constitute an enduring monument of their devotion to peace. What, then, is it that has plunged a people whose antecedent were such as I have described, so peacefully inclined, so adverse to all forms of excitement, into a vortex of unrest which is unparalleled? Edmund Burke has told us—and his dictum has never been challenged, for the reason that it cannot be challenged—that in all controversies between people and their rulers the presumption is that the rulers are in the wrong and the people in the right. (Hear, hear). I say if the matter of this Indian unrest were carefully examined, and there is no tribunal more qualified for the task than the tribunal of the British public, it would be found that the responsibility for this unrest mainly rests, and I am sorry to have to say it, but say it I must, upon the government of the country, (Hear, hear).

I blame no one; I am not here to formulate charges against individuals. Even the most dazzling and brilliant of Viceroys fade out of my recollection before the issues involved. I am here to place the facts before you as they affect my countrymen and to vindicate their character as a peaceful and law abiding people. (Hear, Hear). When you have heard those facts I know you will give your verdict in my favour. (Applause). I am happy to say from the outset England's great mission in the East was realized by the illustrious founders of the Indian Empire. It was not realized by every one, and certainly not by those who went out of India to make money or die of liver complaint—(laughter)—but it was realized by those great and illustrious men whose genius and statesmanship founded the vast and majestic fabric of the Empire of India. Macaulay, speaking from his place in the House of Commons on the occasion of the Charter Act, used language which I for one have ever read with enthusiasm and gratitude. "It may be said," said Macaulay. "that the public mind in India may so expand under our system that it may outgrow that system, and our subjects trained in western civilization may pray for western institutions. I know not whether such a day will come, but if it does come it will be the proudest day in the annals of England." I venture to say that that day has arrived, and great are the responsibilities of England. (Hear, hear and applause). Lord Metcalfe, the liberator of the Indian Press, used similar language when replying to a deputation which waited upon him. "We are not here," he said, "merely to keep the peace and collect taxes . . . we are here for a higher and nobler purpose, to pour into the East the knowledge and culture and the civilization of the West." (Hear, hear). The Earl of Shelburne the great grand-father of Lord Landsdowne, who opposed the insertion of Clause 3 into the Indian Councils Bill, said on the occasion of the debate in the House of Lords on the Charter Act of 1833 that their lordships would be remiss in the discharge of their duties if they did not offer to the Indian people ample opportunity for developing the high moral and intellectual qualities with which they had been endowed. These utterances embodied a noble policy, and such a policy pressed steadily into the view of the Indian Government by the most illustrious of Indian administrators has resulted in higher education being introduced into our midst, the Press liberated, local self-government, and the setting up of councils. But can you tell a people whom you have so liberally educated and plentifully supplied with the environments which stimulate public life that thus far shall they go and no further ? (Hear, hear). Yet that has represented the attitude of Anglo-Indian Government for the past twenty years.

There you have the beginning of Indian unrest, which has now assumed such vast proportions. Can we overlook the wondrous change which has taken in Asia; changes have been brought about by the victories of Japan over Russia, which had strengthened the confidence of Asiatics in themselves. (Hear, hear). We have a mighty wave sweeping over Asia which carries with it high ideals and aspirations. India would be false to herself, her ancient culture which she so largely imbibed, and the education she has received if she did not feel revivified in the example of oriental nations struggling for consideration and self-government. (Hear, hear). On the top of all this excitement came a period of reaction, in which the legitimate aspirations of the people were ignored and trifled with. The people were counted as nothing, we were counted as nothing, we were good for nothing, and we were to do nothing; everything was to be done for us. The generous policy of Lord Ripon was reversed. Local self-government was modified, and the universities, centres of humane and beneficent influence, were officialised, despite the protests of the people. Then on the top of all came the crowning piece of folly—the partition of Bengal. (Hear, hear).

It is true the situation has been somewhat eased by Lord Morley's reform, but this reform scheme has given rise to some considerable diversity of opinion amongst us, (Hear, hear). There are those representing a section of Indian opinion who hold that it lacks the essential element of genuine reform; that it will serve no useful purpose, and that whatever merits it might have possessed have disappeared in the recommendation of a system of class legislation. (Hear, hear). On the other hand, there are those who hold a different view altogether.

They declare that the scheme makes lavish concessions—concessions which were never before thought of, and which represent an entirely new and remarkable departure. As an Indian speaking on behalf of my countrymen, I say at once that I totally dissent from this view. The scheme contains no concessions which have not been sought for. So far from the scheme being lavish, I still say that it does not come up to our expectations in regard to many matters which vitally concern the power of the purse. We want definite control at least over some of the great departments of the State; over sanitation, education, and the public works department. Are you not aware that hundreds of thousands of my countrymen die every year from preventable diseases, such as malaria and cholera? ("Shameful!") Yes, I think it is very shameful indeed. We have been pressing the importance of the matter upon the Government for years. We have cried aloud, but who will listen to us? (Hear, hear.) If we had some effective control over finance, or at least over sanitary measures to be employed, I am convinced that we could prevent to some extent the appalling rate of mortality which desolates homes in Bengal. (Hear, hear). The expenditure on education is inadequate. The great bulk of it is not being spent for education at all but upon inspection. (Laughter). As for elementary education, well, the less said the better. (Hear, hear). If we had any control over finances in regard to education we should devote the money to a useful and profitable purpose. We want the power of the purse and a definite and effective method of self-government. (Cheers). This we have not got; all the scheme does is—and let me be perfectly candid in the matter—to provide machinery by which representatives of the people would be in a position to bring to bear upon the Government not a direct influence but an indirect moral pressure. (Hear, hear).

At the same time we have accepted the scheme as a beginning. We recognise that there is such a thing as the growth of public institutions. (Hear, hear). You cannot make a law, be it good or bad, which is not at once subject to a process of transformation under the operation of immutable moral laws. These are hopes which have gathered round the scheme. They may be fulfilled, or dark clouds may gather the force of reaction may be in the ascendant so that these aspirations which we have fondly cherished may fall away like shadows. All the same, we do cherish these hopes, and we pray that they may be realised (Hear, hear). In Bengal the situation has taken a somewhat strained and difficult aspect. In the firmament of that province there is a cloud which is no bigger than a man's hand, but which threatens to overshadow the beautiful prospect pointed out by Lord Morley's scheme. Lord Morley has recently said that he will be no party to the withdrawal of the partition of Bengal. I hope that pronouncement does not preclude him from considering proposals for the modification of the partition. (Hear, hear). If any one were to tell me, no matter how high and exalted might be his position, that there is no hope for the modification of the partition of Bengal, I should venture to tell him in the name of my countrymen, that then there is no hope for the conciliation of Bengal, or for the cooperation of our people in the working of the reform scheme. (Applause). This partition is our greatest grievance, and in our judgement it is the root cause of the present discontent in India. (Hear, hear). When it was first announced it invoked the united opposition of the Hindus and the Mahomedans alike. The opposition was so wide spread and so intense that it would have sealed the fate of any measure in this country. But the methods of the Government in India are different from the methods of the Government in England. (Hear, hear). For the opposition the Indian Government had its revenge. A wider scheme of partition was announced, which had been deliberated on in the secret recesses of the Secretarial Bureau. It was resolved upon in secret and fell like a bolt from the blue upon the astonished people of India. It gave rise to an agitation the parallel of which I have never before witnessed, (Hear, hear). It is four years since the partition was accomplished, but the wound to-day is as fresh as if at were only inflicted yesterday. (Hear, hear). There are those who say that the feeling against the partition is on the wane, but we are in the position of unfortunate beings suffering from a painful disease. It has its moments of cessation, but the patient knows no rest or peace so long as the root cause of the disease lies ingrained in his system. The anniversary of the date of the partition is a day of mourning. The shops are closed, and all business is suspended. The people go about the streets bare footed, interchanging amongst themselves the mystic ribbon of eternal love, and the vow to carry on the agitation from generation to generation until the partition has been abolished.

I ask you, ladies and gentlemen, is it right to allow a grievance of this kind to foster in the depths of a national life? The longer you permit it the wider becomes its mischievous operation and the deeper grows the discontent (Hear, hear). They say it is a sentimental grievance. Be it so. A sentimental grievance is one which is worthy of consideration. What I should like to know, would be the feelings of the people of England under the identical circumstances. But far more so is the question of sentimental feeling important when it is a question of governing an oriental nation (Hear, hear).

But ladies and gentlemen, this grievance is more than a sentimental grievance, and I desire to lay before you some of the most practical considerations which ought to operate for a modification of this partition. The partition was entered into in the name of efficiency. No finance, I venture to hope, is a crucial test for efficient administration. (Hear, hear). What, however, do you find with regard to Bengal? It is a bankrupt province, unable to meet its demands, and compelled to rely upon subsidies from the Government of India in order to supply its most urgent needs. (Hear, hear). If Bengal remained united she would have been financially prosperous and financial prosperity means prosperity all round. (Hear, hear). Let me take another consideration and not a sentimental consideration. For generations, the Hindus and Mahomedans have lived together in peace, but the partition has thrown the apple of discord into their midst, and has created an alienation of feeling which has led to great disturbances and breaches of the peace. Lord Ripon, of blessed memory, strongly condemned the partition on the ground that it had caused deep discontent among the population—meaning the population of which I have the honour to belong. Contentment of the people is the strongest asset of the British Government, Great Queen Victoria taught us the utmost importance of this in the proclamation of 1858, which she closed with these words: "In the contentment of our people lies the strength of our rule." (Hear, hear). It is useless for me to disguise the fact that universal contentment in Bengal has become a thing of the past. Any one who knows Bengal will tell you that it is a province of peaceful people. Why, then, is it now the centre of disaffection and discontent ? It is the partition. (Hear, hear). I have, ladies and gentlemen, the confirmation of official testimony. You will remember that the persons in the Alipore bomb case were charged with conspiring against His Majesty, and it was stated that the day fixed upon was October 16. That date is important because it happens to be the date of the partition of Bengal. (Hear, hear).

I think, therefore, the partition stands confounded from the mouths of those who support it. What does Lord Morley say? I desire to speak of him with the utmost respect. I have read his work again and again, and I teach them to my scholars and saturate their minds with lofty principles of political wisdom, (Hear, hear.) But if I respect Lord Morley, I love my motherland far more. (Hear, hear and applause). Therefore in the interest of my native land, I must enter into the arena and contend against my political guru. Lord Morley says it is merely a matter of the adjustment of boundaries, and yet he also says that the partition is a settled fact. (Hear, hear). A statesman need not be logical, but he is bound to be reasonable and just, and cannot override the paramount claims of the people. Righteousness is the vital breath of Imperial statesmanship, and a single act of unrighteousness is more disastrous to British rule in India than a great reverse sustained upon an Asiatic battlefield. (Hear, hear). I cannot conceive anything more disastrous to the credit of the British administration than such a proceeding as the partition. It is calculated to shake Indian confidence in the integrity and sense of fairness of the Government. (Hear, hear). Lord Morley says the partition is a settled fact. Then I say on behalf of my fellow-countrymen that we decline to accept it as a settled fact. We decline to accept what is admittedly a blunder and what we feel to be a cruel law and wrong to the sentiment of the people. (Applause). We will continue this agitation and we want your sympathy in our great struggle. (Hear, hear). Will you extend to us the right hand of friendship and sympathy in this matter—(Cheers), that this deplorable blunder has become obvious by the supplement of a policy of oppression which has become necessary to combat the feeling which has been evoked? Take away this partition and then the oppressive policy will become unnecessary.

So far as this policy of repression is concerned I say this, it came to us in the light of an unpleasant surprise. We are accustomed to associate English administration especially controlled by the Imperial Government, with the most scrupulous observance of the right of personal property. Your history and literature and poetry are saturated with the rights of personal liberty. (Hear, hear). No one could read the glowing pages of English history without imbibing a passionate love for such liberty; yet it would seem that we are not to be allowed to enjoy it. By secret reports of a secret police the sanctity of our homes is invaded, domiciliary visits are made, and nine gentlemen, some of them men of light and leading are wrested away from the bosom of their families and held in detention in goal under personal discipline, without the purpose being communicated to them, any explanation given or a chance given of making a defence. ("shame"). And what is the character of these police? The most unscrupulous in the world. (Hear, hear). Sir Lawrence Jenkins, the Chief Justice of Bengal in the Court of Appeal, found that the police had deliberately put a bomb in the house of the accused with a view of fabricating evidence, and Mr. Weston, Magistrate of Midnapur, caused the arrest of the father of one of the accused with a view to extorting a confession. ("Shame!"). It is a shame, and it is a matter of bitter irony that these things should be done under a Government presided over by a Secretary of State of the pronounced liberalism of Lord Morley. (Hear, hear). "Liberalism," said Mr. Gladstone, "was trust in the people, tempered with discretion." Such proceedings as this, however, involve the gravest distrust of the people, and if you will not trust the people they will not trust you.

"Coercion is an evil instrument of government," said Edmund Burke in the eighteenth century, and so said John Morley in the nineteenth ! It exasperates and does not solve, but leaves wounds which take years of conciliatory administration to heal. How did you pacify India after the Mutiny? You did so by the rejection of all coercive measures and by the application of conciliatory methods, (Hear, hear). With all the emphasis I can command, in the name of common sense, on behalf of the people of India and the credit of British rule I do earnestly appeal to you to do all that lies in your power to bring about a speedy abrogation of this oppressive partition, which sits like a nightmare upon the troubled bosoms of our people; and I might also be permitted to make another appeal to you, not to accept the official version that the feeling against the partition is on the wane. (Hear, hear). The patient himself as the best judge of the painfulness of his malady, and we are the patients in this instance.

(Hear, hear). My countrymen are suffering, and in their name and upon their behalf I urge you to do all in your power to bring about a modification of the partition of Bengal. I am sure my appeal will not fall upon heedless ears, but will go forth from this meeting accompanied by a volume of sympathy which will have the effect of redressing our grievance and restoring many millions of my countrymen to contentment. (Applause).

ROMESH CHUNDER DUTT
(1848-1909)

ROMESH CHUNDER DUTT

Social Progress in India

Speech at the Annual Meeting of the National Indian Association in England on 25 March 1901

The Resolution which I have the honour to second has been explained by Sir Ropor Lethbridge, and I have very little to add to what he has said, except that as an Indian myself I feel great pleasure in seconding it. The Resolution is for making increased efforts in support of the Association's funds with the object of promoting female education in India. It is well known—speaking at least for the part of India from which I come, and with which I am most familiar—that for the last thirty or forty years or more, a great deal has been done by the people of India themselves in the cause of social progress and of female education. A great deal has been done, not ostentatiously, but by quiet work at home, to help the cause of social progress; and anything like a lasting and abiding improvement in the country must be done in the future, as has been done in the past, by the people themselves. (Hear, hear). I think many of the gentlemen present here, who have passed a great many years of their lives in India, like my friend Sir Charles Steevens who has moved the first Resolution, are familiar with the names of prominent Indian Gentlemen who devoted their lives to the cause of education and social reform. I need only mention the names of Pandit Iswar Chandra Vidyasagar and Keshub Chunder Sen of Bengal, and of Justice Ranade of Bombay whose recent death has filled the people of India with sorrow. They were prominent men in India who, in spite of various duties which they had to perform, devoted a great part of their time to the cause of social progress and social reform, and were careful to adopt methods which were consistent with our Eastern life, because they knew that all reforms in order to be abiding, must be consistent with our Eastern

Customs and life. (Hear, hear). This is a point, ladies and gentlemen, which we should always remember—we who try to work in the cause of social reform. The people of India gratefully accept help from all true friends in the cause of reform; they avail themselves of the schools and teachers you provide; they benefit by your sympathy and your support; but nevertheless all abiding reforms must be worked out by themselves, consistently with the life they live. It is not desirable and it is not possible, to Europeanise Indian life (Applause). The people of India are well able to judge for themselves, what is best for themselves, and Indian life and Hindu life has always proved itself capable of assimilating what is good for itself. It is because we have been able to assimilate all needful reforms from generation to generation and from age to age, that our ancient Hindu life still exists in India when so many phases of ancient life have passed away in other countries like Rome and Greece, like Persia, Egypt and Babylon. Therefore sir, our best helpers and our truest friends are those who, while they offer us their help and their sympathy, can at the same time sympathise with Eastern life and Eastern institutions. And it is because this Association is trying to cooperate with our own endeavours, to help us where we are in need of help, to provide teachers and schools for the education of our wives, sisters, and daughters, that we gratefully accept its sympathy, its services, and its help. And I have great pleasure, sir, in seconding this Resolution, because the truest progress that we can make, and the truest line upon which we can make that progress, is the extension of female education in India. It is necessary that our women should be familiar with modern institutions, with modern knowledge and with modern history; a sound education like this is needed to smooth the path of our future progress.

LAL MOHAN GHOSE
(1849-1909)

LAL MOHAN GHOSE

We Shall Not Be Parted

Speech in Madras in 1905 at the 19th Session of the Indian National Congress

Brother-delegates, ladies and gentlemen,—After the inspiring strains of *Bande Mataram* it is meet and proper that this resolution should be placed before this house, the subject matter being one which has convulsed the whole of Bengal (A voice: "The whole of India"). I rejoice to learn that our griefs, our sorrows, our disappointments and our trials are sympathised with by brother-delegates throughout the rest of the country. (Cheers). I think, Sir, I am not guilty of the slightest exaggeration when I say that no question has, within the life of this generation, so profoundly stirred the hearts of our countrymen or has given rise to such widespread and intense dissatisfaction, irritation and indignation as the Partition of our Province—our beautiful Motherland. In our Province this question is the talk of the market-place; it is the gossip of the family circle; it is the burden of popular song; it is the theme of the inspiring eloquence of popular oratory. (Cheers). I never knew until now that my language, the language of my mother, the language she spoke to me and I spoke to her, was capable of such marvellous use for the purpose of explanation, of argument and inspiration. (Cheers).

Sir, the year 1905 is one of the darkest and saddest in our annals, relieved by the reflection that it witnessed an upheaval of national life and an awakening of national consciousness without parallel in our history. (Loud cheers). Lord Curzon has divided our Province ("Shame!"); he has sought to bring about the disintegration of our race ("Shame!") and to destroy the solidarity of our popular opinion. Has he succeeded in this novel endeavour? ("No, No"). He has built better than he knew; he has laid broad and deep the foundations of our national life (Cheers); he has stimulated those forces which contribute to the up-building of nations (Cheers); he has made us a nation ("Hear, Hear!"); and the most reactionary of Indian Viceroys will go down to posterity as the architect of the Indian national life. ("Hear, Hear"). That will be the authoritative, final judgement of history and posterity on the work of Lord Curzon's Government and administration. Sir, the year 1905 opens, as far as this Partition question is concerned, with a great public meeting held at the Town Hall of Calcutta. It was presided over by Sir Henry Cotton (Prolonged Cheers), a name honoured in Bengal as well as in India. (Cheers). Great as are obligations to Sir Henry Cotton, they have been accentuated and enhanced by his strenuous efforts to avert the Partition of Bengal, and now that it has been accomplished, by still more arduous labours to undo it, he will be reckoned for all times to come, amongst the greatest benefactors of the Bengali people and races. ("Three cheers to Sir Henry Cotton!").

Sir, at that meeting held at the Town Hall we confessed to a sense of relief at no decision having been arrived at in connection with the Partition question, and we expressed the hope that if there was any modification of the scheme it would be submitted for public consideration. We were living in a fool's paradise, for, at the time when we held this public meeting and were felicitating ourselves upon our good luck, the judgement of Lord Curzon had been pronounced upon the Partition question, though we knew nothing at all about it; for on the 4th of July Mr. Brodrick, replying to a question in the House of Commons, said that the had already given his sanction to the Partition proposals of the Government of India which had been received by him on the 18th February last. It, therefore, stands to reason that these proposals must have been submitted and sent to England towards the end of January. On the 12th January, Sir Henry Cotton forwarded his proposals to the Government of India. He received an acknowledgment in three weeks time; that was about the beginning of February. The Government of India had our resolutions before them; they were dealing with those resolutions; they knew that we had confessed to a sense of relief at the Government not having arrived at any pronouncement with regard to the Partition question. They knew that we were under a false impression. It was their duty to have removed that impression. They did nothing of the kind. ("Shame!"). They lent countenance to the false impression which prevailed in the public mind. They became a conscious party to that false impression. Now, Sir, if a private person had dealt by me in that fashion I should have called him a dishonest fellow. Are we to understand that the code of morality that governs the proceedings of the Government of India is meaner and baser than the code which governs the relations of private life? (Laughter). And if that be so, then what are we to think of those lofty principles of morality which were enforced with such consummate eloquence by the Chancellor of the Calcutta University on the Convocation Day? (Ironical cheers).

Sir, in the early days of the controversy some deference was shown to public opinion. The proposals of the Government were published in the newspapers; conferences were held in Belvedere; my friend was one of the shining lights of this conference. I do know that much came out of them, but they used to be held at Belvedere and Lord Curzon went down to the Eastern districts to ascertain public opinion by personal conference and examination. Sir, if the truth has to be told, Lord Curzon went to the Eastern districts not to learn but to teach, not to ascertain what the public felt but to compel the public to adopt his views and sentiment. He failed. The people of the Eastern districts are a manly and stubborn race, possessed of much grit. They are prosperous and they exhibited the independence which prosperity brings in its train. I see before me the representatives of those districts. Brothers from East Bengal, from North Bengal, we had been parted by that fiat of an autocratic power, but the stroke of autocracy has brought our hearts nearer to you. (Cheers). We are, and we shall always remain, of one mind, of one soul, animated by kindred hopes and aspirations, marching side by side towards the accomplishment of our common destinies. (Cheers). Who can sunder those that are tied by the bonds of Nature? The omnipotence of Government quails before the Majesty of Heaven and ties of Nature. (Cheers).

When, Sir, Lord Curzon failed, and when he failed to compel the people of the Eastern districts to adopt his views, the tactics of the Government underwent a great change. Then were held those secret conferences, those private deliberations of which the public knew nothing; they were not allowed to know anything. We knew nothing about the decision of the Government till the 4th of July last. I knew nothing about the particulars of the scheme till the proclamation of the 20th of July. We begged, we prayed, we protested, but all in vain. No one would listen to us. Ours was a voice crying in the wilderness. ("Shame!"). And then in utter desperation, as a last resort, we were driven to the adoption of the boycott (Cheers)—the policy of passive resistance which represents a memorable departure in our political programme. ("Hear, Hear"). It was a protest, nothing more than a protest, against the indifference of the British public in regard to Indian affairs, and the consequent contemptuous treatment of Indian public opinion by the Government of India. The protest went home! It was marvellously effective. What we could not achieve in 500 meetings extended over two years' time we secured by a boycott lasting for a period of three months. (Cheers). Those who came to scoff remained to pray. The members of the Manchester Chamber of Commerce, which felt a grandfatherly interest in our concerns (Laughter), sent a gratuitous piece of advice to us to give up the boycott, but at the same time they exerted all their influence upon the Secretary of State to cancel the Partition of Bengal. ("Hear, Hear!"). I have the best reason for believing, I said so publicly, I said it to the Viceroy of India, I said so publicly, that a wire was sent by Mr. Brodrick to Lord Curzon on or about the 12th of October asking him if possible to postpone the Partition till the meeting of the Parliament. (Cheers). Lord Curzon declined to accept the suggestion. ("Shame!"). With that exuberant love for the Bengalis and for the Indians he would not conciliate them. He added that the agitation was childish, and that it was about to subside. That was said on the 12th of October, today it is the 29th of December: the agitation will not subside ("No, No!" and cheers), the agitation will not subside till the Partition is cancelled. Today an immense meeting is being held in Calcutta to attract the Prince's attention to the consequences of the Partition. (Cheers). The agitation will not subside: it shows no signs of abatement until that perennial source of irritation—the Partition—has been modified or withdrawn. (Cheers).

Well, gentlemen, the boycott is a political instrument in our hands. We resolved to use it when necessary, subject, of course, to the safeguard that it is only to be used in extreme cases when there is a sufficiently powerful body of public opinion to justify its use and to ensure its success. It is a perfectly legitimate and constitutional weapon. ("Hear, Hear!"). If our rulers will not listen to us, if they will treat Indian public opinion with contumely and disrespect, and if they will trample under foot the constitutional usages which constitute the guarantee of the British power and have given us so much contentment and happiness, they must make up their minds to part with some portion of their trade with India, and they must not be surprised if we decline to fill their pockets with gold.

Well, Sir, the Partition was carried out on the 16th October last despite the pledge which Mr. Brodrick had given to the House of Commons to the effect that he would lay the papers on the table of the House, a pledge which involved the undertaking that the Partition would be postponed pending the final pronouncement of Parliament. The 16th October is a memorable day in our annals. I trust it will be a memorable day in the annals of India. ("Hear, Hear!"). It was a day of universal mourning, of universal fasting and universal fraternising; Hindus and Muhammadans embracing each other in public streets (Cheers), or in private places, vowing the vow of eternal love and concord. (Cheers and loud applause). The shops were closed, the domestic hearth was not lit, food was not cooked, Calcutta presented the aspect of the City of the Dead. A spirit of desolation seemed to hover the scene. The genius of the Motherland was incarnate amidst this bewildering scene of grief and sorrow. Thousands, tens of thousands, hundreds of thousands of pious Hindus, and Hindus who were not pious, rushed to the waters of the Bhagirathi in order to purify themselves for the sins of their rulers. (Cheers). Thousands, tens of thousands, hundreds of thousands of people walked through the streets of Calcutta bare-footed, clad in the garb of woe. Amidst the wild scene of excitement, the National Fund was started; amidst this wild scene of excitement the foundation—stone of the Federation Hall was laid (Cheers) by one who was our President and occupied that place which you now, Sir, adorn. Prostrate on the bed of illness, scarcely capable of moving, my illustrious friend, Mr. Anand Mohan Bose (Cheers), came in a litter attended by Dr. Nilaratan Sircar, to lay the foundation-stone; perhaps the last function which he will be privileged on this side of the grave to perform, and thus conferred another obligation upon his countrymen.

Well, gentlemen, while public excitement was so great, what was the Government doing? Forging instruments of repression, laying the foundations for the inauguration of a reign of terror. ("Shame!"). Yes, it is a matter of inexpressible shame. Within eight days of the 16th October, Mr. Carlyle issued his famous Circular. ("Shame!"). Under the terms of that Circular, students are prohibited from taking part in public demonstrations ("Shame!") and if they did, what then? They were not to be punished, but the institutions to which they belong were to be disaffiliated, grants-in-aid were to be withdrawn from them and their teachers were to be exalted to the dignity of Special Constables! ("Shame!"). A more outrageous scheme of vicarious punishment never entered the imagination of the greatest autocrat of the middle ages. But it was in the new Province that the reign of terror was inaugurated after the latest and most approved Russian pattern. In the new Province public meetings in public place have been prohibited; Sankirtan parties are not permitted to march through public streets; the singing of *Bande Mataram* (Shouts of "Bande Mataram"—a voice "Once more!" and then jointly *Bande Mataram* was sung by a large section of the audience rising to their feet)—the singing of the *Bande Mataram* which you have just sung with so much zest and devotion is punished as a crime and offence. ("Shame!"). Respectable people have been degraded by being enrolled as special constables. ("Shame!"). Not long ago a veritable reign of terror was established at Sirajganj and Barisal, and the police were let loose in the streets, indiscriminately assaulted the people, selecting the leaders of the Anti-Partition Movement as objects for special vengeance. When an aggrieved complained to the Sub-Divisional Officer of Sirajganj the courts were closed against him. Magistrates would not receive the complaint.

At Rajshahi the other day a public meeting was dispersed at the point of the bayonet. I use the words "at the point of the bayonet", advisedly. In a place, in a private place, fifty policemen armed with rifles and bayonets commanded by a posse of inspectors and sub-inspectors marched down to the place of the meeting, ordered the leaders of the meeting to disperse. My friend, Mr. Abul Kasim, I do not see him here (A Voice: "He is here"); he was addressing the meeting and a gun was pointed at him. ("Shame!" Voices "Let us see him", "Let him come on the platform"). My friend asked the inspector to produce his authority, and the inspector said that he had received confidential orders from the Magistrate which he declined to produce. Very properly then he ordered the meeting to dissolve. Since the news of the incident arrived in Calcutta, Mr. J. Chaudhuri and six others, every one of them resolved to go to jail if necessary (Loud and prolonged cheers) went down to Rajshahi in order to test the authority of the police and to vindicate the right of public meetings. ("Hear, Hear"). They held a meeting, the largest ever held at Rajshahi, but the police would not submit to the test, the brave fellows that they were! (Ironical cheers). They were conspicuous by their absence, and since then we have been holding a meeting every day at Rajshahi. (Cheers). Our boys are being prosecuted, and some of them even sent to jail. ("Shame!"). I heard the other day a touching incident regarding the pluck and heroism of young men—the pillars of popular movements whom I always regard with a sense of affectionate and paternal interest. (Cheers). About half a dozen of them were locked up in jail in one of the towns of the Eastern districts. As soon as they found themselves inside the lock-up they made the walls resound with the echoes of their patriotic songs (Shouts of "*Bande Mataram*"). The jailors were touched. They brought them food which they declined to accept. (Cries of "*Bande Mataram*"). If our rulers think that they will repress us in this way, kill the Anti-Partition Movement by having recourse to despotic Russian methods, they are greatly mistaken. Repression will not daunt us ("Hear, Hear!"); rather it will stiffen us in our opposition to the Partition and our support of the Swadeshi Movement. (Cheers). The blood of the martyrs is the cement of the church (Cheers); and our cause will be consecrated by the sufferings of our martyrs. We regard that cause to be of divine origin. Rightly or wrongly we believe ourselves to be humble instruments in the hands of the Almighty Providence (Cheers), walking under the illumination of the Holy Spirit. Call it delusion; call it fanaticism; reckon us among the deluded maniacs of mankind. You have read lessons of history in vain if you do not realize the fact that men fortified by such belief and working under such conviction are irresistible and invincible; there is no danger which they are not ready to brave, no difficulty which they are not prepared to surmount.

The Partition is now an accomplished fact; it has been carried out, but we at any rate do not regard it as an accomplished fact. The resolution says that the Bengalis have exhibited considerable disinclination to regard it as an accomplished fact, and the resolution says truly. And, gentlemen, if you read the resolution you will find that the essence of our prayer is that we want the entire Bengali community to be placed under the same common administration. We do not want to be separated from our kith and kin. Is that not an aspiration which is reasonable and righteous, and is there any one who will not respond sympathetically to an aspiration of that kind? May we not, therefore, appeal to Lord Minto and Mr. John Morley, the new Secretary of State, to reverse the decree which has been passed upon us by Lord Curzon? May we not be permitted to indulge the hope that Lord Minto's mission in India is to conciliate, to throw oil upon the troubled waters, to undo the mischief wrought by his predecessor? His illustrious ancestor who ruled over us about one hundred years ago gave us peace amidst war. May we not appeal to him to emulate the example of his illustrious ancestor and spread the blessings of peace, contentment and happiness throughout the length and breadth of the country? As regards Mr. John Morley, we are all more or less his disciples. We have sat at his feet; our intellectual and moral natures have been fed, stimulated and ennobled by the great lessons which he enforced with such consummate eloquence. He has taught us in his life of Edmund Burke that Asiatics have rights and Europeans have their obligations in India. He has taught us the paramountcy of moral laws in the government of human affairs. May we not ask him to apply his own principles to the solution of the Partition problem and the solution of other Indian problems? Above all, we must learn to depend upon ourselves. To native strength and native devotion and native courage dominated by the spirit of constitutionalism, we must look forward for our eventual emancipation. You know for the moment we have lost; for the moment we have been defeated; but let us not despond. The Irish have been fighting for Home Rule for over 100 years and they have not yet got it, but they are within a measurable distance of success. Let us emulate the courage, the enthusiasm and heroic self-sacrifice of the children of the Emerald Isle. Bear in mind that we are living through critical and great times. The sun has risen in the East. Japan has hailed the rising Sun, but that Sun of Asia will pass in its meridian course over this hapless land and shed upon us its brilliance and lustre. Even now we feel the first fluttering of an awakened national consciousness. Oh! let us strengthen them and invigorate them, ennoble them for the glorification of our Motherland, for the lasting credit of the great race to which we belong and for the permanence upon broad national lines of that great administration which in the past was fired with lofty ideals of duty towards India, but which, in the present moment, we are anxious to rescue from the reproach of reaction and retrogression. (Loud and prolonged cheers).

KASHINATH TRIMBAK TELANG
(1850-1893)

KASHINATH TRIMBAK TELANG

The Ilbert Bill

Speech in Bombay in 1883 to Assess the Ilbert Bill then before the Viceregal Council

Mr. Chairman and Gentlemen,—The resolution which has been entrusted to me runs as follows:—

"That the Committee of the Bombay Branch of the East Indian Association be also requested to take steps to have the memorial, with the necessary alterations, forwarded to the Honourable the House of Commons in England."

In proposing this resolution, it would be wrong, on more than one ground, if I were to detain you with any lengthy speech of my own at this late hour, and especially after the able speeches which have been addressed to you. But the subject which we are met to consider to-night is one of such great importance that I trust the meeting will bear me while I make a few remarks on it. I do not propose to travel over the ground occupied so well by the speeches of Mr. Budrudin and Mr. Pherozeshah and the speakers who followed them. Nor, for obvious reasons, shall I say anything about the recent doings of our European friends in the Town Hall of Calcutta. These doings were of such a nature that, to borrow the language used on a celebrated occasion by a distinguished man, now no more, the best rebuke we can administer to these gentlemen is to refrain from following so dangerous an example. (Cheers). There was, however, one point, gentlemen, made, I believe, at the Calcutta Town Hall, and certainly made in the public press since, to which I feel bound to refer. It has been asserted that the Bengalis entertain feelings of hatred and hostility to the British nation. Well, gentlemen, having had the honour, as you are aware, of being appointed to serve on the Education

Commission, I had recently to spend a few months in Calcutta. And during the period of my stay there I came into close, intimate, and frequent contact with the leaders of thought and the leaders in public affairs of the Bengali nation. And, having frequently had frank conversations with many of them, having thus seen them in a sort of mental undress, so to speak, I venture to affirm, and to affirm very confidently, that this hatred and hostility is a mere figment of some alarmist brain, and has no existence in reality. (Loud cheers). I think that, believing this, as I do believe it, to be the truth upon the subject, I am bound, if not by any other obligation, at least by gratitude for the kindness which I received from my Bengali brethren while I was among them, to make this statement to correct misapprehension. I need not, however, dwell any further on this point, and therefore I shall turn at once to the main subject to which I wish to address myself. As I have said, I do not intend now to go into any of the positive argument in favour of the Jurisdiction Bill. But I propose to examine the main points made by an eminent man, Sir Fitz-James Stephen, in his letter on the subject. Sir Fitz-James Stephen has held high office in this country, and now occupies a distinguished position on the English Bench. He is not only a lawyer, but a writer on Jurisprudence and a political philosopher who has thought out the ultimate principles of the political creed which he holds. (Hear, hear). And, therefore, I need not say that his authority on such a subject as ours is very high, and I should be the first in ordinary circumstances to defer to it, but in this case I must say that if I was an opponent of the Jurisdiction Bill, I should be afraid of Sir Fitz-James Stephen's championship. Many years ago he wrote a work entitled "Liberty, Equality, and Fraternity" which, I think, may, with substantial accuracy, be characterised as the gospel of force. (Cheers). In that work he set himself in obtrusive antagonism to the doctrines of modern liberalism, by which I do not mean what is called by that name in the jargon of English party politics. But I mean liberalism in the broader and higher sense as signifying those political principles, which, for us here in India, are embodied in the great proclamation of 1858. Well, as he holds those opinions, it is plain that even his support, if he supported any measure of Government which involved any of those principles, would be an occasion of embarrassment. But apart from these general considerations, let us see for an instant what Sir Fitz-James Stephen does say. His first proposition, not first in order in his letter, but first in importance is that the policy of Lord Ripon's Government is shifting the foundations of British power in this country, or to use his own expression, is inconsistent with the foundations on which British power rests. Now, I deny this entirely, I say that the principles of Lord Ripon's administration, as pointed out in our memorial, are in consonance with the long-established principles of the British Government as laid down by Parliament and the Crown. (Loud cheers). And I say, further, that those principles are in accord with the lessons to be derived from the study of past history. I remember being struck many years ago, in reading the history of the Romans under the Empire, with a passage in which the author said that one great lesson to be deduced from the history of Rome was that all conquering nations, in order to render their Government in the conquered countries stable and permanent, must divest themselves of their peculiar privileges by sharing them with the conquered peoples. Now, gentlemen, we all know that it is the proud and just boast of Englishmen that they are the Romans of the modern world, and that the British Empire is in modern days what the Roman Empire was in ancient times. If so, are we wrong, are we unreasonable in asking that the lessons of Roman history, and, as Mr. Merivale points out, the lessons of the history of other ancient Governments also, should be adopted by our British rulers? (Cheers). It is not quite proper and reasonable for us to ask that the countrymen of Clarkson and Wilberforce, of Gladstone and John Bright—(loud cheers)—should not only adopt those lessons but improve upon them, and rise superior to the countrymen of Marius and Sylla, the Triumvirs and the Caesars? I venture to say, gentlemen, that if Britons are now content to fail to carry out those lessons, and to fall short of the generosity of the Romans, it will be regarded as not creditable to them by the future historian. And as a loyal subject of the British Government I should be sorry for such a result. (Loud and prolonged cheers). We next come to Sir Fitz-James Stephen's second point. He says—Oh ! it is all very well to ask for the abolition of these special privileges to Europeans, but every other section of the Indian community has its own privileges which the law recognises. And he gives as an instance the fact that Hindus, Mahomedans, &c., have their own special laws of inheritance administered to them. Now, I venture to say that no fair comparison can be made between laws of inheritance and laws of criminal procedure. The former does not affect any one save the special community to which it is administered. What does it matter to John Jones whether the property of Rama, or Ahmed, or Muncherjee goes on his death to his sons or his daughters, his father or mother or widow? But the law of criminal procedure, as has been already pointed out by other speakers, affects the other communities in a most important respect. It is plain, therefore, that the two cases which Sir Fitz-James Stephen treats as identical, are really distinguishable on essential points. Besides, it must be remembered that no other class privileges are recognised in the criminal law of British India; it is only in the civil law that they are so recognised. But, further, I am surprised at Sir Fitz-James Stephen not alluding in his letter to one point relevant to this branch of the subject to which reference is made, in his own volume already referred to. He has there pointed out that the British Government in India is, involuntarily it may be, but still actually, interfering with the personal laws of natives, even in matters connected with their religious beliefs, and is applying as Sir Fitz-James Stephen puts it, a constant and steady pressure to adapt them to modern civilization—so that the Government, as Sir Fitz-James Stephen himself puts it, is really heading revolution. If then the Government is actually interfering with the personal laws of us unenlightened and uncivilized natives, is there anything wrong in their interfering with those of the enlightened Britons, with whose views and opinions, feelings and wishes they are much more familiar, and in much greater sympathy? Is there any thing unfair if we ask that the same measure should be dealt out to both? Sir Fitz-James Stephen next refers to the Special Tribunal for Europeans maintained in Turkey and other countries. But there the European is protected from foreign courts to be subjected to British courts. Here he is protected from one class of British courts to be subjected to another. The difference is quite manifest between the two cases. Further, Sir Fitz-James Stephen says it is only natural that everyone charged with a criminal offence should wish to be tried by one of his own race and colour. But this leads to a difficulty, namely, that natives may have a similar wish. And how does Sir Fitz-James Stephen meet that? Why he says that while no native understands English sufficiently to conduct a trial in that language properly *attempts* are made—mark the expression, attempts are made—to get European officers to study the vernaculars of the country. Now, gentlemen, I think it is not egotistical to say that the first part of the statement is the reverse of the truth. (Cheers).

For every one European that can be shown competent to conduct a criminal trial in a vernacular language, we can show at least one hundred natives even more competent to do so in English. (Loud cheers). And as to the second part, we have not to rely only on our personal experiences. As we say at Law *habemus optimum testem confidentem reum*. Many years ago a book was published by a Bengal Civilian, called "Life in the Mofussil," in which he very candidly admitted that though he passed the examination in Bengali, he knew little or nothing of the language. (Loud laughter). Here we have a test of the success of the *attempt* to which Sir Fitz-James Stephen refers. I do not think, gentlemen, I need further detain you with Sir Fitz-James Stephen's arguments. His principal points have, I venture to say, been satisfactorily answered. There is, however, one argument to which I should like to refer before sitting down. It is put forward in the *Times of India* by a gentleman who signs himself "Maratha," but whose nationality, from internal evidence, seems to be European and not Maratha. However, on the principle of measures, not men, we shall consider his argument, as it deserves to be whether it emanates from a veritable Maratha or not. He says natives are not fit and competent judges of Europeans, because the native papers are writing about the cases of deaths of natives at the hands of Europeans as if they were all cases of deliberate murder and the explanation of a ruptured spleen always untrue. He argues that as this view of the native papers has not been disavowed by educated natives, it indicates the state of their feelings towards Europeans, and renders them unfit judges for trying Europeans. Now, I am not one of those who believe that this explanation of the ruptured spleen is always untrue. (Laughter and applause). I have no doubt that in many cases it is true, and that the language of many of our native papers on the subjects is exaggerated and without justification. But having admitted that, I do not admit the correctness of "Maratha's" argument. I will not, however, analyse it now, but put another argument on the other side. We all know that many Europeans have spoken of the native communities in a way which means that they consider us all as, on the whole, a people given to perjury. This opinion, publicly expressed by some members of the European community, has not been disavowed by others. And, therefore, according to "Maratha's" logic, the true conclusion to be derived from this is that Europeans are not fit judges for natives. (Cheers). This broad conclusion follows according to "Maratha's" principles. Certainly, in cases where natives are charged with perjury Europeans would be, on those principles, unfit judges. Because whereas, according to the presumption of English law, the accused would have to be treated as innocent until the contrary was proved, in the mind of the European judge the native prisoner would be guilty until he proved the contrary. Mark, I don't say this would be a correct result. But I say it follows, if "Maratha's" argument is sound, I use it only as an *argumentum ad hominem*. See then the deadlock. You cannot have European judges, and you cannot have native judges. How then is the administration of justice to be secured? (Laughter and cheers). I do not think, gentlemen, that I ought to detain you any longer. We have a very good case; let us take it before the House of Commons. It has been taken there already, in fact, by the opponents of the Bill. Let us place our view before the House. (Cheers). By past experience we know that in such matters we can trust to the justice and sense of fair play of the British House of Commons. (Loud cheers). Let us leave this matter also to their judgment, in the full confidence that it will be there decided on considerations free from all local passion and local prepossession. (Loud cheers).

BAL GANGADHAR TILAK
(1856-1920)

BAL GANGADHAR TILAK

The National Demand

Speech at the Calcutta Session of the Congress in 1906 Supporting the Resolution on Self-government

I have not the eloquence of my friend Mr. Banerjea, nor of my friend Mr. Jinnah, nor the trumpet voice of Mr. Bipin Chandra Pal. Yet I have to do a duty, and I mean to place before you without any introduction a few facts in support of the resolution which has been so ably moved by the proposer, seconded by the Hon. Mr. Jinnah and certainly not amended but intended to be amended by my friend Mr. Bipin Chandra Pal. The resolution, as you all know, is about Self-government or Home Rule for India. The first paragraph of it says: 'This Congress expresses grateful satisfaction for the pronouncement made by His Majesty's Secretary of State for India on behalf of the Imperial Government that its object is the establishment of Responsible Government in India'. The speaker who preceded me—I mean Mr. Bipin Chandra Pal—seems to think that it is not yet time to be grateful for the declaration of policy. To a certain extent I share in that view, but, at the same time, I cannot say that the wording of the resolution is not adequate. For gratitude, as you know, is defined by one of the best ethical writers of England to mean expectation of favours to come: and grateful satisfaction, translated in view of that definition, means satisfaction at the pronouncement attended with an expectation that the later stages of it will come in course of time as early as possible. That is how I interpret 'grateful satisfaction'. I am satisfied for the present that a thing that was not pronounced before has been declared now, and I hope, at the same time, nay expect, that it will be followed up by higher stages of development in time to come.

All talk about further stages is out of place at present. What should be the first step is the point that I want you to understand. A very simple definition of Home Rule which any of You, including a peasant, can understand is that I should be in my own country what an Englishman feels to be in England and in the Colonies. The simplest definition is that, and that is the whole of it. All those bombastic phrases, such as 'partnership in the Empire,' 'terms of equality,' etc., mean that I want to be in my country not as outlander but as master in the same sense that an Englishman is a master in his own country and in the Colonies. That is complete Home Rule, and if anyone is going to grant it to-morrow, I shall be very glad for its introduction, for it will be Indian Home Rule granted all at once, but I see that it cannot be done. Some compromise has to be made with those who are not in our favour and with some of our friends.

The British power in India was introduced by a compromise, by a Charter. In fact, the first step in a province which you have not conquered is always with consent and compromise, and what the first step should be is explained in this resolution. All talk about future progress, about the establishment of Responsible Government in the Provinces and afterwards in the Central Government is very good talk with which I fully sympathise but which I am not prepared to demand as the first step of the introduction of Home Rule in India. That is the difference between myself and Mr. Bipin Chandra Pal. He wants the whole hog at once., I say it should be granted to you by stages: demand the first step so that the introduction of the second step would be much easier than it is at present.

The Government in the pronouncement has used the words "Responsible Government", not Home Rule or Self-government. Mr. Montagu in the declaration and the Government of India in their Proclamation have deliberately used the words "Responsible Government" unfortunately without defining it, because Responsible Government as naturally understood means Executive Government responsible to the Legislature. But in one place in Mr. Curtis's pamphlet I find that "Responsible Government" is defined to be one where the legislature is subject to the executive. You will see that it is quite necessary to define the words "Responsible Government", otherwise words may be interpreted quite contrary to our intention and it may be said: "We promise you Responsible Government but a Government where the Legislature ought to be under the control of the Executive". And the more it is placed under the control of the Executive the more responsible it will become according to this. I must state frankly here that this is not the kind of Responsible Government that we want. We understand by the words "Responsible Government", a Government where the Executive is entirely responsible to the Legislature, call it Parliament or by any other name, and that Legislature should be wholly elected. That Responsible Government is what we want. When I say that the Executive should be under the control of Legislature, I go so far as to say that even Governors and Lieutenant Governors must be elected by legislative bodies. That, however, will be the final step. But in the present circumstances I shall be quite content, and so I think most of you will be content, if the first step that we demand is granted to you immediately, and Self-government at an early date. And by 'early stages' I do not think that any sane man would understand to be anything which would be attained in fifty years, because a period extending to fifty years is not 'early'. Anything that exceeds the time of one generation is not 'early'. 'Early' means, certainly in ordinary parlance, ten or fifteen years. I should have liked that a definite number of years should have been introduced in this resolution. However, we do not lose much. I say that no sane man can understand 'early date' to mean other than ten or fifteen years. But some men thought that it would be rash to ask for Home Rule or Responsible Government in ten or fifteen years. It was dropped. Never mind. At any rate, the sense is there.

I must draw your attention to the pronouncement made. What is it? It is that full Responsible Government or merely Responsible Government without any qualification—that means the same thing —Responsible Government without any limiting qualifications will be granted to you in ten or fifteen years. That part of the answer given by Mr. Montagu we note with grateful satisfaction in the sense in which I have just explained it. There are certain other conditions. That pronouncement says that it will be granted to you by stages. We also agree to it.

The third part of the declaration is that these stages would be determined by the Government of India. We do not agree to that. We want the stages to be determined by us and not at the sweet will of the Executive. Nor do we want any compromise about it but insist on definite stages and the time to be fixed in the Act itself so that the whole scheme may work automatically. There we differ from the wording of the declaration: however, it is not said here in so many words but the second paragraph of the resolution demands it: it demands a Parliamentary State to be immediately passed definitely, settling and fixing the time when the goal is to be reached, not leaving it to the Government of India to determine when and at what circumstances and in what stages they will grant full Responsible Government to us: definite time should be named in the statute which will be passed about the subject very soon., So, the second part of the resolution is practically a suggested modification of the declaration about which we have expressed our grateful satisfaction in the first part of the resolution. In the third paragraph of the resolution we stick to what was passed last year at Lucknow both by the Congress and the Muslim League. It has been said that that scheme is objectionable and that after a year's experience we should have modified it at this Congress. I hold a different view. I am glad that we all hold the same view. That will be determined when we take the votes. If we unanimously pass the resolution it may be that I shall be speaking for you when you pass the resolution without a dissentient voice.

I hold that the Congress-League scheme is the minimum which might be granted to us to satisfy our aspirations at present and to make a decent beginning in the introduction of Home Rule in India. I tell you why. There have been a number of schemes suggested at various places in India by Congressmen and non-Congressmen, by Muslim League men and non-Muslim League men and by backward and forward classes as they call themselves and by other different communities, and all these representations have been sent up to the Secretary of State. What do you find if you analyse them? The majority of them say that they approve of the Congress-League scheme but they want something more, and if you take vote, you have all the votes for the Congress-League scheme and one vote for each scheme in the country. I say that that itself is an indication that the Congress-League scheme is approved all over the country and we are not going to swerve from it an inch. It has been said that the Government is prepared to grant to you Responsible Government but that you do not ask for it because the Congress-League scheme does not make the Executive removable at the pleasure of the Legislature; it cannot be technically said to be responsible. The pronouncement is that "Responsible Government" will be granted to you, that it should be granted to you by stages, so that the first stage also must have something of Responsible Government. I do not think that that argument is right. The Government meaning is that one stage will be Municipal and Local, the second stage Provincial and the last stage Central Government. That is not the meaning that I attached to it. I say that the Congress-League scheme does not provide for the removal of the Executive at the will of the Legislaure; true, but it gives you all the control over the Executive. We say that the Executive should be under the control of the Legislature and that four-fifths of the legislative body should be elected. What does it mean? It means that the Legislature which the Congress-League scheme demands will not be fully responsible in the sense of being able to remove the Executive, but it can transfer the Executive. If the Executive-will not obey the Legislature they may be transferred to some other post. Why should you ask that the Executive should be removed? Once the bureaucracy understand that they are wise enough, intelligent enough to shape their future conduct accordingly; they are not fools. A beginning of the responsibility is made. The Executive are held responsible and they must take their orders from elected Legislative Councils. So, to say that the Congress-League scheme is not a beginning of Responsible Government is merely deceiving oneself and others by a use of words with which always wise and selfish men try to deceive the masses.

The second objection urged against the Congress-League scheme is that it is better to begin from below; that it is better to build up from foundation, than to begin with the top, so that you must begin with your Municipality, gradually have District Boards under your control, then bring Provincial-Government. Even that argument is fallacious. The case may apply to the building of a new house where you cannot build the top without foundation, but the simile of a house does not apply to a political building, especially in the case of India. We, in India, are not children to be promoted from standard to standard until we pass our graduation either in Arts or in Law. We are full-grown people. We have had experience of governing Empires and Kingdoms in the past. We have learnt those principles and how to use those principles, having watched them so far in civilised countries. Are we not capable of carrying on the Government of India from to-morrow if the Government is given into our hands? When we say that Responsible Government should be granted to us by stages we cannot be meant to suppose that we should have training in Municipalities first, in District Boards afterwards, Provincial Legislative Councils next and then in the Supreme Legislative Council. There is no parallel between the two.

The case of India is like that of an emasculated man who had lost or was made to lose all his nervous power. In the case of a nervous disease, there is emasculation of the whole body and you have to begin the treatment with the brain and not with the toe. If you want to restore a man to health at once you give tonic to the brain, the centre of all nervous system. So it is with India. If the present Government is unfit for the administration of the country in the best interests of the Empire, the best remedy is to give tonic to the brain and that is Simla or Delhi. Unless that centre is made sound soon you cannot expect that any local remedy applied to the different parts of the body—to the foot or hand or other parts of the body—would be of any avail.

So the Congress-League understanding provides that we must have certain powers in the Central Government. If it is not made removable, we must at least be placed on a footing of equality. Half the members of the Executive should be our representatives, i.e., they should be elected by the people. Thus we must go on building from the top. We do not want to divide the political Government in this country into parts, horizontal or vertical. We want to treat the whole man, and we want such cure to be administered as will cure his brain first and power over the lower limbs will gradually be restored. Our scheme provides for that. To talk of Provincial Government when speaking of Imperial autonomy is to talk nonsense. We must have a share of the power in the Central Government. The control over the Municipalities remains with the Central Government, and you know how that power is being exercised and what actual independence you have in Municipality. If you mean to have local Self-government you must have power all through from top to bottom, *i.e.*, Responsible Government from top to bottom.

In the Congress-League scheme it is provided that the Imperial Legislative Council should have four-fifths of its members elected and one-fifth nominated and that the Legislature should have control over the Executive. I admit that this is not Responsible Government but it is really the beginning of Responsible Government. Take the case of a minor whose estate is in charge of the Court of Wards. The minor having attained majority claims the estate from the Court of Wards. Suppose the defence of the Court of Wards is that they will transfer the power by parts, say, the stables outside the house. What is the result? When that is done, the Court of Wards will say, "We shall then think at the later date of transferring the whole house to the man". That defence would not be good enough in a Court of Law; any judge will throw it away. The same is the case in the political struggle between the bureaucracy and the Nation. Bureaucracy is the trustee of our interests. We have attained the age of majority; we claim our estate from bureaucracy and men like Mr. Curtis are prepared to tell us: "Yes, we know that we shall have to transfer the whole power to you, but we shall see that it is transferred to you gradually when proper electorates are brought into existence, and that at some time in the course of a century or two when the preparations are-complete or according to the Hindu time, some time in this *Kali Yuga* we shall transfer the power to you". That kind of defence ought not to be allowed for one moment. We are entitled to the possession of the whole house, and if we allow you to share our power with you in that house, it is a concession made for you in the hope that you will soon clear out of it. You have managed the house so long ; you have been living in the house, we will allow you to live in the house for a longer time, but eventually you must acknowledge that from to-day we are masters of the house; then alone can there be any compromise; otherwise, none.

The first merit of the Congress scheme is that it asks for a transfer of power to the elective body in a Central Government itself. Without a share—an equal share—in the Central Government, it is hopeless to be able to govern the smaller portions of the Empire, such as Municipalities, Local Boards, etc., with any sense of Responsible

Government. You must banish from your mind the idea of building from the bottom. That is not the analogy applicable to our scheme. We consent to nothing less than what is embodied in the Congress-League scheme. "We must have control over the Central Government". The Government of India is one body from the gods of Simla to the lowest policeman in the village. If You want to grant our right, if you think that our claims are just, we must have a share at the top. All these arguments against our scheme are intended to deceive you and are advanced by people whose idea is to remain in possession of the house even though we have attained our majority and are entitled to the possession of the whole house. Mr. Bipin Chandra Pal admitted that we must have the whole Congress scheme plus something more. I also want the plus and not the minus. But I claim the first term of this equation to begin with, the other terms will follow, and I shall be one with him when we fight for the second stage, and I ask him and entreat him to be one with me in fighting for the first. The second merit of our scheme is that it tries to build upon the existing foundation. It is not a new scheme requesting the Government to introduce any modification in the machinery of the Government. The machinery has been in existence for hundred years or more. We want the Secretary of State, we want the Imperial Government, we want the Local Governments, we want the Municipality, we want the District Board, and we also want the bureaucracy to stay in the land and not to go out of it. We all want these, but we want certain transference of power, a decentralisation which will vest people with power, in every one of these institutions. We do not want to change the institutions. We do not say that India should be governed by a Crown Prince from England or that the administration should be transferred to any Native Chief. We say "Retain your administrative machinery as it is". Our question is not with machinery but with power.

The Government of India is composed of Legislative and Executive. We want not changes in Governor, Governor-General and also Executive Councils but we want that the power that vests in the Executive should be transferred to the Legislature. We do not want to disturb the machinery. We do not want a new machinery to be introduced. What we want is that there are certain wheels in the machinery which have appropriated to themselves the power of regulating the machinery, and we want that power to be transferred to other wheels. It is no new scheme; it is a tried scheme, a tried machinery. All that is required is transfer of power from one part of the machinery to another. The Secretary of State should be in India. What next? The bureaucracy also agrees with us that power should be transferred by the Secretary of State to the present Government of India. We want it transferred to the Government of India and that the Executive should be under the control of the Legislature. At present about half the members are elected in the Legislative Council. What is the objection to electing a few more? All objections fall to the ground when you remember that so many Imperial Council members are elected now and do their work often to the satisfaction of Government. All that we ask for in our scheme is to have a few more members of that kind and give them power to control the Executive. We are to build upon the existing foundation. The objection that our scheme is unworkable, untried and that it has never been tried in other countries is useless and harmful to our interests if the objection is put in a language which may deceive the unwary. The second objection was that if we have half the Executive elected and half the Executive nominated, there would be a deadlock. It is said that one half of the Executive will be fighting against the other half and that the conflict would make the administration nugatory. I say No. Our scheme says that the Governor shall have the power of veto and he would decide which side is correct and the administration will not be hampered in any way at all. We have made provision for it, and that provision does not suit the bureaucrats who are in power and they think that when power is shared like that they must act with greater respect to popular opinion.

Lastly, I say that, our scheme is better than any other scheme for another reason, and that reason is that no other scheme will be so compatible with the wishes of the British Parliament as ours. Mr. Curtis and Sir Valentine Chirol have been forced—and I do not think quite willingly—to accept the pronouncement of the Government as the basis of future work. Government having declared the policy—those two gentlemen would have been very glad if the Government had not declared their policy—they have accepted that policy. But what are they trying to do with it ? Given that proclamation, how much of it, in fact, what is the lowest proportion of it, that can be conceded to the people? They wish to draw the minimum length provided for in that proclamation. That is the problem before Mr. Curtis and Sir Valentine. Our problem is how long can the line be drawn. I must warn you not to accept any other scheme or to be carried away by it simply because the author of it professes to limit it. 1, therefore, commend this resolution for your unanimous acceptance.

BIPIN CHANDRA PAL
(1858-1932)

BIPIN CHANDRA PAL

The Swaraj Ideal

From His Third Public Speech in Madras in 1907

Last night I considered the ideal of Swaraj, but I am often times told, "Why do you talk of the ideal? Swaraj is an excellent thing, but it is not within the range of practical politics. It is an excellent academic subject, but not a subject which need trouble us so far as the actual work that we have to do is concerned." I do not, Mr. Chairman, I cannot subscribe to this view, and for this simple reason: unless you are sure as to what you want, you cannot now adopt the necessary means, the instruments for securing that which you want. You are walking, but walking is not progression. Walking may be away from the goal as well as it may be towards the goal and you ought to know what your destination is with a view to determine what your work and duty, what your direction must now be. Practical politics means the adoption of practical measures for the amelioration of the political condition of the people. But unless you have a clear conception of the ultimate end, you run the risk of being carried away by the passions, the temptations, the prejudices, the difficulties, the obstacles of the hour, from your goal. Here is, for instance, a particular wrong that has to be remedied. Take, for instance, the misappropriation of a certain public fund by the Government—the misappropriation of the Famine Fund, the misappropriation in Bengal of the Road Cess Fund. When the Road Cess was first introduced in Bengal, it was regarded by the people of the Province as a practical violation of the Permanent Settlement obtaining in that country. It was a cess imposed on land, and according to the terms of the Permanent Settlement the Government had given the undertaking that no further assessment would be imposed upon land and yet this Road Cess was practically an impost on land, and the Government said, 'No, it is not a part of

Land Revenue, it is a special cess levied for a specific purpose', and accordingly they defined these purposes. They said that sinking wells, digging tanks, keeping and repairing and constructing public roads, looking after village sanitation, establishing a system of proper drainage in the village areas—these are all the objects to which this fund shall be applied. Lastly, however, they refused to grant any money out of this Road Cess Fund for the removal of water scarcity in the rural areas of Bengal. They said, 'No, we will not give any money for sinking wells or digging tanks. We shall spend it on other purposes.' Here was a distinct misappropriation of public funds, and you may do at once one thing: You may appeal to the Government, you may memorialize to Government, you may bring friendly pressure upon the Government with a view to induce them to take to sinking wells, digging tanks and looking after village sanitation. If you do this, a particular grievance will be removed. If the Government sink wells, dig tanks, water scarcity will be partially removed, and so far as it is removed the lot of the people will be easy. It will be some relief to the people, but the question is, will this temporary relief contribute to your progress towards the particular goal upon which you have set your heart? A school-boy is running to his school. He is feeling very thirsty. He has got only one minute's time during which he has to get into his school. He is feeling thirsty. A man offers him a cool drink, and says, 'Here is a cocoanut tree. I am going to the top of it, and I shall give you a drink of a tender cocoanut, wait here.' If the school: boy waits here, he will relieve his thirst, no doubt. He will find it very pleasant to have a drink of the tender cocoanut, but by going to enjoy a drink he will miss his lesson at his school; will he not?

Similarly, by seeking to relieve the present distress, you may be missing an opportunity of creating those forces in the community by the application of which, ultimately you may be able to attain Swaraj or autonomy. If you do not care for Swaraj, yes, Sir, let the partition be removed, let the cess be repealed, let a few more seats be given to us in the Legislative Councils. These are palliatives. These are local applications, and he is a quack doctor who, when the disease is a constitutional disease, wastes time by local application. In politics also, therefore, it is essential that you should know what is that you desire to have. In the politics of free countries, the ultimate principles are well established. There the goal is kept in view, whatever party comes into power. The increase of the political power, the commercial prosperity of the British nation, is the one end towards which Liberals or Conservatives both equally try to move and lead the country. Therefore, the goal being fixed at that point, there being no chances of misconception in the public mind, they are entitled to look after little things, to improve the details of the administration, to try palliatives, to make local applications for the removal of local maladies. But your malady is not a local malady. It is not the removal of one cess or another cess, it is not the securing of a few appointments here or a few honorary posts there. The evil under which you suffer is fundamental, a radical and a constitutional evil, and, therefore, it is all the more necessary for you to keep in mind this constitutional, this fundamental, this radical character of the problem that faces you, so that you may not run off from the right course by the passing temptations of the hour, this way or that way. I told you yesterday that when there is a conflict between the Government and the people, the right policy to follow for those who care for popular progress and popular freedom is to insist upon the Government to adopt and follow the policy of laissez faire, to restrict the operation of the Government, to restrict the activities of the Government within the narrowest possible limits. But when you seek this isolated individual redress, you do actually this—you increase the hold of the Government upon the mind of the people. I should rather wish, Sir, that our people went without good drinking water for 25 years, if that is necessary. I should think it far more desirable that, like the Israelites of old, the Indian people shall pass through the desert, parched up desert, for 25 years together, drawing water at the end of the Prophet's rod out of hard stone, rather than have wells sunk and tanks dug by this foreign authority, who by distributing this water to you will captivate your heart.

What is the real objective of the conflict between the educated community in this country and the Government? What is it, Sir, what is the objective of this conflict that has been going on for the last quarter of a century between the people, the representatives of the people, between the educated class—the enlightened class in India on the one hand and the foreign bureaucracy on the other? What is that objective? What is the citadel which both the parties are trying to capture and occupy? What is that top of the hold to which both the parties are trying to get up the soonest they can possibly do so? Is it merely the amendment of certain laws? Is it merely the removal of certain grievances? No. It is the heart, the mind of the people, of the masses, that is the objective. Lord Curzon saw it, and all his measures were directed towards capturing the popular mind in India. He organized his pageants to appeal to the imagination of the man in the street. He inaugurated rural reforms, agricultural banks and other things with a view to capture the mind of the teeming masses; and the intense scrupulousness with which he tried to do justice in cases of individual wrongs, his punishment of the 9th Lancers, his desire to see British justice maintained in this country—all these things were directed towards one great end, and that end was to secure for themselves, for the foreign bureaucracy, for this alien administration in this country, if not the allegiance, at least the passive, the generous acquiescence of the general mass of the population, and the battle must be waged around that citadel. The Government will try to capture the mind of the masses, and he is a foolish politician in India who allows the Government to capture the mind of the masses to the exclusion of his own influence, of his own countrymen. And what do you do if you make the administration easy? What do you do if you cover the wheel of the British administration with cotton and wool? It moves on and it grinds us small, but the padded wool makes it less painful to you. That is all. Good government is not only no substitute for self-government, it is an exceedingly evil thing when the authority of the State rests in the hands of an irresponsible power. Of all kinds of despotism, a benevolent despotism is the worst, because the benevolence makes people acquiesce in the despotism, and it is, therefore, necessary that you and I should have a clear vision of what we want. Do you want good government, Sir? If you want good government, you can have it. You will have it. Things will be made easy for you, but if you want self-government under existing conditions in India, good government will be absolutely opposed to the promotion of self-government, because, as I said last night, our trouble is with ourselves. Our trouble is with our own mind. Our trouble is with our own sentiments. Our trouble is with our own wills, with our own inertia, and good government will help to continue it if it does not increase the *Maya.* Pleasures of the world help to increase the hold of *Maya* on human beings, and it is, therefore, that he who wants to get rid of *Maya is* asked to cultivate *vairagya,* cultivate abstemiousness, cultivate dis-attachment.

You talk of Swaraj. The knowledge of Swaraj is absolutely impossible without a consciousness of the present *pararashtra.* The knowledge of Self is absolutely impossible unless the Self comes in contact and conflict with the not-Self. So, the knowledge of Swaraj is absolutely impossible unless there is not a *pararashtra. Para* is directly against the *Swara.* It is in the conflict between *Swara and Para,* it is in the conflict between the Self and the not-Self in political affairs, that the conception of the real Self-Government grows, and keen has become the conflict between the Self and not-Self in political matters and in proportion to the keenness of this conflict will the desire for Swaraj grow. Therefore, the conflict must be kept up. You must have a clear conception of what you want. Swaraj, your raj, is your *Shastra,* and the first thing is, discrimination between the Self and not-Self,—in political and civil matters, between the national Self and that which is not the national Self. The ideal of Swaraj has been revealed to us only recently, and, why, because for nearly a hundred years and more we never looked upon the British Government in India as *a pararashtra,* as a foreign Government. When the Congress was started we looked upon this Government as our Government, only it was not so good as we should have liked it to be. Before that we regarded this Government as our Government, because we had been brought up under English ideals, brought up in English traditions. Not only have our territories been conquered by England, but by this English education even our mind, our mental ideals, our ethical ideals, our spiritual aspirations, all these had been got hold of by this foreign Government, this foreign culture, this foreign civilization. And because we looked upon this Government and their institutions in this light, there was no possibility of the growth of the conception of Swaraj in our midst, in proportion as there grew a conflict first in the political field, then in the field of religion, in the field of social reform, in the field of economics, all over the national life, in proportion as there grew in the consciousness of the Indian people the presence of a conflict between ourselves and those who govern the country, between ourselves and the British people; in proportion as this conflict grew, in that proportion, by slow degrees, grew this ideal of Swaraj, until the conflict grew almost unbearable.

The full realization of the ideal of Swaraj came to us after the departure of Lord Curzon from this country and was proclaimed by

Mr. Dadabhai Naoroji from the chair of the Congress last year. If this be so, if this be a fact, Sir, then applying the principles of psychology to the consideration of our political problems, if we find that it is necessary that we should recognize this conflict between the people and the Government, it is also necessary that we should do nothing that will make this Government easy for us, because if the Government becomes easy, if it becomes pleasant, if it becomes good government, then our sense of separation from it will be gradually lost. And when the sense of separation is lost, you contemplate all the good things that this Government can do for you, you meditate on the honours that the Government can shower on you, you meditate on the high offices which the Government may give you. You may get a High Court Judgeship here, a Membership of the Legislative Council there, an Advocate Generalship in another part of the globe, a Legal Remembrancership in a third place, an Executive Membership of the Council possibly again. Now you think of all this, and thinking of all this you feel an attachment for this and feeling an attachment for this, you desire to have this, and the feeling of the desire to have this kills your consciousness of separation from this. And, therefore, good Government, pleasant Government, pleasurable associations with the Government, whatever else, however moderate or temperate they may be, they can never make for Swaraj, because the first thing in Swaraj is the perception of this, that there is an eternal, a natural conflict between the self and the not-self in the political affairs in this country. It is for this reason that I always tried to impress the ideal of Swaraj upon my countrymen, because once you have the ideal before you it will be possible for you to judge of the particular methods or measures in the light of that ideal. Do you want an expansion of the Legislative Council? Let us see if it will help you for Swaraj. Do you want that a few Indians shall sit as your representatives in the House of Commons? Let us see if half a dozen, or a dozen, or two dozens or 40, 50 members in the House of Commons representing the interests of India, elected by the Indian leaders, will make or not make for Swaraj. Do you want a large number of Indians to be in the Civil Service of the Government? Let us see, whether 50, 60, 100, 200 or 300 Civilians will make the Government our own. At one time we thought, Sir, that this was the method. At one time we thought that by slow degrees by participating in a small measure in the work of the administration with the Government of the country, with the foreign rulers of the land, we shall not only be trained in discharging rightly and properly the duties of the administration, but we shall also gradually oust them, replace the English agency by Indian agency. What, Sir, if you replace the agency? What about the principal? He is the primary factor and we, his agents. The whole Civil Service might be Indian, but the Civil Servants will have to carry out orders. They cannot direct. They cannot dictate policy. The policy is dictated by those who stand above them; and you replace, as I have said, the agency, but the agency implies presence of an original, a principal, and if, instead of 200, 300, 2000 Englishmen being the agents of the British nation and the British Parliament in India for the Government of India, you have 2000 natives, will that alter the state of things? I know it will not. We have had a number of Indian Civilians. Have they altered, at any rate, the character, the nature, the traditions of British Government in India? We have just now in Bengal an Indian Civilian who is the Senior Member of the Board of Revenue. 100 or 1,000 Civilians in the service of the British Government will not make that Government Indian. There are traditions, there are laws, there are principles, there are policies to which the Civilian, be he black, brown or white, must submit, and as long as these traditions have not been altered, as long as these principles have not been amended, as long as that policy has not been radically changed, the supplanting of European by Indian agency will not make for Self-Government in this country.

I doubt it very much if it would make for good government either. Why? You seem to think that a larger number of appointments in the Civil Service or in the Subordinate Service will improve the administration. I deny that it will be so, and it is for this simple reason. An Englishman, whatever else his fault is, is trained in the free atmosphere of England. An Englishman, whatever may be his attitude towards you and me, still knows this, he can stand upon his own rights. He never bends his knee unjustly, cringingly, after the manner of the sycophant, even before the highest official superior. But can you say the same of your Indian Civil Servants? And why? Because the Indian Civil Servant knows that there is no one behind his back to support him. The English Civil Servant knows there is behind his back the public opinion of England, the freedom of England, to stand him in good stead. Our Police is corrupt and they sometimes say, "O! What a perfect officer the policeman in London is!" Transplant the London Policeman in India and see where his perfection goes; and what is the reason? Why is it that the London Police is so honest, so painstaking, so respectful to the rights and liberties of the people of London? Because he knows that he is the servant of the public of London. In India every red turban knows that and feels that he is not your servant, but he is your master. And why does he feel it? Because he receives his *sannad* not from your hands, but from the foreign ruler of the land. It is to him that the policeman is responsible and not to you. It is to him the Civil Servant is responsible and not to you. It is to him that the District Magistrate is responsible and not to you. It is to him the Inspector, the Civilian, the District Magistrate and the Police constable and every officer of the Government, in fact, looks to, and naturally looking to his own interest he sees that, if he can please the officials, his interest will be best served, and if he displeases you he will not in the least suffer in his own interest. Therefore, there is such weakness, inefficiency, such disregard of the rights, liberties and the privileges of the people in the service of the Government in this country. Therefore, I say, if you have a larger number of officials native officials that may make things easy for a few families, get a few more coppers into their chest than otherwise, perhaps, they would get, it might make things easy for a few individuals, but for the nation at large it will not improve their lot. It is, therefore, necessary, I say, from whatever point of view you look upon this question, you will find that the consideration of the ideal, the creation of the right conception, the creation of strong convictions in regard to the goal, is essentially necessary for the right conduct and management of what you call practical politics.

It is said, Sir, are you fit for Swaraj? I put the question of fitness entirely out of court, because I am not going to apply to anybody else for granting me Swaraj. It is only when you have to make an application to somebody else to give you a certain thing that you have to prove your fitness for getting it. When you have to make an application to the Registrar of the High Court for a clerkship in the High Court or to the Police Magistrate there for some office at his disposal, you have to say, "Sir being given to understand that a clerkship is vacant, I beg to apply myself as a candidate for the same." And then you have to say, "As regards my qualification, I have passed F.A. or B.A. examination of the Madras University", but I say that when you want to open a shop with your own money, or the money left to you by your father or grandfather, do you in any application say you are qualified or not? Why not? Because you do it yourself. Therefore, you are not called upon to prove your fitness for the thing before you do it before anybody else, and those who ask us to prove our fitness for Swaraj forget that we have abjured the programme of petitions and prayers for good. They forget that we do not ask, nay, not even the benign Government of Great Britain in India, to grant us Swaraj. We do not pray to them for these things; and I would say more, Sir, if the Government were to come and tell me today, take Swaraj, I would say, 'Thank you for the gift, but I will not have that which I cannot acquire by my own hand,' because, my dear friends, in real growth, which is organic growth, there is absolutely no room for gift. Evolution, whether in the case of individuals or of nations, admits of no gifts from outside. We must grow from within, and I am surprised to find, Sir, that those eminently prudent and wise gentlemen, who, the moment we talk of social reform, come up to us and say, 'O, Social reform must be a growth from within', when we talk of Swaraj, call us to prove our fitness. They take it for granted that we must get it from outside. If social reform is to be a growth from within, I accept it unreservedly. There can be no reform, social or economic or political, that can be got from outside. You must gradually acquire your rights and in the acquisition of your rights you develop your character, you equip yourself with those forces and resources which will enable you to protect and to use those rights properly when you have got them. Lord Ripon's generous scheme of Local Self-Government has been a failure, more or less, I should say, out of regard for the tender susceptibilities of our Municipal Commissioners and Local Board Members. And why has it not succeeded? Sir, simply because it was a gift from the Government. If we had grown into it, if we had acquired it by our own strength, if we had organized our village lives ourselves, if we had organized our municipal life ourselves, if we had organized our *taluka* life ourselves, why Local Self-Government would take its stand upon self-determination, self-exertion, self-recognition of the civil duties by the peoples themselves. Such a Local Self-Government would not be a mushroom growth, would not be like an orchid that has no root on the ground, but hangs on the tree of a foreign Government. It will not be like that. The partial or complete failure of the scheme of Local Self-Government inaugurated by Lord Ripon proves my contention that for the exercise of civic rights it is essentially necessary that the people should desire to exercise those rights, should acquire them, and in the acquisition of these rights, they prove their fitness for the exercise of these rights. It is foolish politics, excuse me for that expression, to demand a priori reason and argument for proving the fitness of the people for Self-Government. No man knows, no one can say, that a nation is fit to Self-Government or is not. The proof of the pudding is in the eating thereof, and the proof of the fitness of the people is in their capacity to achieve the institution of Self-Government by their own exertion, by their own strength, by their own combination, by their own determination and by their own readiness to sacrifice themselves.

MOTILAL NEHRU
(1861-1931)

MOTILAL NEHRU

Desire for Swaraj

Speech in the Legislative Assembly on 8 February 1924

I shall simply lay a few broad facts. It will be seen, as I have submitted, that there is a deep seated desire for Swaraj in the country. I do not think any one will doubt that that desire proceeds from the natural cravings of the human heart for freedom. I do not think any one will seriously deny. That being so, I say the first and the last requisite for full responsible government is completely established. According to all modem conceptions, what you have to look to, is a genuine desire proceeding from the natural instinct to which I have referred and the determination to attain that desire. That is all that entitles a nation, that is all that has ever entitled a nation, to complete self-government and complete responsibility. But I am not going to put my case so high to-day. The desire for Swaraj, as all must be aware, has passed through the usual stages of ridicule and intimidation, rather unusually prolonged, and has now, it may be said, and properly said, emerged from an ordeal of fire unscathed and pure. That desire has led different sections of my countrymen to different courses of action. It is all a question of the intensity of the feeling of each section, the point of view of each section and the mentality of each section of my countrymen. That each has been prompted and guided by the best of motives there can be no doubt whatever. The question then is: have we made out a case for the realisation of that desire? What I ask for is, without mincing words, a complete overhauling of the Government of India Act.

Now, what is the great argument that has always been employed against any further advance in political rights to be given to Indians? It is said that those who desire any further advance are precluded by the Government of India Act itself from making the demand, because the Preamble sets out in clear words that responsible Government will only be granted by successive stages and that the parliament shall be the sole judge of the manner and measure of each advance, or words to that effects. And it is that you have no business to come forward and ask for anything. It is for you to satisfy Parliament, to satisfy us who are the agents of Parliament here—I mean the Government—that you deserve a further advance and you shall have it but not before that. Now, our answer, straight and clear, as unequivocal as the Preamble, is that that Preamble is bad, the whole law, the whole Act is as bad as could possibly have been devised to postpone, to stifle and to suppress the natural desire which I have already mentioned. That is what we say and we are perfectly entitled to say so. We feel that we must say so. What answer is it that the Act provides so and so, when the one reason why we do not want it is precisely because it provides so and so. It is arguing in a circle. We say that the Act has done a great injustice to us in that Preamble and in the subsequent provisions of it which refuse to us the full rights of Responsible Government that we demand. It is said: "you will not have them because the Act does not allow you to ask for them, but leaves it to the judgment of Parliament alone." Now, I ask what special sancity is there in this particular Act of Parliament that we must not say a word against it? Wherein does it differ from other Acts of Parliament all of which may be modified or repealed at any time? We ask for modification of this Act—or for its repeal, whatever may be necessary, and in doing so I really do not know what unconstitutional or improper act we are guilty of. Well, if it is true that we may ask for the modification of a piece of legislation which we take exception to, we are not going beyond our rights.

Then, the next question is, "Is the modification that we ask for Justified under the circumstances?" That really is the crux of the whole matter. It has been said—and I have been hearing a considerable amount of loose talk during the last three or four days—that the Act contains within itself enough to give us that from which we can grow, from which we can acquire more by the building up of conventions and things of that sort. I wish at once to dispose of that argument. I say that, so far as I am concerned, it will take very strong authority, and that of the weightiest character, to convince me that any coventions can grow so as to defeat the express provisions of a statute of Parliament. They are simply talking as if this statute did not exist. But even if such conventions could grow, I submit we are not content to let them grow in the way in which it has been suggested. We wish that our rights should be formulated, recognised and clearly admitted, and not only admitted and recognised, but actually conceded to us.

Now as for the steps, the argument is that the Government are in fact doing the very thing that the resolution and the amendment ask for, because what is called the working of the reforms constitutes the steps which are to be taken to secure the ultimate revision of the Government of India Act, and, in insisting upon the working of the reforms as they stand, we are doing all that is necessary to secure the revision of the Act and the inevitable establishment of Responsible Government after all the steps mentioned in the Act have been taken. Now, our submission is—we in the Congress have demanded ever since the year 1919 full responsible government; call it Swaraj, call it Dominion Status, call it anything you like. The Hon'ble Home Member has not paid attention to one very important fact that after the year 1919 the Congress has committed itself to a policy and a programme which were quite new and which had not been adopted before that year. I submit that it will serve no useful purpose except perhaps that of historical research to cite what the Congress said or what the leader of the Congress said in the years 1916, 1917 and 1918 and in previous years. From the year 1919 up to the present day the demand has been consistent that what we require is responsible government, that the Government of India Act is wholly inadequate and disappointing. The Congress has said that it will not rest until it has obtained either a revision or a repeal of that Act. That was the position under which the Act came into force and that is the position under which now it begins its second course. As I have said, we have got to see other things besides the provisions of the Act itself if we wish to come to a right conclusion as to whether the time has come for its revision or not. What are we suggesting? We are not asking for complete responsible government to be handed over to us tied up in a bundle? We say we are quite capable of it, we are quite fit for it, but what is it that my amendment is suggesting?

What we are asking for is not intended to convey something by way of a threat as has been believed in certain quarters. We are putting before the Government an honest and a fair demand. It is not fair to tell us that you can only do this or you cannot do that. It is not fair to treat our demand as a threat and to threaten us in return with dire consequences if we dare to make it. What I say is this; whatever we can do in this House, it is quite obvious that it must be done within the rules and within what is called the constitution. Personally speaking, I say there is no constitution for India. I refuse to believe in this constitution. I do not think that anything deserves the name of a constitution for a country in the making of which the people of the country did not have a voice, and for that reason I say that I do not give it the dignity of a constitution, although I submit to the rules. Now, if we submit to the rules, it is open to us to do certain things under these rules in this House and in the Provincial councils. If we can obstruct you under the rules, what is there to prevent us from doing so as an answer to the attitude that you adopt? I may at once say that the Swarajya Party has sought the suffrage of the electorates not to engage itself in the humdrum business of putting questions and getting answers and acquiescing in the process marked out in the Act itself for further stages of advance and similar things.

We have come here to do something which we have not been doing so far. We have come here to offer our co-operation, non- co-operators as we are, if you will care to co-operate with us. That is why we are here. If you agree to have it, we are your men, if you do not, we shall like men, stand upon our rights and continue to be non-co-operators. Now what threat is there in this! When I say what I am, what threat do I convey? Am I conveying any new idea? If we conform to the programme of non-co-operation, are we doing something that we have not been doing? We have so far been working outside the councils and this Assembly with a definite object. That object we have still in view, that object we consider perfectly legitimate. But we have come here because the dust and heat of the controversy which has been raging for the last three or four years, in fact ever since the inauguration of these reforms, has obscured the real issues.

We have come here and our coming here affords an opportunity to clear those issues as no other opportunity can. We are here for that purpose. We are not here simply to wreck or to destroy. We have been referred to as a party of destruction and wreckers. Yes, we are out to wreck and destroy things of evil, and, rightly or wrongly, we think that the present reforms are a thing of evil. We have come to ask you to meet us so that we may put our heads together,—to hear us and to let us hear you and then to come to some definite conclusion. If we agree, well and good; if we do not, we shall agree to differ, and the issues will be clarified. That is the thing. It is no business of ours to wreck things which we believe are doing good to the country. At least it will be admitted that we have no personal motives. We have not any axes of our own to grind. We believe in a certain principle. We believe that our country has reached a particular stage, and that at that particular stage it is entitled to certain rights, which rights are being withheld from it. We say that we cannot get those rights by an armed revolution, by delivering a great thumping blow, which alone in other countries has gained freedom for the people of those countries. In the very nature of things we can not do that and therefore we say, we shall simply not assist you. What law, what reason, is there which can compel us to co-operate with people who do not co-operate with us? However, I am not here, to justify the principles of non co-operation, but I certainly am here to say that we claim to be as much bound by our own principles as any honourable body of men has ever claimed to be, and that is all.

Now, it is said that the Act has been passed and the policy of the Act been approved by a series of Prime Ministers. We are told by His Excellency in his speech from the throne that, during less than four years of the period he has occupied his exalted office, there have been no less than four Prime Ministers in England and four Governments and that each Prime Minister and each government has approved the policy of this Act. Now, that is so. But I should like the honourable Home Member to answer the question; suppose there had been a dozen Prime Ministers and a dozen Governments in this interval of four years, would these reforms have been three times as good as they are to-day? I do not understand, I say with due deference what has the change of Government or the change of Prime Ministers to do with a good or bad piece of legislation or with the fact whether it is suited to the circumstances of the country or not. Well, I think I would attach more value to the opinion of the Honourable Home Member than I would to those of all the Prime Ministers that have held office ever since the beginning of Parliament up to this date. Why? Because he knows what I know, perhaps more. My only trouble with him is that I cannot get him to feel as I feel. My trouble with Parliament, with Prime Ministers and with the British public is that I cannot impart to them the knowledge which my friend the Honourable Home Member possesses. Then there is the British public. It has been said that the British people must also be taken to have set their seal of approval upon these reforms, because there have been these frequent changes of Government. Well, Sir, I should have imagined that this rapid succession of Prime Ministers and Governments only went unmistakably to show that your home politics are in a hopeless muddle and that you cannot either afford the time or have the inclination to pay attention to matters outside, strictly speaking, the circle of your home politics, such as India and Dominion Status for India. But however that may be, it is a fact which I know personally, and which my friend Pandit Madan Mohan Malaviya also knows, as we have both tried to gain a hearing at the bar of the august body known as the British people or the British public, that it is impossible under the best of conditions for Indians to secure a hearing in that great tribunal. We tried to do so and everybody knows how miserably we failed. It is impossible for us to approach that body. We can approach the Prime Mister, we can approach the Secretary of State, we can approach the Hon'ble Home Member here and the other government Members but the British public is altogether intangible and is something like the will-o'-the-wisp, which the further we follow the further it recedes. That is our experience. We therefore decided for want of any thing better to depend upon our selves and that is what we are doing.

Now the process laid down is nothing, I submit, but a reversal of the natural order of things. What the Government of India Act provides is that an extraneous authority has the right to determine the stages, the manner, the measure and the time for the advance of a nation to attain its freedom. I do not think there is anyone who will question now or seriously argue against the proposition that if there is anything by which nations and communities—big and small—

should be governed and should be guided, it is there own will. Clause III of my amendment has a direct reference to and is suggested by the right of self-determination. Now, that is the principle which we want the British Government and Parliament to accept. That is the principle which it will be for the Round Table Conference first to say whether it is prepared to recommended and then for the new Legislature which I propose in the third clause of my amendment to accept.

Now, I may briefly explain. It will be observed that we have left out all details and we did so because we thought they would more properly form the subject of subsequent negotiations and subsequent conversations. But I must make it perfectly clear that the representative Round Table Conference be really representative. It was intended at first to mention certain proportions but it was subsequently decided to drop them and to leave the word 'representative' there. That I submit, is an essential condition of that clause of the amendment. Then, we come to clause III. That clause affords the only reason for having a conference and provides the only way by which you can ascertain the will of the people.

Another reason why we want this new Legislature to be elected is the same as was put forward by the Hon'ble Home Member. He wants the best of India to agree to anything that is to be done so that there will be no future difficulties on the scene of the constitution or of the rules or of the exact rights which are going to be taken by us or given by the Government as it likes to put it. Now, I want also the best of India to come to this Legislature. As we are all aware, many of our best men are suffering from disqualifications and have not been able to contest the elections. I want them to be here. As for the proposal of my friend, the Home Member, that he wants the best of the people to agree to the arrangement, I can only say that it will all depend upon the manner in which the best of India is approached, as if, I may put it the other way, in which the advances or the approach made by the best of India are received by the Government.

Now, I shall try to answer the questions which have been put by the Hon'ble Home Member. I will first make the general observation that all these questions are really answered by the terms of the amendment which I have put forward before the House, because there is nothing in that amendment, as I said before, which asks that something should be done to-day without consulting the very interests, the very persons, which, the Hon'ble Home Member mentions, are very necessary to be consulted. His first question was, is this Dominion Status to be confined to India or will it include Indian States as well, and if so, on what terms? I say it all depends on our preliminary conversations. If the Indian States want to come in, let us have their representatives too. If they do not want to come in, we do not want them. All the questions that have been put are, I submit, sufficiently answered by one or the other clause of my amendment.

Then the next thing was that Dominion Status of course implies protection of the Dominion by its own armies. I do realise that and we are perfectly willing to confer with you as to how that may be done. We do require men to protect our Dominion with our own armies, but is it at all fair on your part to turn to us whom you have deprived even the use of arms, who cannot even have such training in the use of arms as you give in your schools and colleges? And why, because you have prohibited it, I say is it fair of you to turn round and tell us "you have got to be armed; you have no army and therefore you cannot have Dominion Status". What army have you got? Is it not the Indian Army—I do not say it is the Sole Army that protects us but is it not the largest factor in the British Army in India? I need not go in to what the Indian Army has achieved because that is a very long story and everybody knows it.

When it comes to the carrying on of the Government, I find three distinguished countrymen of mine in the Government Benches. You talk of Hindu-Moslem differences. Well, without trying to go into official secrets, I think I may ask for information whether these three gentlemen—one from Bengal, the other from the Punjab and the third from Madras—whether these gentlemen, when deciding matters relating to the administration, have been flying at each other's throats in the Executives Council Chamber. I mean what is there that can not be done if of course the proper steps are taken: and it is the taking of the proper steps upon which we lay special insistence. The steps may take some times; I do not say that everything has to be accomplished in a night. But to say that you are not entitled to it and you will not get it because we have said so—that is a position of great unfairness to which we are not going to submit.

Then the next question is, there are these communal differences. Of course, communal differences there are. Unfortunately they exist. We have not denied them.

Now the strong hand of Britain is the 'British Civil Service in India'. Remove the cause of 'division, strife, conflict and anarchy' and you take away the sole justification for the continuation of that distinguished service. There can be no question that inter-communal differences constitute the sole cause of 'division, strife, conflict and anarchy' and that inter communal amity which means the removal of that cause means also the removal of all justification for the continuance of the Civil Service.

But, it is said by my learned friend that inspite of these differences he is willing to have some sort of inquiry. He has excluded certain things, however, from that inquiry, namely, the question of the immediate grant of Dominion Status, and he has not given us full information as to what are the questions on which he would go to this Committee for inquiry. He has indicated that the advance that is necessary may be found within the four corners of the Act itself or that it may be necessary even to recast some portions of the Government Act; but not wholly modify it as is demanded by the resolution of my friend and by my amendment. That is a question, which does not arise at the present moment.

I should like to say one more word, and that is that the opportunity which should not be thrown away either by the Government or by us. It will serve no useful purpose to continue the state of things which has existed during the last few years. The Government is very well aware that there is a section of the public in India which can not be entirely ignored and which demands for the country certain rights and is prepared to put those rights before you, but is not likely to be frightened away by threats. It is not prepared to submit to conditions which are foreign to its policy but is fully prepared to bear all the consequences of its action, action which it has decided upon after mature and deliberate consideration. I have said already, and I repeat it again, that we are not hear to threaten anybody, nor even in our activities outside is it any part of our business to threaten anybody, and I submit that what is taken as a threat certainly was not intended to be a threat. All that we want is that you should consider the proposition which we place before you in the same mood without saying that this thing or that thing will happen to us. It must be remembered that we, some of us at least, have burnt our boats behind us. We take our stand upon these rights, and it does not matter to us in the least what happens so long as we go on rendering such service to our country as we believe our country is entitled to.

MADAN MOHAN MALAVIYA
(1861-1946)

MADAN MOHAN MALAVIYA

Swadeshi Movement

Speech in Calcutta in 1906 in Seconding the Following Resolution of the Twenty-Second Indian National Congress

This Congress accords its most cordial support to the Swadeshi movement and calls upon the people of the country to labour for its success by making earnest and sustained efforts to promote the growth of indigenous industries and to stimulate the production of indigenous articles by giving them preference over imported commodities even at some sacrifice.

Brother delegates, I have very great pleasure in seconding the resolution. I have every hope that you will carry it with acclamation. I am sure of that. Of all the resolutions which have been laid before the Congress, there is none which needs less of supporting, less to be said about, to commend it for your acceptance than this resolution. As you have been told, the Swadeshi movement is an old movement in this country. It is not born either of Partition or after Partition and it is extremely desirable that this should always be looked upon as entirely independent of any political considerations. When political considerations come in, you pass your resolutions without mincing matters; but where you deal with a question which is more of economic importance than political, bring a mind free from all other considerations to a consideration of this. (A voice "louder please"). I have had to shout out so much during the last few days that I cannot speak louder! Well, gentlemen, what does Swadeshi mean? There is a lot of misunderstanding about it. What is Swadeshi? The Swadeshi movement is a movement to promote the use of manufactures of our own country and to promote the growth of the manufactures of our own country. How does it arise, and why does the movement arise?

It is born of our poverty. It is born of the industrially weak and deplorable position which we are placed in. Prosperous countries, like England, will not for a moment think of starting a Swadeshi movement. If they happen to be driven to face, for a time, an unfavourable position, they will, of course, resort to Swadeshi movement; but, at present, the countries which are industrially prosperous and thriving will not think of the Swadeshi movement. What is it that drives us to think of it? As I have said before, our extreme and deplorable poverty. The condition of the people is most deplorable. Millions die of famine; millions fall victims to plague; millions never attain to manhood, but die slow, premature deaths by reason of not being able to get sufficient to live upon. That is the condition of the people! The one cause of it is that poverty about which we have been speaking so incessantly for these many years. There is no question that deaths from famine are preventible, deaths from plague are preventible. I say so from personal knowledge of what happened in my own city where people who moved out of the city to live in what is called the Civil Station where bungalows have been built, they were free from plague. Deaths from famine and plague are all the results of poverty. How is that poverty brought about? You know that 20 crores have to be paid every year in the shape of salaries, and pensions, etc. That is one large drain, no doubt, of the country's wealth; and you know that there is a much larger drain in the shape of the price that is paid for manufactures. Now, the total exports of the country are about 120 crores; the total imports are, roughly speaking, 85 crores. You will find, then, that articles of foreign manufacture, of great and immense value, are flooding the markets of the whole country. These have to be paid for. The raw-material of the country is exported and after being finished in other countries, it is brought back and we have to pay tremendous prices for it ! That is another very large drain. It is eating the vitals of the Nation. Our position is easily understood when you find that the annual income of our people per head of population is only £2 a year, as against £40 in England. That being so, the question arises what are we to do? Of course, if we had a potent voice in the administration of the country, I am sure, we should have rejoiced to introduce Protection. We have it not. England did so when it was necessary to do so. The United States of America did so, Australia did so, Germany did so and every country has adopted

Protection in order to let its nascent industries grow. But we are situated differently.

The Government cannot easily be persuaded to adopt Protection for this country, because England is a Free-trader. Ever since, England attained the advantageous position of being able to put its own manufactures at great advantage into other countries' markets. That being out of question, you have to see what you can do to help yourselves. Herein lies the great difficulty and the great opportunity. You can really and truly help yourselves immensely in this matter by promoting the Swadeshi movement. We are asking for Self-government and we are asking for many other privileges. It may be that we may obtain them soon, or it may be that we may obtain them after a long time, but in this matter of promoting the Swadeshi movement there is absolutely no bar which stands in our way. It is our solemn duty to promote it. What do we do to promote it? Australians found not long ago that they could not compete with other foreign people in the matter of manufactures; Australians, with open eyes, resolved to purchase country-made cloths which were coarse and which were dear in preference to cloths of foreign manufacture (hear). Not only that; but when there was a depression of trade in England in 1882, Lord Dunraven, if I remember aright, raised a great debate in the House of Lords, actually advocating the adoption of the policy of Protection. *The Pioneer* advocated the adoption of the "Swadeshi vow" by Englishmen. It actually said that if Englishmen want to find food for their own countrymen, who are starving for want of food they will have to resort to such a movement. That being so, the duty is plain before you. There is not a man, not a sensible man, who can take objection to it, and we need not be concerned with the opinions of those who are not sensible. Now, gentlemen, I look upon it as a part of a religious duty which we owe to our fellowmen. I consider it the Religion of Humanity and, our own particular religion; the Religion of Humanity demands that you should promote the Swadeshi movement to the utmost extent of your power. In purchasing a piece of cloth manufactured by a countryman of mine, I have often felt and am feeling now, that I am helping him to obtain at least a morsel of food to enable him to live (cheers). The yarn may have come from a foreign country, but the labour he had bestowed upon it, will surely enable him to get a portion, half the price or one-third or some portion of the gain in order to feed himself and those that depend upon him. When you find such terrible suffering around you, when you find the drain so great and the income of the people so small, their resources so poor, I say, it is a religious duty cast upon every man of healthy feelings to promote, to the utmost extent, the production of Indian manufactures by giving them preference, wherever he can find them, over foreign commodities, even at some sacrifice (cheers). Gentlemen, the idea of sacrifice sanctifies the resolution ! It is involved in it;— you may express it in words or you may not express it, it involves the idea of sacrifice. Unless you are prepared to do that, where will you stand? I will only tell you what the consequences are, what are the forces arrayed against you that you have partially to combat against. The Germans have partially destroyed the indigo-manufacture. The Germans are flooding the markets with foreign sugar; 7½ crores worth of sugar was imported into this country last year. There is enough of sugar-cane growing in this country. Do you imagine, for a moment, what the importation of sugar to the value of 7½ crores means to your people? (at this stage the President sounded the gong). It means that thousands upon thousands of the people have been thrown out of employment and have added to the number of those who are living on insufficient food. Will you allow this kind of thing to continue without doing your utmost to check it or prevent it? Then, the question arises: How to checkmate it? I look upon it that it is a sacred duty to do, the utmost we can, not merely by using Indian-made articles, but that time has come when capitalists must be induced to come forward to invest money in introducing machinery, in trying to produce manufactures just as they are produced in foreign countries. The educated men and men of capital must combine to bring about the growth of Indian industries. There must also be the utmost encouragement given to the consumption of Indian-made articles in order that capitalists might readily be induced to build up more industries. Gentlemen, I do not think that there can be two opinions as to the result of this movement. There is no element of ill-will or hatred involved in the Swadeshi movement. We love to promote it, because it is our duty to our suffering countrymen to do the utmost we can for them. There is no political bias, no political feeling involved in this matter. I hope and trust that it will be worked up in that spirit and working in that spirit, it is a sacred duty which rests upon us not to throw away lightly any help which we can receive from any direction in building our industries or in promoting the Swadeshi movement. Speaking personally, I say, I thank those who contribute in any small or in any measure at all, to the building of the Swadeshi Movement. The Government have done something. They have started the Commerce and Industrial Department. Let us hope that some good will result from it. It is our duty that we must not throw away help which we cannot substitute with something else. Government's help and people's help must all be combined,—must be combined in one sacred effort to find more bread and employment for the people to diminish the poverty which is eating up any number of our people, (at this stage the President again sounded the gong) and to promote the Swadeshi movement.

RABINDRANATH TAGORE
(1861-1941)

RABINDRANATH TAGORE

Rammohun Roy

Speech at the Rammohun Roy Death Centenary Meeting at the Senate House, Calcutta, on 18 February 1933

RAMMOHUN ROY inaugurated the modern age in India. He was born at a time when our country, having lost its link with the inmost truths of its being, struggled under a crushing load of unreason, in abject slavery to circumstance. In social usage, in politics, in the realm of religion and art, we had entered the zone of uncreative habit, of decadent tradition, and ceased to exercise our humanity. In this dark gloom of India's degeneration Rammohun rose up, a luminous star in the firmament of India's history, with prophetic purity of vision, and unconquerable heroism of soul. He shed radiance all over the land; he rescued us from the penury of self-oblivion. Through the dynamic power of his personality, his uncompromising freedom of the spirit, he vitalized our nations being with the urgency of creative endeavour, and launched it into the arduous adventure of realization. He is the great pathmaker of this century who has removed ponderous obstacles that impeded our progress at every step, and initiated us into the present era of world-wide co-operation of humanity.

Rammohun belongs to the lineage of India's great seers who age after age have appeared in the arena of our history with the message of Eternal Man. India's special genius has been to acknowledge the divine in human affairs, to offer hospitality to all that is imperishable in human civilization, regardless of racial and national divergence. From the early dawn of our history it has been India's privilege and also its problem, as a host, to harmonize the diverse elements of humanity which have inevitably been brought to our midst, to synthetize contrasting cultures in the light of a comprehensive ideal. The stupendous structure of our social system with its intricate arrangement of caste testifies to the vigorous attempt made at an early stage of human civilization to deal with the complexity of our problem, to relegate to every class of our peoples, however wide the cleavage between their levels of culture, a place in a cosmopolitan scheme of society. Rammohun's predecessors, Kabir, Nanak, Dadu, and innumerable saints and seers of medieval India, carried on much further India's great attempt to evolve a human adjustment of peoples and races; they broke through barriers of social and religious exclusiveness and brought together India's different communities on the genuine basis of spiritual reality. Now that our out-worn social usages are yielding rapidly to the stress of an urgent call of unity, when rigid enclosures of caste and creed can no more obstruct the freedom of our fellowship, when India's spiritual need of faith and concord between her different peoples has become imperative and seems to have aroused a new stir of consciousness throughout the land, we must not forget that this emancipation of our manhood has been made possible by the indomitable personality of the great unifier, Rammohun Roy. He paved the path for this reassertion of India's inmost truth of being, her belief in the equality of man in the love of the Supreme Person, who ever dwells in the hearts of all men and unites us in the bond of welfare.

Rammohun was the only person in his time, in the whole world of man, to realize completely the significance of the modern age. He knew that the ideal of human civilization does not lie in the isolation of independence, but in the brotherhood of interdependence of individuals as well as of nations in all spheres of thought and activity. He applied this principle of humanity with his extraordinary depth of scholarship and natural gift of intuition, to social, literary and religious affairs, never acknowledging limitations of circumstance, never deviating from his purpose lured by distractions of temporal excitement. His attempt was to establish our peoples on the full consciousness of their own cultural personality, to make them comprehend the reality of all that was unique and indestructible in their civilization, and simultaneously, to make them approach other civilizations in the spirit of sympathetic cooperation. With this view in his mind he tackled an amazingly wide range of social, cultural, and religious problems of our country, and through a long life spent in unflagging service to the cause of India's cultural reassertion, brought back the pure stream of India's philosophy to the futility of our immobile and unproductive national existence. In social ethics he was an uncompromising interpreter of the truths of human relationship, tireless in his crusade against social wrongs and superstition, generous in his cooperation with any reformer, both of this country and of outside, who came to our aid in a genuine spirit of comradeship. Unsparingly he devoted himself to the task of rescuing from the debris of India's decadence the true products of its civilization, and to make our people build on them, as the basis, the superstructure of an international culture. Deeply versed in Sanskrit, he revived classical studies, and while he imbued the Bengali literature and language with the rich atmosphere of our classical period, he opened its doors wide to the spirit of the age, offering access to new words from other languages, and to new ideas. To every sphere of our national existence he brought the sagacity of a comprehensive vision, the spirit of self-manifestation of the unique in the light of the universal.

Let me hope that in celebrating his centenary we shall take upon ourselves the task of revealing to our own and contemporaneous civilizations the multi-sided and perfectly balanced personality of this great man. We in this country, however, owe a special responsibility, not only of bringing to light his varied contributions to the modern age, but of proving our right of kinship with him by justifying his life, his maintaining in every realm of our nation's existence the high standard of truth which he set before us. Great men have been claimed by humanity by its persecution of them and wilful neglect. We evade our responsibility for those who are immeasurably superior to us by repudiating them. Rammohun suffered martyrdom in his time, and paid the price of his greatness. But out of his sufferings, his power of transmitting them to carry on further beneficent activities for the good of humanity, the modern age has gained an undying urge of life. If we fail him again in this day of our nation-building, if we do not observe perfect equity of human relationship offering uncompromising fight to all forms and conventions, however ancient they may be in usage, which separate man and man, we shall be pitiful in our failure, and shamed for ever in the history of man. Our futility will be in the measure of the greatness of Rammohun Roy.

SWAMI VIVEKANANDA
(1863-1902)

SWAMI VIVEKANANDA

Response to Welcome

At the World Parliament of Religions, Chicago, on 11 September 1893

Sisters and Brothers of America,

It fills my heart with joy unspeakable to rise in response to the warm and cordial welcome which you have given us. I thank you in the name of the most ancient order of monks in the world; I thank you in the name of the mother of religions; and I thank you in the name of millions and millions of Hindu people of all classes and sects.

My thanks, also, to some of the speakers on this platform who, referring to the delegates from the Orient, have told you that these men from far-off nations may well claim the honour of bearing to different lands the idea of toleration. I am proud to belong to a religion which has taught the world both tolerance and universal acceptance. We believe not only in universal toleration, but we accept all religions as true. I am proud to belong to a nation which has sheltered the persecuted and the refugees of all religions and all nations of the earth. I am proud to tell you that we have gathered in our bosom the purest remnant of the Israelites, who came to Southern India and took refuge with us in the very year in which their holy temple was shattered to pieces by Roman tyranny. I am proud to belong to the religion which has sheltered and is still fostering the remnant of the grand Zoroastrian nation. I will quote to you, brethren, a few lines from a hymn which I remember to have repeated from my earliest boyhood, which is every day repeated by millions of human beings: *"As the different streams having their sources in different places all mingle their water in the sea, so, O Lord, the different paths which men take through different tendencies, various though they appear, crooked or straight, all lead to Thee."*

The present convention, which is one of the most august assemblies ever held, is in itself a vindication, a declaration to the world of the wonderful doctrine preached in the Gita: "*Whosoever comes to Me, through whatsoever form, I reach him; all men are struggling through paths which in the end lead to me."* Sectarianism, bigotry, and its horrible descendant, fanaticism, have long possessed this beautiful earth. They have filled the earth with violence, (drenched it often and often with human blood, destroyed civilisation and sent whole nations to despair. Had it not been for these horrible demons, human society would be far more advanced than it is now. But their time is come; and I fervently hope that the bell that tolled this morning in honour of this convention may be the death-knell of all fanaticism, of all persecutions with the sword or with the pen, and of all uncharitable feelings between persons wending their way to the same goal.

LALA LAJPAT RAI
(1865-1928)

LALA LAJPAT RAI

Towards Freedom

Speech in Bombay on 20 February 1920 in Response to the Public Welcome Accorded to Him on His Return to India

I Cannot adequately thank you for the very affectionate and kind reception you have accorded me all this day. I cannot accept it as due to any of my merits, but as a manifestation of that great spirit which animates this country from one end to the other. I accept that manifestation as a great finger-print from the heavens that we are destined to become great and that this country of ours will once more rise in the scale of nations. As such I give the credit not to this man or that man but to the spirit in you, my friends. Why? India was like a sleeping lion. Once it wakes, it wakes with a momentum that carries the force of its ancient greatness. We have never been, in spite of many revolutions that we have undergone, a selfish people, we have never been an oppressive people. We have behind us the righteousness of scores of generations and hence though we may be fallen, though we may be downtrodden, though we may be weak, though we may be treated with humiliation, we have the potentialities to rise and be great once more. It is that potentiality that you are expressing, it is that potentiality which is finding its expression in this manifestation I am seeing today.

This is not the time for me nor the occasion to give you my opinion of the present political situation in this country. I shall beg leave of you to give me time before I express myself on the subject. But there are some fundamental truths which I have learnt to my pleasure in my travels abroad which I am going to place before you as my message to "Young India". My friends I must tell you that henceforth we should recognise it as a fundamental doctrine that the unity of the Hindus and Mahommedans will be a great asset to our political future. In this unity we shall not be guided by the temporary benefit of this community or that. We shall not adopt it as a measure of political expediency. But we shall adopt it as a fundamental doctrine of our faith, to stick to, to our death-beds until we win our freedom. Not till then only, but thereafter too, we shall live in this country as brothers determined to work together, determined to resist together, and determined to win. That is one of the fundamental doctrines which we must adopt as a first article of our political faith.

Now to come to the second article. I must tell you, do not place any faith upon anybody but yourself. You can rise only by your own efforts. Remember "Nations are by themselves made". We shall welcome co-operation. We shall welcome advice. We shall welcome guidance also, in certain matters. But we shall resent patronage and dictation. We are not babies. We have behind us the grown wisdom of six thousand years at least, not to say more.

Then I may tell you I have travelled now practically all over the world and I have seen three of the great self-ruling nations of the world at least, the Japanese, the Americans and the Englishmen. And take it from me, that except perhaps in the requirements of modern knowledge, we are inferior to none on the face of the earth. I shall, if I have time, take you department by department and show to you that in no department of associated life, private life, are we inferior to any nation of the world. What are we inferior in? We have been inferior in the capacity to unite, we have been inferior to a certain extent in adaptation to the modern requirements, we have been inferior in learning the lesson of modern diplomacy. Therein lies our inferiority. If we had learnt the art of telling lies on a broad scale, if we had swept away all our past and had entered into the great arena of violence, if we had done all these things, which at the present moment represent Power in the world, we might have been considered by the great nations of the world as worthy of self-government. But we have been lacking in these qualities.

And there is one of these qualities which I want you to learn. We have been a righteous nation in all our history and we shall continue to be righteous and to win on the basis of righteousness. I want you to be true to your civilization. Seek truth, speak truth and act truth and I promise you shall win. The modern world is being managed, modern politics are being based upon the rights of the superior and the inferior. We recognise no superior and no inferior. We don't want for our country anything that we are not prepared to concede to the other people of the globe. What we want is the position of equality and nothing else.

There are some friends of ours who are often tempted by the term Imperialism. They want to be partners in the great Imperial system. I don't want it. Ladies and gentlemen, there is no word coined by the genius of man, more vicious, more sinful, more criminal than Imperialism. And I may tell you that I for one don't want to be a partner in any Imperial system. All that I want for my country is a position of equality first in the British Commonwealth and then in the nations of the world.

With our connection with Great Britain, we want to cooperate with those British statesmen and politicians, thinkers and workers, who want to convert the British Empire into a British Commonwealth. And I may tell you that the world movements foreshadow coming events and unless the British Empire is soon converted into a British Commonwealth it will go to the dogs as other Empires have gone. The safety of the British Empire lies in converting it into a British Commonwealth and we as Indians, as constitutional workers, as Indians believing in the destiny of the whole world, we are prepared to co-operate, constitutionally with the whole of our thinking force, with the whole of our character at the back of it to convert that Empire into a Commonwealth of equal and free nations. My dear friends, there are some people who tell us that the opinion of other people does not count for much. They tell us that the opinion of the British people who are the present rulers of this country naturally matters for our progress. I do not accept that dictum.

The League of Nations which is at present a humbug, has been established as a fact. It is a fact, and we are a Member of that League of Nations. We want to be a Member of the League with a vengeance. We want to be a living Member of the League of Nations and not a sleeping partner. Ladies and gentlemen, if we become a living Member of the League of Nations, we have to work up the world opinion in our favour, and to show the world that the calumnies that are being circulated against us of our unfitness, of our divisions, of our weakness of character or all these things, that those calumnies are baseless and untrue. And how can we repudiate those calumnies unless by work in foreign countries in co-operation with those joyous world spirits which in every country are trying to raise the world into a humanity from the hell that it is at the present moment. We must cooperate, we must mix our voice with them, we must put our soul force with them side by side to enable them to push the world from the world of unrighteousness into the world of righteousness and equality for every human being, be he of any continent, or any colour, or of any caste, or of any creed. My friends, I beg of you, my young friends, I entreat you with all the earnestness that I can command and with all the love that I bear you, that this is a most critical time in the history of our nation, not only in the history of our nation, but in the history of humanity.

This is a turning point—humanity is taking a turning point. Shall we, or shall we not, take our legitimate part as one-fifth of the human race, as the descendants of the mighty ancient Aryans, as the followers of Mohammedan leaders, shall we or shall we not take our part in the making of the new world? And if we had to take our part in the making of the new world, we must make every effort to make a united stand, to make a truthful stand, to make a righteous stand, to make an unrelenting stand, come what may. The Western world powers have lately in the last war shown you an example. What for did they fight? They said they fought for democracy. They said they fought for the empire of the world. They said they fought for equal justice. Yet we know what they fought for. And if they won with all that they could die in millions, lose all their property, sacrifice their children, give up their women, why shall we not, when we stand for the cause of righteousness and truth only? There are people who speak from the mouth true words of great moment and when the occasion for action comes, they eat them up. Even the greatest men of the world have done that. We know what happened at Versailles, Paris. We know how the world is now treated with peace of Statesmanship.

My friends, do not aspire to be statesmen. Try to be honest men, try to be good men, and last but not least, try to be true to yourselves and to the country which gave you birth. We do not want politicians, we will leave them to America. We will leave them to England. Let them settle their differences. We will even leave them to France, my friends, we will also leave them to Japan. We do not want politicians. We want honest, plain-speaking, truth-speaking men and women. That is all. And if we secure that, our salvation is very near. The difficulty is how to convince you of becoming plain-speaking truthful men. Now, I can tell you one thing. The world has been fighting for material goods. The world has been fighting for the control of capital. The world has been fighting for the control of land. The world has been fighting for the control of markets. The world has been fighting for the control of labour. Capital, wealth, labour, markets, where are they leading the world to? Do you hear the cry from Europe?—that nation is dying, that nation is starving, that nation has become bankrupt, that nation is selling its women, that nation is doing this and that nation is doing that. We have been starving for a hundred years. Thank God we have not done any of these things. Don't be carried away by false ideals.

All the capital of the world cannot save you, cannot bring you freedom. Let me tell you from my experience. We think that these countries are very free. You from here think that England and America and Japan and France are the freest countries on the face of the globe. Well in certain respects, they are. But in certain other respects, let me tell you, take it from me, that they are the most servile people on the face of the globe. Why? Few amongst them can speak the truth. Few amongst them have the spirit of abnegation for higher causes. Where in the world shall we find another man equal in spirit, self-sacrifice and righteousness, equal to Mahatma Gandhi. We may or may not agree with his views. We may or may not follow him. But I challenge the whole world to produce another man like Mahatma Gandhi. Who has produced him? Twentieth century India. He is not alone. I can name several other names whose equals you will not find in any other land. Gentlemen, I have tried my very best to take the most generous view, to take the most liberal view of the other nations, but let me tell you honestly, absolutely honestly, that in the power of self-abnegation, in the power of sacrifice for higher causes there is no other country on the face of the globe which can beat us, only if we direct that spirit of self-sacrifice and self-abnegation to rightful purposes and rightful ends. That is the only thing that is wanted. We have been told here that our politics are corrupt, our politicians are divided; Hindus and Mohammedans are constantly fighting with each other; each caste is prepared to cut the throat of another caste. We have been flaunted with the picture of the depressed classes before us.

But let me tell you that this is all Imperial talk. Why? The two great Imperial assets are: first to change the psychology of the people whom they want to govern and secondly, to change their own psychology. They want it to be believed that they are the choice of the world, and then want to believe that you are the refuse of the world. Therein lies the whole Imperial psychology. You have unfortunately for the 150 years been believing that you are really inferior to other people.

Rise up, Young India, you are inferior to none. In our common men, in the men who till our fields and produce our food, in those men who do not get sufficient to eat twice a day, you have a wealth which no other country on the face of the globe possesses. There are souls ready to redeem them. Even though they will die, even though they will starve, they will never dare to steal one mouthful of food from the house of the rich. Where on earth is that character to be found? If this state of things were to continue in any other country—I only admire the righteous phase of it—if in any other country the thing were to happen, you will find all the capitalists concealing themselves in the wine cellars to protect themselves and their property. This is actually happening in Europe at present. I, therefore, beg of you, young men of India, your motherland is at the present moment lying prostrate, because of your lack of faith in yourselves, in your people and in your country; prostrate because of your weakness of mind and weakness of character. Raise up your minds, enthuse yourselves with the electricity of self-confidence and self reliance. And this race will rise sphynx-like and spread all over the world. Remember one-fifth of the human race possessing the intelligence of you, possessing the arms of you, these arms (pointing to his arms) not swords and pistols—you must be careful in your language, you see. Now, our masters tell us that we are wanting in practical intellect. What is that practical intellect? That subtlety which makes two and two appear five. Well I may tell you that is a dangerous game. If they goad us today like that, who knows what young India may not do? But at the same time I do not want you to make your intellect so subtle as that. I want you to be honest and say two and two make four.

I have told you two or three fundamental principles which I believe in. The unity of the Hindus and Mahommedans, the belief in yourselves—faith in yourselves, as I call self-faith—and the belief that you and you alone shall raise your country. Others can give you numbers. But they shall not give you soul. What we want is not the crumbs, but the soul? We want the soul of the body politic. And what is the soul of the body politic? Perhaps I am treading on dangerous ground. The soul of the body politic is the power of the purse and the power to defend one's own country. Let me tell you that that man is insane, who tells you not to take advantage of every opportunity that is offered to you for the service of your country in whatever direction it might lie handy. But let me tell them—they may take it from me that we shall never be contented unless we get self-government. Constant, unending, unrestrained, uncontrolled vigil, controlled only by self-discipline, controlled only by righteousness, is the price of liberty. Young men of India, are you prepared to pay that price? Do you only say or do you mean it? Well you shall have it. The moment you mean it, you shall get it. At present you only say "yes" half-heartedly. I wish you mean it. (Loud cries from the audience of "We do"). When you mean it you will get it.

I am returning to my country with full faith in the righteousness of my cause. I want you, my countrymen, to work in the open, with absolute frankness, discarding secret methods and all methods of violence. If we don't win by soul force, if we don't win by the force of will and determination of three hundred and fifty millions of human beings, we don't deserve to win it by violence. If one-fifth of humanity cannot win their liberty by the force of their will, by the power of their soul, by the power of their determination, they deserve to be swept off the face of the earth; and no power on earth can save it. Why, think of your power? Think of your potentiality. Think of the force in your hearts. We need not talk of violence, we need not talk of force. Only cowards do that, not the descendants of the ancient Kshatriyas and the descendants of ancient Mughals. One who is working in the open need not be afraid. I may tell you that the moment I change my opinion, I will give notice to the Government that I have done so. I will never do a thing in the purdah. We want all women to come out from the purdah, and not the men to go into the purdah. No, Sir, that won't do for us. We shall not bring a slur upon the names of our forefathers. But subject to that qualification, subject to that reservation, there is nothing on earth which we shall leave undone to win our rights and to gain what is ours. We don't want anything which belongs to anybody else. We are prepared to give whenever anybody is in need and wants it in a spirit of proper co-operation. But we shall not give by force, we shall not give by dictation. We will rather not work, we will die in the fields, than let others exploit and take from us what we do not want to give. That is a lesson which I want Young India to lay at heart. My friends, we have talked much. We have talked a lot, we have talked a great deal. There are orators in India, at almost every corner of the streets of Bombay or Calcutta. There are men who in the flow of oratory want to be Imperial partners. There are men who are proud of things which ought to put them to shame. But there is an awakening.

There is a dawn of a new day, the dawn of a new spirit. The year 1919 shall be memorable in the history of India not for the Reform Act, but for Jallianwalla Bagh. The Reforms we shall utilize to the fullest extent. We do not intend to boycott them; as I have told you it shall be vain to boycott them. We shall utilize every possible avenue, every possible opportunity left to us. To do otherwise would be unwise and insane. But at the same time the shrine in our hearts which shall live for ever in golden letters shall be Jallianwalla Bagh and not the Reforms. That is the shrine we shall worship and that is the shrine we shall offer flowers at, until that wrong is righted and righted in the right.

Ladies and gentlemen, as I told you in the beginning of my speech, I come to this country back after six years. I know that sometimes aspersions have been cast upon my work abroad. It is not my purpose to defend myself. I consider it to be beneath my dignity. No one has a right to ask me to give an account of my actions but my countrymen, and when the demand comes from them, I shall tell them everything. I shall conceal nothing because I have nothing to conceal. But, in the meantime I may tell you that not a single pie of any public fund or from any fund taken from any supporters, has been utilised by me for my personal use. I had plenty of money sent to me by my son, and I have lived a frugal life. I may tell you, it is no secret—that I disdained to do no work, have cooked my food with my hands. I have cleaned my own room. I have at times gone with five cents of bread for the evening meal. Not that I had no money. There were thousands of public funds in my hands, but I would not spend one cent of it for myself. I say this not in vindication of my character because up to this time I have not heard a single countryman of mine questioning my character in that direction; and as I told you I owe no apology to anybody else. But I just want to give this piece of information. In my life from the beginning to the end I have been entrusted by you with numberless funds. I challenge my bitterest enemies to come forward and say that any action of mine has been affected by any considerations of money or property. I don't want to continue in this strain, it is painful and it is humiliating. But when a man is traduced unfairly, sometimes he has to speak a word of truth in his own defence.

One last piece of advice that I want to give you is this. Learn to do your work with your own hands. Do not depend upon servants. Do not depend upon property. Do not imitate other people. That will be extremely foolish and suicidal. The more you are free, the more you have the capacity of suffering, the more you have the ability to live a simple life, the more you will be free. Freedom comes from want of Independence. Freedom does not come by an Act of Parliament. Remember that. If you continue to depend for your means of livelihood, upon this department or that department, upon this Honourable or that Honourable, upon this Excellency or that Excellency, you shall always be slaves. But the moment you take the *kurhad* and go and cut the tree, the moment you take the broom and go and sweep your room without being tempted with offerings of money and service, you are free, free from all the bondages with which you have been afflicted so far. Learn to be free.

What is progress? Progress is nothing but progress towards freedom. Your ancestors have taught to you the lesson that freedom is taken away the moment you have the feeling of dependence. Lessen your dependence at any rate, if you cannot give it up. Cultivate the habit of self-dependence, self-reliance, not in a spirit of aggression or offensiveness, but in a spirit of manliness, manliness, of which we have many examples in the history of India; and, my friends, I tell you, you will never require any speeches to emulate you.

You will never require any measures by any body to free you. Freedom must come from within. Freedom must come from within of the Mother of India. Freedom won't come from without. Freedom won't fall from the heavens. Freedom will rise Goddess-like from our earth; and we shall rise, and with our own hands we shall offer flowers and we shall worship her. I thank you once more.

GOPAL KRISHNA GOKHALE
(1866-1915)

GOPAL KRISHNA GOKHALE

Womesh Chunder Bonnerjee

Speech at a Memorial Meeting in London on 21 July 1906

MR. CHAIRMAN, LADIES and GENTLEMEN,—We are assembled here to-day to give public expression to our grief that the hand of Death has removed from our midst our illustrious countryman,—Mr. Womesh Chunder Bonnerjee. The event, it is true, has not come upon us as wholly unexpected. For some time past it was well known that Mr. Bonnerjee's health had been completely shattered, that there was no hope of recovery, and that continued existence in that state was to him only a prolongation of agony. However, now that the end has actually come, and we are forced to realise that our great and trusted leader, whom it was a joy to love no less than to follow, is no more with us, the mind feels as completely bewildered and overwhelmed as though the great Destroyer had come with stealthy and noiseless steps and had inflicted on us our loss without warning, and with the shock of a sudden blow. Ladies and gentlemen, Mr. Bonnerjee was a man whose death would leave humanity the poorer in any age and in any part of the world. To India, in her present stage of transition, with difficult and complicated problems arising on all sides, his passing away is a national calamity of the first magnitude, and we indulge in no exaggeration when we say that our loss is truly irreparable. It is not my purpose to-day to attempt here an estimate of the character and career of our great countryman. Our loss is still too fresh and our sense of it too acute and poignant to permit of my undertaking any such task in a meeting of this kind. And all I beg leave to do in commending this resolution to your acceptance is to say a few words expressive of my profound admiration of the many noble qualities, both natural and acquired, of our departed leader, and of my humble appreciation of the great, the signal services which he has rendered to our national cause. Ladies and gentlemen, we all know that Mr. Bonnerjee was one of the most distinguished, as he was one of the most successful, lawyers that our country has produced. Now, if he had been only that and nothing else, even then his title to a public expression of our admiration and respect would have been unquestioned. National life to be complete must be many-sided; and a man who brings honour to the Indian name, no matter in what field, advances thereby our national cause and deserves to be honoured by us on national grounds. But Mr. Bonnerjee's claim to our admiration and gratitude rested, of course, on a much wider basis than his pre-eminent attainments as a lawyer. He was, in addition, an ardent patriot, a wise and far-sighted leader, an incessant worker, a man whose nobility of mind and greatness of soul were stamped on every utterance and every action of his life. His intellectual gifts were of the very highest order. Endowed with an intellect at once critical, vigorous, and comprehensive, a truly marvellous memory, luminous powers of exposition, captivating eloquence, great industry, and a wonderful habit of method and discipline, Mr. Bonnerjee was bound to achieve, in whatever field he chose to work, the most brilliant success. Then he had a wide outlook on life, deep and earnest feeling and a passionate desire to devote his great gifts to the service of his country. And added to these were a fine presence, an extraordinary charm of manner, and that combination of strength and restraint which made him one of the most manly men that one could come across. Such a man must tower above his fellow-men wherever he is placed. In a self-governing country he would, without doubt, have attained the position of Prime Minister. We in India twice made him President of our National Congress, and what was more, when the great movement was started twenty-one years ago and the first Congress ever held in India assembled in Bombay, the delegates unanimously elected Mr. Bonnerjee to guide them in their deliberations. And since that time down to the moment of his death, Mr. Bonnerjee, with two or three others, was the very life and soul of that movement. He ungrudgingly gave to the cause his time and his resources—and this far more than is generally known. He cheerfully bore all its anxieties, his exertions for its success were unwearied, and no man's counsel was valued higher by his countrymen, where the Congress was concerned. His courage was splendid, and it rose with difficulties, and his nerve and his clear judgment were a theme of constant admiration among his countrymen. With Mr. Bonnerjee at the helm, everyone felt safe. His was the eloquence that thrills and stirs and inspires, but his was also the practical sagacity that sees the difference between what may be attained and what cannot, and when the need arose no man was firmer than Mr. Bonnerjee in exercising a sobering and restraining influence. I can recall at this moment more than one meeting of the Subjects Committee of the Congress, at which really all important deliberations take place, where Mr. Bonnerjee's far-sighted wisdom and the great weight attaching to his personality steadied the judgments of wilder spirits, and established harmony where discord was apprehended. The loss of such a leader, no word that I can employ can adequately describe, and he has passed away at a time when he was more indispensable than ever, in view of the signs one sees of the vessel of the Congress being about to encounter somewhat rough weather. Ladies and gentlemen, it is really superfluous that I should dwell at any length before an assembly composed so largely of my own countrymen on the distinguished services rendered by Mr. Bonnerjee to our national cause. And, if I refer briefly to one or two of them, it is because they are not very widely known, and they illustrate how immense is the debt that we owe him. You are aware that no Englishman has ever served India more nobly or more zealously than the late Mr. Bradlaugh. Now, it was Mr. Bonnerjee who enlisted Mr. Bradlaugh's sympathies on our side and secured his powerful championship for our aspirations. Then the part Mr. Bonnerjee has played in keeping together all these years the British Committee of the Congress and in maintaining unimpaired its activity in this country, will always constitute one of his best claims to our affection and gratitude. Very few, indeed, of our countrymen have any idea of the difficulties that have had to be overcome from time to time in this connection, of the worries they have involved, and of the sacrifices they have required. But if our great friends, Sir William Wedderburn and Mr. Hume had been here to-day, they would have told you, as, indeed, our venerable chairman may, if he speaks a few words at the end, how invaluable have been Mr. Bonnerjee's co-operation and assistance in this matter. Ladies and gentlemen, I do not wish to detain you longer. Many of us lose in Mr. Bonnerjee not only a great leader, but also a warm generous friend. Who that has ever enjoyed the hospitality of his beautiful home at Croydon—now, alas, plunged into the depths of grief—will forget the singular charm of his personality, the charity of his judgments, his touching devotion to those around him, or the kindness he loved to lavish on all whom he admitted to the privilege of his friendship ! And, speaking in this connection, may I say how our hearts go out to-day to the bereaved family, whose loss is beyond words, and especially to that stricken lady whose life has now been rendered desolate and to whom the world will never he the same again ! One word more and I have done. Mr. Bonnerjee has now crossed the line which there is no recrossing. But he is not altogether gone from us. He has left us the precious inheritance of a noble example. He has left us his name to honour, his memory to cherish. Above all, he has left us the cause—the cause he loved so dearly and served so well. Our very sorrow to-day speaks to us of our duty to that cause and no tribute that we can offer to the memory of the departed will be more truly fitting than a resolve to recognize and an endeavour to discharge this duty according to the measure of our capacity and the requirements of our country.

V. S. SRINIVASA SASTRI
(1869-1946)

V. S. SRINIVASA SASTRI

Dinshaw Wacha

Speech in Bombay on 9 April 1940 at Unveiling the Statue of Late Dinshaw Wacha

You have done me conspicuous honour in assigning to me the principal part in to-day's ceremony. I do not deserve it either by intimacy of association with the illustrious man whose statue I am about to unveil or by a high position in the public life of the country. The meaning of your invitation, as I understand it, is that Sir Dinshaw Edulji Wacha did not belong to Bombay alone, but that distant Madras, as indeed every part of India, can claim his memory as a cherished possession. During the last ten years or so of his life Sir Dinshaw was unable to take prominent part in the public affairs of India. And let it be admitted that the liberal party, of which he was one of the leading lights, has for some years lost the influence which should properly belong to it by reason of its past record and by reason also of the personal merits of its members. Nevertheless, a review of the main features of the long and honourable career of one of its luminaries will not be without profit, even to the present generation, which repudiates the political doctrines that are the immediate parents of its own school of thought.

Sir Dinshaw was 92 years old when he passed away in 1936. He was born into a period of our history very different from to-day, so different indeed that it would take a great effort of the historical imagination for a young man to form a just picture of it in his mind. Let us remember that Wacha was well in his teens when the Great India Mutiny occurred and led to the famous Proclamation of the Queen of 1858. Political agitation and indeed political aspiration had hardly assumed definite shape. Our hero had entered on his forties when he was called upon to take his share in the proceedings of the gathering of Indian leaders which subsequently took the great name of the Indian National Congress. The social reform and the educational movements were then in a rudimentary state. The city of Bombay had already started on its career of commercial prosperity, but no one could have predicted that its destiny was to become within a generation or so the second city of the British Empire. Nor was the Bombay corporation anything like the pattern of municipal efficiency and civic enlightenment that it is to-day. Wacha had the rare distinction of seeing things grow from the humblest beginnings all through the stages of trial and error, of hope and hesitation, of careful planning and haphazard growth, of rising tides of prosperity and struggle against adverse circumstances. In this drama of exciting change and spirited endeavour, Wacha was no mute and unconscious sharer, no mere passive observer, but an active and brilliantly active participant. Of his early education we have a few glimpses from his own vivid pen. In a volume of reminiscences written over the humorous name of "Sandy Seventy," a few chapters describe the early efforts of Christian missionaries and a few private bodies to give the elements of education to their children before the duty of public instruction was recognised as part of the functions of government. This volume is a rich mine of information regarding Bombay of a hundred years ago, which may be recommended to a student of original records. Wacha went, like many promising students before him, to the famous Elphinstone institution, but was not destined to complete the course that was available. This circumstance he seems to have regretted. To one who marks the vividness and vigour of his style, the copiousness and power of his diction, and the range and depth of his observations, it does not appear that he suffered any real loss by the premature end of his scholastic education. At twelve he recited an English piece so well before Lord and Lady Canning that Her Excellency patted him on the back. He heard the great Proclamation of Queen Victoria assuming the direct sovereignty of India read aloud to the assembled citizens by Lord Elphinstone who stood on the spacious verandah of the Town Hall surrounded by the dignitaries of the day arrayed in robes of state. Who would not envy his good fortune when he saw and heard that prince of African explorers, Dr. Livingstone, led into the Town Hall by Sir Bartle Frere of happy memory? He does not fail to mark the changes that time has wrought in our dress and manners, changes not always observed as they take place with exceeding slowness in society. We learn from the luminous pages of the book called by the picturesque name of "Shells from the sands of Bombay" that in his boyhood Indian gentlemen of all classes, Hindus, Mahomedans, Christians, and Parsis appeared on formal occasions in snow-white and flowing *Jama* and *Pichoree* or *Kumerband*. We learn also to our astonishment that there was a time when even Parsi ladies were content to remain within doors and in ignorance. The year 1858 and the occasion of the Queen's Proclamation deserve to be remembered not only for their own intrinsic importance, but as the time of emancipation for Parsi womanhood. For they came out for the first time in open carriages, venetians down, mark you! to view the illuminations, which were on a grand scale. Our chronicler writes boastfully that they were attired in rich silk saries and bejewelled and that the Purdah was literally lifted. Amongst his early inspirations was a study of Sir Joseph Arnauld's classic judgments in the Maharaja Libel case and in the Aga Khan case—judgments which no student either of Indian law or of Indian social history should omit to read. Sir Dinshaw tells us that he acquired his passion for the study of economics and finance from a certain Professor Hughlings, who had fitted up a reading room at his own cost, where he would often sit with Sir Dinshaw and explain learned articles in the 'Economist' of James Wilson, who afterwards became the first Finance Minister of India. Of this original inspiration we have the mature fruits in the writings and speeches which he poured forth in abundance during a long life of conscientious and devoted study. What a lad of fine sensibility and high enthusiasm he must have been to write as he does of the emotion that warmed his breast when first he visited the hallowed precincts of that great house of thought, that great temple of learning, a valhalla where lay buried the great thoughts of great men of all the centuries, which is his own description of the Literary Society founded by Sir James Mackintosh! Only on two other occasions did our hero feel a similar exaltation of spirit, once when he visited the library of the British Museum and again when he was within the precincts of Westminster Abbey. Is it any wonder that with such subtle and powerful stimuli Wacha acquired a voracious appetite for knowledge, which made him to the end of his days a great buyer and reader of books? Nor was he a mere acquirer of all kinds of knowledge. He gave freely to the public out of his vast store of information. There is hardly a man within my recollection who has written and spoken so abundantly as Sir Dinshaw Wacha. His output if we could assemble it all, would easily equal that of any two of his compeers in public life. Anonymously, pseudonymously and over his own proper name, he was an untiring contributor to magazines and newspapers of every degree of influence. And the marvel is that he never took a pie of remuneration for it all. I have it on good authority that he never employed a stenographer, but wrote always in his own hand. His private correspondence was of colossal proportions. He wrote regularly to friends in England and innumerable people in India. As often as a thought occurred to him, I fancy he took pen and paper and wrote it down for somebody's benefit. I fancy also he wrote nearly as fast as he thought. He did not pause for the most appropriate word or the most inoffensive phrase. I have had occasion to read a good deal of his manuscript, for he wrote often and with complete freedom to Gokhale. I do not remember a scratch or an erasure. It was the same even, parallel-lined, fine-looking, fluent calligraphy. The attraction, however, was only on the surface. The trouble started as soon as you put on your glasses and began to read. You came up against an illegible scrawl and could make progress only with many a stumble and many a break, to which you said to yourself you would come back when your organ of vision had regained its tone.

In his public work Wacha was associated with several colleagues of similar calibre. And it used to be said that for many years Bombay had the singular good fortune of having a galaxy of brilliant men who placed their talents at the disposal of the community. In civic matters the ascedency of Sir Pherozeshah Mehta, extending over nearly two generations, was an advantage which other cities of metropolitan rank might have envied. His great example of devotion to municipal duties drew to the service of Bombay a wealth of talent and experience, which might else have been dispersed among diverse small interests and yielded little public benefit. Of about the same age, Wacha seconded his friend with his own uncommon ability. It is a just claim made on their behalf that their unsurpassed influence in the corporation was never perverted to any jobbery or patronage, but exerted to keep policy and principle free from all taint of unworthy ends. In many quarters Pherozeshah Mehta's domination excited jealousy and resentment. But be it said to the honour of Sir Dinshaw and many others that they were not only content but glad to rally round him like soldiers round a brave and gifted general. Wacha in particular regarded his eclipse as a dedication. I was anxious soon after Gokhale's death to call on the notables of Bombay. I was ushered into a room where Pherozeshah Mehta sat beaming among his accustomed companions. Naturally backward in speech. I felt hushed in the great presence, but soon a number of kindly queries broke my reserve; and as the talk flowed easily over a wide range, I remarked how every now and then Mehta would turn round and appeal to Wacha for confirmation of what he had said, and Wacha would assent without using too many words. His book on the Municipality of Bombay, especially the chapter dealing with the inauguration in 1888 of the present constitution, gives due meed of praise to Lord Reay, Mr. Telang, Mr. Forbes Adam and other stalwarts of the time, but accords first place ungrudgingly and convincingly to Pherozeshah Mehta whose vigilance, intrepid advocacy and far-seeing vision transmuted the halting and timid proposals of the authorities into a golden measure of local government, which has nobly stood the test of time and furnished a model of municipal government throughout India. Wacha outlived his great friend by more than 20 years, during which period he was called upon to occupy the vacant place of primacy as far as he could. This was the case not only in the Corporation, but in the Legislature first of Bombay and then of All-India, in the Bombay Presidency Association and in the Indian National Congress. It might be said of this brilliant pair, in greater measure than of any others in the country, that their eminence in municipal affairs led as a natural and almost inevitable consequence to equal eminence on the broader stage of national affairs. Be it also recorded for the benefit of other patriots that they never allowed their zeal for the civic welfare of Bombay to be dimmed or diminished in any way by larger and may be more exalted pre-occupations. Wacha was one of the seventy odd leaders of India who laid in 1885 truly and well the foundations of the Indian National Congress. His interest in this organisation grew with its growth. He was its Secretary for many years and President at the 1901 session in Calcutta. He took a prominent part in its debates, and congressmen of all ranks soon learned to appreciate and love the sterling qualities of the small lively figure who seemed to frisk and jump on the platform as he denounced, in a squeaking voice and apparently through very thick spectacles, the military policy and expenditure of India in vehement accents and with torrential eloquence. His utterance could not be commended for distinctness or melody of tone, but his earnestness and mastery of facts and figures ensured for him patient and respectful attention. Before the Welby Commission on Indian Finance be made a gallant stand for equitable apportionment of charges between England and India, and along with Gokhale gave invaluable support to Dadabhai Naoroji, who was a member of the Commission as well as the most learned and formidable witness on the Indian side. As an economist Wacha belonged to the school of Cobden and John Stuart Mill; and though in later years he countenanced the policy of discriminating protection for the industries and manufactures of India, his original homage to the pure water of free trade was a lifelong obsession. He was instrumental, along with Mr. Manmohandas Ramji and others, in founding the Indian Chamber of Commerce on this side of the country, and when other Chambers had sprung up elsewhere, he induced them all to join together and act as a Federation of Indian Chamber of Commerce and industry. Nothing could be more eloquent testimony to his lofty principles and his unselfish and unworldly character than that throughout his life, though money lay all about him, he never possessed more then a competence and for some time before his death he was without even that competence. It would be a mistake to suppose that, while he specialised in finance and economics, he neglected other aspects of study. His pronouncements on education are entitled to respectful consideration, and he was no mean authority on history in general and international affairs. Writing over the pseudonym of "Rajduari," he surveyed for many years in the "*Indian Review*" the course of events as they shaped themselves in the world, with a wealth of detail and a sureness of grasp which were the admiration of readers.

Wacha's was a simple nature. There was never any difficulty in understanding him. He was subject to strong emotions and expressed his likes and dislikes with disconcerting candour. As Secretary of the Indian National Congress he had to collect monies, call for reports and require conformity to ordinary canons of public business. In the discharge of these duties he had to reprove, to dun, to scold, to threaten. People complained bitterly of the severe terms in which he castigated slackness or evasion of duty. To the end he never learned how to suffer fools gladly or temper the wind to the shorn lamb. Especially in recent years few of his colleagues or correspondents altogether escaped his verbal chastisement. I had my share. But we all remembered how like a child he was and how utterly innocent of the arts of polite circumlocution and of pretended friendship. If he was quick to scold, he was equally quick to forgive and to befriend. As he himself said in one place, if he was a lion in the chase, he was a lamb at home. For my part, while I seldom remember the sharpness of phrase with which he expressed his disapproval of my doings, I recall with mingled pride and pleasure his appreciation of the unresting vigilence with which, as captain of volunteers at the Congress session of 1908 in Madras, I guarded the proceedings, which were in special danger in consequence of the animosities and bickerings of Surat.

Experience will have taught many of you here, as it has taught me, that, ever since the two schools of moderation and of extremism emerged with more or less defined frontiers, nearly every moderate has been suspected at one time or another by his orthodox compatriots of leanings towards the wrong side. In the Servants of India Society that has been the fate of almost all. I sometimes think that the suspicion under which I lay at the beginning still clouds my name, and Gokhale was never wholly sure of me in his inmost mind. Gokhale himself, if the truth be told, would not have been raised to the Cardinalate in the Vatican of Bombay. Going higher still, was not Pherozeshah Mehta accused by the archangels who surrounded the viceregal throne of introducing a new spirit of question and cavil in those serene regions where seemliness and perpetual obeisance were the attributes of the chosen denizens? It was the esoteric belief of the moderates of Bombay, Madras and U.P. that most of our compatriots in Bengal were tarred with the extremist brush and could not be admitted into the *sanctum sanctorum*. Pride must not blind us to the danger lurking in the nature of us all, a tendency, whenever we have unchecked power, to erect the stake and light the fire of inquisition. Wacha was particularly subject to this frailty. Markedly when he was young and less markedly when he had attained middle age, he was playfully and not untruthfully called the firebrand of western India. His views were strong, and the words he chose to express them were stronger. No one could listen to his early speeches or read his early writings without being struck by the uncommon range and sweep of his vocabulary of disapprobation and denunciation. His finger could in those bounding days read the pulse of popular feeling unerringly. If his private letters could be recovered and arranged in the order of date, they could furnish a faithful chronicle of the various phases of feeling through which the general mind passed on the questions engaging it. One instance I may be pardoned for mentioning to-day. His letters to Gokhale during the years 1906, 1907 and 1908 are a mirror in which could be seen vividly reflected the initial hope, the scepticism, the bewilderment, the indignation, the despair and finally the reviving hope and satisfaction with which the eager Indian politician watched the changing moods and fancies and slowly evolving reform proposals of Lord Morley. Gokhale was by no means unaffected by the vagaries of the political barometer; but because of his proximity to the central orb of the firmament, his faith never wholly disappeared, but shone like a star, now bright, now dim, but always there. He gently reprimanded us for failure to make full allowance for Morley's difficulties and misgivings, and it is pleasing to recall now the happy ending of the episode when he expounded the main features of the coming constitution to the Congress of 1908 and successfully communicated to the audience his own expectations of a happy prosperous future.

Wacha is a striking and forceful illustration of the sobering effect of time. We could see how he gradually shed his optimism, moderated his demand and saw things through authoritarian glasses and weighed events in the scales provided by Government. This swing-over is noticeable in the careers of other politicians as well. I can recall more than one occasion on which the late Sir B. N. Sharma and I were roundly censured by him in the Council of State for attacking the Government of the days. But we were amused and half consoled when in his own turn he would get up and belabour Government with the verve characteristic of the redoubtable oppositionist we had known and admired of old. At such times he reminded me of a fond but temperamental mother who might beat her child mercilessly when she was angry, but, if anybody else threatened violence to it, would fly at his throat in a fit of fury.

The year 1918 marked a crucial turn in the fortunes of the Congress. When it became apparent that the extreme section of our politicians had made up their minds to denounce and declare unacceptable the Montagu-Chelmsford proposals of reform, the elder statesmen, if one may be pardoned for appropriating that term, decided to secede from the Congress and create an organisation for themselves. After much anxious consultation and frequent searchings of the heart, of which the memory is still poignant, the members of the Servants of India Society threw in their lot with the All-India Liberal Federation. The two mighty pillars of the movement were Wacha and Surendranath Banerjea. At the end of the inaugural session in Bombay I likened them to those unchanging hills in the landscape by which Sri Rama identified the various regions of the Indian continent when, during his return home after fourteen years of exile, he found no other distinguishing marks, for they had all, rivers and plains and forests and the habitations of men, shifted enormously and obliterated all boundaries. That similitude seems to me not inapt after the twenty-two years that have since passed. A few of us, alas, a continually diminishing few, still stand where we stood, pointing the finger of warning, like Wordsworth's "Peele Castle" amidst the wreckage of a fearful storm.

Rather a succession of fearful storms. For many years now our country has not known tranquillity except for brief periods. While we sit here, tens of thousands of people all over the country are preparing for mass civil disobedience, and the campaign may begin any day. However non-violent it may be, the authorities cannot afford to look on, but must meet it by violent measures. Not improbably communal discord may add itself to the disturbance and convert civil disobedience into something like civil war. The demand for partitioning India into two political entities with separate national interests staggers the imagination and makes it impossible even to guess the next step in our movement. Has the teaching of Sir Dinshaw any guidance for us in this predicament? The answer is not for a moment doubtful. We have all heard of the claim made in Congress circles that, if Dadabhai Naoroji and Gokhale could be brought back to life among us, they would take their stand with the author of non-violent non-co-operation and mass civil disobedience. It is difficult to say how many that actually knew these departed worthies would allow to claim. I do not allow it. In Wacha's case nobody would dream of advancing such a claim. It is well known how Sir Pherozeshah Mehta and he did not countenance in the faintest degree the Home Rule League movement started by Mrs. Besant and how they endeavoured to induce our Grand Old Man to withdraw the consent that he had given to be its President. To Mrs. Besant as a political force in India they had an invincible antipathy. Of Gandhiji's aims and methods Wacha had an instinctive dread. His condemnation would have been clear, complete and caustic. He had no patience with the judicious frame of mind which weighs pros and cons with meticulous precision, and after marking full allowance for purity of motive, pronounces a half-hearted verdict against the particular method at the particular time. I confess to a natural aversion from cocksure, uncompromising, final judgment in any sphere of human conduct. One can never know enough to judge aright. Still, when one is racked by doubt and appalled by the prospect of disaster, one is drawn by the sovereign instinct of safety to the voice of a leader of men who sees clearly into the future and points the way with confidence. In the interests of posterity we cannot afford to let Sir Dinshaw Wacha's fame become dim or his example cease to inspire coming generations. That is why Sir Chimanlal Setalvad and his Committee have in their wisdom erected Wacha's statue on this prominent spot, within hailing distance, in case the shades of great men should wish to commune with one another, of Tata, Mehta, Naoroji, Ranade, Gokhale and Montagu.

MAHATMA GANDHI
(1869-1948)

MAHATMA GANDHI

God is Truth

Speech at a Public Meeting at Lusanne on 8 December 1931

You have asked me why I consider that God is Truth. In my early childhood or youth I was taught to repeat what in Hindu scriptures is one thousand names of God. Among the several little things one of the religious teachers my family had was a little pamphlet which contained these thousand names of God. But these thousand names of God were by no means an exhaustive list. We believe and I think it is the truth—that God has as many names as there are creatures and therefore we also say that God is nameless and since God has many forms we also consider Him formless, and since He speaks to me through many tongues we consider Him to be speechless and so on. And so when I came to study Islam I found that Islam too had many names, but I had not come to recognize God for my personal satisfaction as Truth. I would say for those who say God is love, God is love. But deep down in me I say God may be love, but God is Truth. If it is possible for the human tongue to give the fullest description of God, for myself I have come to the conclusion that God is Truth. But two years ago I went a step further and said Truth is God. You will see the fine distinction between the two statements: God is Truth and Truth is God. And that conclusion I came to after a continuous relentless search after truth which began so many years ago. I found that the nearest approach to Truth is through love. But I found also that love has many meanings in the English language at least and human love in the sense of passion becomes a degrading thing also. I found too that love in the sense of ahimsa and non-violence has only a limited number of votaries in the world. And as I made progress in my search I made no dispute with "God is love". It is very difficult to understand "God is love" (because of a variety of meanings of love) and love in the sense of human passion becomes a degraded thing, but I never found a double meaning in connection with truth and not even atheists have denied the necessity or power of truth. Not only so. In their passion for discovering truth they have not hesitated even to deny the very existence of God—from their own point of view rightly. And it was because of their reasoning that I saw that I was not going to say "God is Truth" but "Truth is God". Therefore I recall the name of Charles Bradlaugh—great Englishman—who lived 50 years ago. He delighted to call himself an atheist. But knowing as I do something of his life I never considered him an atheist. I would call him a god fearing man although he would reject the claim, and I know his face would redden. I would say: No Mr. Bradlaugh, you are a truth-fearing man, not a god fearing man, and I would disarm his criticisms by saying "Truth is God" as I have disarmed criticisms of many a young man. Add to this the great difficulty that millions have taken the name of God and have committed nameless atrocities in the name of God. Not that scientists do not very often commit cruelties in the name of truth. I know today in the name of truth and science inhuman cruelties are perpetrated on animals when men perform vivisection. To me it is a denial of God whether you recognize Him as Truth or by any other name. So I know that there are these difficulties in one's way, no matter how one describes God. But human mind is a limited thing, and you have to labour under limitations when you think of a being or entity who is beyond the power of man to grasp. But we have another thing in Hindu philosophy *viz.*, God alone is and nothing else exists. Now the same truth you find emphasized and exemplified in the *kalema* of Islam. There you find it clearly stated—a Mussalman has to recite it at all his prayers—that God alone is and nothing else is and that is the same about truth. And the name that Sanskrit has for truth literally means that which is—*Sat*. For these and several other reasons that I can give you I have come to the conclusion that the definition "Truth is God" gives me the greatest satisfaction. And when you want to find truth as God; the only inevitable means is love, non-violence—and since I believe that ultimately means and ends are convertible terms—I should not hesitate to say that God is love.

What is Truth?

A difficult question, but I have solved it for myself by saying that it is what the voice within tells one. How then, you ask, different people think of different and contrary truths?

Seeing that the human mind works through innumerable media and that the evolution of the human mind is not the same for all, it follows that what may be truth for one may be untruth for another and hence those who have made these experiment have come to the conclusion that there are certain conditions to making experiments. Just as for science there is an indispensable course common for all, even so is it true for persons who would make experiments in the spiritual realm—they must submit to certain conditions. And since everybody says it is his inner voice which speaks, you must listen to the voice, and you will then find out your limitations as you go along the path. Therefore we have the belief based upon uninterrupted experience that those who would make diligent search after truth—God—must go through these vows: the vow of truth—speaking and thinking of truth, the vow of *brahmacharya*, of non-violence, poverty and non-possession. If you do not take this five vows, you may not embark on the experiment. There are several other things which were prescribed but I must not take you through all those. But those who have made these experiments know that it is not proper for every one to claim to hear the voice of conscience and it is because we have at the present moment everybody claiming the right of conscience without going through any discipline whatsoever that there is so much untruth being delivered to a bewildered world. All therefore that I can in all humility present to you is that truth is not to be found by anybody who has not got an abundant sense of humility. If you would swim on the bosom of the ocean of truth, you must reduce yourself to a zero. Further than this I may not tonight go along this fascinating path.

CHITTARANJAN DAS
(1870-1925)

CHITTARANJAN DAS

The Meaning of Freedom

Excerpts from the Presidential speech at the Ahmedabad Session of the Congress in 1921

I come from a city which has felt the full force of the wrath of the Government. Measures for stifling political life have been taken, as I believe in order to coerce the people to receive His Royal Highness the Prince of Wales; but it is the imprisoned soul of Calcutta that will greet His Royal Highness on the 24th of December. I come from the struggle which has just begun in Calcutta chastened and purified and, if I have no worldly wisdom to give, I at least bring before you unbounded enthusiasm, and a resolute determination to see this struggle through.

Freedom in the first place, does not imply absence of all restraint. . . . in the second place, freedom does not necessarily imply absence of the idea of dependence. . . . But though there is no necessary opposition between freedom and restraints and freedom and dependence, it must be remembered that restraint that does not deny freedom can only be such restraint as has the sanction of the people behind it; and dependence consistent with freedom can only be such dependence as is willingly suffered by the people for its own protection.

What is then freedom? It is Impossible to define the term; but one may describe it as that state, that condition, which makes it possible for a nation to realise its own individuality and to evolve its own destiny. The history of mankind is full of stirring stories as to how nations have struck for freedom in order to keep their nationalism and their individuality inviolate and untarnished. To take only modern instances, one may refer to Finland and Poland, Ireland, Egypt and India. Each of these nations has offered a determined resistance to the imposition of a foreign culture upon it. . . .

We stand then for freedom, because we claim the right to develop our own individuality and evolve our own destiny along our own lines, unembarrassed by what Western Civilisation has to teach us and unhampered by the institutions which the West has imposed on us. But here a voice interrupts me, the voice of Rabindranath, the poet of India. He says, "The Western culture is standing at our door; must we be so inhospitable as to turn it away or ought we not to acknowledge that in the union of the cultures of the East and the West is the salvation of the world?" I admit that if Indian nationalism has to live, it cannot afford to isolate itself from other nations, but I have two observations to make on the criticism of Rabindranath: first, we must have a house of our own before we can receive a guest; and, secondly, Indian culture must discover itself before it can be ready to assimilate Western culture. In my opinion, there can be no true assimilation before freedom comes, although there may be as there has been, a slavish imitation. The cultural conquest of India is all but complete; it was the inevitable result of her Political conquest. India must resist it. She must vibrate with national life and then we may talk of the union of the two civilisations.

I must dispose of another objection, this time of my Moderate friends. "You concede,"—I hear them say, "that freedom is not an end in itself but a means to-an end, the end being control; why not work out your destiny within the British Empire?" My answer is that so long as India occupies the position of a dependency in the British Empire, the task cannot be undertaken. Go into the villages, the heart of India, and see the life that is lived by the average Indian. They are sturdy men and fearless men, they are men of whom any country could be proud; but the degradation that must inevitably follow subjection is writ large on their brow and their lot is made up of caste troubles, petty squabbles, and endless pursuit of litigation for litigation's sake. Where are now the institutions that made them self-dependent and self-contained? Where is the life that enabled them to earn their livelihood and yet left them free to worship the God of their fathers? . . . I think that we should solemnly declare, in open Congress, that Freedom is inherent in every nation and that India has and possesses the right to develop her own individuality and to evolve her own destiny unhampered by what the

British Parliament has decided or may decide for us. I think that we should recognise that any power that in any way hampers or embarrasses the self-realisation and self-fulfilment of the Indian nation is an enemy of India and must, as such, be resisted. I am willing to co-operate with England but on one condition only, that she recognises this inherent right of India. That recognition you will not find anywhere in the Government of India Act, and 1, for one, will not he a party to the perpetuation of British domination in India. But my Moderate friends tell me that though the freedom of the Indian people, in the sense in which I understand the term, has not been recognised in the Act of Parliament, still, if we work the Reforms, it will not be in the power of Parliament to deny us freedom. I do not doubt the wisdom of my friends nor deny their patriotism; but the question, in my opinion is entirely irrelevant. My position is this, that however willing I may be to enter into a compromise with the English Government in matters of detail, and I am willing to make great sacrifices, I will not enter into any compromise on the question which I hold to be fundamental. Freedom is my birthright, and I demand a recognition of that right, not by instalments nor in compartments, but whole and entire. I do not doubt that victory will be on our side, but supposing we fail; we would at least have preserved inviolate our national self-respect and dignity. We would at any rate have repudiated the insult on which the Government of India Act is based. The difference between the Indian National Congress and the Ministers who are working the Reform Act seems to me to be fundamental, in that it has its eye fixed on the ultimate and would reject as essentially false anything that does not recognise the freedom of the Indian people, whereas the Ministers have their eyes fixed on the departments of which they are in charge, and hope to attain freedom through the successful working of those departments. . . .

This then, is the scheme which is being worked by the Ministers, and we have been solemnly assured by the Moderates that the beginning of Swaraj is to be found in the scheme. Much as I would like to end all unnecessary conflict, I cannot recommend to you the acceptance of the Act as a basis for cooperation with the Government. I will not purchase peace with dishonour, and so long as the Preamble to the Government of India Act stands and our right, our inherent right, to regulate our own affairs, develop our own individuality and evolve our own destiny is not recognised, I decline to consider any terms of peace.

The only other method of warfare open to us is Non-cooperation; and that is the programme which we adopted at two successive Congresses. We are devoted to the doctrine of Non-cooperation, and you will not require me to discuss with you its ethics. . . .

This is the essence of the doctrine of nationalism for which men have been ready to lay down their lives. Nationalism is not an aggressive assertion of its individuality, distinct and separate from the other nations, but it is a yearning for self-fulfilment and self-determination and self-realisation as a part of the scheme of the universal humanity by which alone humanity can fulfil itself, determine itself and realise itself. Non-cooperation, therefore, though it does not refuse cooperation with the English because they are English, will refuse to cooperate with any power or institution which embarrasses in any way the growth of the individuality of the Indian nation or hampers its self-fulfilment. Non-cooperation again does not reject Western culture because it is Western culture. But it recognizes that there must be rejection in order that there may be wholehearted acceptance. . . .

What then is Non-cooperation? I cannot do better than quote the eloquent words of Mr. Stokes: "It is the refusal to be a party to preventable evil; it is the refusal to accept or have any part in injustice; it is the refusal to acquiesce in wrongs that can be righted, or to submit to a state of affairs which is manifestly inconsistent with the dictates of righteousness. And as a consequence it is the refusal to work with those who on grounds of interest or expediency insist upon committing or perpetuating wrong."

But it is argued that the whole doctrine is a doctrine of negation, a doctrine of despair. I agree that in form the doctrine is one of negation, but I maintain that in substance it is one of affirmation. We break in order to build; we destroy in order to construct; we reject in order to accept. This is the whole history of human endeavours. If subjection be an evil, then we are bound to non-cooperate with every agency that seeks to perpetuate our subjection. That is a negation; but it affirms our determination to be free, to win our liberty at any cost. Nor do I agree that the doctrine is one of despair. It is a doctrine of hope and of confidence and of unbounded faith in its efficacy. One has only to look at the faces of the sufferers as they are led to prison to realise that victory is already ours. It is not for nothing that Mohamed Ali and Shaukat Ali, courageous and resourceful, have lived and suffered; it is not for nothing that Lajpat Rai, one of the bravest of spirits that ever faced the sun, flung the order of the bureaucracy in its face, and marched boldly into the prison that awaited him. . . .

This, then, is the philosophy on which the Non-cooperation movement is based: to defy with absolute constancy the hostile powers that would hamper in any way our growth and self-fulfilment as a nation, to keep its evil always in view, not hating it, but recognising the evil as an evil and refusing no pain that power can invent. . . .

The fact that disturbances have taken place is no argument against the essential truth of our movement. We must meet the situation with courage and devise means to prevent the recurrence of those disturbances; but I cannot and I will not advise you to stay your hand from the Non-cooperation movement. The fact that India has remained calm in spite of the recent arrests shows that the Bombay lesson has gone home. The recent manifestation of courage, endurance and remarkable self-control has in my opinion demonstrated the efficacy and the necessity of non-violent Non-cooperation. And nothing can stop our onward march if the same spirit is still further developed and retained to the end. . . .

Lord Reading is obviously in error in suggesting, as he has done, that the arrests now being made in Calcutta and in other parts of India are under the ordinary criminal law of the land. . . . Rightly or wrongly, the Congress has adopted the policy of Non-cooperation as the only legitimate political weapon available for its use. That is not breaking the law. Rightly or wrongly, the Congress has decided to boycott foreign goods and especially foreign cloth. That is not breaking the law. Rightly or wrongly, the Congress has decided to boycott the visit of His Royal Highness the Prince of Wales. That is not breaking the law. Now, in what way is the Congress to carry on its work except through the voluntary organisations which you have proclaimed unlawful under the Indian Criminal Law Amendment Act? In striking at these voluntary organisations, you strike at the Congress propaganda which, you are, bound to admit, is not unlawful. Why should it puzzle Your Excellency, assuming you credit us with the same amount of patriotism which you have, that we have solemnly resolved to disobey your orders and court imprisonment? I assert that it is you who have broken the law and not we. You have transgressed the law which secures to every subject freedom of speech and action, so long as the speech and the action do not offend against the ordinary criminal law of the land. You have transgressed the law which secures to the subject the unrestricted right to hold meetings, so long as these meetings do not degenerate into unlawful assemblies. These are the common law rights of the subject which you have transgressed, and I would remind Your Excellency that it is on the due observance of these elementary rights that the allegiance of the subject depends.

But then, it is said that these associations interfere with the administration of the law and order. If they do, then the ordinary criminal law is there, and it ought to be sufficient. I have heard of no instance of violence in Calcutta; certainly none was reported to the police. Charges of violence can be investigated, and therefore, they were not made. But charges of threat and intimidation are easy to make because they cannot be investigated. I would ask the authorities one question : "Was any case of threat or intimidation reported to the police? Has the local Government found, on enquiry, that quite apart from general allegations which can easily be made, there were specific cases of threat or intimidation practised by the non-cooperators on the 'loyalists' of Calcutta? An English journalist, signing himself as "*Nominis Umbra*", gave as his opinion to an English paper in Calcutta that the '*hartal*' was willingly acquiesced in by the people. We read in "A Ditcher's Diary" in *Capital* of the 24th November last: "The people surrendered at discretion, but it was impossible for a careful observer not to see that not only were they, for the most part, willing victims of new *zoolum*, but also that they exulted in the discomfiture of the Sirkar." If that be so, then what case is there for the declaration under Section 16 of the Indian Criminal Law Amendment Act? Was the position in Calcutta on the 17th of November last worse than the position in England when a big strike is in progress? And is it suggested that there resides any power in the Cabinet of England to put down a strike and prevent picketing? No gentlemen, the real object of the application of the

Indian Criminal Law Amendment Act is not to protect society against the threats and intimidation of the non-cooperators, but to crush the Congress and the Non-cooperation movement. It is to such threat that you have to return an answer.

There is another object which the Government has in view; it is to make, by threat, intimidation and coercion, the visit of His Royal Highness the Prince of Wales to Calcutta a success. On your behalf I would respectfully lay before His Royal Highness our wishes of goodwill to him personally. There is no quarrel between us and the Royal House of England; but he comes here as the ambassador of a Power with which we have decided not to cooperate: as such we cannot receive him. Also, we are in no mood to take part in any rejoicing. We are fighting for our national existence, for the recognition of our elementary rights freely to live our own life and evolve our own destiny according to our rights. It would be sheer hypocrisy on our part to extend a national welcome to the ambassador of the Power that would deny us our elementary rights. There is in the refusal to extend a national welcome to His Royal Highness, no disrespect either to him or to the Royal House of England. There is only a determination not to cooperate with the bureaucracy.

AUROBINDO GHOSH
(1872-1950)

AUROBINDO GHOSH

Gita

Speech at Khulana on 25 June 1909

GENTLEMEN, Today I will speak a few words on the Gita. The main object of that philosophy is found in the *Vedanta,* which is the basis of Hindu thought and life, and according to the *Vedanta,* life is dominated by *Maya* or *Avidya*. We are driven into action because we are ignorant of our true selves, of the true nature of the world. We identify ourselves with our bodies, our desires, our sorrows, and spirits. We lose ourselves in our happiness, grief, and pleasures.

By these motives we are driven into action. This life is a chain of bondage which keeps us revolving. We are surrounded on all sides by forces which we cannot control. As man has a perpetual desire for freedom, he is driven by forces he cannot control. Under the influence of these forces within or without, action takes place. The object of Hindu philosophy is to make man no longer a slave, but to escape from bondage and to make human beings free. Hindu philosophy tries to go into the root of things. What is the real beginning of maya?. . . . Whatever we may try, from the nature of the world, we cannot escape from bondage. There is our knowledge by attaining which we can become free.

In the Gita we find that Sri Krishna unites the *Vedanta* philosophy with the philosophy of *Sankhya*. Modern science denies that man has a soul. Science considers only the laws of nature. It regards nature as material, and man as merely a product of nature. It says man is a creation of natural forces. All his actions are results of fixed laws and he has no freedom. According to the *Sankhya,* man has a soul and is essentially the *Purusha* and not matter. The spirit does not act. The soul is calm and motionless. *Prakriti* is always shifting and changing, and under her influence all actions take place. *Prakriti* (nature) acts.

Man can only free himself by recognising that he is the *purusa.* Sri Krishna adopts this theory of *Sankhya* in the Gita, and he also adopts the philosophy of *Vedanta*. He says that man has an immortal soul, but there is also a universal soul. Man is merely a part of God. He is merely a part of something that is eternal, infinite, omniscient, and omnipotent. This eternal power is what really exists, and in all that we see, hear, feel, it is He alone who exists. It is He alone whom we feel and see. *Parameshwara* builds up this world by his *Maya* (illusion). He is the master of the great illusion which He calls *Maya.* This He made to express Himself the One. All these things around us are transitory. Within us is that which cannot change, which is eternally free and happy. If he feels himself miserable, it is because he in his ignorance allows himself to be dominated by egoism (*Ahankara*). He thinks that he is all. He does not realise that God is the master of this *Lila* (God's action). He thinks that it is I who act, am the lord of my body, and because he thinks so, he is bound by his action. By these forces he is driven from birth to birth. The great illusion is that this body which he inhabits is himself; next he identities himself with the mind, and thinks it is I who think, see, and feel. In reality, according to the Gita, God is within the heart of every creation.

The second thing you have to recognise is that you are only a part of Him, who is eternal, omniscient, and omnipotent.

His first answer to Arjuna is that the feeling which has come upon you is not the pure feeling. It is a feeling of egoism. Still Arjuna does not understand how that can be.

How can it be my *Dharma* to kill my own brothers and relations? How can it be to slaughter my nation and house? Sri Krishna answered according to the spirit of Hindu ideas. He says that it is your *Dharma*, because you are a Kshatriya. This is your *Dharma* of a particular kind. The duty of the Kshatriya is not the same as that of the Brahmin, and that of the Kshatriya is not equal to that of the Shudra. If a Shudra adopts the *Dharma* of a Brahmin, he brings the confusion of all laws and leads to the destruction and not to the betterment of mankind. It is nature which teaches you your own *Dharma*. This is your *Dharma*. If you shrink from upholding the cause of virtue, truth, and justice, out of feeling which is inconsistent, you are guilty, you bring in confusion, you encourage yourself to give up your duty. Still Arjuna is not satisfied. Sri Krishna still goes deeper. He says that the whole of our life is determined by *Maya* which is of three kinds—*Sattwa, Rajas* and *Tamas*. Their nature is this. *Sattwa* leads to knowledge, *Rajas* leads to action, and *Tamas* leads to inaction and ignorance. These are the qualities of nature which governs the world. The *Swabhava* which leads you to work is determined by three *Gunas*. Action is determined by *Swabhava*. All action leads to bondage, and is full of defects. What you call virtue or virtues, they have defects in themselves. The virtue of the Brahmin is a great virtue. You shall not kill. This is what *Ahimsa* means. If the virtue of *Ahimsa* comes to the Kshatriya, if you say I will not kill, there is no one to protect the country. The happiness of the people will be broken down. Injustice and lawlessness will reign. The virtue becomes a source of misery, and you become instrumental in bringing misery and conflict to the people. Your duty to your family seems to conflict with your duty to society, that of society to nation, and that of the nation to mankind. How shall we follow the path which leads to salvation? It is difficult to say what is right and what is wrong. How to decide it then? There is one way: do action in Yoga, and then you rise above ignorance and sin cannot touch you, and you rise above all that hampers you and binds you. What is Yoga? No certain process. When we think of Yoga, we think of a man who shuts up himself in a cave and subjects himself to certain practices. He frees himself from all the bondages. But Sri Krishna uses Yoga in a different sense. He says: Do action in Yoga. The first element is *Samata*. *Samata* means you shall look with equal eyes upon happiness and misfortune, praise and blame, honour and dishonour, and success and failure. You shall regard none of these, but with a calm and unshaken mind, the work which you are given to do you should proceed with that, unshaken by the praise or censure of the world. The man who has this *Samata*, has no friends and no enemies. He looks upon all with equal feelings, because he has knowledge, because he has looked into himself and out into the world. He finds himself everywhere and all in himself. He finds himself in all, because God is in all. Whether he looks at the high or low, he sees no difference and sees that in every creature there is *Narayan*. He sees that he is only an *Amsha* (part) of one which is in every matter. If there be any differences, they are only temporary and outward. He is only that through which *Vasudeva* carries on his *Lila* (play). He is not anxious to know what will happen tomorrow, because the action is not guided by laws. The man who has communion with God has no reason to be guided by laws, because he knows God is alone and all. He is not troubled by the fruits of his action. You have the right to action, to work, but not to the fruit. Work and leave the result to Me. Those men whom you shrink from slaying are already slain. These men would all perish. Therefore the fruit is already obtained beforehand by Me. Your anxiety for the result is ignorance. The destiny of the world is fixed. When a man has to do anything he must know that the fruits are with God. Man is to do what God wills.

Yoga means freedom from *Dwandwa*. He is free from the bondage of pleasure and pain, of anger and hatred and attachment, of liking and disliking, because he looks with equal eyes on all. He does not shrink from misfortune or misery, happiness and unhappiness. He rises above the bondage of the body, because no man can give him pleasure or pain, because he has his own source of strength, of delight and happiness. This is the freedom which the Gita says the Yoga gives. The freedom which we ordinarily mean is *Mukti*. This is the freedom which the Gita promises. He says if you act in Yoga, you rise above grief and pain, even above all things. You are free from fear or sin, because you do not act for yourself. You do not act because you will get pleasure, but for the sake of God: that is how you are to reach Yoga. If you wish to be happy, you must give up all your works to God. You must do all your work for His sake, and therefore sin does not touch you. It is only for selfishness that sin touches you. If you realise that *Narayan* is in all, it follows that you lose the smaller, the individual limit itself. You look to wider things. You see yourself in the family, in community, race, humanity, and all things in the world. You forget yourself altogether. You work for the race and others, for mankind. It is not God's work that you follow after your selfishness. The Gita says: "Your welfare is God's business." If you work for Him you have no fear, because God stretches out his hand of mercy to you. It is to that which the Yoga leads. The teaching of the Gita, if it is followed, delivers you from all possibility of sin, of sorrow. He says: "Take refuge in Me, I shall free you from all evil. Do everything as a sacrifice to Me." That is the goal towards which you move. The name of Hari will free you from all evil. This is the way in which Sri Krishna has solved the problem put by Arjuna. Arjuna says that "It is my duty to fight for justice, it is my duty as a Kshatriya not to turn from *Dharmayuddha*, but I am perplexed, because the consequences will be so terrible. The people I am to slay are dear to me. How can I kill them?" Krishna says, "There is no doubt an apparent conflict of duties, but that is the nature of life. Life is itself a problem, a very entangled thread, which it is impossible to undo. But it is I who do all these, am leading you to the fulfilment of your duties. Leave it to Me. If you do your duty it is a thing which I am bringing about. You are not doing it from selfishness. It is a thing necessary for my purpose. It is a thing which is decreed, already done, but it is now to be effected in the material world. Whatever happens, it happens for the best. I now give you my knowledge, the key to Yoga. I remove the evil of ignorance from you. I give you the meaning of Yoga". In the Gita Sri Krishna gives certain rules by which a man may hold communion with God.

The Gita says that man is not a bundle of outward cares and griefs, of things that do not last. Man is a garment which is put off from time to time, but there is within us something which is omniscient and eternal and cannot be drowned.

Sri Krishna gave Arjuna *Divya Chakshu* (Divine eye), with which he saw *Vishwarupa* (the real appearance of God). He now sees *Vasudeva* everywhere. He sees within him things that cannot be seen by the mysteries of science. With this knowledge comes to him that force.

How can I act, yet be free from bondage? The Gita says that the man who has no knowledge, has to do exactly what other men do. He has to live as a man in his family, race and nation. But there is the difference which is internal and not external. By the internal difference he acts in communion with God; others act in pursuance of their desires. He knows by experience how a man can act when he is free from desire. This force of action is the force of God himself. He is not troubled by the result of action: he gets eternal bliss.

This is the whole teaching of the Gita. It is Yoga which gives utter perfection in action. The man who works for God is not shaken by doubts.

The teaching of the Gita is the teaching for life, and not a teaching for the life of a closet. It is a teaching which means perfection of action. It makes man great. It gives him the utter strength, the utter bliss which is the goal of life in the world.

BHULA BHAI J. DESAI
(1877-1946)

BHULA BHAI J. DESAI

Why Is India What She Is Today?

Speech to the University students at Nagpur in 1934

It is not a mere formal expression of gratitude if I tell you that it gives me very great pleasure tonight to come in your midst, particulary as you belong to the University Union. For after finishing my college course, I began my life as a professor in a college. Since I gave up college life, I have always been in touch with University education as a member of the University Syndicate. It was under some unusual and difficult circumstances that I could not stand for election, not being free to do so, on the last occasion. I have not merely, therefore, a sort of living relationship with the student world, but I am one of those who believe—though the idea can easily be overdone—that the youth of the country is the only thing, after all, that matters, with its great future. I have always claimed, notwithstanding my grey hairs, that 1 am in spirit probably younger than most of you present here. But at the same time I am quite willing to concede that in the historical sense the future belongs to you, and in so far as any one of us, by long experience or learning, has got anything to convey to you, it is up to us that we should say so, not in the spirit of a teacher, which I do not and cannot claim to be, but in the spirit of handing on the accumulated experience of the past for the benefit of the future. It is only in that sense of historical continuity that 1 wish to tell you a few things tonight. I have given no name to the subject, for it bears no particular individual name. The only name that I can give is "My experience as a student of the past and as a student of the future." That is what I propose to speak to you about tonight, but let me warn you before hand against any disappointment, as I am not an expert educationist. I am an expert historian still less. An expert economist I happened to be or at any rate claimed to be, some years back, but now I have ceased to be that also. There might have been many, I am sure there have been, who have addressed you before in the true academical style, whether in literature or in science, so let me speak to you as a common man in the street, on the art of life, for it is that which matters more than anything else, except from the point of view of an expert.

As I have told you, you have heard many University addresses. What have you been told at the end of it all? It is that question that I ask myself at the end of an address. I do not believe and expect that all of you, many of you for that matter, will agree with me, but it will give me sufficient satisfaction if at the end of the address there is something that you should like to think over. If only I gave you an idea which you would turn over in your minds, that is enough so far as I am concerned.

I am one of those who are trying to see what Indian history means; not the Indian history as Prof. Sarkar would have it, trying to solve the controversy as between Shivaji and Afzalkhan, or Akbar's attitude towards religious questions, trying to solve only a controversy which perhaps is not a part of the Indian history at all, either at the Universities or in the colleges, although at one time it was a part of the subject.

The Indian history that I learnt consisted of a few chapters of what ancient India was, a few chapters of the mediaeval period in which nothing was given except perhaps some descriptions or inscription of Asoka, coming down to the period where India was divided in the political and military sense, and to the time when during the last some 150 years' succession of Governors-General and Viceroys began. It is in that spirit of succession of the names of people who governed, either well or ill, it is in that way that history has been taught to me. I am only reproducing for you or recreating for you the ancient history of India and it is unnecessary to recreate for you the history of India either during the Mohammedan rule or the shortlived Maharatta Empire. I do not possess that memory which my friends the historians possess. They would be able to rehearse before you, I am sure, the long line of Viceroys, of the measures they passed, the wars they fought, and ultimately how India became what it is to-day. I wish to create for you the Indian history as I want it to be studied.

The way in which I visualise Indian history is, and the question that I wish to propound to you is: what is it that accounts for the present position of India to-day? That is the question to which I do not demand an answer from you to-night, but it is undoubtedly a question which I want you to ask yourselves, not to-night, but as often as you think it your duty to do so. What is it that has reduced India to the position in which it is to-day? It is up to every detached mind studying Indian history to put that question. That is which requires solution, for on its true solution depends our future, near as well as remote. We should not solve the Indian problem by merely saying that we are the inheritors of the most ancient civilisation of the world. We would not solve the problem by saying to ourselves that our forefathers were carrying on the torch of learning when perhaps a considerable portion of the West had not yet learnt to clothe itself in decency, when perhaps the leaves and barks of trees were the only clothing they had.

It is that sort of feeling I remembered that Dr. Besant created in many an audience in which I happened to be present. I had often thought to myself then, and now I ask you to ask yourselves, "What does it matter what our ancestors were, if we, their descendants, are not worthy of their names?" And, therefore, it is that I have propounded to myself the question "Why is it that we are what we are to-day, and what is it that accounts for it?" I won't deal in any spirit of cynicism or bitterness with the political aspect of a matter which is already bitter enough, but I am going to examine the position of India of to-day in order that we may understand ourselves in the fullest sense of the term, and having so understood it will be up to our leaders in times to come so to continue to fashion our life, to mould our conduct and ideas, that we may deserve to be, as we claim to be, the true descendants and of a race of which you may justly be proud. It is that question to which many of my historian friends have not addressed themselves. It is probably not their fault. They study isolated ideas, they study isolated problems, they study isolated questions, great and important in themselves, occupying a great deal of intellectual attention, but leaving at the end of it all a mere feeling that they have learnt history but not the historical lesson; for history matters nothing if it is a mere question of succession of events of all times; history matters if only we are in a position to learn from it something that we may apply to the individual and corporate life of Indian people of to-day.

There are many among you who, I daresay, have already received prizes and medals in the study of the history of Western countries. I suppose you have read in English history of the process, by which, since the time of Magna Carta, England acquired the empire of which she boasts to-day. There are many here, I am sure, among you who have learnt and learnt probably better than I can ever hope to do, the causes of the French Revolution and how it affected Europe. There are many, I am certain, who have studied Roman history, beginning with the earliest democracy of the first Roman Republic, and there are many also who have doubtless studied the history of the Dutch Republic. But at the end of it all, after receiving all those prizes and medals, I ask, has it ever occurred to you to ask yourselves the question: "Has the growth of liberty of England taught a single lesson that you wish to apply to your lives, has the French Revolution taught a lesson that you dare translate into action in your lives?" What do these prizes and medals matter, of what value are they, if after 150 years of University education, you cannot translate into action, you cannot apply to your own lives, the lesson these struggles for liberty have taught you? Have we applied a single lesson from all those struggles for freedom of the human mind? Have you ever attempted to examine the genesis of our situation to-day? If you have not, I regret to say the prizes that you have won are for nothing and do not matter at all.

I say in all humility that I am also one of those who acquired a great many prizes in my academic career, but it is only now that I am beginning to learn, and it is in that spirit of a new student that I am speaking to you to-night, so that you may not waste and divert your energies. I am addressing you tonight so that you may begin rightly, begin again and begin for the first time with all the freshness of energy and enthusiasm. Would you study English history merely in order that you might satisfy your curiosity as to how they attained their freedom? Would you study the French Revolution in order that you may admire Napoleon, or would you study history in the way in which I will now ask you to study?

I have recently been studying Geography and I looked at the map of the world only the other day—and that is the reason why I warn you that you must not expect, and you will be disappointed if you do so, any very great academic address: I want to talk to you as I would talk to myself if I were entering the first year of the college to-day, and it is in that spirit that I want you to follow me—I was looking at the map of the world only a short time ago. What did I see in it? What would you see if you studied? I looked at Africa. I ask you, looking at the colours that every Atlas gives. "Does any part of that vast country belong to the people of Africa?" I asked myself another question. "Is there any part of that country that remains undivided between the races of the West?" I look further to the east. I begin to look at what at one time was the Turkish empire. It may not be an empire to the same extent now, but small though it may be, it is still an empire which can be proud of the narrow limits to which it has drawn itself in order only that it may sustain its original spirit and maintain its liberty. I look at the next country which was a Mandated territory under the Treaty of Versailles. I look at the next country which was nearly under the influence of the West, but which by the mercy of Providence, as a result of jealousy between the western races, escaped. I look at the next land, Afghanistan. I look at our own land, at Burma, Malaya and Java Islands which have been partitioned between the western races and further east up to China. I look also at the map of the frontiers of China, on the eastern side of what are called Concession ports and I come to Japan. I turn round and look at North and South America and that finishes my study of the map.

What came over the world since the year 1815? So far as Africa is concerned, it has been parcelled out as the property of the western countries. What came over the world that we, one-fifth of the human race, have sold ourselves, body and soul and land as the property of the western races? As far as they are concerned, it stands to their credit. Undoubtedly they are entitled to be proud of the great empire they have built. But what about you and me who have become their property? They are rightly proud of the brightest Jewel in the British Crown. Have you found out the reasons for that change, the change that has taken place in your condition historically?

Again I ask myself, and I ask you: Why is India what it is today? It is because of three dominations, two of which at least are entirely in our hands, if not all the three. They are, the domination of the Indian mind by its society, the domination of the Indian spirit by its present religion, and the domination of the people by the foreign races. That is the reaction which finds us in the condition in which we are to-day. It is not for the purpose of blaming those who have acquired that domination that I am narrating the simple facts of history, but it is for the purpose of making you approach life with some sense of reality. What boots it to us if you pass all the examinations and get out of the Universities with B.A., M.A., and other degrees, if only at the end of all that you have learnt, what I would call, a common stock of secular knowledge such as history, mathematics and science in order that you may comfortably settle yourself in some appointment that it is possible to get and that may fall to your lot? For, after all, what is the purpose of education? Is it only to acquire some part of knowledge, all the time ignoring the greatest aspect of knowledge that is, the art of life for yourself? Has that ever occurred to you? I quite agree that the first reaction of foreign rule is the sense of dumbness, a sense of resignation, a sense of almost willing submission, and it continued for a period of a hundred years notwithstanding our education. If freedom is a virtue, it cannot be a virtue for only a limited part of the human race? Why is freedom a virtue to be fought for so far as the West is concerned so that they may be men, so that they may be masters in their own countries, and why is it a crime in so far as India is concerned? For it was considered a crime during the last three years of history of this country when people who dared to fight for their liberty were punished, were thrown into prison, and the spirit of freedom was considered a crime and sought to be suppressed as a crime. If freedom is a virtue, it is a virtue for all mankind.

Why was the war of slavery fought in America? Was it fought in a spirit of Truth, in a spirit of righteousness? Why was the last war fought in Europe? Why did we give everything that we had in our power in order that the Allies may succeed? Because they all the time professed that they were fighting for the liberties of others and for the self-determination of the subject races of the world. Therefore, the first lesson that you have got to learn is this. They did not hesitate to make any amount of sacrifice to preserve their freedom. Millions were wounded and killed in that war, and you are perhaps aware that the wealth accumulated for over a century went into the air as bare exploded gun-powder. Why did men offer themselves? Why did they give all their resources? Because they truly loved freedom in the spirit in which their great poet, whom I admire, Byron spoke of freedom. We call ourselves educated, we recite those poems and get prizes for the recitation, but does it not occur to you that you must in your own lives begin to examine the lessons of literature and history?

It would really be futile to be taught anything in Universities and Colleges, where we spend lakhs and lakhs of rupees, to learn, not as parrots to recite what we have learnt, but as human beings and to put into practice what we have learnt. I am sure that if you truly love freedom, those very people who to-day want to suppress your spirit of freedom would admire you when you have achieved it, for I have not the slightest doubt in my mind that while there must necessarily be a clash between those who have acquired an empire, who naturally want to keep it, and those who want to win their freedom, they truly love freedom and who try to with-hold it from you would be the first to admire you if you only assert yourselves. Therefore the first and foremost lesson that you should learn is that freedom has its own value in and for itself in order that you might rank as men, and not for the gains it brings. It is a deficiency which ranks you down with those things which are lower than men. Freedom is not a mere matter of policies. Freedom is the single aspect of endowment which God has given to us.

There are three kinds of domination as I have told you. Let us take the condition of the domination of the Indian mind by the social conditions into which it exists. What is the duty that you owe to yourself? Are you going to allow yourself to be dominated in every aspect of your lives by the small, narrow, hard, rigid circle to which you happen to belong, or are you going to say that human society on such a basis is but a form of tyranny? The human society which does not rank every single individual member of it as equal to another member is not a society that is based on genuine freedom, and you cannot deny—at least I do not deny—that every single effort that is made towards the cause of the enfranchisement of our minds from the domination of the society to which we belong does require our first consideration, for after all it touches every aspect of our lives. What is the good of your learned Vice-Chancellor conferring a degree upon you, if you do not go back and begin as men, each one of you saying to himself: "Henceforth I am going to take my share in the responsibility of freeing my society from the domination by which my society is kept down from its progress"?

What is the great Harijan movement which is at present, to a very large extent, agitating the Indian world? I do not wish to deal with the narrower controversial aspect of the subject which undoubtedly predominates in every society. What is it that the priesthood of every country does after the spirit of religion has gone out of the ceremonial? When I was young, I read a book of Carlyle which was prescribed as a text-book for the degree of the Master of Arts. All that I remember now is enough to enable me to bring to your notice the great lesson that he taught. The one lesson that he attempts to teach is this. Every form of religion or religious ritual once it has lost its original appeal to the true spirit loses its significance and it becomes a matter of routine. It is the spirit of it which matters.

The next thing is, that the priest, by reason of his ability, influence and learning, the position he occupies in society and last but not the least by reason of his vested interest, predominates the human mind. Perhaps you are aware, whether you belong to Hinduism, Islam or Christianity, what respect is demanded as a matter of right by every man who puts on the robes of a priest. It is because our minds have become mechanically subject to the form of religion and have lost the appreciation of its true spirit, its true purpose of elevation of the soul, and its true and genuine salvation. That is what, in my opinion, and that is how I ask you to look at it, has brought the Harijan movement among us. I am only giving an illustration. In fact, it is being used even for political purposes to day. I never thought that God created religion in order that man may exploit it for political purposes. That is the true position of India to-day. That is the true analysis of ourselves, and it is only if we analyse it in that way that we will realise the fundamental unity on which we ought to stand.

After having told you of the domination of society, I have told you of the domination of religious aspects. It is not religion. It is but the shadow of religion, for after all, a church is not a church, a temple is not a temple, a mosque is not a mosque, unless it teaches you the purest form of Faith to reach your God in your own way. It is not to be used for mundane, secular, narrow and lower purposes.

If you fight the first two dominations, I have not the least doubt that the third will be nearer achievement. If you begin to realise that your society should be based on such a broad basis that it shall recognise no barrier between man and man, I am quite certain that freedom in the political sense is a mere matter of effort and time. And here I must bring you again to the map of the world with which I began. When I was travelling in Europe, lecturing in France, Switzerland and England, I was frequently asked this question. "How can India acquire any title for freedom, because India is not a nation—I will use the expression which is frequently used—it is a conglomeration of heterogeneous people divided by all sorts of ideas which they call religion, speaking numerous languages?" That is what I am told India is. That is why it does not deserve freedom. I began to ask myself "Could it be really as bad as that, notwithstanding the degraded condition, the lower condition, to which we have voluntarily fallen by allowing ourselves to be dominated in the manner I have pointed out"?

Sometime ago, in order to be able to answer the question, I told myself looking at the map of the world, "Let me see the democracy that the world admits to be the greatest, the United States of America, the one state which dared to stand against the combined strength of the world. Is there any state on earth which has not a citizen there, is not there a German, an Englishman, an Italian, a Philippine, Japanese and many other races that I can name, except ourselves, for we are international, so far as our country is concerned. We belong to all but nothing belongs to us, not even our own country. That is the United States of America, that is the United States that fought on the side of the Allies in the last war. I told myself that in whatever way my opponent may look at it—it is to his interest that he should make much of these things—with this illustration before me, he cannot say that we are not a nation on this ground. At least it gives me hope.

If you carefully study the map of India, from Peshawar down to the southernmost coast of India, you will find at least one common form of civilisation, the great Aryan civilisation. The name of which Hitler is proud to-day is the name that belongs to us. The Swastika belongs to us, and yet where do we stand as a nation? Wherever I go in India I find a single form of life and thought. I venture to tell you that it is up to you to realise that you are far nearer each other than many of the western races, notwithstanding the vast expanse of your country and notwithstanding the fact that you are one-fifth of the entire human-race. You have both intellectual and moral equipment, and if you only knew what you were, you would not be what you are.

The next question that I ask myself is, "What does it matter if we have several languages?" I went to a small country called Switzerland, so small that you can traverse the whole country in a few hours. In its Parliament there are three languages used today, Italian, German and French. And yet it is perhaps as small nations go, one of the most cultured and powerful nations in the world. That is the only nation that dared stand neutral in the midst of the greatest conflagration that the world has ever seen. There the number of languages does not matter, at least so far as the making of a nation goes.

Then I was asked about religion. I was asked this question at Oxford. Fortunately for me, I was standing in the place where John Ridley was burnt by reason of his daring to profess his faith. There is a memorial there. Did England deserve freedom the less because the Catholics and Protestants burnt each other when they quarrelled about religion? And yet this is said to be the greatest impediment in the way of India claiming to be a single nation !

But it is our opponents' business to magnify our differences. In fact, the Editor of the *London Times* had to naively admit to me that in the normality of things, when each time a riot took place in a small place, it was promptly telegraphed to London in order that the paper may come out with big headlines of our differences. Matter of religion ! Do you know how many religions there are in Japan, a country not bigger, probably, than Gujarat? There are at least three religions there, and who dare say that it is not a political unit entitled to all honour that a united nation deserves at the hands of the world? If we are what we are, we do not deserve to be respected. But we want to be respected. So it seems to me that religion as a matter of dividing line between you and other men, as a matter of dividing line in politics, is a little overdone in this country, not because of its reality, but because we allowed ourselves to be persuaded falsely.

Christianity is divided into hundreds of sects. Has it come in the way of freedom of Christian nations of Europe? Did the Protestants and Roman Catholics refuse to fight side by side when it came to a question of freedom of their own countries? Let us clearly understand that by the domination of religion in the lower sense of the term, we allowed ourselves to get into this state of mind. It is up to us to think a little more freely for unless we think a little more freely, unless we stand united, we will not be respected.

What did Mr. Baldwin say, What did Mr. Ramsay Macdonald say when our great and honoured friends went there? 'We are sorry, gentlemen, we are quite willing to give you all you want, but you do not seem to agree among yourselves.' Whose fault is it that we do not agree? There must be something radically wrong in us if we cannot agree about a thing that we all desire. It is for you to answer that question during the remaining life that God has given you as a trust. We have among us men of the highest intellect, and yet we are told as if we were school boys "Oh what can we do, you do not agree among yourselves, you are not politicians, you are not statesmen and you do not understand freedom."

We do not want other people's lands. We only want what is ours and what is due to us. It was said to be a trust some years ago. Now it has ceased to be a trust. It has now become a matter of struggle. Therefore, it is in your own hands to take it if you can, and you are asked to take it in a manner that the world has yet to learn. That is the only solution for us. A war of force is only a vicious circle, the vanquished only waiting to become powerful enough to fight again. Do you want any illustration from history for it? Are you so unintelligent, so ignorant of what is happening in the world to-day? Does it not strike you that a war of force must necessarily be, even though it is fought for a most sacred cause, a vicious circle? There are many eminent scientists to-day who are really afraid that the advancement of science, the purpose for which it is put to use, will bring about the destruction of the world. Some day a solution must be reached of this problem of force for the purpose of solving the differences between man and man, country and country, race and race, for you may be certain that the most militant man does not generally love his job. He does it because he believes that he must do it for his country's sake.

But a war of force is needed only for aggression. You need no war of force because all that you have to do is to dare to assert your right for freedom and banish away all ideas by means of which you divide yourself. You will laugh at yourselves if you give some thought to it, but let me tell you that every day, it seems to me, the idea of individualism seems to become more and more powerful in our country, in fact, more powerful than in most of the powerful free countries. I ask myself, "What really is the psychological cause?" Every man says, "I am independent", and the result is, as the proverb goes, where there are twelve men, there are thirteen opinions, and what is more, none of them can agree. When the time for concerted action comes, every one says, "I am going to form my own party, please excuse me, I really cannot do anything, I am very sorry." What is it? Is it not the case of two slaves fighting with each other for something trivial and allowing themselves to be dominated by a third party? I want you to provide an answer. That is the fundamental analysis of the Indian situation to-day.

The other day I read a book on the problems of the East—I want each of you to read it—written by Sir Federick Whyte, who came out here as the first President of the Legislative Assembly. In it he asks why the Indian people are in such a hurry when only 15 years ago they dared assert—the idea that they are entitled to freedom? All they asked till then was "Please mitigate this evil, please mitigate that evil, please relax the Arms Act, please reduce the income-tax and please introduce a few more Indians into the service." As I said in another place, I still remember the time when the late Dada Bhai Naoroji succeeded in getting a resolution passed in the House of Commons to hold simultaneous examinations for admission into the Indian Civil Service, there was not a single town in this country where the people did not pass a vote of thanks and congratulation on that achievement. I am illustrating this, not with a view to minimise the great work of our forebears, but in order only to impress upon you that we have lived through a period when we were parties to a willing submission, to the continuation of foreign rule. My only request to you is that you should learn to remove that domination which now exists, and that you must fight so that you may restore your freedom in society, you must fight in order that you may restore genuine faith, you must fight in order that you may be equals with free men. Begin doing it as early as you can and make it a part of your religion, a part of your duty.

I am addressing you as men who have the future in your hands, as women who have—thanks to the present upheaval in India, women have begun to take an equal part in our struggle for freedom—and am appealing to you that you must recreate India, that you must give a few minutes every day, notwithstanding your daily struggle for existence, for that is given to every man in the inscrutable wisdom of God, you have got to labour, but in the midst of your labour every one of you must make it a purpose in life—not merely to make speeches, not merely to pass resolutions, not merely to argue, for we have argued enough—but to translate your ideas and live up to them in your life. I am sure that you will not disagree with me when I say that there is no man with any spark of manhood left in him who will deny that it is up to every man to fight for his freedom. Therefore, fight for your freedom.

There is no greater virtue, in my opinion, than moral fearlessness, moral courage. What else is it that makes that great man, who is physically the most frail and the most unprotected man, the most honoured man, and the most powerful man in the world to-day? He has risen above all fear. If only he has got to assert the truth, he will stop at nothing and he will dare to go forward against millions of cannons. Each of you must make it your duty to rise to that height of moral courage. It seems to me that what we require is moral courage.

Ladies and gentlemen, if I have awakened in you, in every single individual among you, the faith of your liberation, I shall consider that I have not addressed you to-night in vain.

SAROJINI NAIDU
(1879-1949)

SAROJINI NAIDU

The Battle of Freedom Is Over

Broadcast from the A.I.R. Delhi on 15 August 1947

O world of free nations, in this day of our freedom, we greet you. O, world of nations not yet free, on the day of our freedom we pray for your freedom in the future. Ours has been an epic struggle, covering many years and costing many lives. It has been a struggle, a dramatic struggle. It has been a struggle of heroes; chiefly anonymous in their millions. It has been a struggle of women transformed into strength and power like the Kali, the goddess of strength they worship. It has been a struggle of youth suddenly transfigured into power itself, sacrifice and ideals. It has been a struggle of young men and old men, of rich and poor, the literate, the illiterate, the stricken, the outcast, the leper and the saint. It has been the only revolution in the whole history of the world that has been without bloodshed; and for this we thank one man, one tiny person, who is on this far-off corner of India, wiping the tears of those who feel themselves exiled from our midst. Mahatma Gandhi, our prophet of non-violence, our general of victory, has taught us a new way of deliverance from evil. He had no device on his banner excepting non-violence. He had no weapons for his legions excepting self-sacrifice and suffering. We marched to the tune of faith and hope and charity that forgives all sins of trespassers that ruined our country through the ages. We have to thank him, our leader, whose life is immutable, immortal, in the love of his countrymen, whose days are imperishable, who has created a new civilization for the world to be based in the years to come on his gospel of love, truth and non-violence.

But we wish to offer today our thanks to the men and women of all races who had striven for India's freedom, the scholars of Europe who restored to us our pride and ancient culture, to the antiquarian and the archaeologist who has discovered for us our own ruined cities, to the missionaries of all countries who chose the life of poverty in far-off villages and served the poor and the needy and the desolate. To all we owe thanks. Today I remember those abroad who were the pioneers of our dream of freedom, men who are exiles if they are alive, forgotten if they are dead, who never sought, nor received recognition, nor reward, only privation, persecution and death. But all these today are immortal in our minds. We thank the Englishmen who were our friends, though many Englishmen were our enemies, not personal enemies but the victims themselves of a system of iniquitous imperialism. But those Englishmen who served us, became part of our Indian history, part of our struggle for India's independence. And it seems somehow poetical, it seems somehow romantic, it seems somehow logical that the great-grandson of Queen Victoria, Louis Mountbatten, should have, by grace and generosity, dissolved the empire that Disraeli built for her. All of them we thank.

The battle of freedom is over. The struggle for peace begins. And my country, my India, that has never excluded friend or foe from her hospitality, my India that has taken knowledge from all over the world, that has offered knowledge and wisdom to the world, once more will she stand in the forefront of the world civilization, once more will she bring the message of peace, once more will she carry her lamp into the darkness of strife and struggle and hatred; and the nations of the world who are free, nations of the world who are not free, we pledge you our comradeship, our fellowship, our understanding, our love. Let us move together towards the great world fellowship of which we dream. Let us work together for the peace that will never be ended. Let us work for justice, for equity, for human rights but no privileges, for human duties but no prerogatives, let us be fellow citizens of a great free world of which our ancestors dreamed and for which we have striven. Men and women together, men and women of a common humanity, let no religion, no community, no sect, no tongues divide us, for ours is a common destiny. Ours is a common purpose. Ours is a common wish and ambition to rebuild this broken world into the image of our heart's desire. And which country but India can take the lead in restoring the world to its pristine glory. We who have been the dreamers of dreams, the seers of visions, the creators of wisdom, the followers of renunciation, we who have given the heroes of the independence struggle for India, we have rung through the whole gamut of the world's adventures, of the world's emotions. We are the wise. We are reborn today of the crucible of our suffering.

Nations of the world, I greet you in the name of India, my mother, my mother whose home has a roof of snow, whose walls are of living seas, whose doors are always open to you. Do you seek peace or wisdom, do you seek love and understanding, come to us. Come to us in faith, come to us in hope, come to us believing that all gifts are ours to give. Today, in the name of India, I give for the whole world the freedom of this India that had never died in the past, that shall be indestructible in the future and shall lead the world to ultimate peace.

CHAKRAVARTI RAJAGOPALACHARI
(1879-1972)

CHAKRAVARTI RAJAGOPALACHARI

Election of Committee on Subjects Assigned to the Union Centre

Resolution Moved in the Constituent Assembly at the Constitution Hall, New Delhi, on 25 January 1947

Mr. Chairman,

I beg to move the Resolution standing in my name, which reads as follows:

WHEREAS in paragraph 15(i) of the Cabinet Delegation's Statement of May 16, the subjects assigned to the Union Centre are generally and compendiously indicated under four broad categories,

AND WHEREAS an understanding of the scope of these subjects is necessary for the purpose of framing the Union and other Constitutions, of avoiding as far as possible overlapping and conflicts between the provisions in the Constitution relating to the Union and those in the Constitutions referred to in clause (v) of paragraph 19 of the Statement, and of bringing all the said Constitutions into line with each other.

AND WHEREAS it is necessary to draw up lists of matters included in and interconnected with the subjects assigned to the Union before the framing of the Constitutions referred to in clause (v) of paragraph 19 of the Statement is taken up for consideration;

This Assembly resolves—

(a) that a committee consisting initially of twelve members, elected according to the principle of promotional representation by means of the single transferable vote, be constituted to examine the above matters and to report to the Assembly not later than the 15th of April, 1947, and

(b) that the President may add ten more persons to the committee and that the selection of all or any of these ten additional members be made at such time and in such manner as the President may determine.

Sir, I might take the matter a little in advance and mention that there are three amendments that are going to be proposed to this motion of mine, and those amendments deal with subsidiary matters, Mr. Munshi and Mr. Satyanarayan Sinha will move them in due course and I propose to accept them. So, in order to make the matter easier to understand I shall read the Resolution as it will stand when these amendments are accepted. The first part of the Resolution, *i.e.*, the preamble, stands as before, but the operative part would read like this: . . .

"This Assembly resolves—

(a) that a committee consisting initially of the following members:

1. The Hon'ble Pandit Jawaharlal Nehru
2. Mr. Sarat Chandra Bose
3. Dr. Pattabi Sitaramayya
4. The Hon'ble Pandit Govind Ballabh Pant
5. Mr. Jairam Das Daulatram
6. Sri Biswanath Das
7. The Hon'ble Sir N. Gopalaswami Ayyangar
8. Bakshi Sir Tek Chand
9. Diwan Bahadur Sir Alladi Krishnaswami Ayyar
10. Mr. D.P. Khaitan
11. Mr. M.R. Massani
12. Mr. K.M. Munshi

be constituted to examine the above matters and to report to the Assembly not later than the 15th of April, 1947,

(b) that the President may add ten more persons to the committee, and that the selection of all or any of these ten additional members be made at such time and in such manner as the Presidnet may determine,

(c) that the quorum for the Committee shall be one-third of

the total number of members for the time being of the Committee, and

(d) that casual vacancies in the committee be filled as soon as possible after they occur by nomination by the President from among the members of the Assembly".

Sir, the object of the Resolution is to help this Assembly in framing the Constitution so as not to leave for the future any overlapping or conflicts that might occur if various proceedings took place without correlation in different Sections of the Assembly or otherwise. I may be permitted, therefore, to explain exactly what the possibilities are which we wish to avoid.

This Assembly, Sir, has been entrusted with a very serious task, perhaps more onerous than any Constituent Assembly in the world has had to deal with. The number of differences that have to be settled are enormous; the population that has to be satisfied is enormous; and the problems that are before the Assembly are as difficult as any which any other Assembly has had before it. The British Government's Statement has put things in a farely clear way, but not quite as clearly as we would desire it. If we examine the British Government's Statement, on which this Assembly's programme is based, we will find few matters settled clearly.

No. 1—it is decided that we are to frame a constitution for a united India.

No. 2—we have to frame a constitution where the centre is given the powers over Defence, Communications and Foreign Affairs and also powers necessary to raise the finances required for the above subjects.

And then thirdly another principle has been laid down that the residuary powers, that is to say, all powers which have not been transferred to the Central Government, should remain in the Provinces. Then fourthly, a subsidiary point is laid down also, that such powers as the Provinces agree to transfer to any Groups they may form would go to the Groups. All subjects other than the Union subjects and all residuary powers should vest in the Provinces. The States will retain all subjects and powers other than those ceded to the Union. This is (3) and (4) of Clause 15 of the State. It is further laid down that there will be a ten-year revision of this Constitution and the initiative for that revision is vested in the Provinces. These are the broad principles laid down in Clause 15:

But let us examine this a little more closely. We find in sub-clause (1) that:

"The Union should have all the powers necessary to raise the finances required for the above subject."

Now, what are powers, unless we mean the power actually to enforce the law as prescribed for raising the finances and that would include, Sir, the power of collection and probably also the power of securing the services of a proper judiciary wherever required. No provision has been put down for this purpose. Again, if we examine clause 19 which gives the procedure for carrying out the principles set out in clause 15, we find, strangely enough, a lacuna in sub-clause (v) of clause 19. It is stated that the Sections shall proceeds to settle Provincial Constitutions and then they shall also decide whether any Group Constitution shall be set up, and if so with what provincial subjects the group shall deal. Then the representatives of the Sections and the Indian States shall re-assemble for the purpose of setting the Union Constitution. Now, there is no provision as to how and when the Group Constitution shall be settled. Beyond stating that whether any Group Constitution shall be set up may be decided in the Sections and also that the Sections shall set out the provincial subjects with which the groups should deal there is no provision for settling the Group Constitution itself.

Then, again, if we examine the provisions as to the Advisory Committee on Minorities, we find this. The Advisory Committee shall report to the Union Constituent Assembly upon the list of fundamental rights, clauses for protecting minorities and a scheme for the administration of Tribal and Excluded Areas, and it should advise whether these rights should be incorporated in the Provincial, the Group or the Union Constitutions. Now, it follows logically that when the Advisory Committee has reported to the Union Assembly, the Union Assembly should have the power to see whether it should be incorporated in the provincial or in the Group or in the Union Constitutions. If the Provincial and Group constitutions should be settled beforehand, and at a later sitting for the Union Assembly, they decide that it should be incorporated in the Provincial or Group

Constitutions, what is the procedure to be followed? Therefore, there is a great deal of correlation to be done before we can carry out the intentions of the Cabinet Mission's Statements, or the Resolutions of this Assembly. If we interpret the programme laid down in clause 19 literally and assume that what is asked to be done at the various sittings should be the only things done at this stage and nothing else, we will be landed in a great deal of difficulty at the end in carrying out the explicit intention of the Cabinet Mission's Statement. Considering all these matters, it has been found necessary, we have found it necessary, Sir, to make this motion for the appointment of a committee which shall do the required thinking on these matters and report to this House before we end the preliminary session so that we may frame our programme of future work.

This Assembly has to consider, as I said before, very serious matters, and we will have to do a great deal of thinking. We cannot do our work on the assumption that we are here only to register previously arrived at decisions, opinions and programmes. We have to do a lot of substantial thinking in this constituent Assembly; and in the nature of things, therefore, we require the assistance of a select Committee to consider and advise us on the difficulties that may arise in the course of our work. It is with that object that this Committee has been proposed. It is not with the object of undermining the essential intentions of the Cabinet Mission's Statement or anything of that kind. It is to help us to think out our difficulties and to find solutions for those difficulties.

Sir, if I may venture to put it that way, it is not only a matter of culture or good-breeding, but it is statesmanship to think of those who are absent, to think of other people than ourselves, when we deal with any matter. That is why in proposing every motion, Hon'ble Members have dealt with the intentions and purposes of those who are not yet present in this Assembly. We find a great many possibilities of misunderstanding and we try to anticipate those difficulties and remove possibilities of misunderstanding as far as we can. In this connection I would mention, therefore, that those who are absent should not misunderstand the purpose of this Committee that I am proposing. The Muslim League policy has been to secure a separate, sovereign State of their own. Now, this Constituent Assembly has taken up its task on the basis of the Cabinet Mission's Statement and if one thing is more clearly decided in his Majesty's Government's Statement than anything else, it is this, that there shall be only one sovereign State in India. It has been decided clearly beyond all possibility of doubt that a division of India into two sovereign States is not to be thought of in this connection. That explains many of the things that we are doing and will remove many of the misunderstandings that are likely to arise. If I may put it that way, the League has gone the wrong way for securing their objective. If they had only restricted their claims to what legitimately should be asked in pursuance of their policy, possibly they might have achieved their object and they would not have been in the present difficulty. Let me put it frankly. The greatest difficulty for the Muslim League now is that they have to join this Assembly and thereby, once for all and beyond doubt, accept the single sovereign State of India. That is why they find it difficult to come in, and that is why these postponements. That is why the League fixes its date always after the meetings that the other major parties have programmed for their consultations. That is why we find to-day, even after the last adjournment, the League has been unable to make up its mind and join us. Let us understand the difficulties of the other side. If the league comes in, they come in on the express understanding that India shall be only one sovereign State, abandoning their separatist policy. This is difficult for them to do at once. Let us realise these difficulties and not misunderstand even the delays. We desire to proceed with the work as fast as possible, understanding very well the difficulties of the Muslim League members in the way of their coming and joining us at this stage. Let them think it over. Let us give them ample time to come. But that does not mean that we stop our work, that we stop thinking, that we stop doing anything whatsoever, until they make up their minds. That would lead to indefinite postponement. Hence, Sir, I have no hesitation in recommending this Resolution that we should appoint this Committee of twelve members as proposed, so that they may think out all the difficulties and advise us so that we may frame a constitution for India which will create no difficulties for those who have to work it, and which will be a stable, strong constitution for the Centre with stable and strong constitutions for the provinces, to work under the Centre and in the single State that is being contemplated. Therefore Sir, I move that this Resolution be accepted by the House. As I said before, there are two amendments. One is to replace the election by proportional representation, by twelve members definitily named to the House: and the other is to provide for quorum and another is to provide for casual vacancies. I commend the Resolution with these amendments.

SARVEPALLI RADHAKRISHNAN
(1888-1975)

SARVEPALLI RADHAKRISHNAN

Rajendra Prasad's Election as Chairman of the Constituent Assembly

Congratulatory Address at the Constitution Hall, New Delhi, on 11 December 1946

Mr. President, Sir,

I consider it a great honour to be called upon to be the first speaker after the election of the permanent Chairman of the Constituent Assembly. I offer to him, on behalf of this House, our most respectful congratulations on the unique honour that has been conferred on him.

This Constituent Assembly has met here to frame the constitution, to effect the withdrawal of British control, political, economic and military and to establish a free independent India. If successful, this transfer of authority will be the biggest and the least bloody of all transfers in human history (Cheers).

The first Britisher to arrive in this country was a Jesuit Missionary in 1579. He was followed by merchants who came to trade but stayed to rule. In 1765 the authority was transferred to the East India Company. Later it was gradually subordinated to and replaced by the authority of Parliament and it has been continuing till now on the famous principle enunciated by Cecil Rhodes—the principle fundamental to imperialism and philanthropy. On that principle it has worked. Right through however there were protests against the British rule. All these protests became canalized when the Indian National Congress was established in 1885. It adopted mild methods till the advent of Mahatma Gandhi when it became aggressive and dynamic. In 1930 the Resolution for the Independence of India was passed at Lahore and we are now here to give effect to that resolution. The British are empirics from beginning to end. It was Lord Palmerston who said 'we

British have no eternal principles, we have only eternal interests'. When they adopt any particular line of action you may take it that it is not a willing surrender of power or authority but it is a response to the historic necessities of the case. When the discontent grew up they gave us the Morley-Minto Reforms and they introduced the principle of communal electorates and these communal electorates were intended to keep the people apart. The higher mind of Britain advised the local officials that they would betray the trust placed upon them if they foisted communal electorates. They would inject a poison into the very body politic which could be removed if at all, at the cost of a civil war. We know how those anticipations are getting realized today. We had after that the Montford Reforms and then the 1935 Act, the Cripps' proposals and now the Cabinet Plan. The latest Statement of His Majesty's Government on this question indicates how it is not in human nature to surrender power easily. (Hear, hear). Playing off one section against another is unworthy of a great people. It is much too clever to be permanent and would embitter the relations of this country and Great Britain. (Hear, hear). It is essential for the British to understand that if an act is done it must be done with the utmost grace. All the same we are here assembled to draw up a constitution for future India. A constitution is the fundamental law of the nation. It should embody and express the dreams and passions, the ideals and aspirations of the people. It must be based on the consent of all, and respect the rights of all people who belong to this great land.

We have been kept apart. It is our duty now to find each other. We all deplore—speakers yesterday and day before yesterday deplored—the abstention of the representatives of the Muslim League from this Constituent Assembly. We take it that it will only be temporary, for their cooperation is absolutely essential for the success of any constitution which we may lay down. But in approaching these matters our attitude should be one of realism. Take the problems from which we suffer; our hunger, our poverty, our disease, our malnutrition—these are common to all. Take the psychological evils from which we suffer—the loss of human dignity, the slavery of the mind, the stunting of sensibility and the shame of subjection—these are common to all; Hindus or Muslims, Princes or peasants. The chains may be made of gold but they are still chains that fetter us. Even the Princes will have to realise that they are slaves in this country. (Hear, hear). If they have a sufficient sense of self-respect and exercise a little self-analysis, they will find how much their freedom is fettered.

Again, the people—whether they are Hindus or Muslims, Princes or peasants,—belong to this one country. Earth and Heaven have combined to make them belong to one another. If they try to disown it, their gait, their cast of countenance, their modes of thought, their ways of behaviour, they will all betray them. (Hear, hear). It is not possible for us, to think that we belong to different nationalities. Our whole ancestry is there.

It is essential for any constitution which is drawn up to make all the citizens realise that their basic privileges—education, social and economic are afforded to them; that there will be cultural autonomy; that nobody will be suppressed, that it will be a constitution which will be democratic in the true sense of the term, where, from political freedom we will march on to economic freedom and equity, Every individual should feel that he is proud to belong to this great land.

Apart from all these, a nation does not depend on identity of race, or sentiment, or on ancestral memories, but it depends on a persistent and continuous way of life that has come down to us. Such a way of life, belongs to the very soil of this land. It is there indigenous to this country as much as the waters of the Ganges or the snows of the Himalayas. From the very roots of our civilization down in the Indus Valley to the present day, the same great culture is represented among Hindus and Muslims, we have stood for the ideal of comprehension and charity all these centuries.

I remember how Anatole France went up to the Musse Guimet on the first of May 1890 in Paris and there in the silence and simplicity of the gods of Asia reflected on the aim of existence, on the meaning of life, on the values which peoples and Governments are in search of. Then his eyes fell on the statue of the Buddha. France felt like kneeling down and Praying to him as to a God, the Buddha, eternally young, clad in ascetic robes, seated on the lotus of purity with his two fingers upraised admonishing all humanity to develop comprehension, and charity, wisdom, and love, prana and karuna. If you have understanding, if you have compassion, you will be able to overcome the problems of this world. Asoka, his great disciple, when he found his Empire inhabited by men of all races and religions, said—

> "*Samavaya eva sadhuh.*"
> "Concord alone is the supreme good".

India is a symphony where there are, as in an orchestra, different instruments, each with its particular sonority, each with its special sound, all combining to interpret one particular score. It is this kind of combination that this country has stood for. It never adopted inquisitorial methods. It never asked the Parsis or the Jews or the Christians or the Muslims who came and took shelter there to change their creeds or become absorbed in what might be called a uniform Hindu humanity. It never did this. "Live and let live"—that has been the spirit of this country. If we are true to that spirit, if that ideal which has dominated our cultural landscape for five or six thousand years and is still operating, I have no doubt that the crisis by which we are faced today will be overcome as many other crises in our previous history have been overcome. Suicide is the greatest sin. To murder yourself, to betray yourself, to barter away your spiritual wealth for a mess of pottage, to try to preserve your body at the expense of your spirit—that is the greatest sin. If we therefore stand out for the great ideal for which this country has stood, the ideal which has survived the assaults of invaders, the ideals to which the unheeding world today is turning its attention, if we are able to do it, the flame which has sustained us in overcoming foreign rule, will fire our efforts to build a united and free India.

It is not an accident that our temporary Chairman, Dr. Sachchidananda Sinha and our permanent Chairman, Dr. Rajendra Prasad, both come from Bihar. They are both impregnated with the spirit of the *vihara*—the invincibility of gentleness, the gospel of India. *The Mahabharata* says:

> *Mrduna darunum hanti, mrduna hanti adarunam nasadhyam mrduna kinchit tasmat tiksnaram hi mrduth.*
>
> Gentleness can overcome the hardest things; it can overcome the softest things. There is nothing impossible to be overcome by gentleness, and therefore the sharpest weapon we have is gentleness.
>
> Softness, gentleness,—that is the greatest weapon which will

wear out the highest kind of opposition. We have not been true to it. We have betrayed and done wrong to millions of our own fellow beings. It is now time for us to make atonement for all our past guilt. It is not a question of justice or charity, it is atonement—that is how I would put it.

In Dr. Rajendra Prasad we have one who embodies this spirit of gentleness. (Cheers). He is the soul of goodness, he has great patience and courage, he has suffered. It is not an accident that this year which remarks the sixtieth year of the Indian National Congress, is also the year of the opening of the Constituent Assembly. We have to remember with gratitude all those great souls who worked and suffered for the freedom of this country, for the dawn of this day. Thousands died, more thousands suffered privation, imprisonment, and exile, and it is their suffering that has cemented and built up this great edifice of the Indian National Congress. (Hear, hear). We have to remember them all, Rajendra Prasad is the suffering servant of India, of the Congress, who incarnates the spirit for which this country stands. I only hope that this spirit of amity, concord and harmony which has come down to us from the image of Siva in the Indus civilization down to Mahatma Gandhi and Dr. Rajendra Prasad, will inspire our efforts. (Applause).

JAWAHARLAL NEHRU
(1889-1964)

JAWAHARLAL NEHRU

Asia Finds Herself Again

Speech Inaugurating the Asian Conference in New Delhi on 23 March 1947

FRIENDS and fellow Asians, what has brought you here, men and women of Asia? Why have you come from the various countries of this mother continent of ours and gathered together in the ancient city of Delhi? Some of us, greatly daring, sent you invitations for this Conference and you gave a warm welcome to that invitation. And yet it was not merely the call from us, but some deeper urge that brought you here.

We stand at the end of an era and on the threshold of a new period of history. Standing on this watershed which divides two epochs of human history and endeavour, we can look back on our long past and look forward to the future that is taking shape before our eyes. Asia, after a long period of quiescence, has suddenly become important again in world affairs. If we view the millennia of history, this continent of Asia, with which Egypt has been so intimately connected in cultural fellowship, has played a mighty role in the evolution of humanity. It was here that civilization began and man started on his unending adventure of life. Here the mind of man searched unceasingly for truth and the spirit of man shone out like a beacon which lighted up the whole world.

This dynamic Asia from which great streams of culture flowed in all directions gradually became static and unchanging. Other peoples and other continents came to the fore and with their new dynamism spread out and took possession of great parts of the world. This mighty continent became just a field for the rival imperialisms of Europe, and Europe became the centre of history and progress in human affairs.

A change is coming over the scene now and Asia is again finding herself. We live in a tremendous age of transition and already the next stage takes shape when Asia takes her rightful place with the other continents.

It is at this great moment that we meet here and it is the pride and privilege of the people of India to welcome their fellow Asians from other countries, to confer with them about the present and the future, and lay the foundation of our mutual progress, well-being and friendship.

We welcome you delegates and representatives from China, that great country to which Asia owes so much and from which so much is expected; from Egypt and the Arab countries of Western Asia, inheritors of a proud culture which spread far and wide and influenced India greatly; from Iran whose contacts with India go back to the dawn of history; from Indonesia and Indo-China whose history is intertwined with India's culture, and where recently the battle of freedom has continued, a reminder to us that freedom must be won and cannot come as a gift; from Turkey that has been rejuvenated by the genius of a great leader; from Korea and Mongolia, Siam, Malaya and the Philippines; from the Soviet Republics of Asia which have advanced so rapidly in our generation and which have so many lessons to teach us; and from our neighbours Afghanistan, Tibet, Nepal, Bhutan, Burma and Ceylon to whom we look especially for co-operation and close and friendly intercourse. Asia is very well represented at this conference, and if one or two countries have been unable to send representatives, this was due to no lack of desire on their part or ours, but circumstances beyond our control came in the way. We welcome also observers from Australia and New Zealand, because we have many problems in common, especially in the Pacific and in the South-East region of Asia, and we have to co-operate together to find solutions.

As we meet here today, the long past of Asia rises up before us, the troubles of recent years fade away, and a thousand memories revive. But I shall not speak to you of these past ages with their glories and triumphs and failures, nor of more recent times which have oppressed us so much and which still pursue us in some measure. During the past two hundred years we have seen the growth of Western imperialisms and of the reduction of large parts of

Asia to colonial or semi-colonial status. Much has happened during these years, but perhaps one of the notable consequences of the European domination of Asia has been the isolation of the countries of Asia from one another. India always had contacts and intercourse with her neighbour countries in the North-West, the North-East, the East and the South-East. With the coming of British rule in India these contacts were broken off and India was almost completely isolated from the rest of Asia. The old land routes almost ceased to function and our chief window to the outer world looked out on the sea route which led to England. A similar process affected other countries of Asia also. Their economy was bound up with some European imperialism or other; even culturally they looked towards Europe and not to their own friends and neighbours from whom they had derived so much in the past.

Today this isolation is breaking down because of many reasons, political and other. The old imperialisms are fading away. The land routes have revived and air travel suddenly brings us very near to one another. This Conference itself is significant as an expression of that deeper urge of the mind and spirit of Asia which has persisted in spite of the isolationism which grew up during the years of European domination. As that domination goes, the walls that surrounded us fall down and we look at one another again and meet as old friends long parted.

In this Conference and in this work there are no leaders and no followers. All countries of Asia have to meet together on an equal basis in a common task and endeavour. It is fitting that India should play her part in this new phase of Asian development. Apart from the fact that India herself is emerging into freedom and independence, she is the natural centre and focal point of the many forces at work in Asia. Geography is a compelling factor, and geographically she is so situated as to be the meeting point of Western and Northern and Eastern and South-East Asia. Because of this, the history of India is a long history of her relations with the other countries of Asia. Streams of culture have come to India from the west and the east and been absorbed in India, producing the rich and variegated culture which is India today. At the same time, streams of culture have flowed from India to distant parts of Asia. If you would know India you have to go to Afghanistan and Western Asia, to Central Asia, to

China and Japan and to the countries of South-East Asia. There you will find magnificent evidence of the vitality of India's culture which spread out and influenced vast numbers of people.

There came the great cultural stream from Iran to India in remote antiquity. And then that constant intercourse between India and the Far East, notably China. In later years South-East Asia witnessed an amazing efflorescence of Indian art and culture. The mighty stream which started from Arabia and developed as a mixed Irano-Arabic culture poured into India. All these came to us and influenced us, and yet so great was the powerful impress of India's own mind and culture that it could accept them without being itself swept away or overwhelmed. Nevertheless, we all changed in the process and in India today all of us are mixed products of these various influences. An Indian, wherever he may go in Asia, feels a sense of kinship with the land he visits and the people he meets.

I do not wish to speak to you of the past, but rather of the present. We meet here not to discuss our past history and contacts, but to forge links for the future. And may I say here that this Conference, and the idea underlying it, is in no way aggressive or against any other continent or country? Ever since news of this Conference went abroad some people in Europe and America have viewed it with doubt imagining that this was some kind of a Pan-Asian movement directed against Europe or America. We have no designs against anybody; ours is the great design of promoting peace and progress all over the world. Far too long have we of Asia been petitioners in western courts and chancelleries. That story must now belong to the past. We propose to stand on our own feet and to co-operate with all others who are prepared to cooperate with us. We do not intend to be the playthings of others.

In this crisis in world history Asia will necessarily play a vital role. The countries of Asia can no longer be used as pawns by others; they are bound to have their own policies in world affairs. Europe and America have contributed very greatly to human progress and for that we must yield them praise and honour, and learn from them the many lessons they have to teach. But the West has also driven us into wars and conflicts without number and even now, the day after a terrible war, there is talk of further wars in the atomic age that is upon us. In this atomic age Asia will have to function effectively in the maintenance of peace. Indeed, there can be no peace unless Asia plays her part. There is today conflict in many countries, and all of us in Asia are full of our own troubles. Nevertheless, the whole spirit and outlook of Asia are peaceful, and the emergence of Asia in world affairs will be a powerful influence for world peace.

Peace can only come when nations are free and also when human beings everywhere have freedom and security and opportunity. Peace and freedom, therefore, have to be considered both in their political and economic aspects. The countries of Asia, we must remember, are very backward and the standards of life are appallingly low. These economic problems demand urgent solutions or else crisis and disaster may overwhelm us. We have, therefore, to think in terms of the common man and fashion our political, social and economic structure so that the burdens that have crushed him may be removed, and he may have full opportunity for growth.

We have arrived at a stage in human affairs when the ideal of One World and some kind of a World Federation seem to be essential, though there are many dangers and obstacles in the way. We should work for that ideal and not for any grouping which comes in the way of this larger world group. We, therefore, support the United Nations structure which is painfully emerging from its infancy. But in order to have One World, we must also, in Asia, think of the countries of Asia cooperating together for that larger ideal.

This Conference, in a small measure, represents this bringing together of the countries of Asia. Whatever it may achieve, the mere fact of its taking place is itself of historic significance. Indeed, this occasion is unique in history, for never before has such a gathering met together at any place. So even in meeting we have achieved much and I have no doubt that out of this meeting greater things will come. When the history of our present times is written, this event may well stand out as a land-mark which divides the past of Asia from the future. And because we are participating in this making of history, something of the greatness of historic events comes to us all.

We seek no narrow nationalism. Nationalism has a place in each country and should be fostered, but it must not be allowed to become aggressive and come in the way of international development. Asia stretches her hand out in friendship to Europe and America as well as to our suffering brethren in Africa. We of Asia have a special responsibility to the people of Africa. We must help them to their rightful place in the human family. The freedom that we envisage is not to be confined to this nation or that or to a particular people, but must spread out over the whole human race. That universal human freedom also cannot be based on the supremacy of any particular class. It must be the freedom of the common man everywhere and full opportunities for him to develop.

All over Asia we are passing through trials and tribulations. In India also you will see conflict and trouble. Let us not be disheartened by this; this is inevitable in an age of mighty transition. There are a new vitality and powerful creative impulses in all the peoples of Asia. The masses are awake and they demand their heritage. Strong winds are blowing all over Asia. Let us not be afraid of them, but rather welcome them, for only with their help can we build the new Asia of our dreams. Let us have faith in these great new forces and the dream which is taking shape. Let us, above all, have faith in the human spirit which Asia has symbolized for those long ages past.

BHIMRAO RAMJI AMBEDKAR
(1891-1956)

BHIMRAO RAMJI AMBEDKAR

On the Resolution Regarding Aims and Objects of the Constituent Assembly

Speech at the Constitution Hall, New Delhi, on 17 December 1946

Mr. Chairman,

I am indeed very grateful to you for having called me to speak on the Resolution. I must however confess that your invitation has come to me as a surprise. I thought that as there were some 20 or 22 people ahead of me, my turn, if it did come at all, would come tomorrow. I would have preferred that as today I have come without any preparation whatsoever. I would have liked to prepare myself as I had intended to make a full statement on an occasion of this sort. Besides you have fixed a time limit of 10 minutes. Placed under these limitations, I don't know how I could do justice to the Resolution before us. I shall however do my best to condense in as few words as possible what I think about the matter.

Mr. Chairman, the Resolution in the light of the discussion that has gone on since yesterday, obviously divides itself into two parts, one part which is controversial and another part which is non-controversial. The part which is non-controversial is the part which comprises paragraphs (5) to (7) of this Resolution. These paragraphs set out the objectives of the future constitution of this country. I must confess that, coming as the Resolution does from Pandit Jawaharlal Nehru who is reputed to be a socialist, this Resolution, although non-controversial, is to my mind very disappointing. I should have expected him to go much further than he has done in that part of the Resolution. As a student of history, I should have preferred this part of the Resolution not being embodied in it at all. When one reads that part of the Resolution, it reminds one of the Declaration of the Rights of Man which was pronounced by the French Constituent Assembly. I think I am right in suggesting that, after the lapse of practically 450 years, the Declaration of the Rights of Man and the principles which are embodied in it has become part and parcel of our mental make up. I say they have become not only the part and parcel of the mental make up of modern man in every civilised part of the world, but also in our own country which is so orthodox, so archaic in its thought and its social structure, hardly anyone can be found to deny its validity. To repeat it now as the Resolution does is, to say the least, pure pedantry. These principles have become the silent immaculate premise of our outlook. It is therefore unnecessary to proclaim as forming a part of our creed. The Resolution suffers from certain other lacuna. I find that this part of the Resolution, although it enunciates certain rights, does not speak of remedies. All of us are aware of the fact that rights are nothing unless remedies are provided whereby people can seek to obtain redress when rights are invaded. I find a complete absence of remedies. Even the usual formula that no man's life, liberty and property shall be taken without the due process of law, finds no place in the Resolution. These fundamental rights set out are made subject to law and morality. Obviously, what is law, what is morality will be determined by the Executive of the day and when the Executive may take one view another Executive may take another view and we do not know what exactly would be the position with regard to fundamental rights, if this matter is left to the Executive of the day. Sir, there are here certain provisions which speak of justice, economical, social and political. If this Resolution has a reality behind it and a sincerity, of which I have not the least doubt, coming as it does from the Mover of the Resolution, I should have expected some provision whereby it would have been possible for the State to make economic, social and political justice a reality and I should have from that point of view expected the Resolution to state in most explicit terms that in order that there may be social and economic justice in the country, that there would be nationalisation of industry and nationalisation of land, I do not understand how it could be possible for any future Government which believes in doing justice socially, economically and politically, unless its economy is a socialistic economy. Therefore, personally, although I have no objection to the enunciation of these propositions, the Resolution is, to my mind, somewhat disappointing. I am however prepared to leave this subject where it is with the observations I have made.

Now I come to the first part of the Resolution, which includes the first four paragraphs. As I said from the debate that has gone on in the House, this has become a matter of controversy. The controversy seems to be centred on the use of that word 'Republic'. It is centred on the sentence occurring in paragraph 4 "the sovereignty is derived from the people". Thereby it arises from the point made by my friend Dr. Jayakar yesterday that in the absence of the Muslim League it would not be proper for this Assembly to proceed to deal with this Resolution. Now, Sir, I have got not the slightest doubt in my mind as to the future evolution and the ultimate shape of the social, political and economic structure of this great country. I know to-day we are divided politically, socially and economically. We are a group of warring camps and I may go even to the extent of confessing that I am probably one of the leaders of such a camp. But, Sir, with all this, I am quite convinced that given time and circumstances nothing in the world will prevent this country from becoming one. (Applause). With all our castes and creeds, I have not the slightest hesitation that we shall in some form be a united people. (Cheers). I have no hesitation in saying that notwithstanding the agitation of the Muslim League for the partition of India some day enough light would dawn upon the Muslims themselves and they too will begin to think that a United India is better even for them. (Loud cheers and applause).

So far as the ultimate goal is concerned, I think none of us need have any apprehensions. None of us need have any doubt. Our difficulty is not about the ultimate future. Our difficulty is how to make the heterogeneous mass that we have to-day take a decision in common and march on the way which leads us to unity. Our difficulty is not with regard to the ultimate, our difficulty is with regard to the beginning. Mr. Chairman, therefore, I should have thought that in order to make us willing friends, in order to induce every party, every section in this country to take on to the road it would be an act of greatest statesmanship for the majority party even to make a concession to the prejudices of people who are not prepared to march together and it is for that, that I propose to make this appeal. Let us leave aside slogans let us leave aside words which frighten people. Let us even make a concession to the prejudices of our opponents, bring them in, so that they may willingly join with us on marching upon that road, which as I said, if we walk long enough, must necessarily lead us to unity. If I, therefore, from this place support Dr. Jayakar's amendment, it is because I want all of us to realise that whether we are right or wrong, whether the position that we take is in consonance with our legal rights, whether that agrees with the Statement of May the 16th or December 6th, leave all that aside. This is too big a question to be treated as a matter of legal rights. It is not a legal question at all. We should leave aside all legal considerations and make some attempt, whereby those who are not prepared to come, will come. Let us make it possible for them to come, that is my appeal.

In the course of the debate that took place, there were two questions which were raised, which struck me so well that I took the trouble of taking them down on a piece of paper. The one question was, I think, by my friend, the Prime Minister of Bihar who spoke yesterday in this Assembly. He said, how can this Resolution prevent the League from coming into the Constituent Assembly? Today my friend, Dr. Shyama Prasad Mookerjee, asked another question. Is this Resolution inconsistent with the Cabinet Mission's Proposal? Sir, I think they are very important questions and they ought to be answered and answered categorically. I do maintain that this Resolution whether it is intended to bring about the result or not, whether it is a result of cold calculation or whether it is a mere matter of accident is bound to have the result of keeping the Muslim League out. In this connection I should like to invite your attention to paragraph 3 of the Resolution, which I think is very significant and very important. Paragraph 3 envisages the future constitution of India. I do not know what is the intention of the mover of the Resolution. But I take it that after this Resolution is passed, it will act as a sort of a directive to the Constituent Assembly to frame a constitution in terms of Para 3 of the Resolution. What does para 3 say? Para 3 says that in this country there shall be two different sets of polity, one at the bottom, autonomous Provinces or the States or such other areas as care to join a United India. These autonomous units will have full power. They will have also residuary powers. At the top, over the Provincial units, there will be a Union Government, having certain subjects for legislation, for execution and for administration. As I read this part of the Resolution, I do not find any reference to the idea of grouping, an intermediate structure between the Union on the one hand and the provinces on the other. Reading this para in the light of the Cabinet Mission's Statement or reading it even in the light of the Resolution passed by the Congress at its Wardha Session, I must confess that I am a great deal surprised at the absence of any reference to the idea of grouping of the provinces. So far as I am personally concerned. I do not like the idea of grouping. (hear, hear). I like a strong united Centre, (hear, hear), much stronger than the Centre, we had created under the Government of India Act of 1935. But, Sir, these opinions, these wishes have no bearing on the situation at all. We have travelled a long road. The Congress Party, for reasons best known to itself, consented, if I may use that expression, to the dismantling of a strong Centre which had been created in this country as a result of 150 years of administration and which, I must say, was to me a matter of great admiration and respect and refuge. But having given up that position, having said that we do not want a strong Centre, and having accepted that there must be or should be an intermediate polity, a sub-federation between the Union Government and the Provinces I would like to know why there is no reference in para 3 to the idea of grouping. I quite understand that the Congress Party, the Muslim League and His Majesty's Government are not ad idem on the interpretation of the clause relating to grouping. But I always thought that,—I am prepared to stand corrected if it is shown that I am wrong,—at least it was agreed by the Congress Party that if the Provinces which are placed within different groups consent to form a Union or Sub-federation, the Congress would have no objection to that proposal. I believe I am correct in interpreting the mind of the Congress Party. The question I ask is this. Why did not the Mover of this Resolution make reference to the idea of a Union of Provinces or grouping of Provinces on the terms on which he and his party was prepared to accept it? Why is the idea of Union completely effaced from this Resolution? I find no answer. None whatever. I therefore say in answer to the two questions which have been posed here in this Assembly by the Prime Minister of Bihar and Dr. Shyama Prasad Mookerjee as to how this Resolution is inconsistent with the Statement of May 16th or how this Resolution is going to prevent the

Muslim League from entering this Constituent Assembly, that here is para 3 which—the Muslim League is bound to take advantage of and justify its continued absentation. Sir, my friend Dr. Jayakar, yesterday, in arguing his case for postponing a decision on this issue put his case, if I may say so, without offence to him, somewhat in allegalistic manner. The basis of his argument was, have you the right to do so? He read out certain portions from the Statement of the Cabinet Mission which related to the procedural part of the Constituent Assembly and his contention was that the procedure that this Constituent Assembly was adopting in deciding upon this Resolution straightaway was inconsistent with the procedure that was laid down in that Paper. Sir, I like to put the matter in a somewhat different way. The way I like to put it is this. I am not asking you to consider whether you have the right to pass this Resolution straightaway or not. It may be that you have the right to do so. The question I am asking is this. Is it prudent for you to do so? Is it wise for you to do so? Power is one thing; wisdom is quite a different thing and I want this House to consider this matter form the point of view, not of what authority is vested in this Constituent Assembly, I want this House to consider the matter from another point of view, namely, whether it would be wise, whether it would be statesmanlike, whether it would be prudent to do so at this stage. The answer that I give is that it would not be prudent, it would not be wise. I suggest that another attempt may be made to bring about a solution of the dispute between the Congress and the Muslim League. This subject is so vital, so important that I am sure it could never be decided on the mere basis of dignity of one party or the dignity of another party. When deciding the destinies of nations, dignities of people, dignities of leaders and dignities of parties ought to count for nothing. The destiny of the country ought to count for every thing. It is because I feel that it would be in the interest not only of this Constituent Assembly so that it may function as one whole, so that it may have the reaction of the Muslim league before it proceeds to decision that I support Dr. Jayakar's amendment—we must also consider what is going to happen with regard to the future, if we act precipitately. I do not know, what plans the Congress Party, which holds this House in its possession, has in its mind? I have no power of divination to know what they are thinking about. What are their tactics, what is their strategy, I do not know. But applying my mind as an outsider to the issue that has arisen; it seems to me there are only three ways by which the future will be decided. Either there shall have to be surrender by the one party to the wishes of the other—that is one way. The other way would be what I call a negotiated peace and the third way would be open war. Sir, I have been hearing from certain members of the Constituent Assembly that they are prepared to go to war. I must confess that I am appalled at the idea that anybody in this country should think of solving the political problems of this country by the method of war. I do not know how many people in this country support that idea. A good many perhaps do and the reason why I think they do, is because most of them, at any rate a great many of them, believe that the war that they are thinking of, would be a war on the British. Well, Sir, if the war that is contemplated, that is in the minds of people, can be localised, circumscribed, so that it will not be more than a war on the British, I probably may not have much objection to that sort of strategy. But will it be a war on the British only? I have no hesitation and I do want to place before this House in the clearest terms possible that if war comes in this country and if that war has any relation to the issue with which we are confronted today, it will not be a war on the British. It will be a war on the Muslims. It will be a war on the Muslims or which is probably worse, it will be a war on a combination of the British and the Muslims. I cannot see how this contemplated war be, of the sort different from what I fear it will be. Sir, I like to read to the House a passage from Bruke's great speech on Conciliation with America. I believe this may have some effect upon the temper of this House. The British people as you know were trying to conquer the rebellious colonies of the United States, and bring them under their subjection contrary to their wishes. In repelling this idea of conquering the colonies this is what Burke said:—

> "First, Sir, permit me to observe, that the use of force alone is but temporary. It may subdue for a moment; but it does not remove the necessity of subduing again; and a nation is not governed, which is perpetually to be conquered.
>
> My next objection is its uncertainty. Terror is not always the effect of force and an armament is not a victory. If you do not succeed, you are without resource, for conciliation failing, force remains;

> but, force failing, no further hope of reconciliation is left. Power and authority are sometimes bought by kindness; but they can never be begged as alms by an impoverished and defeated violence. . .
>
> A further objection to force is, that you impair the object by your very endeavours to preserve it. The thing you fought for is not the thing which you recover; but depreciated, sunk, wasted and consumed in the contest.

These are weighty words which it would be perilous to ignore. If there is anybody who has in his mind the project of solving the Hindu-Muslim problem by force, which is another name of solving it by war, in order that the Muslims may be subjugated and made to surrender to the Constitution that might be prepared without their consent, this country would be involved in prepetually conquering them. The conquest would not be once and for ever. I do not wish to take more time than I have taken and I will conclude by again referring to Burke. Burke has said somewhere that it is easy to give power, it is difficult to give wisdom. Let us prove by our conduct that if this Assembly has arrogated to itself sovereign powers it is prepared to exercise them with wisdom. That is the only way by which we can carry with us all sections of the country. There is no other way that can lead us to unity. Let us not have doubt on that point.

SUBHASH CHANDRA BOSE
(1897-1945)

SUBHASH CHANDRA BOSE

Give Me Blood and I Promise you Freedom

Speech to a Mass Rally of Indians in Burma on 4 July 1944

Friends ! Twelve months ago a new programme of "Total Mobilisation" or "Maximum sacrifice" was placed before Indians in East Asia. To-day I shall give you an account of our achievements during the past year and shall place before you our demands for the coming year. But, before I do so, I want you to realise once again what a golden opportunity we have for winning freedom. The British are now engaged in a world-wide struggle, and in the course of this struggle, they have suffered defeat after defeat in so many fronts. The enemy having been thus considerably weakened, our fight for liberty has become very much easier than it was five years ago. Such a rare and God-given opportunity comes once in a century. That is why we have sworn to fully utilise this opportunity for liberating our Motherland from the British yoke.

I am so very hopeful and optimistic about the outcome of our struggle, because I do not rely merely on the efforts of three million Indians in East Asia. There is a gigantic movement going on inside India and millions of our countrymen are prepared for maximum suffering and sacrifice in order to achieve liberty.

Unfortunately, ever since the great fight of 1857, our countrymen are disarmed, whereas the enemy is armed to teeth. Without arms and without a modern army, it is impossible for a disarmed people to win freedom in this modern age. Through the grace of Providence and through the help of generous Nippon, it has become possible for Indians in East Asia to get arms to build up a modern army. Moreover, Indians in East Asia are united to a man in the endeavour to win freedom and all the religious and other differences that the

British here tried to engineer inside India, do not simply exist in East Asia. Consequently, we have now an ideal combination of circumstances favouring the success of our struggle— and all that is wanted is that Indians should themselves come forward to pay the price of liberty.

According to the programme of "Total Mobilization," I demanded of you men, money and materials. Regarding men, I am glad to tell you that I have obtained sufficient recruits already. Recruits have come to us from every corner of East Asia from China, Japan, Indo-China, Philippines, Java, Borneo, Celebes, Sumatra, Malaya, Thailand and Burma.

The only complaint that I have is that considering the population of Indians in Burma, the number of recruits from Burma should have been larger. You will, therefore, have to exert yourselves still more in future in order to furnish more recruits from this part.

With regard to money, you remember that I demanded 30 millions from Indians in East Asia. I have actually got much more in the meantime and, from the arrangements that have been made, I am confident that a steady flow of money will be maintained in future.

From my experience of more than 20 year's work inside India, I can properly assess the worth and value of the work done here. I must, therefore, warmly thank you for the hearty co-operation that you have extended to me. At the same time, I must draw your attention to the work that still lies ahead of us.

You must continue the mobilization of men, money and materials with greater vigour and energy, in particular, the problem of supplies and transport has to be solved satisfactorily.

Secondly, we require more men and women of all categories for administration and reconstruction in liberated areas. We must be prepared for a situation in which the enemy will ruthlessly apply the scorched-earth policy, before withdrawing from a particular area and will also force the civilian population to evacuate as was attempted in Burma.

Last, but most important of all, is the problem of sending reinforcements in men and in supplies to the fighting fronts. If we do not do so, we cannot hope to maintain our success at the fronts. Nor can we hope to penetrate deeper into India.

Those of you who will continue to work on the Home Front should never forget that East Asia—and particularly Burma—form our base for the war of liberation. If this base is not strong, our fighting forces can never be victorious. Remember that this is a "Total War"—and not merely a war between two armies. That is why for full one year I have been laying so much stress on "Total Mobilization" in East.

There is another reason why I want you to look after the Home Front properly. During the coming months I and my colleagues on the War Committee of the Cabinet desire to devote our whole attention to the fighting front—and also to the task of working up the revolution inside India. Consequently, we want to be fully assured that the work at the base will go on smoothly and uninterruptedly even in our absence.

Friends, one year ago, when I made certain demands of you. I told you that if you give me "Total Mobilization" I would give you a "Second front." I have redeemed that pledge. The first phase of our campaign is over. Our victorious troops, fighting side by side with Nipponese troops, have pushed back the enemy and are now fighting bravely on the sacred soil of our dear motherland.

Gird up your loins for the task that now lies ahead. I had asked you for men, money and materials. I have got them in a generous measure. Now I demand more of you. Men, money and materials cannot by themselves bring victory or freedom. We must have the motive-power that will inspire us to brave deeds and heroic exploits.

It will be a fatal mistake for you to wish to live and see India free—simply because victory is now within reach. No one here should have the desire to live to enjoy freedom. A long fight is still in front of us.

We should have but one desire today—the desire to die so that India may live—the desire to face a martyr's death, so that the path to freedom may be paved with the martyr's blood.

Friends ! My comrades in the War of Liberation ! To-day I

demand of you one thing, above all. I demand of you Blood. It is blood alone that can avenge the blood that the enemy has spilt. It is blood alone that can pay the price of freedom. Give me blood and I promise you freedom.

SHYAMAPRASAD MOOKERJEE
(1905-1953)

SHYAMAPRASAD MOOKERJEE

Greatness of India

Speech at Patna University Convocation on 27 November 1937

You will forgive me if I do not make educational reconstruction the main theme of my discourse today. So much has recently been said on the subject that it may perhaps be more useful if we cease for a while from speculating on theories and concentrate on carrying out our declared policies, keeping in view the cardinal truth that India stands in need of a wide and progressive expansion of educational facilities from the lowest to the highest stage and not their curtailment in any form whatsoever.

As I stand in the historic city of Patna, the ancient Pataliputra, I feel tempted to trace some of the fundamental features of our civilisation in the majestic march of Indian history, not with the knowledge of a historian—for I lack such qualifications—but as a layman, an humble worker, who takes pride in the glories of our past history and longs for the day when this great land of ours may again claim her rightful place among the nations of the world and provide for the millions of her sons and daughters a higher and nobler life in all spheres, social, political, economic and cultural.

India has been styled an epitome of the world. This city which was the capital of the Imperial Mauryas and the Guptas, the scene of the activities of Bhadrabahu and of Sher Shah and the birthplace of Guru Gobind Singh, may well be described as an epitome of the land of Hindus and Muslims, of Jains and Sikhs. From time immemorial, it has been known for its toleration and catholicity, its love of learning and love of men. From the region where the waters of the Sone unite with the main stream of the Ganges, issued those messages of overflowing love towards men and even dumb animals which made the name of Asoka immortal. His edicts carved on rock and pillar throughout his vast empire served as a source of inspiration to rulers, statesmen and philanthropists. To the city of Pataliputra flocked merchants, diplomats, savants and sages, students and enquirers from all quarters of the civilized world.

The welcome extended to the visitors from distant lands was only equalled by the solicitude shown for the material comfort of the humblest among men. The free hospitals of the metropolis were open to all, irrespective of caste or creed. Toleration and concord were the watchwords of the rulers; benevolence and righteousness inspired their subjects at large. The province that boasted of Pataliputra included within its boundaries Uruvilva and Nalanda, Uddandapur and Bikramasila, the centres of Gautama's enlightenment, of Silabhadra's discourses, of Gopala's piety and of Dharmmapala's charity. The massive towers and fairylike turrets of Nalanda and her sister cities were visible symbols of that solid learning, high aspiration and conspicuous talent for which those great seats of the spiritual and intellectual life of India were justly famous.

India has had a splendid past. Many were the epochs when she lay safely anchored in a haven. But at times, storm and wind battered her masts and threatened to throw her precious burthen overboard. Nature, while impressing on her the stamp of unity by encircling her with lofty mountains and rocking seas, left gaps through which successive waves of invasion swept into the interior and brought ideals and ways of life that did not always fit in with her environments. In the interior itself, the hand of nature has drawn lines by rock and wood that proved serious impediments in the way of developing a common national life. But in spite of these, our forefathers did not despair of their country and we have had brilliant epochs in the history of India when she could justly claim respectful attention from the civilized world. There were times when the political unification of the country ceased to be a mere dream of poets and patriots and came near a historical reality, resulting in an outburst of activity in the domain of religion, literature, science and art, comparable to that of the Greece of Pericles or the England of Elizabeth.

That splendour was by no means ephemeral. Indian culture has retained its vigour and vitality and has found a worthy place among the civilisations of all ages. The pyramids bear mute testimony to a vanished civilisation on the banks of the Nile, the winged bulls are but lifeless relics of another culture that once flourished on the banks of the Euphrates and the Tigris, the ruins of Persepolis and Susa are today but subjects of antiquarian interest. Greece has achieved her political independence but the old Hellenic civilisation has disappeared for good like the Medusa and the Minotaur.

Here in our land, however, the Hindu still chants the Vedic hymns on the banks of the sacred rivers; the Buddha, Sangha and Dhamma are still invoked by millions of devotees from the mysterious heights of Fuziyama to far-off Adam's Peak. The civilisation of India is still alive; its philosophy and teachings still inspire millions of human beings, although Indian culture no longer finds its stimulating support from an independent national state. We must attribute its success to its catholicity and universal sympathy.

The ancient Aryans did not revel in destruction for its own sake, they believed in assimilation and improvement. The Macedonian and the Greek, the Saka and the Kushan came to conquer and slay but remained to wonder and pray. It has been often asserted that the polytheistic Hindu failed to establish a spiritual kinship with the monotheistic Muslim who held much that is Indian in scorn and still seeks his spiritual inspiration abroad. How can we say that India ignored the teachings of Islam when we find saints like Nanak and Chaitanya, Namdev and Tukaram, preaching the brotherhood of man and the futility of caste in matters spiritual? Although attempts on Hindu culture and institutions fill the pages of Indian history, how can we assert that Muslims ignored the appeal of Hindu culture when we find Muhammad Jayasi weaving a beautiful romance to illustrate the teachings of Hindu philosophy, when we read the simple devotional hymns of Kabir and Sheikh Farid, who refused to recognise the barriers of caste and creed on the high road to God's kingdom? "Utter not one disagreeable word," said Farid, "since the true lord is in all men. Distress no one's heart for every heart is a precious jewel." In the same strain did Kabir proclaim, "There is the same God for the Hindu as for the Muslim." A rejuvenated India found an Akbar to put an end to political chaos and social disharmony and a Shah Jahan to dream a dream in marble the like of which is not to be met with in the world.

India did not confine her attention to her adopted children alone. Whenever the stranger stood in need of spiritual solace, she ungrudgingly gave of her best. Did not she send a prince and a princess from this very city more than two thousand years ago to the land of the Yakshas to teach them the supreme truth that the only way to happiness lies in nonviolence and renunciation? Did not the Imperial ascetic send the same message to the far-off lands of Egypt, Asia Minor and Greece? Did not this country spare her very best, Dipankara, when Tibet and Sumatra stood in sore need of him? That tradition is not altogether dead even now. Only the other day, Swami Vivekananda bore the message of Paramhansa Ramkrishna and of India's storied past and taught the true path to peace and happiness to a struggling materialistic world, suffering from the evils of its very greatness. And today every civilised country in the world finds in Mahatma Gandhi a new messenger of peace, an embodiment of truth and non-violence who can brave the wrath of the mightiest and suffer nobly and patiently for the sake of his ideal. Do we not find again in Sister Nivedita and Mira Ben the representatives of those pilgrims who have been coming to us all through the ages in search of the truth eternal?

It may be asked that if such has been the greatness of India as a home of culture and thought, why is it that she has lost her political independence and has become a subject nation? Would it be true to say that the catholicity and universal sympathy which contributed so much to the everlasting freshness of India's civilisation, concealed in them the germs of her political downfall? Did they engender that other-worldliness which spelt ruin to the prospect of India's freedom? History supplies the answer. Did not India produce Chandragupta and Samudragupta, Pratapsingh, Sivaji, and Ranjit Singh, in spite of the pacific teachings of our ancestors? Did not the nameless but illustrious heroes, the Indian Argonauts, who explored the mysteries of the unchartered seas and spread Indian culture to the furthest East, prove that Hindu pacifism did not eliminate enterprise and love of adventure? Indian sages and philosophers never suggested that cowards and weaklings would ever be the torchbearers of India's great heritage. None but the valiant can achieve salvation. India's culture has not been responsible for India's bondage. That culture transplanted to the Himalayas and beyond has not taken the edge off the martial spirit of Mongolian races.

Is it then her climate that deteriorated the sturdy Aryan, Turk and Afghan in turn? If this were so, how are we to account for the rise of the Mahrattas and the Rohillas, the Jats and the Sikhs? How are we to explain the resurrection of the Rajputs? How could Hyder Ali of Mysore hold his own against the Mahrattas and the English? It is not the climate; it is not the culture; we must seek the cause of our downfall elsewhere.

India fell mainly because her people were at the critical hour divided and disorganised. Her influence waned when the forces of disintegration, political and social, were at work. If we left our neighbours alone, we revelled in internal strife which ceased for a time when great kings like Asoka and Akbar ruled over the destinies of India—mighty men, who sought to unite the teeming millions of this vast sub-continent by the bond of a common aspiration and a passionate longing for the eternal code of righteous conduct, charity and understanding. A strong and united India fearing none and loving all, brought messages of peace and goodwill to a distracted world. But as soon as the scepter dropped from their hands, when their grip over the country was loosened through weak and short-sighted successors, when narrow selfishness and mutual jealousy and distrust overpowered our souls, when local feuds and religious strife raised their ugly heads giving rise to social exclusiveness and moral decadence, unity was lost; freedom, man's priceless treasure, disappeared; the country broke into fragments and relapsed into a state of conflict and struggle. While the national and political unity of India was successfully achieved by great individuals, the masses did not at all times feel an abiding interest in its preservation. Thus although our culture has survived the storm and stress of time, we find ourselves in the strange and tragic position of the representatives and exponents of an ancient civilisation, yet alive but in bondage.

We may pertinently ask ourselves at this stage whether the forces of disruption that had effectively blocked the path of Indian progress in the past, have reacted more satisfactorily to their present environments, social, political and economic. It is obviously not possible for me here to deal with the history of British connection with India except to make some very general observations. The English came to India as traders and ultimately remained as masters of an empire.

During the last century and a half, we have witnessed the progress of India in various directions. Stability, peace and order have been generally restored. The benefits of science, which have revolutionised civilisation and have affected the lives of men and nations to an unprecedented extent, have penetrated into this great and ancient land, leading to considerable material progress. Western education has helped to broaden our outlook, deepen the sense of patriotism and laid the foundation of a political consciousness. Ideas of liberty and equality have slowly but steadily percolated from one corner of Hindustan to another and we witness the ever-increasing vitality of Indian nationalism. A spirit of inquisitiveness has captured the minds of Indians who have proved their worth in various domains of thought and activity. Many social evils have been uprooted and there is a general desire for uplifting the masses so that they may live more useful and noble lives.

While the progress of Indians on such lines is attributable to a large extent to western influence, no self-respecting Indian can ignore the vital defects and limitations of our national life. We must boldly take stock of the things that we have lost and yearn for. We find a general decay of the creative Indian arts which once triumphantly flourished in this land, and produced the frescos of Ajanta and the Taj of Agra. Indian music, Indian art and architecture, and Indian literature were not systematically and adequately patronised and that they have not entirely disappeared today is due mainly to the persistent efforts of individual workers. We witness the decline and disappearance of the indigenous industries of India which mainly thrived in her towns and villages. Such cottage industries, if they are to be revived, developed and saved from foreign competition require the unstinted support of the state. We find also deplorable neglect of the health and welfare of the villages of India which are today but shadows of their former affluence and happiness. Indeed much of India's poverty and distress, is traced to a systematic pursuit of an economic and industrial policy which has not been prompted and administered in the sole interest of India and her inhabitants.

One of the most staggering features of Indian life of today is the illiteracy and ignorance of more than 90 per cent of the people and for this no plea or excuse will ever be accepted by any impartial historian. One other vital weakness about which Indians feel bitterly is that they have not been adequately trained to defend their own hearth and home. An autonomous India is unthinkable without a national army and a national navy controlled and manned by Indians themselves. It is not correct to assume that many of the peoples of India are devoid of military or naval traditions. Indian history gives ample evidence of individual and collective courage and heroism. If there are parts of the country where the youths have today become feeble in health and energy, surely the remedy lies not in condemning them for eternity but in training them up for competent service.

I do not forget that in recent times efforts are being made to meet some of our vital needs. But no reforms of a radical character in any field of activity will ever be possible, nor can India rise to her full stature spiritually and economically, until and unless she takes her rank among the free nations of the world. No material gain, no earthly possession can ever compensate for the loss of man's liberty. The conflict of ideals and interests between a subject-race and the power that wants to hold it in its leading strings is as old as history itself; it can be solved peacefully and amicably only if the latter accords to the former the same treatment as it demands from others in respect of its own rights and privileges.

In defining freedom I can do no better than follow the language of a British peer, a statesman and philosopher, who has dealt with the question with remarkable lucidity in one of his recent books. What, he asks, is the ultimate goal of enlightened man? The answer is that one of the aims is that nations should be free from alien domination. What, he asks, should be the pattern set for civilised mankind? The answer is, within the nation the individual should be free, free to think, worship, speak and act as he would, subject to the similar rights of others, free under the protection of equal justice to pursue his lawful business as he chooses. Men should no longer be bound down from birth to death by the hampering restrictions that come from bondage, poverty, overwork and environment. Freedom consists not only in the absence of restraint but also in the presence of opportunity. Liberty is not a single and simple conception. It has four elements: national, political, personal and economic. The man who is fully free is one who lives in a country which is independent; in a state which is democratic; in a society where the laws are equal and restrictions at a minimum; in an economic system in which national interests are protected and the citizen has the scope of a secure livelihood, an assured comfort and full opportunity to rise by merit.

This freedom, so truly and courageously defined, is not ours today and until this condition is reached, India will never achieve true greatness or happiness, based on the glorious features of her past civilisation.

The Indian universities, if they are to play their role in the rebuilding of a new India, must not regard themselves as exclusive institutions which exist apart from the currents of the country's life. Let them train their alumni in a worthy manner, saturate them with the lessons of Indian history and civilisation, instil into them unity and reason, strength and dauntlessness, inspire them with skill and knowledge and teach them to apply themselves devotedly and unselfishly to the service of their fellowman. Let the teachers of the universities consider it their sacred duty to be the interpreters of India's heritage, the seekers of truth and knowledge, and prove to the world that Indian scholars are second to none in their efforts to serve the cause of the humanities and the sciences in relation to the unfettered progress of India and of human civilisation itself.

Bibliography

Ahluwalia, B.K., ed. *M.K. Gandhi: Selected Speeches*. Delhi: Sagar Publications, 1969.

Andrews, C.F. *Mahatma Gandhi's Idea*. London: George Allen and Unwin, 1949.

Ayer, S.A., ed. *Selected Speeches of Subhas Chandra Bose*. Delhi: Publication Division, 1992.

Azad, Abul Kalam. *India Wins Freedom*. New Delhi: Orient Longman, 1959, revised edition 1989.

Bal Gangadhar Tilak. Madras: G.A. Natesan, 1918.

Ball, Upendranath. *Rammohun Roy: A Study of His Life, Works and Thought*. Calcutta: U. Roy and Sons, 1933.

Bonerjea, Hiranmay. *Iswarchandra Vidyasagar*. Delhi: Sahitya Academi, 1994.

Banerjea, Sir Surendranath. *A Nation in Making*. Bombay: Oxford University Press, 1925.

Bayly, C.A., ed. *The Illustrated History of Modern India* 1600-1947. Bombay: Oxford University Press, 1991.

Bhattacharya, Bhabani. *Gandhi, The Writer*. New Delhi: National Book Trust, 1969.

Bonnerjee, Sadhona. *Life of W.C. Bonnerjee*. Calcutta: Calcutta University, 1944.

Bose, Amalendu. *Michael Madhusudan Dutt*. Delhi: Sahitya Academi, 1981.

Bose, Nemai Sadhan. *Swami Vivekananda*. Delhi: Sahitya Akademi, 1994.

Bose, Subhas Chandra. *Indian Struggle*. 2 vols. London: Wishart and Co., 1935.

Brown, D.M. *The National Movement in India: Political Thought from Ranade to Bhave*. Berkeley: University of California Press, 1970.

Bruce, Carlisle Robertson. *Raja Rammohun Roy: The Father of Modern India*. Delhi: Oxford University Press, 1995.

Carpenter, Mary. *Last Days in England of the Rajah Rammohun Roy*. London: 1866.

Chakravarty, Satish Chandra, ed. *The Father of Modern India: Commemoration Volume of the Rammohun Roy Centenary Celebration*. Calcutta, 1933.

Chand, Feroz. *Lajpat Rai: Life and Works*. Delhi: Publications Division, 1993.

Chander, Satish. Chief Editor. *Jawaharlal Nehru Souvenir*. Delhi: Jawaharlal Nehru Souvenir Committee "Cultural Meet", n.d.

Chandra, Bipan, et al. *Indian Struggle for Independence* 1857-1947. New Delhi: Penguin, 1989.

Chandra Bipan. *Modern India*. New Delhi: Orient Longman, 1981.

Chatterjee, Saral Kumar. *Bipin Chandra Pal*. Delhi: Publication Division, 1984.

Chaudhury, P.C. Roy. *Gandhi and His Contemporaries*. Jullundhur: Sterling Publishers, 1972.

Chibber, V.N. *Jawaharlal Nehru: Man of Letters*. New Delhi: Vikas, 1970.

Chintamani, C.Y., ed. *Speeches and Writings of Sir Pherozeshah Mehta*. Allahabad : Indian Press, 1905.

The Collected Works of Mahatma Gandhi: 100 volumes. Delhi: Publications Division, 1958 to 1994.

Congress Presidential Addresses. 2 vols. Madras: Natesan G.A., 1931.

Constituent Assembly Debates: 9.12.1946 to 24.1.1950. New Delhi: Lok Sabha Secretariat, Third Reprint, 1999.

Cousins, Norman, ed. *Profiles of Gandhi*. Delhi: India Book Co., 1970.

Dada Bhai Naoroji's Speeches and Writings. Madras: Natesan, d.n.

Dutt, Michael Madhusudan. *The Anglo-Saxon and the Hindu, Lecture 1*. Madras : Pharooh and Co., Atheneum Press, 1854.

Elphinstone, Mount Stuart. *The History of India*. With Notes and Additions by Cowell, E.B. London: John Murray, 1889.

The English Works of Raja Rammohun Roy: Centenary Edition. Calcutta: Social and Educational, 1933.

Fischer, Louis. *The Life of Mahatma Gandhi*. Stuttgart: Tauchinty, 1953.

Gandhi, M.K. *An Autobiography*. Trans. Mahadev Desai. Ahmedabad: Navajivan Trust, 1995 reprint of 1927 edition.

Ghose, Sankar. *Leaders of Modern India*. New Delhi: Allied Publishers, 1980.

Ghose, Sisir Kumar, ed. *Faith of a Poet: Selections from Robindranath Tagore*. Bombay: Bharatiya Vidya Bhavan, 1983.

Ghose, Sisir Kumar. *Rabindranath Tagore*. New Delhi: Sahitya Akademi, 1986, reprinted 1994.

Ghosh, Devaprasad, ed. *Pandit Motilal Nehru: His Life and Work*. Calcutta: Modern Book Agency, 1934.

Gopal, S. *The Mind of Jawaharlal Nehru*. Madras: Sangam Books. 1980.

Great Men and Women of India. New Delhi: Publications Division, 1973.

Grover, Verinder, ed. *Balgangadhar Tilak*. Delhi: Deep and Deep, 1992.

Grover, Verinder, ed. *Bipin Chandra Pal*. Delhi: Deep and Deep, 1992.

Grover, Verinder, ed. *Dada Bhai Naoroji*. Delhi: Deep and Deep, 1992.

Grover, Verinder, ed. *Mahadev Govind Ranade*. New Delhi: Deep and Deep, 1991.

Grover, Verinder, ed. *Rajagopalachari*. Delhi: Deep and Deep, 1992.

Grover, Verinder, ed. *Raja Rammohun Roy*. Delhi: Deep and Deep, 1992.

Grover, Verinder, ed. *S. Radhakrishnan*. Delhi: Deep and Deep, 1992.

Grover, Verinder, ed. *Sri Aurobindo Ghose*. Delhi: Deep and Deep, 1993.

Grover, Verinder, ed. *Subhas Chandra Bose*. Delhi: Deep and Deep, 1991.

Gupta, Hemendranath Das. *Deshbandhu Chittaranjan Das*. New Delhi: Publications Division, 1977.

Gupta, Padmini Sen. *Sarojini Naidu*. Delhi: Sahitya Akademi, 1974, rpt. 1989.

Gwyer, M. and Appadorai, A., eds. *Speeches and Documents on the India Constitution*. 1921-1947. Delhi: OUP., 1957.

Hutchins, Francis. *The Illusion of Permanence: British Imperialism in India*. Princeton, New Jersey: Princeton University Press, 1967.

The Indian Nation Builders. 3 vols. n.d.; rpt. Delhi: Mittal Publications, 1989.

Iyenger, K.R. Srinivasa. *Indian Writing in English*. New Delhi: Sterling Publishers, 1985.

Jagdisan, T.N., ed. *Letters of the Right Honourable V.S. Srinivasa Sastri*. Bombay: Asia Publishing House, 1963.

Jagdisan, T.N., ed. *My Master Gokhale: A Selection from the Speeches of Rt Hon'ble V.S. Srinivasa*. Madras: Model Publications, 1946.

Jeejeebhoy, J.R.B., ed. *Some Unpublished and Later Speeches and Writings of The Hon. Sir Pherozeshah Mehta*. Bombay: The Commercial Press, 1918.

Jha, Amarnatha. *Sarojini Naidu: A Personal Homage*. Allahabad: The Indian Press, n.d.

Jog, N.G. *Lokmanya B.G. Tilak*. New Delhi: Government of India, Publications Division, 1970.

Joshi, V.C., ed. *Lala Lajpat Rai: Writings and Speeches*. 2 vols. Delhi: University Publishers, 1966.

Kripalani, Krishna. *Tagore: A Life*. Delhi: National Book Trust, 1986, reprinted 1997.

Kuber, W.N. *B.R. Ambedkar*. Delhi: Publications Division. 1990.

Kumar, Ravindra and D.N. Panigrahi, eds. *Selected Works of Motilal Nehru*, 3 vols. Delhi: Vikas Publishing House, 1984.

Kundu, Kalyan, Bhattacharya, Sakti and Sircar, Kalyan, eds. *Rabindranath and the British Press* (1912-1941). London: The Tagore Centre, 1990.

Lala Lajpat Rai on Non-Co-operation. Madras: G.A. Natesan, n.d.

Madras-Speeches of Bipin Chandra Pal. Madras: Ganesh, 1907.

Mansingh, Surjit. *Historical Dictionary of India*. Delhi: Vision Books, 1998.

Masani, R.P. *Dada Bhai Naoroji*. Delhi: Publications Division, 1975.

Majumdar, J.K., ed. *Indian Speeches and Documents of British Rule 1821-1918*. Calcutta: Longmans, Green and Co., 1937.

Mascreen, P.J. *Makers of Modern India*. New Delhi: Kalyani Publishers, 1983.

Mishra, Ganeswar and Satapathy, Sarat Chandra, eds. *A Modern Seer: Selections from Nehru*. Hyderabad: Orient Longman, 1989.

Mitter, Raj Jogeshur, ed. *Speeches by Rajendra Lala Mitra*. Calcutta: Lahiri, 1892.

Modi, Homi. *Sir Pherozeshah Mehta: A Political Biography*. Bombay: Asia Publishing House, 1921.

Mohammad, Shan. *Writings and Speeches of Sir Syed Ahmad Khan*. Bombay: Nachiketa, 1972.

Mookerjee, Girija K. *Subhas Chandra Bose*. Delhi: Publications Division. 1992.

Moon, Vasant, ed. *Writings and Speeches of B. Ambedkar*. 10 vols. Bombay:

Government of Maharashtra, 1989.

Moorhouse, Geoffrey. *India Britannica*. 1983; rpt. London: Paladin, 1984.

Moraes, Frank. *Jawaharlal Nehru*. Bombay: Jaico, 1978 Impression.

Mukherjee, Arun Kumar. *Keshub Chunder Sen*. Delhi: Publications Division. 1992.

Nag, Kalidas and Debajyoti Burman, eds. *The English Works of Raja Rammohun Roy*. Parts I to VI. Calcutta: Sadhoran Brahmo Samaj, 1945-1951.

Naik, M.K. *A History of Indian English Literature*. New Delhi: Sahitya Akademi, 1982.

Nanadkumar, Prema. *S. Radhakrishnan*. Delhi: Sahitya Akademi, 1992.

Naoroji, Dada Bhai. *Poverty and Un-British Rule in India*. 1891; rpt. New Delhi: Commonwealth Publishers, 1988.

Narasimhaiah, C.D., ed. *The Essential Nehru*. Delhi: Macmillan, 1985 impression.

Narasimhaiah, C.D., ed. *Selections from speeches by Jawaharlal Nehru*. Madras : Macmillan, 1959.

Naravane, V.S. *Sarojini Naidu: Her Life, Work and Poetry*. Delhi: Orient Longman, 1980, rpt. 1996.

Nehru, Jawaharlal. *Autobiography*. 1936; rpt. Delhi: OUP, 1962.

Nehru, Jawaharlal. *The Discovery of India*. 1946; rpt. Delhi: OUP, 1982.

Nehru, Jawaharlal. *Glimpses of World History*. 1934-35. rpt. Delhi: Oxford University Press. 1996 impression.

Nehru, Jawaharlal. *Speeches*. 4 vols. Delhi: Publications Division, 1993 impression.

Nirvedananda, Swami, ed. *Swami Vivekananda on India and Her Problems*. Calcutta: Advaita, 1988.

Nivedita, Sister. *The Master as I Saw Him*. Calcutta: Udbodhan Office, 1991.

Nizami, K.A. *Sayyid Ahmad Khan*. Delhi: Publications Division, 1965.

Panikkar, K.M. and Pershad, A., eds. *Voice of Freedom: Selected Speeches of Pandit Motilal Nehru*. Bombay: Asia Publishing House, 1961.

Pantham, Thomas and Deutsch, Kenneth L., eds. *Political Thought in Modern India*. New Delhi: Sage, 1986.

Parekh, Manilal C. *Brahmarshi Keshub Chunder Sen*. Rajkot: Orient Christ House, 1926.

Parry. Benita. *Delusions and Discoveries*. 1972; rpt. Delhi: Orient Longman, 1974.

Parvate, T.V. *Bal Gangadhar Tilak*. Ahmedabad: Navjivan, 1958.

Parvate, T.V. *Makers of Modern India*. Jullundhur: University Publishers, 1964.

Prabhu, R.K., ed. *An Anthology of Modern Indian Eloquence*. Bombay: Bhartiya Vidya Bhavan, 1960.

Rabindranath Tagore: A Centenary Volume. Calcutta: Tagore Centenary Citizens' Committee, 1961.

Rabindranath Tagore: A Centenary Volume, 1861-1961. New Delhi: Sahitya Akademi, 1961, reprinted 1992.

Radhakrishnan, S., ed. *Mahatma Gandhi: Essays and Reflections on His Life and Thought*. Allahabad: Kitabistan, 1944.

Rajagopalachari, C. and Kumarappa, J.C., eds. *The Nation's Voice*. Ahmedabad: Navajivan Publishing House, 1958.

Rajgopalachari, C. *The Voice of the Uninvolved*. New Delhi: National Book Trust of India, 1960.

Raja Rammohun Roy: His Life, Writings and Speeches. Madras: Natesan, 1925.

Ramakrishna, D., ed. *Indian-English Prose: An Anthology*. New Delhi: Arnold-Heinemann, 1980.

Ranade, Mrs. Ramabai. *Miscellaneous Writings of the Late Hon'ble Mr. Justice M.G. Ranade*. Delhi: Sahitya Academi, 1992.

Ray, Prithwis Chandra Ray. *Life and Times of C.R. Das*. London: Oxford, 1927.

Robertson, Bruce Carlisle. *Raja Rammohun Roy*. Delhi: Oxford University Press, 1995.

Rolland, Romain. *The Life of Vivekananda and the Universal Gospel*. Calcutta: Advaita Ashrama, 1931, reprinted 1988.

Rolland, Romain. *Mahatma Gandhi*. Trans. C.D. Groth. 1924; rpt. Delhi: Publications Division, 1990.

Saggi, P.D., ed. *Life and Works of Lal, Bal and Pal*. New Delhi: Overseas, 1962.

Saiyid, Matlubul Hasan. *Mohammad Ali Jinnah: A Political Study*. Lahore: Shaikh Muhammad, 1945.

Samagra Lokmanya Tilak 7 vols. Pune: Kesari, 1974-76. [Collection of Marathi and English Writings and Speeches]

Sarkar, Hem Chandra. *A Life of Ananda Mohan Bose*. Calcutta: A.C. Sarkar, 1910.

Sarkar, Jedunath. *India through the Ages*. 1928; rpt. Calcutta: Sangam Books, 1979.

Sastri, Srinivasa. *Life and Times of Sir Pherozeshah Mehta*. Madras: The Madras Law Journal Press, 1945.

Sen, S.P., ed. *Dictionary of National Biography*. 4 vols. Calcutta: Institute of Historical Studies, 1972-74.

Sharma, B.M. and Choudhry. *Expanding Dimensions of Freedom*. Agra: Oriental Publishing House, n.d.

Sharma, Jagdish Saran. *The National Biographical Dictionary of India*. New Delhi: Sterling Publishers, 1972.

Sheean, Vincent. *Mahatma Gandhi*. New York: Alfred A. Knopf, 1965.

Dr. Sinha, Sachidananda. *Some Eminent Indian Contemporaries*. Patna: Janaki Prakashan, 1976.

Sitaramayya, Pattabhi. *History of the Indian National Congress*. 2 vols. Bombay : Padma Publications, 1947.

Smith, A. Vincent. *The Oxford Student History of India*. Revised by Rawlinson, H.G. London: Oxford University Press, 1962.

Spear, Percival. *A History of India. vol. 2 from the Sixteenth Century to the Twentieth Century*. 1965; rpt. London: Penguin, 1990.

Speeches of Bhula Bhai Desai: 1934-38. Madras: G.A. Natesan, 1938.

Speeches of C.R. Das (1917-18). Calcutta: Banerjee Das and Co., 1918.

Speeches and Writings of Gopal Krishna Gokhale. Madras: G.A. Natesan, 1908.

Speeches and Writings of Mahatma Gandhi. Madras: G.A. Natesan, 1931.

Speeches and Writings of Sarojini Naidu. Madras: G.A. Natesan, n.d.

Speeches Delivered by H.E. Sri Chakravarti Rajagopalachari. Calcutta: West Bengal Government Press, 1948.

Speight, E.E., ed. *Indian Masters of English*. London: Longman, Green and Co., 1934.

Sri Aurobindo Birth Centenary Library Popular Edition. Pondicherry: Aurobindo Ashram Trust, 1972.

Swaminathan, K. and Patel, C.N., eds. *A Gandhi Reader*. Madras: Orient Longman, 1988.

Tagore, Rabindranath. *The English Writings*. Ed. Sisir Kumar Das, 3 vols. New Delhi: Sahitya Akademi, 1996.

Tagore, Rabindranath. *Lectures and Addresses*, ed. Anthony X Soares. Madras: Macmillan, Pocket Edition, 1988.

Tagore, Rabindranath. *Nationalism*. New Delhi: Rupa, 1994 (first published by Macmillan and Co., 1917).

Tagore, Rabindranath. *The Religion of Man*. New Delhi: Indus, 1994 (first published by George Allen and Unwin, London, 1931).

Tagore, Saumyendranath. *Raja Rammohun Roy*. Delhi: Sahitya Academi, 1989.

Thompson, Edward. *Rabindranath Tagore: Poet and Dramatist*. Delhi: Oxford University Press, 1989.

The Trumpet Voice of India: Speeches of Babu Surendranath Banerjea. Madras: Ganesh, n.d.

Toye, Hugh. *The Springing Tiger: Subhas Chandra Bose*. Bombay: Jaico, 1984.

Vivekananda, Swami. *Complete Works*. Calcutta: Advaita Ashrama fifth reprint, 1992.

Vivekananda, Swami. *Lectures from Colombo to Almora*. Calcutta: Advaita Ashrama, Fifth impression. 1984.

Wacha, D.N. *Speeches and Writings*. Madras: G.A. Natesan, 1918. *The Way to Swaraj: Speeches of Deshbandhu Das in Madras*. Madras: Natesan, 1923.

Williams, H.M. *Indo-Anglian Literature 1800-1970: A Survey*. Bombay: Orient Longmans, 1976.

William, L.F. Rushbrook, ed. *Great Men of India*. Delhi: Gian Publishing House, 1985.

Wolpert, Stanley. *Tilak and Gokhale: Revolution and Reform in the Making of Modern India*. Berkeley: University of California Press, 1962.

Writings and Speeches of Bipin Chandra Pal. 2 parts. Calcutta: Yugayatri Prakashak, 1954.

Zaidi, A.M., ed. *Grand Little Man of India, Dada Bhai Naoroji: Writings and Speeches*. New Delhi: S. Chand, 1984.

Index